Experiential Learning

Fourth Edition

Experiential Learning

A practical guide for training, coaching and education

Colin Beard and John P Wilson

Publisher's note

Every possible effort has been made to ensure that the information contained in this book is accurate at the time of going to press, and the publishers and authors cannot accept responsibility for any errors or omissions, however caused. No responsibility for loss or damage occasioned to any person acting, or refraining from action, as a result of the material in this publication can be accepted by the editor, the publisher or the authors.

First published in Great Britain and the United States in 2002 by Kogan Page Limited as *The Power of Experiential Learning*
Second edition published in 2006 as *Experiential Learning*
Third edition 2013
Fourth edition 2018

Apart from any fair dealing for the purposes of research or private study, or criticism or review, as permitted under the Copyright, Designs and Patents Act 1988, this publication may only be reproduced, stored or transmitted, in any form or by any means, with the prior permission in writing of the publishers, or in the case of reprographic reproduction in accordance with the terms and licences issued by the CLA. Enquiries concerning reproduction outside these terms should be sent to the publishers at the undermentioned addresses:

2nd Floor, 45 Gee Street	c/o Martin P Hill Consulting	4737/23 Ansari Road
London	122 W 27th St, 10th Floor	Daryaganj
EC1V 3RS	New York, NY 10001	New Delhi 110002
United Kingdom	USA	India

www.koganpage.com

© Colin Beard and John P Wilson, 2002, 2006, 2013, 2018

The right of Colin Beard and John P Wilson to be identified as the authors of this work has been asserted by them in accordance with the Copyright, Designs and Patents Act 1988.

ISBN   978 0 7494 8303 6
E-ISBN   978 0 7494 8304 3

British Library Cataloguing-in-Publication Data

A CIP record for this book is available from the British Library.

Library of Congress Cataloging-in-Publication Data

Names: Beard, Colin (Colin M.), author. | Wilson, John P. (John Peter), 1955 August 11- author.
Title: Experiential learning : a practical guide for training, coaching and education / Colin Beard and John P. Wilson.
Description: Fourth edition. | London ; New York : Kogan Page, 2018. | Includes bibliographical references and index.
Identifiers: LCCN 2018017822 (print) | LCCN 2018020891 (ebook) | ISBN 9780749483043 (ebook) | ISBN 9780749483036 (pbk.)
Subjects: LCSH: Experiential learning–Handbooks, manuals, etc. | Active learning–Handbooks, manuals, etc. | Employees–Training of–Handbooks, manuals, etc.
Classification: LCC BF318.5 (ebook) | LCC BF318.5 .B43 2018 (print) | DDC 153.1/52–dc23
LC record available at https://lccn.loc.gov/2018017822

Typeset by Integra Software Services, Pondicherry
Print production managed by Jellyfish
Printed and bound by CPI Group (UK) Ltd, Croydon, CR0 4YY

References to websites (URLs) were accurate at the time of writing. Neither the authors nor Kogan Page are responsible for URLs that may have expired or changed since the manuscript was prepared.

CONTENTS

01 A brief introduction to experiential learning 1
Experience: a bridging concept 5
More than social and cultural 8
Experience and the problem of language 11
More about this book 13
An overview of the chapters 14

PART ONE Experiential learning: foundations and fundamentals 21

02 Practical answers to some theoretical questions 23
Introduction 23
Question 1: Experiential education and experiential learning – are they virtually the same? 24
Question 2: Is experiential learning (EL) simply the sum of experience (E) plus learning (L)? 27
Question 3: What are the more popular models currently being used to explain experiential learning? 32
Question 4: What are the main criticisms of experiential learning? 41
Question 5: Has the notion of the experience society contributed to our understanding of experiential learning in any way? 45
Conclusion 50

03 Designing, delivering and evaluating experiential learning 53
Delivering a learning experience 54
Learning experience design 62
Using the Learning Combination Lock 73
The review and evaluation of experiences 78
A brief reminder of the chapters that follow 80

PART TWO The Learning Combination Lock model 83

04 The outer-world learning environment: other humans, other living creatures, and spaces and places (the belonging dimension) 85

Introduction 85
Indoor learning: the new classroom 91
Outdoor learning 96
Disappearing boundaries: indoor–outdoor, natural–artificial 98
Reaching out: learning in city space 101
Artificially created learning spaces 104
Pedagogy and personal development 106
The advantages of simulated recreation environments 110
Empathetic strategies and the outdoor therapeutic 'effect' 112
Outdoor environments: therapeutic experiential learning 114
Sustainable learning environments 117
Conclusion 120

05 Experiential learning activities, behaviours and actions (the doing dimension) 121

Introduction 121
Planned or unplanned experiences? 123
The evolving milieu 125
The Great Escape 125
Outdoor adventure learning 126
Dramaturgy 127
Designing experiences: a simple experiential typology 130
Adventurous journeys 132
Expeditions 134
Sequencing learning activities 136
Mind and body 138
Rules and obstacles 140
Constructing and deconstructing 141
Handling physical objects 142
Learning activities: exploring reality 143
What is a real experience? 143
Fantasy 150

Play and reality 153
Suspending reality: drama and role playing 156
Rafts and planks… or real projects? 161
Metaphors and storytelling 162
Management development and cartoons 165
Using photographic images and computer software 167
Reflections on reality: reading and writing 168
Doing and reviewing 169
Conclusion 171

06 Sensory experience and sensory intelligence (SI) (the sensing dimension) 173

Introduction 173
Amplification and habituation 174
So what is sensory intelligence? 177
Language and the human sensorial experience 179
Interpreting and misinterpreting words 183
Going 'away': outdoor sensory-awakening experiences 184
The senses in higher-education teaching 187
Digital games and the design of multisensory experiences 191
Sensory stimulation in learning and therapy 191
Sensory stimulation, emotions and mood 193
Nature-guided therapy 193
Inner sensory work: presence and anchoring 196
Conclusion 197

07 Experience and emotions (the feeling dimension) 199

Introduction 199
Fast thinking 201
Communicating with feeling 202
Emotion and experiential learning 206
The power of the emotional state 209
Emotional waves 211
Experiencing emotional calm 211
Flow learning 214
Experience, learning and 'identity' 216
Practical ways to access feelings 219
The emotional climate: mood setting and relaxed alertness 219
Overcoming fear 221

Mapping and accessing emotions 224
Using trilogies in emotional work 227
Using humour and other positive emotions 229
Accessing emotions through popular metaphors 231
Conclusion 236

08 Experience, knowing and intelligence (the knowing dimension) 238

Introduction 238
Human learning: is it really all in the mind? 239
Thinking with the body and thinking with feeling 242
The organizing mind: patterns and creative thinking 243
What is intelligence? 246
The many forms of intelligence 249
Neglected forms of intelligence 253
Sensory intelligence – SI 253
Emotional intelligence – EQ 254
Spiritual intelligence – SQ 257
Naturalistic intelligence – NQ 261
Creative intelligence – CQ 264
Wisdom 270
Conclusion 271

09 Deeper learning (the being dimension) 273

Introduction 273
The experience of being human 275
Well-being 276
Mindfulness 277
Single- and double-loop learning 288
Using problems and challenges 289
Problems and painful learning 291
Action learning 292
Experience and the inner game 298
Being, becoming, transforming: the experience economy 302
Conclusion 304

PART THREE Experiential learning and the future 305

10 Imagining, experiencing and learning from the future 307

Introduction 307
We are imagining all the time 308
Imagination 309
Imagination versus action 312
Mental fitness for the future 313
Imagining the future 314
Imagination and the child 315
A chronology of experiential learning 317
Prospective learning: reflecting on the future 323
Functional equivalence and virtual reality 326
Conclusion 327

References 329
Index 351

A brief introduction to experiential learning

01

A key characteristic of the human mind is that it has a tendency to organize, sequence, differentiate, classify, and to generally explore patterns and connectivity. LAKOFF AND JOHNSON (1999)

Experiential learning is a *category* of learning, and the quotation above highlights how we humans have a strong tendency to categorize and organize. We like to know where things belong, and why, and so this chapter will do just that; we will explore the basic ideas behind the philosophy and practice of experiential learning.

It is no wonder those sticky, coloured labels posted on walls and whiteboards are so popular with facilitators, trainers and teachers: it is because they can be moved, and so they help us to organize things! Categories of good and bad, safe or dangerous, exciting or dull are simple examples of categories, but they are remarkably hard to define. In a similar way we also categorize learning, such as *adult learning, lifelong learning, problem-based learning* and *life-wide learning*. We also have categories of learning that involve 'experiential' approaches, and so these too are categorized: they might include, for example, *experiential learning, experiential education, outdoor learning, adventure learning, gamification* and *experience-based training and development*. This new fourth-edition is all about these 'experiential' categories of learning that are becoming more widely utilized in many different ways around the globe.

Many of these *experiential* categories of learning overlap, as we will explore in more detail in Chapter 2. They are particularly difficult to clearly define and differentiate. When we explore the defining parameters we begin to engage in what some people call the 'theory': however, even the categories of *theory* and *practice* are also hard to distinguish. It can be argued that there is no practice without theory, and no theory without practice. Furthermore, most, if not all, practitioners will have their own views on, for example, the question of what is good practice, and their ideas are therefore their own 'theories in use'. In this edition we not only offer practical suggestions and advice, we also explain our underlying reasoning. Much of our thinking behind this book has come about not just by considering what other people have written about in books, but also from our ideas that have evolved from our own experiences, our interactions with other practitioners, and in the conduct of our practice around the globe.

There are many ways people learn from experiences, for example through parents, everyday life, risky adventures, or by going to events. But are all these experiences 'experiential learning' (after all, they are all potential learning *experiences*)? The answer is no, and so we must therefore ask, *what exactly is experiential learning*? Edward Cell, in his book *Learning to Learn from Experience*, refers to a basic definition of experiential learning by Keeton and Tate back in 1978. Cell was highlighting the differences between 'academic learning' and 'experiential learning' when he offered the following definition of experiential learning:

> Learning in which the learner is directly in touch with the realities being studied. It is contrasted with learning in which the learner only reads about, hears about, talks about, or writes about these realities but never comes into contact with them as part of the learning process. (Keeton and Tate, 1978, in Cell, 1984: viii)

This definition is limited in terms of what it really tells us about the nature of experiential learning. It implies that reading and listening are not experiential learning, but of course these 'activities' could be. One practical experiential learning approach described in Chapter 4 is a choreographed experience designed to generate a genuine interest in reading, whereby learners investigate a question by exploring a wide range of interesting material on the topic. Armed with refreshments participants go off and find relaxing spaces to read 'papers', sometimes newspapers and sometimes academic or professional papers. When they return from the solo reading experience they engage in a group conversation, to generate and consider their collective thinking about a particular topic under investigation. It is called Coffee and Papers.

We suggest at this point that experiential approaches to learning consider the role of 'experience' as somehow special, as having a certain quality: the experience is regarded as central to the learning process. The experience takes centre stage, as it were. In experiential learning the *experience* is the foundation *of*, and the stimulus *for*, learning. Experiential learning is not about a deliberate intention to teach by just telling or presenting: experiential learning is when there is a clear intention to utilize specific experiences for people to learn. The reasoning behind this is that the richest resources for learning originate in the learners themselves. Furthermore the experience can be a powerful memory trigger; a good learning experience is easily recalled, enabling or triggering access to the learning that occurred as a result of the experience. In practical terms this means that we must attend to two particular aspects of *experience*. There is the experience that is designed or utilized *for* learning that requires skill and expertise to design and facilitate. Then there is the experience *of* learning; the processes of learning have to be considered, so we need to know and understand how humans learn, and how people *experience* their own learning.

We are not only of the view that the quality of the experience *of* and *for* learning has to be considered; we also believe we should consider each person as a whole person, as a sensing, thinking, feeling human being. This introduces a second dimension to experiential learning. The learning experience is taking place within our *inner private world*, and there is also the experience we have of the *outer (public) world*, in the environment 'out there'. In experiential learning both of these worlds need to be understood in terms of how they influence human learning. These two worlds continually interact with each other, and we *experience* life rather like our own unique film, with all the clips and storyline put together with information from both these two worlds. These ideas, of four key components (for, of, inner private world, outer public world) to the experience, are our basic start point to both our philosophy and our easy-to-use holistic model of experiential learning, called the Learning Combination Lock, which is presented in Chapter 3. However, at this stage we will build our ideas about experiential learning a little further, step by step.

Figure 1.1 sets out the '2 × 2' elements of experiential learning, of the inner and outer world of the learner, and of the experience *for* and *of* learning. These are central to a definition of experiential learning taken from *The Experiential Learning Toolkit,* which contains 30 practical activities (Beard, 2010):

> A sense-making process involving significant experiences that, to varying degrees, act as the source of learning. These experiences actively immerse and reflectively engage the inner world of the learner, as a whole *being* (including physical-bodily, intellectually, emotionally, psychologically and spiritually) with their intricate 'outer world' of the learning environment (including belonging and acting (conative) in places, spaces, within the social, cultural, and political milieu) to create memorable, rich and effective experiences for and of learning.
> (adapted from Beard, 2010: 17)

Figure 1.1 The 2×2 experiential learning quadrant

The four core interactional dynamics of experiential learning	
The experience designed *for* learning is experienced in the inner world of the human	The experience designed *for* learning is experienced in the outer world
The experience *of* learning is affected by the inner world of the human	The experience *of* learning is affected by the outer world interactions and conditions

The definition highlights these four core interactional dynamics including the foundational relations between the *process* and the *person*. A closer examination of the definition above also reveals more views on what experiential learning is, and is not: it appears to involve *active immersion*, *reflective engagement* and *significant experiences*. These words represent ideas about the need for the person(s) to be motivated to learn. Another definition, created by Boud, Cohen and Walker (1993: 8), clearly draws on the work of John Dewey to develop these motivational aspects when they comment that:

> We found it to be meaningless to talk about learning in isolation from experience. Experience cannot be bypassed; it is the central consideration of all learning. Learning builds on and flows from experience: no matter what external prompts to learning there might be – teachers, materials, interesting opportunities – learning can only occur if the experience of the learner is engaged, at least at some level. These external influences can act only by transforming the experience of the learner.

When experiences have significance for the learner, there is engagement and therefore potential for change to the person, the 'self'. But this, as these authors say, is a central concern for all learning, and so it is not a core defining issue for experiential learning, despite this idea being found in other definitions. Two other notable contributions that signpost other ideas about experiential learning come from Tom Boydell in the 1970s, and David Kolb in the 1980s. Boydell explores the necessity for the experience to be engaging, with a sense of *exploration* or *investigation* by the learner:

> Experiential learning... is synonymous with 'meaningful-discovery' learning... which involves the learner in sorting things out for himself [*sic*] by restructuring his perceptions of what is happening. (Boydell, 1976: 19, 20)

> [Experiential learning is] the process whereby knowledge is created through the transformation of experience. Knowledge results from the combination of grasping and transforming experience. (Kolb, 1984: 41)

The idea of the transformation of the experience is interesting, and it clearly focuses on processes *of* learning and change. Here David Kolb, who created the experiential learning cycle (see Chapter 2) reinforces the idea that reflecting on the experience can potentially lead to a transformation as a result of the experience(s). Ultimately it is our inner being that is transformed and this we explore further in Chapter 9. This transformation can come about by both positive and negative experiences: it is sometimes a painful process to change our long-held beliefs and habits.

Experience: a bridging concept

The concept of experience is the bridge that connects the person and the object involved in an interaction, and this can be observed in some of the definitions above where there is reflection on the process involving a person and their external environment. Indeed, Cuffaro (1995: 62) emphasized: 'Action and thought are not two discrete aspects of experience. It is not to undertake an activity and then at its end to contemplate the results. What is stressed is that the two must not be separated, for each informs the other.'

Dewey is, arguably, the foremost exponent of the use of experience for learning, and the word experience occurs in a number of titles of his books, including *Experience and Nature* (1925), *Art as Experience* (1934) and *Experience and Education* (1938). Cuffaro (1995) explained that Dewey used experience as a lens through which he could analyse the interactions of people and their environments and it becomes clear that experiencing something is a linking process between action and thought (Figure 1.2). Dewey (1916: 144–45) argued:

Thinking, in other words, is the intentional endeavour to discover specific connections between something which we do and the consequences which result, so that the two become continuous. Their isolation, and consequently their purely arbitrary going together, is cancelled; a unified, developing situation takes place.

Figure 1.2 Experience: a unifying concept

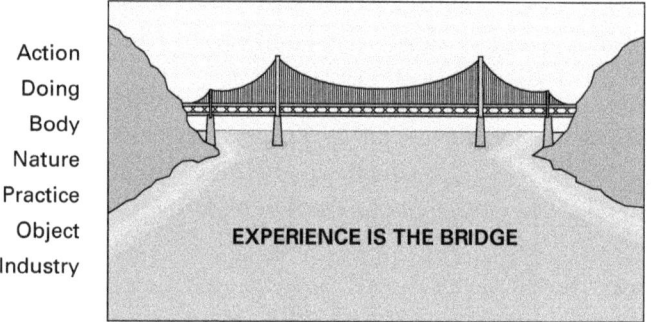

Our theories are abstract conceptualizations of how thoughts and external objects relate to one another in a consistent manner. They inform and guide us in our practice, and enable us to gain insights into the various events in which we are involved. If our practical experience does not match our theory of how we think things should be, then we often revise our theories or sometimes revisit the experience in order to see if it can be fitted into our *weltanschauung* – our way of seeing the world. Thus there is a continual interaction of theory and practice in which each informs the other.

In this way Dewey was able to connect opposites or dualities, eg person and nature, subject and object, knowing and doing, mind and body, etc. These polarities become connected and the concept of experience creates an organic whole of continuity, process and situation.

Our ideas about experiential learning are now becoming more substantial. More defining parameters of experiential learning are now emerging:

- *Experience* is central to the learning process, and it takes centre stage.
- The *experience* of learning has potential for the transformation of the 'self', our being.

- The *experiential* dynamic is fourfold: *of* and *for*, affecting the whole person through the *inner* and *outer* world interactions.
- The conditions for learning, learner motivation, active engagement and immersion in the experience are all significant.
- *Experience* acts as the bridge unifying typical dualisms such as action and thought, doing and knowing, body and mind, nature and person, practice and theory.

We would suggest at this introductory stage that the difficulties of completely tying down the defining parameters of experiential learning should be acknowledged, and, to an extent, accommodated. We should be comfortable with the fluidity of the concept of experiential learning, as experience and learning are not static phenomena. Using the metaphor of *fluidity* suggests that experience is like a river, in the sense that it is always on the move and so it is not possible to step into the same water twice. There are times when we allow the waters to flow past us, to enjoy being present in the moment as an experience of just 'being', without any intention to grasp that experience, or indeed to consciously learn from what is happening. The *film* metaphor suggests the experience is a complex composition, but in this metaphor we can use the idea of playback and memory to *reflect in* and *reflect on* the experience and take another look at it: we can rerun, rethink and reinterpret experiences. Metaphors, however, can not only illuminate, they can also distort, so we must be careful which metaphors we choose when communicating with others. We now have more ideas to add to our understanding of experiential learning:

- Learning is a fluid, ever-changing process, derived from and linked to other *experiences*: it is like a *river* or a *film*.
- *Experience* and *learning* are constructed as a complex composite of the inner-world and outer-world experiences.
- The *experience* should ideally be significant and memorable.

At this point we will cease generating more ideas and add a word of caution. Michelson acknowledges the incoherence of experiential learning, suggesting this is fruitful because experiential forms of learning have their roots in alternative practice. Experiential learning, she suggests, is 'liberatory precisely because it is unstable and provisional, because it is collective and not individual, because it always contains an insurgent element that resists categorization and management' (Michelson, 1999: 142). The idea of experiential learning as 'liberating' is an interesting point. This is not always the case, as experiential learning can also be used to oppress, and this is something that has to be kept in mind and avoided when designing experiential learning activities. Telling people what they should learn, by imposing fixed and uncomplicated truths, without allowing critical thinking, is just one example where oppressive forms of experiential learning can thrive.

More than social and cultural

In this book we take a broad, multidisciplinary approach to the understanding of experiential learning (for a more detailed exploration of multidisciplinary views of experiential learning see Beard, 2015). Many people have explored experiential learning, each viewing it through their different lenses of understanding. However, the majority of books on education and learning are written by authors whose focus is on people, culture and society. They adopt a *sociological* perspective, arguing that learning is socially constructed, and that humans are 'free agents', having control of their actions. This stance rejects the idea of *biological determinism*, a view that our biology directs and determines our actions. Boud, Cohen and Walker (1993), for example, position learning as socially and culturally constructed, arguing that learning is shaped by the socio-emotional context in which it occurs. Likewise Illeris (2009: 401) and Jarvis (2006: 13) argue that learning occurs through social situations, whereby humans interact with other humans in what they refer to as a 'material environment'. Indeed Jarvis (2006: 5) notes that 'existence, then, is never unchanging and always social; we live and move and have our being in a social context'. We do not support this anthropocentric view, rather we take into account both the human world and the human interactional dynamic with the 'more-than-human world'; in this way we recognize other living creatures within the ecosystems of the planet not just as a 'material' backcloth, but very much alive, and as such significant in determining our human way of *being* and *belonging* in the world. We argue that to fully understand experiential learning it has to be viewed though the many lenses of, for example, the psychology of learning, the neuroscience of learning, the biological processes and the influence of planetary processes on learning, in addition to the social and cultural lenses of the human world. We will therefore take into account the fact that we share the planet, our home, our environment, with many millions of other species. Below is a case study to explore how organizations and individuals interact with this 'more-than-human' living world and in doing so apply experiential learning to influence individual, societal and planetary change.

CASE STUDY Kadoorie Farm and Botanic Garden, Hong Kong

Kadoorie Farm and Botanic Garden (KFBG) is based in the rural New Territories of Hong Kong (www.kfbg.org). The organization is located on the northern slopes of Tai Mo Shan, Hong Kong's highest mountain. It was set up by the Kadoorie brothers who were part of a well-established business family who saw wealth as a sacred trust to benefit mankind. Long ago they helped many thousands of refugees to rebuild their lives. Now it is a unique public–private partnership, funded by the Kadoorie Foundation to the tune of over 130 million Hong Kong dollars per year (US $16.6 million). The organization works closely with the public, governments, academia, non-governmental organizations (NGOs) and businesses to protect our common future. As the lead author of this book it has been a privilege for me to provide staff training and development on a regular basis to an organization that has a remarkable set of values within their core mission statement to 'harmonize our relationship with the environment'. Their vision for the future is 'a world in which people live sustainably with respect for each other and nature'.

These are their seven headings of values: sustainable living, justice, love, participation, professionalism, learning and happiness. The details behind the value of 'love' are as follows: having self-awareness and understanding of the interrelationship of all things. Having compassion and respect for life. Recognizing that our outer discord is a reflection of inner discord. Striving for inner silence. The details under the heading of 'learning' are as follows: being adaptive and flexible to changing circumstances. Having a holistic outlook. Being practical, objective, creative and insightful.

KFBG offers a series of public experiential learning events each year that work with the four Hs: head, hands, heart and home. These remarkable events work with experiences involving interactions with the 'more-than-human world' (MTHW) and can be more complex to design. The programme includes, for example, a half-day and a full day such as a 'Day of Mindfulness'; working with sustainable farming methods that use the 24 solar rhythms of the Chinese calendar; a 'Talk to Plants' programme; and many other experiential 'encounters' with the more-than-human world.

Their half-day and day courses of Day of Mindfulness have attracted many hundreds of people in the last few years. The event involves facilitators taking participants through a peaceful and uplifting experience in the serene surroundings of the beautiful forest and gardens of KFBG. The core physical activity is a slow walk, sometimes barefoot, a small pilgrimage as others have done for perhaps 1,000 years, to the summit of Kwun Yum Shan, a spiritual mountain at an altitude of 552 metres. On the way the participants experience mindful walking, sitting silently in nature, storytelling, deep circular breathing, stretching activities, studying individual plants close up from all angles, drawing and sometimes singing and sharing. During the journey they may visit a herb garden and pick a selection of what catches their attention, with which to make a herbal tea half-way up the mountain. Sometimes they have a ceremony to release a wild bird of prey, once injured and then treated and rehabilitated at KFBG's Wild Animal Rescue Centre. At the summit of Kwun Yum Shan they show silent gratitude to nature, or listen to music, watching the sunset.

Many participants remarked that sitting listening to the sounds of flowing water was very special to them. In the instructions sent to participants people are 'requested to respect other participants by maintaining silence throughout the journey'. Participants report experiencing a quieting of the mind, a special closeness to nature, an inner peace and well-being. A significant number of people experiencing these events expressed a desire to return, and to do more of these experiential encounters.

The above case study reveals an organization that works extensively with experiential learning: it is a component within their mission, and vision. The organization takes environmental and planetary issues right to the heart of its purpose, ways of working and ways of being in the world. They also use the experiential learning model presented at the end of Chapter 3 to guide the design of their extensive programme of public events. This case study is the first of many within this new edition that offer practical solutions to support the understanding of experiential learning.

Whilst this book is a detailed practical guide, we continually connect with, clarify and make readily available our underlying philosophy. In addition we will signpost and guide you towards an extensive body of literature so that you can explore and expand knowledge and practice in other directions. We venture into, borrow and learn from many other disciplines: we include ideas and integrating concepts from fields such as psychotherapy, evolutionary psychology, education, corporate training, organizational development, adventure and outdoor studies, event management and leisure. We consider the role of thinking and feeling in the experience *of* learning, and the role of the body, as well as the phenomenal experiences of the beautiful living world that surrounds us every day. These are some of the many dynamics influencing personal and organizational change: factors that influence how we think, what we do, and how we conduct ourselves and behave in the world.

Experience and the problem of language

When we teach, train, facilitate or coach it is important to be conscious of the words we use in our work. Certain ways of communicating can help the brain to navigate and understand complicated things. In the case study above we might reflect on one traditional concept and way of working that originated as an approach within Outward Bound, notably to 'let the mountains (the experience) speak for themselves'. The natural world has a powerful 'voice', it speaks to us if we listen and let the voice in. The suggestion, then, is that there are times when a facilitator should be silent, not take on the voice of the mountains, but to simply let the mountain speak to people. This leads to the question of whether all people can hear the experience speaking to them, and this might be viewed as the extent to which people can *experience their experiencing*. This in turn relates to our levels of *consciousness of our experiences*, and the extent to which we are conscious of the way we learn from our experiences. These issues are all significant to our understanding of experiential learning.

When we speak, or write, the metaphors we use send specific signals, relating to the way we experience the world: this can be a sensory metaphor, a bodily metaphor or a spatial metaphor, for example. This is illustrated as follows: I am feeling a bit *down*, you have your life *in front of you*, she works in *higher* education, they are *weighed down* with work, the government *rushed* the law through parliament. In this book, as we have already stated, we take the view that the human experience is a complex and fluid process of interaction. These interacting worlds, between and within humans, occur through a system of bodily signals, and spoken and written words. Writing, speaking and gestures are all bodily acts and, furthermore, we continually use these bodily metaphors, as well as time and space metaphors, in our speech.

Language is significant to the way we experience the world, not only from the perspective of social interactions, but also because we have multiple voices and conversations from our multiple selves speaking almost continually in our heads. You will notice that the act of reading this text takes the form of one such voice within your head!

Our ability to be conscious of or describe our *experience* of the world is limited, and we refer to this as *the problem of languaging experience*. This can be illustrated by the experience of Robert Kull who tried to write about his experience of solitude whilst living on a remote island of Argentinian Patagonia. He was trying to write notes for a PhD when he recalls how his words marched statically across the page, and he dropped his pen, perhaps out of frustration, when he realized that there was no dance between world and word. Here lies a further difficulty underlying the act of writing about and describing experiential learning.

To recap so far, we have the following understanding of experiential learning:

- *Experience* is central to the learning process, and it takes centre stage.
- The *experiential* dynamic is fourfold: *of* and *for*, affecting the whole person in terms of their *inner* and *outer* world experiencing.
- There must be a certain *quality* to the experience so as to *engage* the learner, and be *memorable*.
- The *conditions* for learning, and learner *motivation*, active *engagement* and *immersion* are significant.
- There are many elements that make up the *learning experience*, and they are not only social and cultural; there are emotional, sensorial, cognitive and conative dynamics relating to our human sense of belonging, becoming and being in a human and more-than-human world.
- The richest resources for learning originate within the learner.
- The *experience* of learning has potential for the transformation of the 'self', our being.
- Learning flows, and is derived from other *experiences*: it is continuous, flowing like a *river*, with a script and complex composition, like a *film*.
- *Experience* is a complex composite, made up of information from the constantly interacting inner world and outer worlds.
- Human language, the film *script*, is limited in terms of its ability to describe experience(s).
- Experiential learning acknowledges the issues affecting power and control: learners take responsibility for leading their own learning.

- *Experience* acts as the bridge unifying typical dualisms such as action and thought, doing and knowing, body and mind, nature and person, practice and theory.

More about this book

These deliberations about the nature of experience are not merely academic, with no practical application. It is only by considering what we mean by *experience* that trainers, educators, facilitators and developers of human potential can gain insight into one of the most powerful means to learning that currently exists: learning from experience is one of the most fundamental and natural means of learning available to everyone. This natural form of learning has become increasingly popular whether it operates at the individual, group, organizational or societal levels – and for this reason it deserves close examination. We are attempting to get closer to terms like *experience*, *education* and *learning* so as to create a more coherent, relational understanding, where theory and practice connect to each other. The book is divided into three parts. Part One is an introduction to experiential learning, about the foundations and fundamentals. In Part Two the chapters deal with each of the component parts or dimensions of our model of human experience called the Learning Combination Lock. In Part Three we explore the future and the world of imagination, mental fitness, virtual and augmented reality, and gamification.

Few books other than novels are designed to be read from cover to cover, and this book is based on the pick-and-mix principle. You will have your own particular requirements and should, therefore, dip in and out to select the areas that have most value to yourself. Below we provide a brief description of each of the chapters, to help guide you through the book and to support your personal learning and topic investigations. The book offers techniques that help learners make sense of their experience, as well as methods to develop and practise new behaviours. The techniques include mood setting, drama, creative writing, art, meditation, environmental modification and routine rituals. Much more detailed accounts covering over 30 practical experiences are found in the sister book, *The Experiential Learning Toolkit* (Beard, 2010). We seek to help you as a coach, developer, educator or trainer, to focus on new ideas, and we explore ways to improve professional practice and ethical responsibility through self-monitoring and feedback techniques. Many of the theories and practical methods presented in this book apply equally to all parties involved; indeed, as practitioners, we too are learners, and good practice emanates from our ability to learn from our own experiences.

An overview of the chapters

Part One

Chapter 2: five big questions about experiential learning

In this chapter we will scrutinize in more detail what we mean by the category *experiential learning*. To do this we examine the roots of experiential learning, its constituent parts, and we will say more about what it is, and what it is not. A number of basic models of learning are provided to illustrate how experiential learning has evolved. We also critique the notion of experiential learning, the learning cycle and learning styles. We compare experiential learning with experiential education and other experiential approaches to learning. Experiential learning, while superficially a relatively simple concept, becomes more complex as we probe the subject more deeply. We investigate the many dimensions of experience, and explore the reason why experience is often considered as a synonym for learning. In this chapter we explore these issues by asking what we are calling the 'Big Questions'.

Chapter 3: designing, delivering and evaluating experiential learning

In this chapter we introduce our overarching whole-person philosophy through an easy-to-use model. We also look at the navigational tools that can support the experience *of* learning with a new idea of *making learning visible*. 'Human experience mapping' is introduced as a design and evaluative method for practitioners.

Part Two

This part of the book has chapters covering each of the six dimensions of the Combination Lock model.

Chapter 4: learning environments – people, spaces and places

The belonging dimension of the learning experience Learning is about interactions with other people. It is a social process, reaching out into communities and beyond. In this chapter we not only explore the social processes of learning, we explore how we interact with the world beyond human beings, the so-called 'more-than-human' world. Experiential learning occurs in places and spaces, and these can be indoors, or outdoors, and in natural or artificially constructed environments. We have witnessed student nurses being filmed interacting with dementia patients within specially constructed classrooms: simulated homes, with a lounge and kitchen area similar to the real homes that these patients might traditionally live in. In this chapter we show how the design and use of artificial and natural learning environments can maximize learning. Computer simulations, simulated ice-walls, artificial mountains, simulated catering kitchens and law courts, indoor climbing walls, artificial caves, tall ships, school classrooms, ski slopes, concrete white-water rafting courses and many other places are used for experiential learning and many of these will be explored as illustrative case examples. We will show how the rich and varied spatial ecology for learning that is constantly evolving: many different spaces are currently being utilized for experiential learning.

Chapter 5: experiential learning activities

The doing dimension of the learning experience Doing what, and why? Doing less, or doing more? The *doing* of activities *for* learning has been a main focus for some experiential learning providers and we explore how this focus is changing. However, as we saw from our first case study, there is always choice and personal and organizational responsibility attached to the act of *doing* when understood as the way we behave in the world, and how we conduct ourselves.

This chapter guides you through a range of design ideas for particular forms of planned experiential learning. We recognize that much learning occurs in an unplanned way, and that learning outcomes are often not the ones anticipated. The chapter also explores the many different types of activities that people do so that they can learn from their experience. We systematically analyse some of these learning activities to create a 17-point checklist. We also examine stories and journeys, planned and unplanned learning, real versus simulated learning, the use of objects and obstacles, sequencing and pacing, flow, challenge and support.

The main theme of this chapter is that there are many new and emerging trends that signpost the endless possibilities for experiential providers to enhance the delivery of any experience for educational, training or developmental purposes. In this chapter we also consider the way in which the degree of 'reality' can be altered to benefit learning. Learner perceptions of reality can be applied to many aspects of experiential learning, including the learning process itself, the perceived reality of the activities and the perceived reality of the location in which the experience takes place. We show examples where reality can be manipulated as a key consideration in the design and delivery of experiential learning, including the alteration of elements of realness in a negotiating training programme, as well as the altering of reality in play, drama, sculpture, art and fantasy.

Chapter 6: sensory experience and sensory intelligence

The sensing dimension of the learning experience The senses are the means through which information from the outside and inner bodily world reach our bodies and brains. The senses are the conduits connecting the outer public world with our inner private world, shaping our raw unprocessed experience. This chapter acknowledges that when we use more senses in our experience of learning then the stronger the possibility of learning being more memorable, with increased depth. For this reason, the senses are considered, one by one, with strategies for enhancing and enriching them. The chapter also recognizes that the senses can be overwhelmed by data and we provide advice on the benefits of mindfulness, solitude or silence through sensory input reduction.

The senses can be viewed as providing the basic data, which is profoundly important for learning. In compassionate communication (Rosenberg, 2003), and in other forms of complex communication, learning to observe without emotion-based judgement means developing a strong sense awareness, to get to know our bodies and the feelings we experience. This experiencing our experiences often involves suspending thinking. In this chapter we offer many practical examples where the senses can be used to enhance learning, including sensory work to develop higher mind states, and sensory applications for work with complex learning needs, or for therapeutic work. Sensory data significantly influence the learning experience and there is a need for more research into the way sensory intelligence affects learning.

Chapter 7: experience and emotions

The feeling dimension of the learning experience Emotional experiences and emotional intelligence underpin learning, yet many educators and trainers have only recently given more attention to emotional capability. Emotional intelligence, according to Goleman (1996), is at the core of all success. Emotions are played out in the theatre of the body, and experiential learning will always have an emotional dynamic as part of the experience. This chapter begins with an examination of how emotions and moods underpin experiential learning. The concept of emotional intelligence is examined and set in context with other types of intelligence. The chapter examines the nature of emotional waves, including the troughs, with balance as a central theme: different waves, different sizes and different frequencies all create the essential roller-coasters that form the emotional self. Emotions influence our sense of self and so we examine the role of emotional blocks to learning such as fear and risk taking. The positive and negative aspects of emotional engineering are also considered. In this chapter the Learning Combination Lock shows how the senses form the basic conduit for an external experience to be translated into an internal stimulation. The stimulation of the senses creates a parallel affective response, one that is a powerful determinant of subsequent learning. Helping people to be conscious of this emotional experience can allow people to manage and intensify their own learning. The chapter offers ways to read and work with key emotional signs and to understand the emotional nature of unfulfilled need within conflict. We suggest methods to access the roots of emotion and ways to surface feelings and challenge emotions, and we further explore how humour, metaphors, trilogies and storytelling can be used to access and influence the emotional connection to learning. Helping learners to sense, surface and express both positive and negative feelings rather than to deny or censor them requires great skill and care in group work. It enables the colour and richness of the feelings of learners to be expressed and considered in a controlled way so as to maximize learners' understanding of the learning processes.

Chapter 8: experience, knowledge and intelligence

The knowing dimension of the learning experience Which is best: thinking slowly or thinking fast, thinking superficially or thinking with depth, thinking too little or thinking too much? How important is the human body in the process of thinking? We address many of these core issues in this chapter. We explore the historical period when the idea of the brain as operating like a computer was the dominant view of human learning, and we consider new developments. Howard Gardner's book *Frames of Mind* (1983) drew attention to the validity and importance of multiple intelligences (MI), eg musical intelligence, linguistic intelligence. This chapter considers the range of intelligences, including the difficult areas of spiritual intelligence, naturalistic intelligence and creative intelligence. Each of the three intelligences – spiritual, naturalistic and creative – is theoretically discussed and descriptions of skills are listed. As with the rest of the book, there are frequent illustrations of practical examples that link theory and practice, thus applying the essence of experiential learning.

Chapter 9: experience, learning and change

The being dimension of the learning experience It could be said that all learning contributes to the construction of our very being: we learn to become different. Learning is fundamental to the transformation and change to our self, our being. Thinking is a way of learning; sensing and observing are ways of learning; doing and acting are ways of learning; and belonging and interacting are ways of learning. We learn and so contribute to the changes in our being, therefore we are continually becoming, and we do this in a number of ways. If we call ourselves human beings, then what do we mean by being? These are some of the issues we explore in our penultimate chapter. We consider conditioning, conduct and consciousness and the dangers of not knowing our self. We also return to the idea of life as a film, where we write the script, and put the clips of our life experiences together to form our own unique footage. We are always becoming in the life-long and life-wide journey of learning to be. This final part of the Learning Combination Lock model is the most difficult area to explore, but arguably the most important.

Part Three

The final section of the book contains a single closing chapter.

Chapter 10: imagining and experiencing the future of learning

It is not only through considering past and present experiences that we can learn. It is also possible to imagine multiple futures and rehearse alternative scenarios in our minds. This gives us the possibility to minimize the potential for failure and increase the chance of success. Thinking about future possibilities tends to develop the neural connections in the brain and further increase the likelihood of success. We look at how the conscious part of our brains can interfere with the subconscious to undermine our performance, and use the game of tennis as an example. Furthermore, we predict that some of the experiential forms of learning and working might influence the development of the human brain:

To find that point, that reason for our doing and our being, it helps to build on three senses – a sense of continuity, a sense of connection and a sense of direction. Without these senses we can feel disoriented, adrift and rudderless... We shall need all the help we can find to recognize our place and role in it. These senses are the best antidote I know to the feelings of impotence that rapid change induces in us all. (Handy, 1994: 239)

The book is dedicated to making the art and science of experiential learning explicit at the individual, group and institution, and societal levels.

PART ONE
Experiential learning: foundations and fundamentals

Practical answers to some theoretical questions 02

Learning is an experience. Everything else is just information.
ALBERT EINSTEIN

Introduction

In this chapter we consider concepts and theoretical underpinnings to experiential learning by asking five simple practical questions, and we are calling these the Big Questions. The chapter explores some 'need to know' topics before we proceed further in the book to consider a range of practical topics that underpin the design, delivery and evaluation of experiential learning. At the end of this chapter we will summarize our thoughts about the core distinguishing features of experiential learning. The five questions are as follows:

Question 1: Experiential education (EE) and experiential learning (EL) – are they virtually the same?

Question 2: Is experiential learning (EL) simply the sum of an *experience* (E) plus an intention to *learn* (L)?

Question 3: What are the more popular models currently being used to explain experiential learning?

Question 4: What are the main criticisms of experiential learning?

Question 5: Has the notion of the *experience society* contributed to our understanding of experiential learning?

Question 1: Experiential education and experiential learning – are they virtually the same?

As we have already noted in Chapter 1, the ability to define any categories is fraught with problems. The quotation below is taken from Fenwick (2000: 5), who commented on a number of conceptions of experiential learning:

> The different categories presented here may appear as natural and given, when in fact they are highly constructed. All dimensions of classification derive from some perspective held and imposed by the classifier, thus constructing a world arranged according to the preferred order of things derived from the classifier's viewpoint. In this assertion, I simply admit the constraints of my own logic. In particular, Western classificatory logic embeds its knowers with the deep assumption that there is such a logic, seeking to know the differences between things, and to separate them accordingly. I cannot presume to hide my own interests in cognition and my own preferences for particular learning theories behind these dimensions as if they are neutrally presented simply as different types. I am also aware that my own desires for conceptual control are reflected in the act of rendering these perspectives as manageable, comparable threads of intellectual thought.

To illustrate the points above, and to answer the question of whether experiential learning and experiential education are virtually the same, first read the following three definitions and then decide which is a definition of experiential learning and which is a definition of experiential education.

> **A:** The combination of processes throughout a lifetime whereby the whole person – body (genetic, physical and biological) and mind (knowledge, skills, attitudes, values, emotions, beliefs and senses) – experiences social situations, the perceived content of which is then transformed cognitively, emotively or practically (or through any combination) and integrated into the individual person's biography, resulting in a continually changing (or more experienced) person.

> **B:** A holistic philosophy, where carefully chosen experiences supported by reflection, critical analysis and synthesis are structured to require the learner to take initiative, make decisions and be accountable for the

results, through actively posing questions, investigating, experimenting, being curious, solving problems, assuming responsibility, being creative, constructing meaning and integrating previously developed knowledge.

C: A sense-making process involving significant experiences that, to varying degrees, act as the source of learning. These experiences actively immerse and reflectively engage the inner world of the learner, as a whole *being* (including physical-bodily, intellectually, emotionally, psychologically and spiritually) with their intricate 'outer world' of the learning environment (including belonging and acting (conative) in places, spaces, within the social, cultural and political milieu) to create memorable, rich and effective experiences for, and of, learning.

'A' is a definition of lifelong learning, taken from *Towards a Comprehensive Theory of Human Learning*, by Jarvis (2006: 134), and quoted in *The International Handbook of Lifelong Learning* (2009: 10). 'B' is a definition of *experiential education*, taken from Itin (1999: 93) and it is part of a comprehensive 150-word definition that captures the essence of John Dewey's (1938) sophisticated thinking on experiential education. 'C' is a definition of *experiential learning*, adapted from *The Experiential Learning Toolkit* (Beard, 2010). The similarities of the defining parameters of experiential learning, lifelong learning and experiential education are evident; the category boundaries are clearly blurred and rather fuzzy, and so we will further explore the question a little more.

Both experiential learning and experiential education are terms, or categories of learning, that contain the word experiential, and they continue to be used interchangeably, with aspects of their defining parameters 'mirroring each other' (Itin, 1999: 91). This is because their historical 'roots' have a common heritage: their roots frequently merge and separate, and are so complex that many authors have resorted to the use of metaphors of tree roots, rivers or ropes, so as to unravel and explain the inherent convolutedness. Roberts, in his book *Beyond Learning by Doing* (2012), utilizes the metaphors of *rivers* and *currents* to illustrate the complex social, political, individual, democratic and market influences that have impacted on the evolution of experiential education. In a chapter titled 'The origins of outdoor and adventure education' in the book *Rethinking Outdoor, Experiential and Informal Education*, Jeffs applies the metaphor of 'a long rope comprising many strands' to explain outdoor and adventure education. Furthermore, the rope, he says 'remains unfinished' (Jeffs, 2018: 1).

The foundations of experiential learning

The deep roots of experiential learning, and experiential education, lie within ancient Eastern and Western philosophies. It is said that the 'West's first conceptual notion of experience' (Roberts, 2012: 17) was derived from ancient Greek philosophical contributions, and that the philosopher Aristotle was the originator or 'progenitor of the experiential learning cycle', developed by David Kolb in the 1980s (Stonehouse, Alison and Carr, 2011: 18). In the Eastern world, however, the ancient but well-known Chinese aphorism '*I hear I forget, I see I remember, I do I understand*' came from Confucian philosophy. This saying laid the early foundations for later interpretations of experiential learning in the West, suggesting that if a learner is simply told, then they forget; if they watch, they might remember; but if they 'do' the 'real' thing then this is the best way for them to learn. But is it? This Chinese aphorism clearly gave rise to the thinking behind the 'Tell–Show–Do' pyramid model of instructional techniques, sometimes known as Dale's Cone of Experience, developed by Edgar Dale (1969). Some people mistakenly regard this as the fundamental underpinning to experiential learning, ie that experiential forms of learning are to do with doing. But what do we mean by 'do', and what is meant by *doing the real thing*? Aphorisms do not offer detail, and so we might usefully challenge these ideas and their interpretations so that we might better understand experiential forms of learning. This Confucian saying is clearly open to interpretation, more so because it was written in Chinese, and therefore in the language of the 'Chinese way'. When the saying was translated from Chinese into English it lost some of its original depth of meaning. 'Doing' is perhaps better interpreted in English as the *whole person immersion in a practice*. Let us offer a slightly more exacting translation of the saying for you to ponder on. I want you to imagine a Confucian philosopher saying the following words:

> *To hear something is better than not to hear it,*
> *To say something is better than just to hear it,*
> *To know something is better than just to say it,*
> *To practise something is better than just to know it...*
> (reproduced from Beard, 2010)

To practise is to actually *experience* it: to feel it, to sense it, to understand it and to *immerse* oneself in doing it, regularly, for oneself. Over time the notion of 'doing' things has become dominant within these simple constructs of experiential forms of learning, and this has created problems.

The textbook title *Beyond Learning by Doing* published by Roberts in 2012 reflects this very concern. Eastern sages suggest that difficulties arise when inherent complexity confuses the signposts with the journey, and that we need to understand that the 'learning doctrine is not the same as practising the wisdom the doctrine is intended to teach' (Stevenson, 2000: 17).

Boundary disputes

These complex histories underpinning the development of experiential learning and experiential education have created frequent boundary disputes. Some authors adopt Dewey's sophisticated ideas about education to make contentious claims that experiential learning, unlike experiential education, 'lacks a philosophy', and that it is a mere 'method' or 'technique' (Roberts, 2012: 4). Roberts, in his defence of experiential education, erroneously argues that experiential learning is merely learning by doing. Others suggest that experiential learning is a subfield of experiential education, possibly even 'redundant' (Smith and Knapp, 2011). Einstein, however, noted that 'the only thing that interferes with my learning is my education'.

In this book we present our own philosophy of experiential learning, and our position is that in an evolutionary sense (phylogenetic), and from the human development (ontogenetic) perspective, *learning* is prior to, and much broader than, the notion of formal, or informal, *education*. In a similar vein, Kidner notes (2001: 20), when people consider nature as a mere backcloth to the social world of humans, nature is 'prior to human existence or activity', and nature 'is a condition of social life rather than a consequence of it'.

Question 2: Is experiential learning (EL) simply the sum of experience (E) plus learning (L)?

Experiential learning is a term consisting of the two words *experience* and *learning*, and it would be sensible to first explore each word separately. When a word or concept is examined in order to write a definition, it soon becomes apparent how elusive its meaning is, and the closer we look, the more indistinct and vague it can become. The word 'experience' is no different in this respect; however, reaching for a dictionary can provide some assistance, and the Oxford Dictionary describes experience as:

> The fact of being consciously the subject of a state or condition; of being consciously affected by an event; a state or condition viewed subjectively; an event by which one is affected; and, knowledge resulting from actual observation or from what one has undergone.

As we commented in Chapter 1 the *experience* takes centre stage as it were: experiential learning approaches consider the *experience* to be the foundation *of*, and the stimulus *for*, learning. However, no matter how hard we try to grasp, categorize and define these substantial, slippery concepts of *experience* and *learning*, there will always be fragments that will remain elusive. The words *experience*, *learning* and *education* open up a diverse and complex range of issues associated with philosophy, ontology, epistemology and methodology when we attempt to define them (Hager, 1999). Big words indeed!

As we noted above the development of philosophical thought about the meaning of *experience* has a long history and can be traced back to ancient Eastern and Western thinking. The development of understanding about experiential learning is therefore deeply grounded in such philosophical thought. Many contemporary writers draw upon this ancient heritage in order to develop their own ideas, including Dewey, Lewin, Revans and Kolb. John Dewey was well known for arguing for a *theory of experience*. Dewey also argued that philosophy should investigate life as humans *experience* it. According to Warren, Sakofs and Hunt (1995), Dewey maintained that, as humans:

> We find ourselves in continual transaction with the physical, psychological, mental, spiritual world, and philosophy should be a systematic investigation into the nature of this experience. (Warren, Sakofs and Hunt, 1995: 11)

Experience as interactional

The continual transactions, in simple terms, involve the inner, private world of a person continuously interacting with the outer, public world. Learners 'explore inner space as well as the physical world, entering deeply into the inner being of the mind and seeking to be fully connected with the outer world' (Fenwick, 2003: 52). This dynamic forms the basic structure for our experiential learning model that we present in Chapter 3. Later chapters of this book will systematically investigate each of these 'worlds' and the multiple transactional processes mentioned in the quotation above relating to human experience, and that is why we propose that our book is simultaneously a philosophy and a practice of experiential learning.

Dewey worked extensively on developing a philosophy of experience. His work was focused on educational contexts, and more specifically schools, though his thinking continues to inform and underpin both experiential education and experiential learning in the 21st century (see Beard, 2018). Dewey presented the notion known as the *continuity of experience*, highlighting how our experiences do not happen in isolation: rather they are linked to previous and future experiences. Experience(s) are also influenced by both the subconscious and conscious thoughts that continually contribute to the construction of the 'self', our *biography*.

Unique experiences

Each individual constructs their own unique experiences, based on their sensory reception and perceptual processing, and so any experience will be influenced not only by past experiences, but, for example, by personal needs, and selective sensory focusing. Experience is constructed by an ever-changing perceptual novelty. This interrelationship between an experience and previous experiences and the selective nature of perception is summed up in the following quotation from Boud, Cohen and Walker (1993: 8):

> Learning always relates, in one way or another, to what has gone before. There is never a clean slate on which to begin; unless new ideas and new experience link to previous experience, they exist as abstractions, isolated and without meaning. The effects of experience influence all learning. What we are attracted towards, what we avoid and how we go about the task, is dependent on how we have responded in the past. Earlier experiences that had positive or negative effect stimulate or suppress new learning. They encourage us to take risks and enter into new territory for exploration, or alternatively, they may inhibit our range of operation or ability to respond to opportunities.

Our memories of experiences are not fixed either, they are dynamic (Baddeley, Eysenck and Anderson, 2009) and, therefore, these new cognitive structures may influence the way in which we view the experience on revisiting it. In other words, as Heraclitus said: 'You cannot step in the same river twice.' Each time we revisit a memory there is the possibility of interpreting it differently from previous understandings. This is because during the intervening period we have new experiences. This difficulty in accurately and precisely pinning down the meaning of experience is discussed by Boud, Cohen and Walker (1993: 7) who commented:

For the sake of simplicity in discussing learning from experience, experience is sometimes referred to as if it were singular and unlimited by time or place. Much experience, however, is multifaceted, multilayered and so inextricably connected with other experiences that it is impossible to locate temporally or spatially. It almost defies analysis as the act of analysis inevitably alters the experience and the learning that flows from it.

In relation to the quote by Einstein at the beginning of this chapter, Rogers (1996: 107) similarly suggests that 'there is a growing consensus that experience forms the basis of all learning', as does Jenny Moon (2004: 119) who maintains that 'all learning is based on experience'. Yet, it is not entirely evident that all learning is as a result of the accumulation of everyday experiences. We possess, for example, some prewired, inherited behaviours. A brief consideration of infant and child development illustrates that when a baby is born they have the natural ability to strongly grip, and even hang from, the fingers of the midwife or parent. The infant also possesses the sucking reflex, and babies will make stepping movements if their feet touch the floor, even though they are unable to support their own weight (Siegler, Deloache and Eisenberg, 2006). It would appear that many of our inner biological functions are already hardwired while other dimensions develop and grow as a result of our experiences. We are not the free agents we believe we are in terms of experiencing the world; our subconscious mind appears to have considerable influence on our experiences (see Swaab, 2014). Furthermore, specific brain areas develop with extensive or repetitive experiences, and this is well illustrated by the growth of the hippocampus area of the brain (as an area related to memory and spatial cognition) among taxi drivers (Maguire *et al*, 2000). In summary, we are saying that the foundation of nearly all of our human learning is the interaction between the inner self and the external environment, in other words our *experience* of the world.

Resistance to description

We noted in Chapter 1 how Robert Kull (2008), in his learning for a PhD in the study of solitude on a remote island in Patagonia, experienced the words of his notes marching static across the page such that there was no dance between *word* and *world*. The difficulties of describing experiences is evident. Furthermore, experience can be variably 'read' so that a complete understanding through language will always be elusive. Burr (2003) suggests that some experiences are resistant to description, and therefore 'extra discursive', and in a similar vein Sheets-Johnstone (2009: 239) notes that the 'gap between experiential and the linguistic is not easily bridged'. What is directly experienced is not easy to communicate in language, despite the fact that we translate our thoughts and experiences by *speaking to ourselves*, in our head. We talk to ourselves and we talk things through, and often this is a way of learning. Indeed there are concerns in education that these processes of learning should be made more 'visible'. One of the methods to support learners is to ask them questions such as: 'what is going on in your head right now?', or 'tell me what makes you think that?' (Berger, Rugen and Woodfin, 2014).

The construction of experience

Many authors have attempted to understand the complex nature of experience, and learning, within their specific fields of study, such as experiential learning, experiential marketing, outdoor leisure and adventure programming, and economics, to name a few. Whilst these fields of study have sought to investigate the key components that make up the human experience, they have done so to differing degrees and the result is that there is much debate concerning the dimensions of experience that are most important for learning. The social sciences are said to be the dominant form within educational research (see Whitehead and McNiff, 2006) and so there is much written about the way learning is *socially* constructed. The extent to which an experience is socially constructed (with other people), psychologically constructed (inner psyche/self), emotionally constructed (feelings), cognitively constructed (mind/thinking), environmentally or otherwise constructed is a contentious topic. Illeris (2002) suggests that learning involves three different dimensions, as a 'tension field' between cognition, emotion and society. We suggest that learning involves more than these three dimensions. Learning derives from the experience of: *thinking* (cognition) as learning, *sensing* as learning (eg this can involve not thinking too much, but merely *observing* the self), *feeling* (affective) as learning, *doing* (conative) as learning, and *belonging* (as social, and the other than human interactions, eg animal, spiritual) as learning. These aspects of learning, including the role of the *conscious* and *subconscious* processes, including our *psyche*, all contribute to changes in our *being*, our sense of self as our *biography* or make-up.

The rich ecology of experience

To add to the complexity, as we have noted already, the meaning derived from any experience is uniquely perceived by individuals, and so experience design is always going to be an inexact science. The nature of knowing, and knowledge, is equally complex. Hughes and Lury (2013: 797) view knowledge as an event, as ephemeral in form: 'we think the term ecology is helpful insofar as it enables us to acknowledge the ongoing and dynamic interrelation of processes and objects, beings and things, figures and grounds'. In this sense there is a growing realization that experiential interactions with knowledge are complex: 'The focus of enquiry is not so much on the components of experience but, rather, on the relations that bind these elements together in action' (Davis and Sumara, 1997: 108). They go on to ask: 'What happens if we were to reject the self-evident axiom that cognition is located within cognitive agents who are cast as isolated from one another and distinct from the world, and insist instead that all cognition exists in the interstices of a complex ecology of organismic relationality?' (Davis and Sumara, 1997: 110). *Experience*, *knowledge* and *learning* are clearly not simple, static phenomena that are easily describable, or definable: they are continually shifting over time and subject to continuous reflective reconstructions. Whatever the exact relation between experience and learning there is little doubt that experience probably provides the most coherent underpinning to any theory of learning.

Question 3: What are the more popular models currently being used to explain experiential learning?

Many educators are unable to articulate a coherent view of what it is that informs and shapes their design of teaching or facilitation, though typically this involves the application of certain models. Despite the 'vast literature on experiential learning' (Moon, 2004: 105), it is said that there is little evidence of experiential learning in the British educational literature prior to 1980 (Mulligan and Griffin, 1992) and that which exists appears to be concerned with a range of principal themes: efficacy, the degree to which it might contribute to wider mainstream educational reform (eg Lindsay and Ewert, 1999), how we learn from experience, and how it can best be facilitated (Edwards, 1994). Significant contributors to the field of experiential learning such as Boud and Walker (1993: 19) note that 'whilst there has been extensive discussion of models in theory building and research, less emphasis has been given to the development of models to aid teaching and learning'. Similarly Brooks and Brooks (1993: 3), in presenting a case for constructivist classrooms, note that many promising educational propositions fail to address the core 'processes of teaching and learning that occur daily, relentlessly, inexorably'.

Experiential learning must be considered against a broader backcloth of human understanding about learning in general. The dominant understanding of human learning has changed over time. Theorizing about how humans learn has thus been subject to continuous reassessment over many years. The continuing sense of an incomplete understanding has led to an unremitting quest for more ideas about how we humans learn. In Figure 2.1 we introduce a quick and simplistic contextual history that can be remembered in the form of a code: BCHSE. The dominant modes of thinking about human learning over time are shown in Figure 2.1.

In a recent text on digital games and learning, Whitton (2014: 181) argues that 'the movement of educational games from adopting a predominantly behaviourist to constructivist model, is, for me, a crucial repositioning of the field'. Let's explore this in more detail to help with an understanding of these changes, relating to past and present ideas about how humans learn, and the terminology that is associated with these periods.

In the early 20th century *behaviourism* (B) emerged as a dominant view, linked to and associated with conditioning (Pavlov, 1927; Skinner, 1974). This was a period with an animalistic focus, where much study was based on stimulating animals to see what the response would be. Conditioned learning was discovered through experiments with animals. Notable were the experiments with dogs who salivated when a bell was rung as they associated this with feeding time. It was thought that if we could learn more about how animal learning came about then we might be able to understand learning in humans. This approach gradually shifted to *cognitivist theories* (C), which began to surface in the late 1950s. The cognitive focus saw the 'human' as unique, highly intelligent and rational, and so computational brain processing – involving *thinking, remembering, analysing* and seeking ways to *explain and make sense of the world* – became the new focus. Major contributors included Lewin (1951) and Gagne (1974), but perhaps the most well known was Bloom (Bloom *et al*, 1956), who developed a spatial hierarchy of cognition. Higher forms of knowing include evaluation and synthesis, whereas lower forms of knowing would involve description. These hierarchical models can be seen as problematic, particularly as some writers relegate experiential learning as a lower level of practical learning by doing (see, for example, Young, 2008).

By the late 1960s *humanist theories* (H) were emphasizing personal agency, personal responsibility and the fulfilment of personal potential. Perhaps the most well-known proponent was Carl Rogers (1969), whose seminal text *Freedom to Learn* expressed a liberating metaphor. For Rogers, feelings, warmth, acceptance, empathy and nurturing were central to

Figure 2.1 A brief and simplified history of the major theories of learning

Time period	1900–1940s	1950s	1960s	1970s	1980s	1990s	2000–
Human learning theories (BCHSE)	BEHAVIOURAL (ethology, animal focus). Early roots of transmission approaches. Conditioning.						
		COGNITIVE (computational, focus on brain as an advanced processor, human as a rational, intelligent being).					
			HUMANIST (empathetic/nurturing). Early roots of transactional approaches. Whole person, as thinking feeling.				
				SOCIAL CONSTRUCTION of knowledge (social interaction, cultural influences).			
	ECOLOGICAL complexity. Embracing rather than rejecting preceding theories of learning.					Rich ecological complexity. Transformational approaches are more widely discussed. Revisionary post-modernism.	

learning: individuals, if treated in the right way, had it within themselves to work towards solutions to problems. These ideas were instrumental in the development of learner-centred methods. But cultural and social context became increasingly recognized as important (eg Vygotsky, 1978), giving rise to a range of *social constructivist* (S) theories, with learning seen as active, and contextualized. Learners were seen not only as constructing knowledge for themselves, as individuals, but also through social interaction. Although social constructivist theories remain highly influential, new thinking is emerging. Social constructivist ideas are now positioned among many other views about how humans learn that have been adopted from multidisciplinary perspectives. Previous ideas are embraced and not discarded as out of date. An example is that conditioning is still being applied in learning. Rich, multidisciplinary interpretations of learning are emerging, and we refer to these views as the new *ecological view* (E). Such interpretations are not dissimilar to the way we understand the workings of the complex ecology of a rainforest.

Many more contemporary contributions continue to add to this brief sketch (BCHSE). The diagram is not meant to be comprehensive and it does not, for example, expose new understanding of the role of hidden desires and fears, as in psychoanalytic theories (Britzman, 1998); the questioning of the outdated notion of single intelligence (Gardner, 1983); advances in brain science (neuroscience) leading to a reassessment of old views about our biology controlling us (known as 'biological determinism') (see Collins, 2016); and, particularly significant to our discussions here, the wider recognition of the role of the body in mental processing (embodiment) (see Lakoff and Johnson, 1999; Sheets-Johnstone, 2009). The senses are also very important to learning (see Abram, 1997), and bodily gestures are also significant to mental processing (Gallagher, 2005). Emotions are also strongly linked to mental processing (Illeris, 2002). Such diverse works illustrate the ongoing search for more integrative and comprehensive explorations of human learning within and across disciplines (Dillon, 2007), where the connective relationship between mind, body and field can be further explored.

Although far from presenting a complete picture, this historical sketch charts a simple trajectory from ethology (basic behavioural studies) to ecology (complex relational processes). Our knowledge about human learning has thus shifted from animalistic simplicity, rooted in predictability and control experiments such as conditioning, towards complex, ecological interpretations across disciplines (see Sterling, 2003). However, note that the shading in the E zone in Figure 2.1 continues across the chart: new ideas do not negate old ideas, they often add to a richer understanding of human learning. Whilst cognitivist and social constructivist views remain dominant, it is the ecological interpretation that aligns with our multidisciplinary, holistic model, called the Learning Combination Lock, which has millions of possibilities or permutations. Ecological theorists Davis and Sumara (1997: 112) outline this new rich complexity by suggesting that all the contributing factors in any learning situation are 'intricately, ecologically, and complexly related. Both the cognizing agent (us as humans) and everything with which it is associated are in constant flux, each adapting to the other in the same way that the environment evolves simultaneously with the species that inhabit it.' Ideas about experiential learning continue to evolve: if we zoom in to examine some of the more recent and popular theories related to experiential learning we can shed further light on our understanding.

Popular models as 'theories-in-use' for experiential learning

We have outlined the origins of the Tell–Show–Do pyramid, or cone (Dale, 1969) derived from Eastern philosophy. There have been many other simple models. Illeris offers a triangular model that shows learning as involving three dimensions, notably the social, the emotional and the cognitive. He goes on to comment that there do not appear to be 'any earlier learning theories that fully recognize and deal with this complexity in its entirety' (Illeris, 2002: 9). Similarly, Heron voices concern about old models of education that 'going back to classical times, dealt only with the education of the intellect, theoretical and applied'. He suggests an integration of emotional, interpersonal and political competence, as 'nowadays we have people who are learning by *thinking, feeling and doing* – bringing all these to bear on the acquisition of new knowledge and skills' (Heron, 2001: 208 – italics added).

Undoubtedly the most popular model and theory of experiential learning is that developed by Kolb (1984). He stressed the importance of his experiential learning theory by stating that it is:

> the foundation for an approach to education and learning as a lifelong process that is soundly based in intellectual traditions of social psychology, philosophy and cognitive psychology… And it stresses the role of formal education in lifelong learning and the development of individuals to their full potential as citizens, family members and human beings. (Kolb, 1984: 3–4)

Kolb's (1984) book *Experiential Learning: Experience as the source of learning and development* has been extraordinarily influential, with the experiential learning cycle, and the subsequent development of learning styles, becoming pervasive. One experiential learning theory bibliography assembled by Kolb, Boyatzis and Mainemelis in 2001 contained 1,004 entries across a range of disciplines: management (207); education (430); information science (104); psychology (101); medicine (72); nursing (63); accounting (22); and law (5). The bibliography was subsequently updated (Kolb and Kolb, 2008a, 2008b) and the original figure had expanded to 2,453 entries (Kolb and Kolb, 2009). 1984 also saw the publication by Edward Cell, *Learning to Learn from Experience* (1984).

Kolb looked at the process of experiential learning and drew on the legacy of the perspectives provided by Lewin, Dewey and Piaget. Kolb (1984) asserted that Lewin's description of the learning process is relatively similar to that of Dewey, which involved *observation*, *knowledge* and *judgement* (see Figure 2.2).

Kolb described how Lewin's action research and T-group training in laboratories was influenced by the concept of feedback that was used by electrical engineers. This feedback process involved: 1) *concrete experience*; 2) *observations and reflections*; 3) *formation of abstract concepts* and *generalizations*; and 4) *testing implications of concepts in new situations* (see Figure 2.3). The similarities with Kolb's learning cycle in Figure 2.4 may be seen.

Figure 2.2 Dewey's learning process

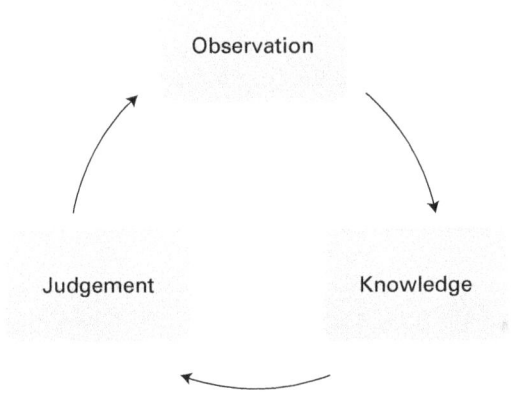

Figure 2.3 Lewin's feedback process

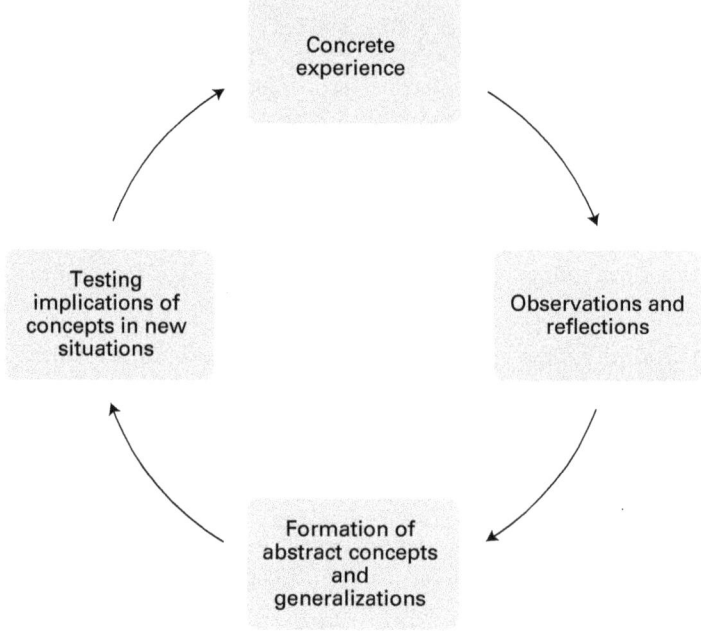

Figure 2.4 Kolb's experiential learning cycle

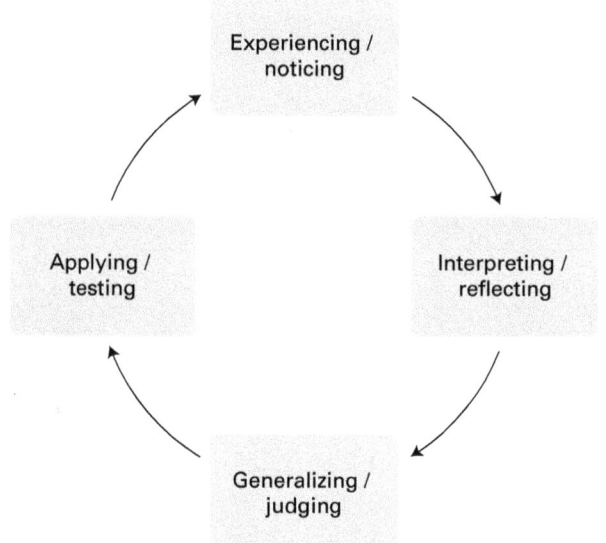

From learning cycle to learning styles

The change in emphasis from teaching to learning has resulted, quite rightly, in a greater consideration being given to personal learning preferences. If a person finds it easier to learn in a particular way then consideration should be given to this although, of course, larger numbers of people can make individualized learning more challenging. In 1971, Kolb investigated learning styles and identified four learning styles: diverging, assimilating, converging and accommodating, and later a learning styles inventory (LSI) was published based around the four stages of the learning cycle (Kolb, 1976). The LSI has been subsequently revised a number of times and it is now composed of nine learning styles (Learning from Experience, 2012).

Learning styles inventories and questionnaires have proliferated and Coffield *et al* (2004) identified 71 different theories of learning styles. A popular questionnaire, based upon Kolb's learning cycle, was developed by Honey and Mumford who stated that 'The term learning styles is used as a description of the attitudes and behaviours which determine an individual's preferred way of learning' (Honey and Mumford, 1992: 1). They argued that two people of similar intelligence and background who undergo a learning opportunity may be affected in very different ways, eg one is enthusiastic while the second person is disaffected. They maintain that the reason for this is that people have particular styles of learning that influence their attitudes and abilities towards learning opportunities. According to Honey and Mumford, people learn in two ways. The first is through teaching, and the second is through experience.

Honey and Mumford described four stages of learning and explained that a person may begin anywhere in the cycle and does not have to begin at Stage 1, eg the person may receive some information and review it (Stage 2), and then draw some tentative conclusions (Stage 3), and then plan a course of action (Stage 4) and finally undertake the course of action (Stage 1). The process is an iterative one and allows people to join the cycle at any point, the main proviso being that they complete the cycle, otherwise the learning process is incomplete, eg they may review the experience that using a hammer to drive in a nail is a painful process to their thumb when they miss the nail, and never learn to use the hammer correctly. They need to complete the cycle by testing the theory and confirming it. Honey and Mumford (1992: 7) used the term 'experience' in three of the four stages, as can be seen in Figure 2.5.

Honey and Mumford explained that there are four types of people and their preferences are shown as four stages in the learning cycle. Although it was recognized that people's learning styles can alter when they change jobs and are therefore not fixed, there is value in taking into account the preferred learning style of a person. This is not only from the point of view of the teacher or trainer but also from that of the learner, who can become more aware of his or her personal process of learning. The various styles are:

- **Activists:** prefer to involve themselves in an experience and do so in an open-minded manner. They involve themselves with the activity first and then weigh up the implications of their actions afterwards.
- **Reflectors:** prefer to gather information and carefully consider it before reaching a conclusion. They are thoughtful and cautious, and tend to reserve judgement in meetings until they are reasonably sure about their conclusions.
- **Theorists:** tend to be systems people who gather information and attempt to develop a coherent theory about the experience. They are logical and prefer to analyse information and produce an encompassing theory.
- **Pragmatists:** prefer to apply theories and techniques to investigate whether they work. Pragmatists are realistic people who seek out improved methods of operating.

Honey and Mumford explained that this cyclical process is a fundamental one, which is similar to the scientific method upon which Revans also based his model. It is also similar to problem-solving and decision-making approaches, as well as the quality cycle. W Edwards Deming was a physicist who used statistical methods to improve the quality of production in Japan after the Second World War. He was a disciple of Shewhart, a statistician

Figure 2.5 Honey and Mumford's learning styles

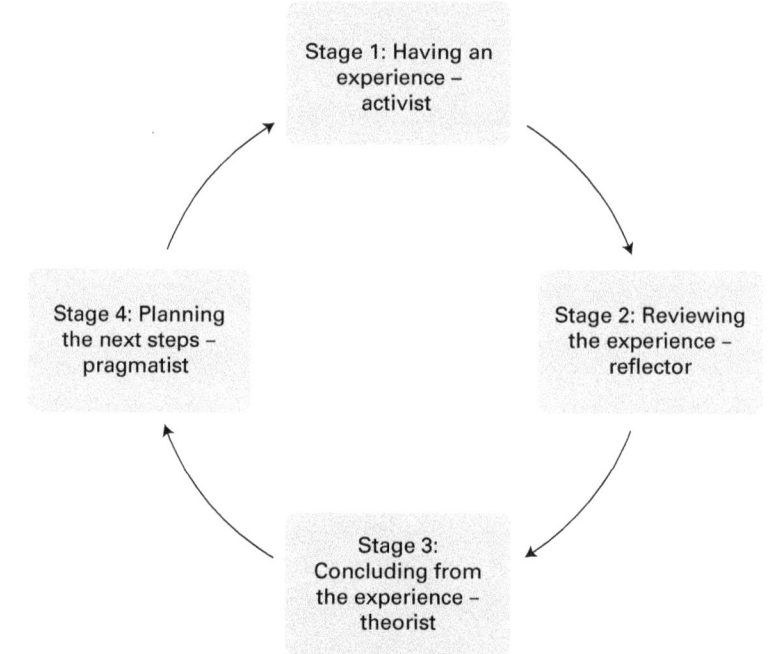

Figure 2.6 The Shewhart/Deming cycle of continuous improvement

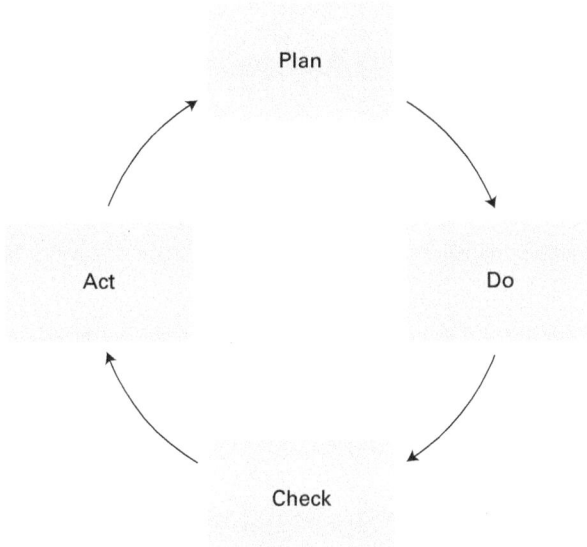

at Bell Laboratories, and he developed the Deming or Shewhart cycle of continuous improvement, which involved a systematic approach to problem solving and was a cyclical process of plan, do, check, act (see Figure 2.6).

That people prefer to learn in different ways is little doubted, but whether these closely match the stages in the learning cycle is open to debate. Coffield *et al* (2004) investigated some of the main learning-styles theories and concluded that they had not been sufficiently validated by independent research. In our experience, the value of these questionnaires/inventories is not in their diagnostic capabilities but in using them with learners to encourage self-reflection about different personal learning strategies.

We saw in Figure 2.1 the linking of theory and practice, which has a strong similarity to the various cycles of Lewin, Kolb, Honey and Mumford, and Deming/Shewhart. While they are all interlinked and have influenced one another, there would appear to be a fundamental principle at work here in which we need to combine thinking with doing or applying in order to create an effective learning process.

Question 4: What are the main criticisms of experiential learning?

So far we have highlighted the problem that some authors see experiential learning as merely *doing* things, or that it is just a method, with no underpinning philosophy. Our preceding discussions have also demonstrated the complexity associated with the terms *experience*, *learning* and *education*, and we have outlined the inability to create definitive defining parameters. Malinen (2000: 15) is similarly critical about these aspects of experiential learning, concluding that:

> Adult experiential learning is a complex, vague and ambiguous phenomenon, which is still inadequately defined, conceptually suspect – and even poorly researched… its theoretical and philosophical foundations are fragmented and confusing… There are too many interpretations and priorities among the theorists and practitioners that no single, clear definition of these foundations could be constructed.

The learning cycle as developed by Kolb (1984) has become compellingly established, as a *taken-for-granted* theory of learning. Whilst the work of Kolb is perhaps the most frequently cited theory of experiential learning, it is also seen as being practically and theoretically problematical. *The Learning Cycle* receives both widespread acceptance and extensive criticism as a pedagogic approach. The criticism centres on the research basis of the model, which is said to be lacking in fieldwork with people from different cultures, gender, ages, socio-economic and educational backgrounds.

Reynolds's (1997) article, 'Learning styles: a critique', and Holman, Pavlica and Thorpe's (1997) article, 'Rethinking Kolb's theory of experiential learning in management education', both argue that although the famous circle (the learning cycle) has been extremely influential, especially in management education in the United States and the UK, it is rarely seen as unproblematic. It locates itself in the cognitive psychology tradition, and overlooks or mechanically explains learning, thus divorcing people from the social, historical and cultural aspects of self, thinking and action. Holman, Pavlica and Thorpe (1997) suggested that the idea of a manager reflecting like a scientist in isolation on events is like an 'intellectual Robinson Crusoe'. They argued that the social interactions of a person were very important to the development of self, thought and learning. Furthermore, they suggested that Kolb's theory was fundamentally cognitivist and had a number of limitations. The main criticism was that the four stages of the cycle – concrete experience, reflective observation, abstract conceptualization and active experimentation – were independent and represented a dualism or tension of opposites, for example the separation of active experimentation and reflective observation. Holman, Pavlica and Thorpe (1997) similarly disagreed with the idea of a sequential progression through the cycle. They argued: 'Learning can be considered as a process of argumentation in which thinking, reflecting, experiencing and action are different aspects of the same process. It is practical argumentation with oneself and in collaboration with others that actually forms the basis for learning' (1997: 145). There has also been much scepticism about learning-styles inventories based on the learning cycle (Hall and Moseley, 2005).

There is also increased recognition that emotion, and individual differences, play a significant role in the ability to learn and such factors are not accounted for in the simplistic learning cycle. From a pedagogic perspective, then, this cyclical model is perhaps always going to be regarded as simplistic, overly mechanistic and formulaic (Rowland, 2000; Moon, 2004). As a result of this criticism, however, Kolb and Kolb (2009: 309–10) recently upgraded the learning cycle into a learning spiral, thus embracing the notion of *continuity* of experience, as developed by Dewey (1938). When a concrete experience is enriched by reflection, given meaning by thinking, and transformed by action, the new experience thus created becomes richer, broader and deeper. Further iterations of the cycle thus continue the exploration, and transfer to experiences in other contexts.

In an article subtitled 'Corn circles in search of a spaceship?' Taylor (1991: 258) aptly sums up many of the limitations of circular models used in the search for meaning:

> They first began to appear about 25 years ago. Neatly laid-out circles in the pages of training textbooks, journals and Industrial Training Board publications. They quickly came to seize the imagination of a growing band of training professionals. They must have been created by a superior intelligence, being so neat and logical and all. There were of course variations in the patterns observed, but these, it was discovered, were due to differing environmental conditions. Being a pragmatic and opportunist bunch the practitioners, although faintly curious about where they came from, what they actually meant, and who controlled them, were so much more interested in associating themselves with the phenomena so as to establish their own professional credibility and status. The mystery and novelty soon became displaced as attempts were made to elaborate and integrate the phenomenon into the known universe. Within a few short years the 'systematic training model' [or 'training cycle' to some] became the orthodoxy of the training profession.

Circles, and other simplistic models of learning such as the pyramid model from Dale (Tell–Show–Do), all have some value for use in experiential approaches to learning, particularly in terms of accessibility and applicability. However, some models, while being more accurate representations of reality, may tend to be underused and sometimes disregarded simply because of their complexity. It could be argued that Kolb's learning cycle is a minimalist interpretation of the complex operations involved in human learning, and therefore it is not surprising that this model is somewhat limited in describing the learning process.

Miettinen (2000) maintains that Kolb's development of the experiential learning cycle, underpinned by previous work by Dewey, Lewin and Piaget, was a selective interpretation that did not really represent the facts. Although Kolb talked about the 'Lewinian Model' of impulse, observation, knowledge and judgement, Miettinen maintained that Kolb's research is based on observations of only a small section of Lewin's work described by Lippit (1949). Miettinen (2000: 68) compared the work of Dewey and Kolb and concluded that Kolb does not take into account Dewey's distinction between habit, 'the great flywheel of society' that enables society to function predictably when faced with recurring challenges, and the habit that tyrannically traps us into behaving in a particular way without thinking of alternatives. The use of habit is very important to our functioning, and Covey (1990: 46) in his book *The Seven Habits of Highly Effective People* states, 'Habits are powerful factors in our lives. Because they are consistent, often unconscious patterns, they constantly, daily, express our character and produce our effectiveness or ineffectiveness.' Habits, because they are often unconscious, tend to be a form of single-loop activity rather than a form of double-loop learning. Miettinen also suggests that Kolb's experience and reflection occur in isolation and that there is a necessity for the individual to interact with other humans and the environment in order to enhance the reasoning and conclusions drawn.

Fenwick, in her text *Learning Through Experience: Troubling orthodoxies and intersecting questions*, offers a rich critical analysis for further reading. In an enlightening chapter titled 'Critiques and debates' many critical perspectives on the broader notions of experiential learning are presented, including the rejection of the core idea that 'knowledge is extracted and abstracted from experience by the processing mind' (2003: 80), and that experiential learning models misrepresent experience as concrete, and knowable. Fenwick discusses five theoretical 'orientations' towards experiential learning that currently exist, notably constructivist theory, situative theory, psychoanalytic theory, critical cultural theories and complexity theory. The latter, complexity theory, has already received some consideration earlier in our answer to Question 3.

Question 5: Has the notion of the experience society contributed to our understanding of experiential learning in any way?

If we explore the literature from a consumer design perspective we see a variety of opinions as to what constitutes the key dimensions of an *experience*. In the events industry Peterson and Getz (2009: 310) argue that 'experiences cannot be fully designed, they are both personal (ie psychological) constructs that vary with the individual, as well as being social and cultural constructs related to influences on the individual and the (often) social nature of events'. However, Schmitt, from a broad consumer perspective, suggests that people do want to have experiences that are not just everyday experiences, but special, to 'dazzle their senses, touch their hearts, and stimulate their minds' (1999: 22). Figure 2.7 highlights the range of thinking about the core dimensions of experience that should be considered when designing

Figure 2.7 The contested and complex nature of human experience

Author(s)	Important dimensions of the event experience	Number of core dimensions
Beard and Wilson (2002)	Social and more-than-human world (MTHW), belonging/interacting, doing, sensing, feeling, knowing, being… as inner and outer world experiences.	7
Thorne (1963)	Sensual, emotional, cognitive, conative, self-actualization, climax/peak experiences.	6
McIntyre and Roggenbuck (1998)	Environment/nature; self and internal thoughts; others; emotions; and task/activity.	5
O'Sullivan and Spangler (1998)	Physically, mentally, emotionally, socially or spiritually.	5
Mossberg (2007)	Emotionally, physically, intellectually, spiritually.	4
Bitner (1992)	Cognitive, emotional, physiological.	3
Mannell and Kleiber (1997)	The cognitive (thinking), the conative (acting/doing) and the affective (feelings).	3
Mannell (1984)	A state of mind.	1

consumer experiences. As can be seen there are differing opinions as to the dimensions of experience that are considered important in the consumer experience. In the figure, seven core dimensions of experience, present in our Learning Combination Lock model, are shown for comparison.

Figure 2.7 is constructed from literature derived from a range of books concerned with the emerging 'experience society', as a new or 'neo-experiential' phenomena (Roberts, 2012). The 'experience society' is a concept introduced by Schultz (1992) in *Die Erlebnisgesellschaft*. Later, Pine and Gilmore (1999) wrote *The Experience Economy*, and in the same year Schmitt (1999) published *Experiential Marketing*. Pine and Gilmore (2011) contend that societies have progressed through a number of stages, ie an agricultural economy, industrial economy, service economy, and the knowledge economy, and they argue that we are now in an 'experience economy'. They argue that although the other economic factors are still present, the experience economy is a main force. Although they briefly mention the importance of experience in educational settings, the arguments presented by Pine and Gilmore are predominantly economic ones. They emphasize the financial benefits and state:

> Relying on the manufacturing of goods and the delivery of services remains the mindset of too many executives (and politicians), prohibiting the shift to more vibrant enterprise offering experiences (and thus more robust national economies). So let us be clear: goods and services are no longer enough to foster economic growth, create new jobs and maintain economic prosperity. To realize revenue growth and increased employment, the staging of experiences must be pursued as a distinct form of economic output. Indeed, in a world saturated with largely undifferentiated goods and services the greatest opportunity for value creation resides in staging experiences. (Pine and Gilmore, 2011: ix)

This economic and societal backcloth of the experience society has indeed influenced thinking about experiential learning in both positive and negative ways. The experience society has led to new thinking and research into the nature of human experiences, particularly within the commercialization and commodification of purchased experiences. The outdoor education and adventure learning communities in particular have drawn attention to this phenomena with some disapproval. Loynes (2002), for example, coined the phrase 'adventure in a bun' to describe the packaged, formulaic, commodified nature of some forms of experiential education that have been influenced and colonized by market forces. This has also variously been referred to as the McDonaldization or Disneyfication of experiences (Ritzer,

2001; Bryman, 1999), and the implication for education is that *any experience* might suffice for the purpose of experiential learning. Roberts (2012: 101) comments that:

> Thus, in a general sense, the neo-experiential variation becomes part of a larger problem rather than a potentially powerful and transformational curriculum response. Prepackaged and sweet (like candy), predictably and efficiently managed (like McDonald's), and slickly produced (like Disney), it can give us only the illusion of freedom.

An alternative view is that in the early 21st century the design of experiences has been heavily influenced by more advanced understandings of consumer behaviour as a result of renewed interest in the commercial applications of neuroscience and evolutionary psychology, thus shifting experience design to a more sophisticated level. A number of companies that focus on experience design are becoming conversant with the considerable body of research about the psychology, neuroscience and chemistry that drives human behaviour. Equipped with this new knowledge, specific human behaviours are being fashioned, and sometimes deliberately designed to be addictive in form. Recent book titles signpost these new trends: *Addiction by Design* (Schull, 2012), *The Power of Habit* (Duhigg, 2012), *Impulse* (Lewis, 2013) and *Hooked* (Eyal, 2014) are all texts that articulate how human experiences can be made or designed to be more compelling by applying habit-forming, persuasive technologies that intentionally mould our lives, as illustrated by a number of social media applications. Indeed the book *Hooked* has a subtitle: *How to build habit forming products.*

To illustrate how this new science underpinning experience design is emerging in society we briefly draw attention to two contemporary examples of the Disneyfication of experiences for learning in the commercial world. The Disney Experience applies new scientific understanding to the design of experiences for children; Loeffler and Church (2015) inform us that Disney's theme parks demonstrate how the Disney experience focuses on four cognitive drivers that release the natural positive emotion drugs that stimulate the human brain, generating pleasure as a reaction to specific experiences. The four natural drugs said to be used to hook children into the experience of pleasure at Disney, receiving specific mention, are serotin, oxytocin, dopamine and endorphin.

KidZania (http://www.kidzania.com) is a much more multifaceted educational-entertainment experience design concept targeted at children and young people, with a broader mix of *play, experience, education* and *learning* as the stated outcomes that are created when participating youngsters interact with a real, scaled-down shopping mall, spending time and money on play and leisure. It was started in Mexico in 1996.

CASE STUDY KidZania

KidZania is all about 'learning by doing' and represents experiential, free-range learning at its best – learning full of teachable moments and actively promoting social interaction. In this *edutainment* concept children and young people aged 4–14 can earn money by doing jobs at sponsored outlets, and they are remunerated for their work in the currency of KidZos, which is transferable throughout other outlets around the globe. They can then spend that money to eat, shop or be entertained. The jobs include, for example, a pilot, firefighter, doctor, police officer, radio broadcaster, Formula One pit-lane engineer, chocolatier, surgeon and estate agent. Each of these job scenarios is sponsored by multinational as well as local industry partners. The registration process mimics an airport check-in, and so in Kuala Lumpur it is sponsored by Air Asia, and in London by British Airways. The kids get a boarding pass, can open a bank account and, of course, get money to start them off. KidZania has internal Zupervisors who facilitate learning and act as 'second teachers'. The commercial sponsors also act in the capacity of third-teacher status; indeed KidZania is encouraging partners not only to consider their *return on investment*, but to explore their *return on involvement*. An educational 'think tank', consisting of internationally renowned educators and other professionals, supports and challenges the educational thinking behind the KidZania concept and development of future ideas.

The kids are empowered to be in charge of their own aspirations, and their own learning journey as KidZania encourages a world-of-work-related independent learning. This approach aims both to enable children to be empowered to learn 'free range', and to aid schools in fulfilling curriculum and statutory requirements through applied experiential learning. Role play is a universal form of play enjoyed by children all over the world. Role play is fun and has very positive educational, psychological and motivational benefits. Indeed psychologists, educators and play experts are extensively consulted during the development of every KidZania location to ensure the learning content matches the local area focus: creativity, critical thinking, communication, confidence and collaboration. By blending learning and reality with entertainment, KidZania provides an authentic and powerful development experience, helping to prepare children to understand and manage their world.

KidZania is developing a strong 'career awareness' focus to its mission, and in this vein their research as to what the kids do when experiencing KidZania has proved particularly interesting. Television producer or hair stylist, pilot or cabin crew? The research reveals that bias in the talent pipeline starts before school age. For example, stereotypes start early on in life as evidenced by the jobs the children choose at KidZania. Data from the London site shows how girls select roles typically held by women, and boys tend to choose jobs designed for older children, whilst girls opt for younger children's activities. The gap between the aspirations of boys and girls widens as they grow older. If KidZania places women in charge of the pit-stop Formula One racing-car engineer role, however, more girls will try out this experience – from role model to role play. The figures also show that children from schools around London in the UK are more likely to choose service roles, such as firefighting and pilot training, whereas children from non-London schools tend to choose manufacturing-related activities.

There are also links with Harvard University's 'Visible Thinking – Project Zero' research, with learning aligned to a 'Connect–Extend–Challenge' concept.

Dr Ger Graus OBE, Global Director of Education, KidZania (http://www.kidzania.com)

A new approach to the application of the science underlying human behaviour, combined with commercial drivers, underpins these neo-experiential designs, as is evident in the above case study of KidZania.

The general notion of 'the student experience' within educational settings has been influenced by 'experience economy' thinking. The experience focus is acting as a driver for change within educational settings, particularly for higher education. Usher and Edwards allude to the positive consequences of consumer perspectives within educational settings by arguing that by 'valuing experience and its potential as a resource for learning, people are enabled to value themselves more fully… The focus on experience gives people a 'voice' they do not otherwise have in the practices of traditional education' (1994: 203). With students seen as consumers in the experience economy, educational institutions such as schools and universities have arguably become more interested in the nature of the 'student experience' of learning, and their sense of belonging within the academe. The educational institutions and the governing political party continually search for the views of students, thus making their voice more visible. One particular impact has been the careful crafting of the student experience of belonging (Baumeister and Leary, 1995) within schools and universities.

As the student 'voice' is increasingly being embraced by educational institutions, ostensibly at least, this in turn has potential to influence the nature of their learning experiences, and thus the design of the learning experience by their educators. These changes have presented a modicum of democracy for the students, sometimes at the expense of the voice of the teacher or lecturer. At the same time these subtle market processes can create the conditions for the students to unwittingly become part of oppressive factors regulating and controlling the curriculum (Usher and Edwards, 1994) in the battle for political ideologies. Dewey (1938) was vocal about such oppressive forces acting upon education. Experiential learning, as with all types of learning, entangles itself with both liberatory and oppressive ideologies: it is always interwoven with the political.

Experiential learning is commonly utilized for work-related, employability-based learning. This is increasingly so within higher education, with universities increasingly 'under scrutiny over what they do to maximize graduates' economic potential upon leaving university' (Tomlinson, 2017). Smith and Betts (2000: 591) divide this employability learning into three main forms, which are interwoven and interrelated:

- learning *about work*, which is informational;
- learning *at work*, which is locational;
- learning *through work*, which is experiential.

It is evident that the application of experiential learning is growing, being applied in a breadth of subjects and locations, and perhaps this is being accelerated by the influence of the so-called *experience society*. The widespread use of experiential learning illustrates the value and benefits that are perceived to accrue from its use and, in some professional areas, such as medicine, it is the foundational learning philosophy, as Dunn and Chaput de Saintonge (1997: 25) state:

> Medical education in the UK differs from that in many other European countries in its emphasis on clinical experience as a means of learning… Experiential learning is therefore at the centre of the education of the pre-registration house officer.

Conclusion

This chapter has added to our understanding of experiential learning, and we have done this by asking five simple practical questions. Question 1 showed that experiential forms of learning have similar philosophical roots, and defining parameters. It has become clear that *experience*, *education* and *learning* are terms that are intertwined, as almost inseparable. They present tautological concerns when paired: *experience* and *learning* might be considered to be one and the same. Question 2 highlighted the way the experience is often resistant to description. The complexity of the notion of experience, as an interactional process, is a result of the unique personal inner world continually interacting with our outer environment of the human and more-than-human world.

Several core interactional dimensions of *experience* of and for learning have now been introduced, such as thinking as learning, doing as learning, sensing and observing as learning, belonging and interacting as learning (human and more-than-human world), feeling as a way of learning, thinking as a way of learning, and being as a way of learning. The reverse is also true for experiential learning, notably the ability to learn to belong, to learn to do and act, to learn to sense, to learn to feel, to learn to think and learn to be. This is surely what we want for the education of our children. When *experience* and *learning* are joined together they form the term *experiential learning*, and something very different is created. Experiential learning, as a category of learning, is fundamentally different from other categories of learning.

Question 3 highlighted some of the main experiential learning models in use, with Question 4 highlighting some of the main criticisms of experiential learning. Question 5 illustrated how the experience society and contemporary market forces are changing our understanding of the design of human experiences from a consumer perspective, in both liberatory and oppressive ways.

With Chapter 1 and 2 combined we are now creating many more distinguishing features underpinning the notion of experiential learning:

- *Experience* is central to the learning process, and in experiential forms of learning it takes centre stage.
- *Experiential* forms of learning have a common heritage.
- The *experiential learning* dynamic is fourfold: 1) *of* and 2) *for* learning, affecting the whole person, their 3) *inner* and 4) *outer* world experiencing.
- *Experience* is a complex composite made up of information from the *constantly interacting* inner and outer worlds.
- The *outer world* includes the human (social/cultural), physical and more-than-human world.
- The *inner world* includes the sensorial, emotive, cognitive and psychoanalytic elements of our being.

- There are many elements that make up the *learning experience*, and they are not only social and cultural; there are emotional, sensorial, cognitive and conative dynamics relating to our human sense of belonging, becoming and being in a human and more-than-human world.
- There is a shift in emphasis in the relationship of teacher-centred teaching and learner-centred experiencing as a co-dependent learning experience.
- There must be a certain *quality* to the experience so as to *engage* the learner, and be *memorable*.
- The *experience of* learning, when of a certain quality, has potential for the transformation of the 'self', our being.
- The *conditions* for learning, such as learner *motivation*, active *engagement* and *immersion*, are significant.
- Learning flows, and is derived from other *experiences*: it is continuous, flowing like a *river*, with a script and complex composition, like a *film*.
- The less-complex models of experiential learning are more commonly used in practice, the less-common modelling tends to be derived from complexity or ecological theories.
- There are a number of criticisms of experiential learning, but most relate to the more simplistic modelling and theories.
- The understanding of the complex nature of human experiences continues to expand and inform experiential learning, in both positive and negative directions.
- *Experience* acts as the bridge unifying typical dualisms such as action and thought, doing and knowing, body and mind, nature and person, practice and theory.
- Teachers and university lecturers are spending an increasing amount of time designing learning experiences, as opposed to simply designing specific content to teach.
- The learner, and their experience of the world, is valued: people are like seeds that can grow and bear fruit, not buckets for filling up.

Designing, delivering and evaluating experiential learning

03

> *There is no more powerful transformative force than education to promote human rights and dignity, to eradicate poverty and deepen sustainability, to build a better future for all, founded on equal rights and social justice, respect for cultural diversity, and international solidarity and shared responsibility, all of which are fundamental aspects of our common humanity.* IRINA BOKOVA, DIRECTOR-GENERAL OF UNESCO (2015)

What is the purpose of experiential education, or experiential learning? As we can see from the quotation above there are important wider issues to consider about the function and wisdom underlying the idea of experiential learning, and experiential education. The notion of responsible citizenship, and the idea that education should make a positive contribution to society, is of considerable importance. Indeed John Dewey (1938) devoted much thought to the notion of education as a major contribution towards a more democratic society.

Experiential learning is certainly not about adding in a few activities or experiences to make education or training more palatable. Sterling (2001: 40) offers a critical perspective on the negative forces that impact on the role of teachers, lecturers and trainers, suggesting that they are increasingly subject to subtle elements of 'deprofessionalization': 'The analogy with the factory is telling: young people and qualifications are produced; there are precise goals and targets; the curriculum provides directives for each stage of production, and teachers are technicians and are therefore substitutable... And workers are not required to think too much.' What counts as *achievement*, he suggests, is being limited to what can be measured.

Handy (1989) suggests that those who are in love with learning are in love with life! Life is full of experiences: bad, good and mediocre. Our life is our own film, our biography. We write our own script, and navigate our own journeys. We can use our knowledge as a compass to guide us on this journey. We can also use our emotions as a compass, our senses as a compass, and our actions and behaviours as a compass. A facilitator, teacher, therapist or trainer can help us navigate through these various journeys of life and learning. Using these metaphors their role might be considered to be that of an 'experiential guide'.

Delivering a learning experience

The art and science of skilled teaching, facilitating or coaching experientially, to precis Dewey's ideas, is very demanding. Good experiential guiding, or teaching, or facilitation has become quite complex, possibly even 'supercomplex' (see Barnett, 2000). When facilitating learning, in adults or young people, learning should be happening simultaneously, for both teachers and students. Indeed some suggest that we cannot properly be involved in transforming others without transforming ourselves (Blackie, Case and Jawitz, 2010).

Categories, titles and names for those involved in supporting learning experientially

> Role model. Mentor. Counsellor. Outdoor Educator. Instructor. Friend. By whichever name they are called, Outward Bound Singapore instructors are, undeniably, a special breed. Their work is not merely the transfer of skills or knowledge, but, more importantly, life values. They challenge participants to see the possibility in impossibilities, to dig deep within themselves for what is seemingly absent, to stretch to greater achievements. (Outward Bound Singapore brochure, undated)

In the United States, the Association for Experiential Education convened a task force of 115 global experiential practitioners and produced a document titled Definitions, Ethics and Exemplary Practices (DEEP) of Experiential Training and Development (ETD) (DEEP, 1999). This document sets out guidelines of good practice, and contains definitions of trainers and facilitators. A facilitator is an 'individual responsible for managing the learning environment to assist individuals/groups to achieve value from the learning process'. A trainer, however, is said to be 'a practitioner who leads and directs prescribed learning for skill development, towards measurable explicit results' (DEEP, 1999: 18–19).

Boud and Miller (1996) offer caution on the use of titles; the word 'facilitator', they suggest, comes with much conceptual baggage, having resonance 'with humanistic psychology and work with individualistic concerns' (1996: 7). They opt for the French term 'animateur', but they are worried about the association with 'acting'. The term 'trainer' is derived from the Old French *trahiner* (to drag) from the Latin *trahere* (to pull). In contrast, the word 'facilitator' has a different flavour or feel to it, and comes from the Latin *facilitas* (easiness). This meaning, then, is to do with making it easier; to help (Bee and Bee, 1998: 1). Allison (2000a: 45) suggests careful use of phraseology, as words portray values. He debates a range of terms and advises equal caution in describing learners as 'kids', 'punters', 'clients', 'youths' or 'participants'. Using the word 'client', he suggests, locates providers in the 'market of consumption'. To find a collective term to describe the role of people involved in supporting the learning of others is clearly problematic.

In Chapter 2 we presented a definition of experiential education by Itin (1999: 93); however, further on in his definition he continues his thinking by commenting that 'the learning usually involves interaction between learners, learner and educator, and learner and the environment'. He not only outlines the complex conditions required for learner engagement with the learning *experience*, he also includes a reference to the tasks of the teacher:

> The educator's primary roles include selecting suitable experiences, posing problems, setting boundaries, supporting learners, insuring physical and emotional safety, facilitating the learning process, guiding reflection, and providing the necessary information. The results of the learning form the basis of future experience and learning. (Itin, 1999: 93)

The notion that *experiences* are central to the learning process, that they take centre stage, means that experience design is now the new focus. There is a shift from too much teaching and telling, towards the design of learning experiences. However, design is not an easy process, as we show in Figure 3.1. There are many complex learner interactions, including sharing, telling, showing, doing, building, solving, creating and so on. The design of experiences *for* learning requires a sound understanding of the experience *of* learning, including how these experiences manifest themselves within the

Figure 3.1 Seven aspects to learning experience design (LED)

1	Outer world experience *for* learning
2	Inner world experience *for* learning
3	Outer world experience *of* learning
4	Inner world experience *of* learning
5	1 + 2 = Focus on the EXPERIENCE DESIGN
6	3 + 4 = Focus on LEARNING DESIGN
7	1 + 2 + 3 + 4 = LEARNING EXPERIENCE DESIGN (LED)

SOURCE Beard (2018)

inner and *outer* worlds. All these dynamics are in continuous interactional flux. Learning experience design has the letters LED, and we are suggesting that this metaphor has some significance. It may be time to throw away the old-fashioned lightbulb, as LEDs are brighter (more illuminating) and more energy efficient (teaching too much is tiring and, after all, the students do need to do the work themselves), and of course LEDs last longer (memory retention)!

Does a facilitator or teacher need to intervene?

The term *education* suggests that a teacher is required, whereas the term *learning* does not have the same connotations. However, the notion of intervening or not is quite complex. The experience itself can lead to learning without a teacher, and this point was recognized by Outward Bound long ago, as they coined the saying: *let the mountains (experiences) speak for themselves*. Outward Bound gradually developed other intervention formats, including speaking for the experience, and debriefing the experience. Sometimes the experience doesn't 'speak', and sometimes people cannot hear what the experience is telling them, and so a teacher, facilitator or coach might consider supporting the understanding of a learning experience by working with the four experiential dynamics we have introduced above in order to maximize the learning potential.

Jeffs and Ord, in their recent *Rethinking Outdoor, Experiential and Informal Education*, include a chapter where Jeffs (2018) (re)introduces the idea of 'informal education'. Formal teacher interaction, he suggests, spills over into other informal spaces, in informal ways. Jeffs notes that the first time the term *informal education* was created was within a textbook by Josephine Brew (1946). He acknowledges that its pedigree lies within dialogical education, such as Socratic questioning, which prospered in Athenian society. However, Brews advocates taking education into places where people congregate:

> Schoolteachers, for instance, were encouraged to perceive the playground as somewhere educational conversations and dialogue with pupils might prosper and the school gate is a venue where they might converse creatively with parents. Outdoor educators might simply try relocating to the back of the minibus to cultivate dialogue and social workers might do the same with clients lingering on the office door step. (Jeffs, 2018: 63)

Intervention then does not always need to be a formal affair. Nature has a powerful influence, and immersion in nature can heal, without a therapist guiding and directing. Nature can act as a partner in the healing process (Berger, 2007). The outdoor 'solo' experience is, as the term implies, an individual, experiential adventure learning process. Recent research by Williams (2012: 137) suggests participants on solo experiential programmes do not 'require a facilitator to tell them what they should be learning and that they will identify for themselves the outcomes that are meaningful and important'. Other examples of self-directed experiences are provided by Macala (1986: 57), who observed:

> If you were to ask a group of adults to talk about their most interesting and exciting learning experience, chances are good that instead of describing a classroom scenario, many of them will talk about a self-directed learning experience that enabled them to learn new information, a skill, theory, or process on their own. Their experiences might have included… learning how to sail a boat by trial and error, or developing leadership or fund-raising skills through committee work… they asked questions, got feedback, did research, took risks, made mistakes, found mentors, informants, helpers, tried out and checked their progress, accuracy, skill; and they grew and changed as they were challenged.

Loynes (2000) explores what he calls 'indigenous learning', which he regards as more authentic, 'real' and 'natural'. He argues that learning should not be overly interfered with. Experiential learning, he suggests, can only occur when people attach meaning and value to their experience, and he regards experiential learning as 'natural' when people do this themselves, or with peers participating in the experience. Intervention by others, he argues, especially when there is an element of imposed theory, morality or judgement, can disturb or interrupt the emergent indigenous learning, thus negating it as experiential learning. This can of course be accidental or deliberate. Loynes

(2000) suggests that instead of imposing prepackaged theories or ideas to generate preprepared solutions, those who follow experiential learning principles should allow people to build their own theory from their own action.

To grant or deny opportunities for people to tell and share their experience, through their own lens of life, is an important psychological issue. McLeod (1997: 100) comments that 'very often the existence of a personal "problem" can best be described as a response to silencing, as an unwillingness of others to hear the story that "needs" to be told'. Central to experiential learning is the notion that individuals need to tell their story.

The question of whether to intervene or not is not a simple dichotomy. We can conclude that there are many ethical issues to consider when making interventions. For example, ethical issues arise in youth development programmes, where the 'highs' experienced on outdoor wilderness adventures can be short-lived, and later they can be experienced as debilitating. Taking young vulnerable people away from dysfunctional environments to experience euphoric outdoor adventures may seem on the surface to be sensible, but these experiences can leave young people vulnerable in the longer term, with feelings of disappointment, and feeling let down on return to their home environment (Davis-Berman and Berman, 1999). Disillusionment and potential crisis can be avoided by careful practice. Barrett and Greenaway (1995) suggest ways to overcome these negative effects, recommending a four-stage realignment approach to change:

- close-to-home introduction;
- Outward Bound away-from-home experience;
- city-bound – working on preparation for the last stage;
- homeward-bound – for supported transfer of learning.

Tenant (1997: 140) argues that there is 'ironically, an unnecessary dichotomous conceptualization of teacher and taught in much adult education literature'. We suggest that the processes of learning and teaching are inextricably interlinked, and so we recommend a co-constructive, interactional approach to teaching and facilitating whereby both learner and teacher are both growing and changing as a result of interactions.

Intervention skills

Allison (2000a) suggests that there are six fundamental characteristics of good practice in (outdoor) learning. He argues that if they are not present then the experience will lack quality. One key ingredient is the authenticity of the facilitator. On this same topic of good practice Wickes (2000) suggests that high levels of peak experience can occur when facilitators 'tread lightly'. Wickes offers a map of 21 key ingredients for excellence in facilitation, including: creating the right climate; getting in – rapport; creating experiences that work; creating engaging, memorable and meaningful experiences; helping people review, articulate and share personal learning; making it easy to disclose and share experiences; maintaining a constructive atmosphere; and creating powerful, emotional and satisfying experiences.

Heron (1990), who conducted extensive research into facilitator interventions, offers a range of interventions, including: echoing, selective echoing, open and closed questioning, empathetic divining, checking understanding, paraphrasing, logical marshalling, following, consulting, proposing or leading, bringing in and shutting out. These interpersonal skills form the essence of good facilitation, and similar behaviours were identified by the Huthwaite Group (Rackham and Morgan, 1977) and used in 'behaviour analysis'. They include: proposing, building, supporting, disagreeing, defending/attacking, testing understanding, summarizing, seeking information, giving information, bringing in and shutting out. In checking understanding, for example, the facilitation phrase might be 'So can I just check this – what you are saying is…?' This gentle checking intervention encourages and checks the story, rather than redirecting it. Selective echoing involves the facilitator in selecting 'some word or phrase that carries an emotional charge or stands out as significant in its context' (Heron, 1999: 266). This is done in order to give the client space to explore, in any direction, the significance of what has been reflected or echoed back to him or her. These interventions require a degree of selective interpretation, without leading the story, so as to help the client focus. McLeod (1997: 114) suggests other interventions:

- **Approval.** Provides emotional support, reassurance or reinforcement. Accepting or validating the client's story.
- **Information.** Supplies information in the form of data, facts or resources. It may be related to the therapy process, the therapist's behaviour or therapy arrangements (time, place).
- **Direct guidance.** These are directions or advice that the therapist suggests for the client, either for what to do in the session or outside the session. Structuring the process of storytelling.
- **Closed question.** Gathers data or specific information. The client responses are limited and specific. Filling in the story.
- **Open question.** Probes for or requests clarification or exploration by the client. From a narrative perspective, open questioning can be used to

invite the telling of a story or to explore the meaning of elements of a story.

- **Paraphrase.** Mirrors or summarizes what the client has been communicating either verbally or non-verbally. Does not 'go beyond' what the client has said or add a new perspective or understanding to the client's statements or provide any explanation for the client's behaviour. Includes restatement of content, reflection of feelings, non-verbal reference and summary. Therapists using a narrative approach may wish to communicate to the client that they have 'heard' the story, or may attempt to focus attention on a particular aspect of a story.
- **Interpretation.** Goes beyond what the client has overtly recognized and provides reasons, alternative meanings or new frameworks for feelings, behaviours or personality. It may establish connections between seemingly isolated statements or events; interpret defences, feelings of resistance, or transference; or indicate themes, patterns or causal relationships in behaviour and personality, or relate present events to past events. This response includes a wide range of narrative-informed interventions, centred on the general goal of retelling the story in different ways.
- **Confrontation.** Points out a discrepancy or contradiction but does not provide a reason for such a discrepancy. This discrepancy may be between words and behaviours, between two things a client has said or between the client's and the therapist's perceptions. In narrative therapy, the client is encouraged to resolve the tension or incongruity between opposing versions of a story.
- **Self-disclosure.** Shares feelings or personal experiences. The therapist gives an account of his or her own story, either in terms of relevant episodes from a personal life story, or framed in terms of a therapeutic meta-narrative, or drawn from a myth and other cultural sources.

High-quality facilitation requires a high level of understanding of a complex range of intervention skills, and experiential facilitators should consider the degree to which they are open and transparent in describing their own values around which they operate; otherwise, because of the power they hold, they can have undue influence on other people's beliefs and values.

Power and control

If as a facilitator we introduce ourselves, then *we* decide what to *say*. If the people attending get together in groups and ask four or five questions per group about the facilitator, then *they* decide what to *ask* as they want to know, and in turn this affects power relations, control and group confidence. The groups also learn about the art of questioning! Power and control are fundamental issues relating to facilitation style. Arising from his investigations into 'expert telling' versus 'finding out and experiencing', Carl Rogers (1969), the eminent US psychologist, made controversial statements about teaching, declaring that anything that can be 'taught' is rather inconsequential. His focus was concerned with the intrinsic limits of what teachers can do. He explored the nature of teaching and learning, expressing concern with the ephemeral nature of what he called the 'jug and mug' approach to learning, where the so-called expert pours knowledge into the mugs, the recipients. His interest lay with the nature of *'learner-centred learning'*, and was concerned that the provider should not always control the agenda. Providers of experiential learning regularly face such issues of power, control and intervention, as Table 3.1 highlights. It has been suggested that facilitators should 'concentrate on providing the resources and opportunities for learning to take place, rather than "manage and control" learning' (Bee and Bee, 1998: 2).

Table 3.1 A dichotomy of power and control

Learner-centred	Provider-centred
Providers work with the natural curiosity and concerns of the learner.	Passive learning is encouraged.
There is a learning contract.	The provider has a rigid syllabus to get through.
Real issues and problems are worked on and used as vehicles for learning.	Trainees learn by memorizing, and use artificial case studies.
Feedback on self-performance is encouraged.	Learning is monitored, examined and assessed by the trainer.
Learners are considered to have a valuable contribution to make.	The trainer is the repository of knowledge.
Learners are trusted to learn for themselves.	The teacher/trainer knows best.
Responsibility for learning is shared with the learners.	Trainees wait for the trainer to lead.
The learning provider offers resources to learn.	Learning is limited to the trainer's knowledge.
Learners continually develop the programme.	The trainer dictates the flow of the programme.

(continued)

Table 3.1 *(Continued)*

Learner-centred	Provider-centred
Learners and providers have joint responsibility and power.	The trainer has responsibility and power.
There is a climate of genuine mutual care, concern and understanding.	Trust is low; trainees need constant supervision, and the trainers remain detached.
The focus is on fostering continuous learning, asking questions and the process of learning, and learning is at the pace of the learner.	Knowledge is dispensed in measured chunks decided by the trainer.
Emphasis is on promoting a climate for deeper, more impactful learning that affects life behaviour.	Emphasis on here-and-now acquisition of knowledge and skills to do the job.
There are no teachers, only learners.	The teacher/trainer is, and remains, the expert.

Poor training, teaching or coaching is often experienced as a form of patronizing behaviours, created at times through an exaggerated ego trip. Good experiential learning providers can help to change hearts and minds, and life values. These issues are explored by Rae (1995) using a three-dimensional grid of skills, concerns and competence to examine a classification of trainer types. With the grid came a range of titles: professional trainer, humble expert, endearing bumbler, shallow persuader, boring lecturer, directive instructor, oblivious incompetent and arrogant charlatan! Trainers have also been variously described as martyrs, science boffins, chat-show hosts, army officers, actors, magicians and many other names. Some of the metaphors used in the book *The Emotionally Intelligent Lecturer* (Mortiboys, 2002) include guru to followers, tour guide to occupants of a tour bus, advocate to the jury, gardener to plants, salesperson to potential buyer, and sheepdog to sheep.

Learning experience design

Discovering the essential ingredients that make an experience profound, and strongly positive for learning, is difficult because of the holistic nature of learning. The design of experiences for learning should consider how the design affects the processes *of* learning, and this requires considerable effort in experiential forms of learning. The consideration of the place and space, the activities, the social and emotional dynamics, sensory stimulation, the stretching of capacities of intellect, the challenging goals and aspirations are some of the salient ingredients that facilitators have to juggle with. We now offer some initial guidance on design approaches by suggesting practical ways to enhance the experience *of* learning.

Bodily learning, movement and gestures

Movement can considerably enhance learning. The body not only has the major sensory organs located on it, the body also contains what we are calling a natural 'GPS system' generating spatial awareness. The body shapes the mind, and the mind shapes the body. Emotions, which are reactions by the brain to experiences, are evident in our bodies. Movement energizes people, and so people need to move around. Furniture needs to be moveable, and space reconfigured. Data, when moved around, can be seen in different ways. Sticky post-it labels are extremely popular for this reason, because information can be easily reorganized. It is also interesting that *gesture*-based technologies are now developing very fast: we swipe, slide and develop a range of movements to control our IT devices.

The body receives information about the world (reception), which is processed (perception) to form the building blocks of understanding and meaning making (conception). Gestures are bodily movements and they work alongside thought; they are vital to communication and social interaction. The body supports the brain and has done long before the creation of languages: the period before languages is often referred to as a 'prelinguistic' period; however, it might also be referred to as *post-kinetic*. Gestures can support cognitive processing (see Gallagher, 2005), and sign language of course is gesture based. The human body also uses about 7,000 facial expressions for communication (Winston, 2003).

Maps to navigate learning

Maps allow us to transcend our direct experience of the world in that they offer a spatial-relational perspective, highlighting multiple relationships (reference–cartographic maps). Schematic maps not only allow us to see things directly, they can help us to see other perspectives, such as 'higher' abstract levels of understanding. Maps can also distort spatial information in some way, because it is of course impossible to capture everything in a complex multidimensional world. In this way maps can be seen as tools that support learning in the way they use spatial arrangements. With maps, when we see the big picture this helicopter view allows us to gain visual access to a greater number of spatial relations. However, whilst this will give others an ability to discover new information, much depends on what it is that is presented, and not presented, within the map.

Harry Beck was a draughtsman who created the wonderfully imaginative and yet simple London Underground map in 1931, in a design format that is now used all over the world to inform people about transport links. Throughout the world, what we now see in many cities is a particular type of map that has been deliberately simplified to help people to navigate their way around the complex reality of built-up areas. The train and bus routes are explained through colour-coded lines, and stations are configured as circles along these lines. This simple map, now replicated around the world, has helped millions of people to navigate their way around a complicated city yet the map has little geographical reality. So if we ask ourselves why these maps are so successful, the answer lies in the simplification of reality: a satellite map would not function in the same way as it would possess too much information. People who have lived in cities for many years do not need to follow the maps; they are familiar with the territory. If you are a novice or a newcomer to the city you will need the map. So it is with learning: colour, shapes and the simplification of reality are key components to these navigational aids. Navigational tools help learners to understand complicated abstract things. However, there is more to consider.

Graphical displays like this are so powerful to convey complex information that would be so hard to explain in other formats. Graphical displays also allow private, mental conceptualization to be made public, so that they can be easily communicated and understood by others (Tversky, 2001). Abstract notions require ways to depict them, to help the brain to grasp and understand. The way things are visually represented and organized, for example, vertically or horizontally, or in front or behind, is very significant.

Mapping is a technique used to bring into view information that would not otherwise be explicitly available. Mapping is a process of making visible the invisible, through, for example, the collaborative construction of a schematic representation. The time and space relationships are key, and learning can be significantly enhanced through the use of a mixture of textual, visual and spoken communication.

CASE STUDY

A customer service *performative* approach described by Beard (2010) is called 'The Four Steps'. In this experience participants experience the tutor acting out a *critical incident* during a business-class flight to Mumbai. The scenario actually happened to the author and the perceived *reality* of the experience is enhanced by showing the real ticket, and exploring the real menu, but the actual in-flight experience is simulated with people sitting in rows as a trolley (a chair!) is wheeled down the aisle. The session involves a great deal of laughter, further cementing the relationship between the facilitator and the participants. One customer (on the actual flight it was the tutor) is served last each time, and for the first two courses the options the customer chose are not available. The chief steward later comes to talk to the customer, who didn't complain. Fun and humour is involved and eventually participants are asked to go away and discuss what they would do in this situation if they worked in the airline industry. The scenario relates to learning approaches to customer service recovery.

Participants share in conversations about the possible solutions they might adopt to recover the situation. Eventually they are asked to create four key stages that their response scenario might go through in terms of this critical incident that they are presented with. The groups write their four stages, in one or two words, on four cards. Participants then look for commonality or similarities amongst the other groups.

When the cards are placed on the floor they are aligned next to four large laminated numbers. The groups are each asked to walk through their own four stages, explaining to the facilitator and their peers what it is they would do in this incident. This walking involves the use of a sensory experience; the seventh sense or the human GPS system. The tutor talks through the cards and then offers four essential steps as a map to guide or navigate the learners through the customer service interactions.

By walking and talking through the solutions, speech is involved, walking and bodily learning through movement is involved, abstract thinking is enhanced, and memory retention is significantly endorsed. It is remarkable how people remember the steps long after the session.

In both the Eastern and Western world some of the great philosophers of the past used walking as a key method for learning. Socrates would often walk whilst asking numerous questions about a variety of topics. In more recent times Charles Darwin, who created the theory of evolution, had a sand-walk made in the grounds around his house, and he regularly walked to get away from his desk where he studied barnacles for many years. It is said that this walking helped his thinking, by first emptying out his mind, and then allowing a synthesis of the complex information he was trying to deal with when progressing his thoughts about his encounters with many species across the globe. The rhythmic routine of walking or swimming is said to clear the mind, and so making way for new thinking (see Wood-Daudelin, 1996). Perhaps this is why so many actors walk up and down whilst rehearsing their lines?

These principles of thinking (aloud), walking (through a route), observing and sharing, can also be used to enhance learning with highly complex material. One technique called 'Walk the Talk' involves learning a particularly difficult topic that has complex spatial and temporal underpinnings that make navigational aids for learning important. 'Walk the Talk' is more completely described in Beard (2010). It was developed as a learning experience design for students studying the evolution of the British environmental movement. The history is particularly difficult to learn as it involves a complex number of events, influencing a complex set of laws under British legislation, and the interaction of many voluntary organizations, key individuals, political lobbying, the designation of special sites and the setting up of government departments. In this example the 'steps' that are walked, though, are not linear in form; there are hundreds of steps and numerous routes. The map, constructed by the students, is like an exceptionally complex version of the London Underground map.

The design of this phase of the learning experience was influenced by research on neuroscience. The 'Walk the Talk' method facilitated a complex exchange of information, not just socially but by the additional use of graphical schema. Lakoff and Johnson (1999) argue that spatial relations are at the heart of our conceptual systems, that concepts and reason are embodied. That is why mapping them out can help learning: sensory and motor systems are put to work in order to develop abstract reasoning (Pinker, 1989), and so movement in a space-and-time frame is intentionally utilized to support the development of abstract thought (Gattis, 2001). Thus the landscape of complex spatial-relational 'data' is understood and navigated through by storied interpretations involving oration (linguistic), walking (motor/corporeal), visual schematics (spatial-relational) and abstract reasoning (higher cognition).

Other navigation approaches

Learning is often made harder than it really needs to be. In the design of learning experiences different kinds of navigation tools can help people to understand complex ideas. 'Navigational tools' include mapping things out, demonstrating, building something, walking through a sequence or map, colour and/or number coding, using metaphors, telling stories, feeling or sensing something, or providing signposts. These are just some of the navigational tools that can be used to support the experience of learning. Facilitators can set out numbers and letters on laminated sheets, or packs of cards with images or photographs on, or sticky post-it labels, objects and coloured arrows to indicate links. These are all resources that support the learning processes – highlighting, for example, time, space, sequence, steps, patterns, stages, connectivity, routines, direction and flow. Sometimes difficulties in understanding arise because relationships are not made visible to the learner. Navigational resources scaffold the learning and so help people to understand inherent complexity.

A language to support learning

Vygotsky (1978: 78) notes that 'the child begins to perceive the world not only through its eyes but also through its speech'. As we have already outlined, language is not only used for communicating with others, it occurs inside our heads also. It is important therefore that in order to support learning there has to be a consciousness and a recognition of the power of words, and the way the chosen words 'mediate, shape, inform and solidify experience' (Ritchhart, Church and Morrison, 2011: 243). Spoken language is complex and it has evolved to support communication and understanding, but at times language alone is insufficient, as we have already suggested. It is problematic in that it is linear; spoken words come out of the mouth one word at a time, and so what is a linear language struggles at times to explain non-linear things and so we need to help the brain to understand. Our human language does, however, help the brain to navigate and understand, and it does this through the use of certain kinds of words. A simple example would be the use of the word *higher* education: the term highlights the educational requirement for '*higher*' (abstract) levels of thinking required in universities.

Many spatial metaphors also help us to understand time (temporal reasoning), and time is often explained in our language in relation to our own bodies. We say things like: you need to put those worries *behind you*,

I am really *looking forward* to that day, *forward planning* is essential. Bodily metaphors are also in common usage: I feel *burdened* by the pressure of work, mathematics is usually a matter of understanding the *step-by-step logic*, the law was *rushed through* by parliament. Thus we can 'see' or derive spatial and/or temporal meanings from these words. These types of words offer clues to the brain and so help with abstract reasoning. Awareness of how language is used in this way, of this linguistic form, is important for good communication in teaching and learning, particularly when we want to *make learning visible*.

Speaking as thinking aloud

One way to facilitate learning is to ask people to describe what they can see, or what they are thinking, or feeling or sensing. This is where our seven-dimensional model, described later, is particularly useful. If we ask such questions then quite naturally learners will move from descriptive to propositional thinking: the thinking conversation within our heads is simply made visible by foregrounding it (see, for example, *Making Thinking Visible* by Ritchhart, Church and Morrison, 2011). This can generate a greater awareness of the experience *of* learning. This is known as meta-cognition, or thinking about thinking. Here are some conversational examples:

> 'Tell me what you can see'; 'Tell me what you are thinking';
> 'What makes you say that?'...
> *I can see an old key, and a plastic swipe card. The key is metal. The key is heavy. The plastic card is light, and it can be reprogrammed and used for a lot of functions... multifunctional, including unlocking doors, for financial transactions such as buying things. It is recyclable. If the metal key is lost, then... plastic keys are more frequently used these days for hotel room keys, for secure access to work, for identification... and this could be seen as an environmental benefit to the use of plastic.*

So it is with neo-experiential therapies. In experience-processing therapies the therapist acts as an experiential guide in a similar way by asking 'what are you experiencing right now?'

Objects, props and icons

The use of objects as props in theatre such as scenery and items for use by the actors all contribute to the sense of reality. It is interesting that children's books increasingly use props. They are also becoming more experiential with the use of interesting more dynamic props, such as pop-ups, moving characters through moving-page *scanimation*, and even train sets built into the book!

Humans regularly interact with simple symbols and icons that easily convey a message across language barriers, such as the iconic disability sign or the toilet signs for men and women. Objects can be used in similar ways, to visualize a concept. A rubber lizard can frequently remind people about their primitive 'reptile' brain operating their threat behaviours. The palm of the hand facing students who are learning about research can have a powerful effect. When asked: 'tell the truth, from where you are sitting, do human hands have knuckles?' The nature of truth is then discussed. If the wrong research methods are used for research then unfortunately the conclusion could be: no, hands do not have knuckles! What is required is a different lens so that the problem can be seen from a different perspective.

These objects are to some extent used as conditioning devices in a basic sense, and as such they also act as 'memory triggers', releasing the learning when reimagined.

Codes

People sometimes struggle to see things and by watching the processes of learning specific support mechanisms or navigational tools can be developed. When we observe people exploring a range of business products, people tend to pick them up and talk about them, looking at similarities, differences, trends and patterns. The sequence we observed is that first they tended to handle them (H), then discuss (D) them. They then organized (O) their thinking about them, often by relating them to each other. These patterns were then analysed (A), and finally a conceptualization (C) emerged. A process code was eventually developed to help future learners, and this code acted as guide to signpost, and to speed up and facilitate the journey from practical descriptive conversations, through to the more difficult theoretical–conceptual conversations. The code we gave out on cards thus became HDOAC.

Stories, sound and film bites

We live our lives by stories, and stories can be very powerful and can make learning engaging or exciting. Stories have specific ingredients and often successful leaders have an ability to tell good stories. In *The Story Teller's Secret*, Gallo (2016), a communication coach for a number of leading corporate organizations, suggests that the brain is hardwired for storytelling, and that inspirational leaders turn their passion into a performance, through their ability to tell brilliant stories. He argues that the latest scientific knowledge can help people to create persuasive stories that win hearts and minds. This can be useful for creating experiences that win the hearts and minds of learners. One of the pieces of advice is to have a hero in the story, and overcoming a challenge or struggle in the story. Another piece of advice is to divide the story into three chunks – and that images, videos, photographs, metaphors and analogies can work like magic. In reality this advice is a mixture of navigational tools for abstract thinking, but also emotional tools to create passion and other feelings. Sound and film bites can also be used in many different ways so as to create an experience for learning.

Developing learning habits

It is significant that we are often not aware of what our brains are doing and this is the case with impulsive behaviours, conditioning and habits. A fairly recent book, *The Power of Habit*, written by Duhigg (2012), suggests that habits are formed by three essential steps of a loop in the brain. In the development of a habit first a cue or trigger is required (C), followed by a routine (R) and finally there is a reward (R) that strengthens the loop. Over a period of time these nerve pathways become well used and therefore the loop becomes more automatic. In this way, it is said, a habit is formed.

Positive learning habits can be developed using this same loop. Let me now illustrate with a practical example. When marking assignments using speech recognition the views of the marker are simply spoken. As the assignment is viewed the marker first scans the document looking for specific things. The sequence of comments can ultimately create positive learning habits. A simple example is as follows: *As I briefly scan your assignment before talking about more specific issues I notice that your layout and presentation are excellent. All the pages are numbered, and the figures and charts are also numbered and titled. There is a comprehensive Contents page, making the structure of your work explicit. Looking through the body of the work there are on average four or five citations per page. For a first-year student this is good and this evidences your ability to engage with wider reading. For the next semester I would like to see you count your citations on each page and move from four/five to an average of seven/eight per page.* Some students will read this and realize that the marker is moving through their document in a particular way, checking the assignment. They will recognize and mimic some of this marking process in their own editing process before submission. They will highlight and count the number of citations per page and look to make improvements if this message is re-enforced by other markers This is not just student feedback; it is also an attempt to create positive habits.

There are other wider applications to these habits. The following is taken from *The Creative Teaching and Learning Toolkit* by Best and Thomas (2007: 93), highlighting how this idea has been carried out within some schools:

> The start to a school day can be very rushed, with assemblies, registers, and the giving out of notices and information. A more relaxed start can provide a pleasant change and lower stress levels. A number of schools operate a system whereby on one or more mornings a week the whole school falls silent and everyone reads – in some schools this even includes the school office and phones are taken off the hook! Reading material is available for anyone who forgets, and comics, newspapers and books of all kinds can be read. The usual announcements are pinned up or displayed on screens instead of read out. These initiatives have helped to develop a sense of calm during what can be a very hectic start to the day, and have enabled students to enter a more appropriate state for learning.

The case study below explores the essence of successful change, based on altering the learning experience within schools.

CASE STUDY Experiential Learning at XP School, Doncaster, Yorkshire

EL (*expeditionary learning*) education is derived from a collaboration between Outward Bound (OB) US, and Harvard Graduate School of Education. The Harvard Outward Bound project (established 1987) sought to increase the profile of *experiential education* at the Harvard Graduate School whilst bringing more academic rigour to Outward Bound's work in schools. Thus EL education is a marriage of the philosophies of Kurt Hahn, the founder of Outward Bound, and the best of the Harvard Graduate School of Education's theoretical and practical approaches to teaching and learning. Demonstration schools began in 1993, and these schools remain rooted in this original heritage, providing teachers and students with academically rigorous *experiences*. The mountain that the students and teachers climb is, however, metaphoric: the mountain is a climb of scholarship, not a physical climb. The ethos is essentially the same as a typical OB wilderness course.

The XP School in Doncaster, a Free School set up in 2013, follows this US-style philosophy, with children embarking on cross-subject learning expeditions. The

Free School idea was set up by the Department for Education to provide potential to respond to what local people say they want. XP School is a Free School with a difference. It was founded by CEO Gwyn ap Harri and experienced headteacher Andy Sprakes, partially because of their own frustrations with the more traditional approaches to education. The school has become an academy trust of three schools, comprising a second new secondary school being built next door, and a local primary school. Ap Harri notes that the curriculum is delivered in a totally different way: 'If you want, for instance, an investigation into the wildlife in your back garden, there are lots of different subjects you can cover. You can do maths in terms of the size of the garden, how many samples you can find, what percentage that is. Then there is the history of the place, the geography, biology and other topics, so you can learn through a really wide project or expedition' (XPschool.org). The school uses an exploration approach to learning, covering the National Curriculum using themes such as '*being human*', a multi-topic exploration of what makes a human (being). Each expedition has a number of essential elements, including fieldwork and the use of external experts, and the presentation and celebration of the student work to significant audiences at the end of their extensive projects.

But there appears to be more reasons behind the early successes of the XP School in Doncaster. The Core Practices guide for EL schools discusses the general development of culture and character, similar to that recommended by Kurt Hahn: kindness, respect, responsibility, courage and active citizenship. The school selected an organization called Relational Schools (www.relationalschools.org) to investigate relationships within the school in terms of teacher with student, student with teacher, and student to student. The findings highlighted how relationships at XP are significantly healthier than the benchmark average. In a report based on 533 school surveys, relational proximity at XP was on average 17 per cent higher than the national benchmark (Report: Building relationships through expeditionary experiences). What makes these results so impressive is that the data included the new students, collected only two weeks after staff and students had met each other for the first time; their relationships were merely two weeks old! The success has been partly attributed to the fact that staff and students don't immediately enter school at the start of the new intake. Instead the children depart on a coach to take part in a four-day Outward Bound outdoor expedition in Wales, where they develop a culture whereby all students are 'crew not passengers'. In Outward Bound terms, of course, a ship is not designed to remain in the harbour; hence the crew of the ship must be ready to be outward bound, for life at sea.

Using the Learning Combination Lock

A model for the design and evaluation of experiential learning

Whilst the design, delivery and evaluation of experiential learning is a complicated process, new knowledge is continually emerging that further informs us about human learning. At this stage of the book we introduce our holistic philosophy with a model that has been created from doctoral research (Beard, 2008), involving a complex interactional mix of multidisciplinary knowledge with practical experience.

We present this model in different visual formats as we realize how this significantly affects reactions to the modelling. Initially, and for a basic practical understanding, we created the 'Learning Combination Lock', which comprises a series of tumblers, each illustrating an almost infinite range of experience possibilities that can be varied so as to have more potential to enhance learning. Some people see this as too mechanical and deterministic, preferring models with less definitive boundaries – and so we also present the model in other visual formats.

Using this visual metaphor of a combination lock, with seven tumblers, the potential number of learning permutations is many millions; indeed it can be expanded to an almost infinite number. Although we are on our guard to avoid mechanistic thinking, we do believe it is robust material and we discuss the theoretical basis of our thinking, as well as offering many practical examples to illustrate the value of learning from experience. This model will help in the understanding of the very complex processes involved in experiential learning.

The model is frequently demonstrated with a rope, placed in a circle on the floor. The circle represents a human. We say the rope itself is the human interface between the outer world and inner world of a person. This interface is the site of the senses of sight, smell, touch, taste and sound. But there are some senses that people are not aware of, such as the ability of the body to sense space, the bodily GPS system as we call it. We ask what happens when sensory data is processed and in doing so we build the inner world of the person, starting with the emotional self, as a fast brain response to incoming data. Data is then analysed by the slower rational response. The human has a core, a 'self', our biography, our 'being' – and this is what learning makes a contribution to.

We then build the outer world. People do things: activities and actions. We live among other humans and we continually interact with others, and generate knowledge with them. We have a deep desire to belong to others and to the world, including the more-than-human world. The inner and outer worlds are in continuous interaction in the creation of a continuous flow of experiences.

Everyone is given a set of six or seven plastic lids and a piece of string or rope and they go off in pairs to build the model themselves. The model building, the walking around the model, and talking it through with others, reinforces meaning and memory. It is simple, yet potentially complex. The model embraces an understanding of experiential learning as much more than social-cultural. Our model, shown in Figure 3.2, embraces the natural and more-than-human world. This is how we build understanding of the experiential learning model.

In building the model called the Learning Combination Lock, we reject, in a similar way to Dewey, the classical dualisms of energy–tension, challenge–support, task–process, male–female, indoor–outdoor, natural–artificial environments and real–simulated activities. We suggest these are in a state of fluidity. These themes illustrate some of the key factors that present countless opportunities in the design of experiential learning.

The model represents our philosophical and conceptual framework for experiential learning. For the first time ever, to our knowledge, the core elements of learning have been brought together in the Learning Combination Lock model. In the past, only some of the human dimensions involved in the experience of learning have been discussed in detail in the literature on experiential learning, and then often in isolation. This has resulted in a partial picture of human experiential learning. The chapters that follow will address in sequence the tumblers or key dimensions of experiential learning that make up the Learning Combination Lock (Figure 3.3); however, we will briefly discuss each of these main categories here in order to provide an overview that will enable you to dip in and out of the book in order to find strategies and answers that apply to the circumstances in which you find yourself.

The Learning Combination Lock (Figure 3.4) in its elementary sense is based on the notion that the person interacts with the external environment through the senses. It is presented as a visual metaphor of six tumblers that represent the complexity of the many possible experiential choices. Beginning on the left of the Learning Combination Lock, the first tumbler involves the question of where, and with whom? The environment consists of the people,

Figure 3.2 A multidisciplinary modelling of the human experience

PRACTICAL AND PHILOSOPHICAL CONSIDERATIONS		
1 Outer world of people and the more-than-human world	2 Sensorial bodily interface	3 Inner world of people

HUMAN EXPERIENCE – SIX DIMENSIONS SPANNING THE NATURAL AND SOCIAL SCIENCES					
1 The environment	2 The activities	3 Senses	4 Affect – emotions	5 Mind reason	6 Change in self

PRACTICAL QUESTIONS (PHRONESIS)					
WHERE? WHO? Where... with whom (relating), including more-than-human world in what contextual circumstances (eg environment /culture/place) does experience take place?	WHAT? What will the people actually do?	HOW? How will people experience the world through their senses? Reciprocity	HEARTS? What is the nature of the emotional engagement in the experience?	MINDS? What is the nature of the cognitive engagement in the experience?	CHANGES IN SELF? How might people be changed as a result of the experience?

PHILOSOPHICAL – PROPOSITIONAL					
BELONGING	DOING (conative)	SENSING (receptive/ perceptive)	FEELING (affective)	THINKING (cognitive)	BEING

←		Focus on tangible 'things'			→
Potential to engage the less tangible					Potential to engage the less tangible
		FORM			
		To do something, sense something, to feel something, to think something			
FORMLESS					FORMLESS

SOURCE Beard (2005)

Figure 3.3 The seven core dimensions of the human experience: an oscillating, interacting flux

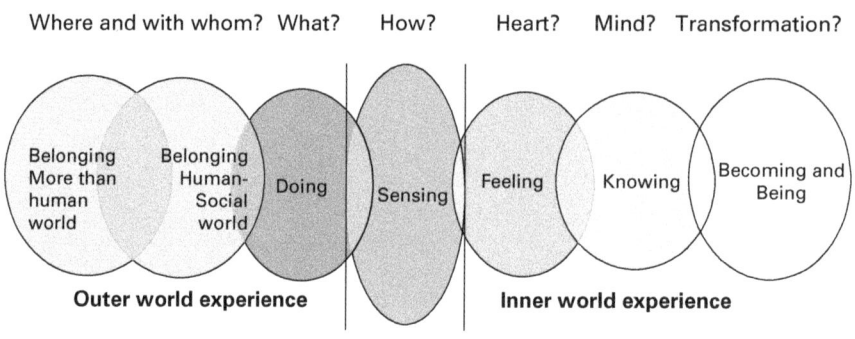

SOURCE Beard (2005)

place and space in which learning takes place, providing the location, external stimuli and ambience for the experience. The next tumbler represents the 'what' of the experience; what is it that people are going to do? Many possible learning activities present themselves in practice; for example, a journey or a challenge. The next group of tumblers are concerned with the how. How is the learning actually received? This tumbler represents the senses through which we receive the various forms of stimuli. The fourth tumbler involves engaging the emotions (heart) where we perceive, interpret and emotionally respond to the stimuli from the external environment; in other words we internalize the external learning experience. The fifth tumbler focuses on the scope and form of intelligence (mind). The final tumbler concerns change and transformation, our becoming, and being. Each of these six tumblers should inform practice, choices, and selection of other tumbler options, so as to avoid a random, one-armed-bandit approach to selecting the possible components for experiential activities for learning.

Experiential learning, when effective, works with the whole person. Colin Beard's work with the Singapore Ministry of Education was due to the significant alignment of this experiential model to their future educational focus, as Singapore was introducing new 21st Century Competencies (https://www.moe.gov.sg/education/education-system/21st-century-competencies). Our model was closely aligned with what was required for the education of children and young people, ie learning to *know* and *think*, learning to *feel*, learning to *sense* and *observe*, and learning to *act* and *behave*, learning to '*belong*', to '*become*' and to '*be someone*' in the world.

If you are involved in providing planned or emergent experiences for learning, be it a teacher, lecturer, facilitator, trainer or coach, the design

Figure 3.4 The experiential Learning Combination Lock model

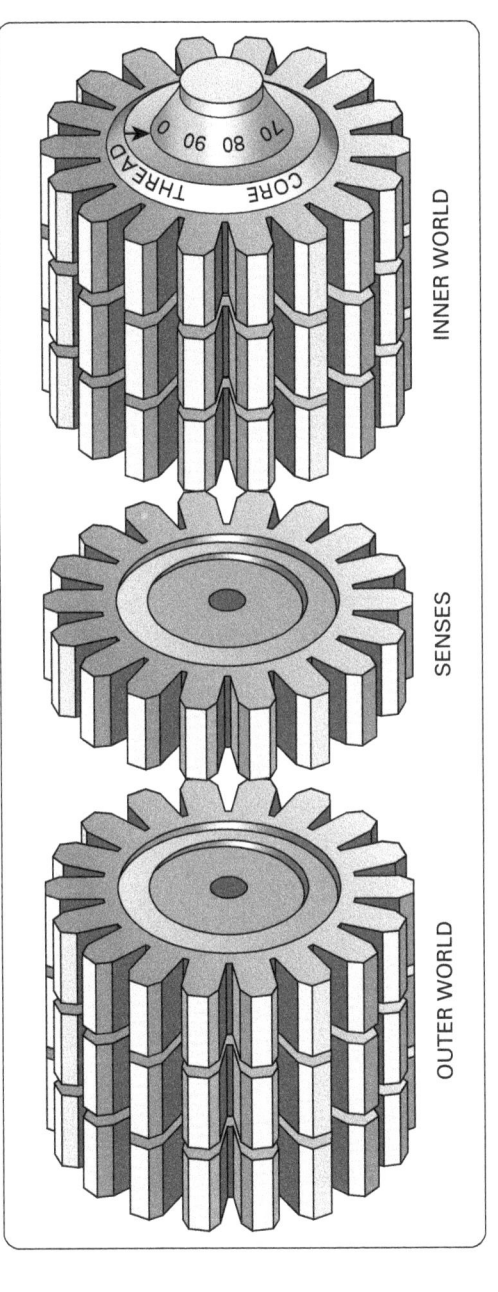

SOURCE Beard (2005)

and facilitation of experiences for these are all areas that are fundamental to good practice. Mastery of practice requires a sound understanding of the way experiences can be the basis *for* and *of* learning. Mastery therefore requires the basic theories and philosophies that were introduced in Chapters 1 and 2 to be understood.

As you read through the book, you may well identify new elements to add to the contents of individual tumblers, and perhaps even add completely new categories of tumblers. We strongly encourage you to create your own personalized Learning Combination Lock to answer and respond to your own obstacles and challenges.

The review and evaluation of experiences

Reviewing is explored in Chapter 5. However, the case study below highlights a process called Human Experience Mapping (Beard and Russ, 2017) as an approach that can offer insight and depth to the understanding of any human experience, and can be of benefit to learning experience design (LED).

CASE STUDY Experience mapping

A higher-education student conducted a small-scale piece of research into the experiences of several women from a UK bank who had volunteered to sleep out on the streets of Sheffield (UK) for just one night. Their experience was designed by a charity as a project to increase awareness of the plight of rough sleepers and homeless people. The information collected by the student relating to their experiences was particularly interesting. The women had subjected themselves to a unique experience that had quite a powerful impact on them. Their guide for the night was a homeless man and his dog, who had slept on the streets for over 20 years.

The student found the analysis of the interview data quite hard to interpret. In order to help the student understand this data I first of all asked him to disaggregate it into a number of dimensions of the human experience, such as their emotional experiences, their sensorial experience, anything associated with knowing and knowledge, etc. He covered the following: 1) knowing, 2) doing, 3) sensing, 4) feeling, 5/6) belonging (people and places) and 7) being (identity, values, etc). These core dimensions of the human experience are related to our model that we present at the end of this chapter.

The student now had two forms of data. The first one was the data from his original interview questions, whilst the second batch represented the same data allocated to the seven dimensions of the human experience. This second 'view' of the data, which was quite easy to complete, helped the student considerably in his interpretive work, yet he was still struggling to really understand the experiences of this group of women. What started to concern me was the fact that traditional academic data, presented in this way to the inexperienced eye, often proved difficult for people without a research background to comprehend with any depth. This was of course made worse by the fact that the many columns of data, as written words in lines, was printed out on several sheets of paper. In this form, data is linear and so it is difficult for the human brain to comprehend, to see how it is all related, and to detect 'patterns'.

I was determined to develop an approach that would allow both the student, and event industry practitioners, to more readily grasp large bodies of data collected in a traditional (academic) way. What I was looking for was a method that would be simple and quick to create a rich picture of the sleepout experience.

I designed a way to convert the original academic data not only into a view of data as disaggregated into the several human experiential dimensions, but more significantly into a spatial-relational map to generate a picture so that the large amounts of data could be understood in a relatively short time.

The method involved three to five people gathering around a sheet of paper 3–4 metres long, and 1 metre wide. They read the original data, as handouts, from the first two approaches and typically people were struggling to grasp it all. People were initially overwhelmed with the six to seven pages of data and so they often got stuck: they had to be pushed to just get on and write something. This was an important step in building confidence. I encouraged them to literally scribble down anything that they found of particular interest in the first instance, and to do this within one of three zones: the experiences before the sleepout, during the sleepout and after the sleepout.

After about 30 minutes people were asked to have a dress rehearsal of their understanding of the participant experiences. They had to walk alongside their scribbles, from the pre-sleepout to the post-sleepout experiences, talking about what they had understood so far. Everyone had to contribute, and so a collaborative narrative emerged.

This trial run led to a period of further understanding as the groups felt they wanted more understanding and so they intentionally looked to fill in gaps. During their final, collaborative, 'walk the talk', completed in front of other peers, the narrative became more complex, taking on a level of critical analysis that showed a considerable depth of understanding. The resulting discussion, and the generation of a rich picture of the event experiences, was quite astonishing. This mapping process has subsequently been successfully tried out in Hong Kong, Singapore, the United States, Malaysia, Slovakia and the Czech Republic.

The creation of a map whilst writing, talking and sharing appears to have been key to this final process. Brain research shows that linear formats limit the capacity to identify spatial-relational connections. London taxi drivers appear to have enlarged areas of the hippocampus due to their work in comprehending and navigating the spatial layout of thousands of roads and streets (Woollett and Maguire, 2011).

This human experience mapping process is not dissimilar to the mapping processes that Harry Beck used to create the London Underground map that is now replicated around the world to depict transport-system complexity in a simple manner.

Is experience mapping a process that can be refined and used more readily by experiential learning practitioners so as to critically explore, evaluate or design participant experiences?

For a more detailed exploration of experiential mapping see Beard and Russ (2017).

A brief reminder of the chapters that follow

The seven core dimensions of learning

Chapter 4 covers the outer world of learning, which involves humans interacting with other humans (social and cultural), and human interactions with the non-human world, including, for example, the physical, spiritual and living natural environments. This dimension is therefore twofold, and we refer to these issues as 'Belonging' in the world. Chapter 5 is concerned with a broad notion of doing, action, activities and agency. It is the dimension of the 'Conative'. Chapter 6 covers work with the senses, including sensing our inner world, and our outer world. This is the 'Sensing' dimension. Chapter 7 explores the way emotions affect learning. The chapter relates to the 'Affective' dimension of learning. Chapter 8 explores thinking, reasoning and intelligence. It is the dimension of 'Cognition'. Chapter 9 explores the nature of our self, our 'Being'. Chapter 10 is on experiential learning and the future.

As we develop many other principles of practice throughout the rest of the book, particularly the seven dimensions of learning (eg tumblers), it should become clear that the number of possibilities for designing or creating learning experiences is almost limitless. While we present you with many ideas and concepts, we strongly encourage you to add to our modelling, or to develop your own learning models as your experience develops through your own practice. We hope this book is a small contribution towards helping you to find creativity and new directions for your work with experiential learning.

PART TWO
The Learning Combination Lock model

The outer-world learning environment: other humans, other living creatures, and spaces and places

04

(the belonging dimension)

The science of designing learning environments is currently remarkably underdeveloped. FEILDEN (2004)

Introduction

Humans have a deep sense of belonging and a deep psychological need to belong (Baumeister and Leary, 1995). The internal sense of belonging is affected by our outer-world experiences. We continually interact with the world around us; other people as well as the living and physical world that is not human. The social aspects are covered in numerous places throughout this book, in particular the way knowledge and learning is socially constructed, and so in this chapter we will give additional focus to the more-than-human world, including the living creatures we share the planet with, as well as the spaces and places where our experience of learning takes place. However, it is also important that the rich and ancient knowledge residing in indigenous or First Nation people is respected and understood. Across the globe these people continue to experience the colonization and theft of their land and their ways of being by the rich and powerful. In this way their experiences are denied or devalued.

Many indigenous cultures have long been based on a natural spirituality, one in which all things are connected and where there is a mutual respect between the land, animals and the natural world. For them, if this balance does not exist then hard times will prevail in their environment, their personal lives and their spiritual lives. Many First Nation people believe their connection with the natural surroundings is one of the strongest relationships they have. This applies to their earth, their planet and their spiritual world. They live by a principle of balance and harmony between all these intertwining elements. These principles underpin their experiences of their world; if all humans want to build sustainable communities then all future generations across the globe will need to learn experientially how to develop such a deep partnership with the natural systems and planet that we share.

The Norwegians have an important concept they call *friluftsliv*, or feeling at home with nature (Barnes, 2000). Native American people, and their beliefs about nature, are discussed in an article called 'Spirit of the earth' (Peard, 1999), which offers an analysis of a speech by a Native American chief, and in doing so offers two extreme perspectives on nature taken by Western civilization and by Native Americans. The dichotomy, although oversimplistic, is presented thus:

Native American	Western civilization
at home in nature	fear
belonging	ownership
community	individualism
spiritual	capital
sustainable	exploitation
freedom	domination

Mohawk (1996) describes how Western fairy tales paint pictures of nature as foreboding and dark. 'Natural' places are where Hansel and Gretel got lost, and where Sleeping Beauty was surrounded by thorn bushes and immense forests. Natural places possessed 'wild' animals and 'savage' people, and both had to be tamed. The psychological origins of these negative mindsets highlighted also in the dichotomy above are not only rooted in ancient folklore, they are also to be found in contemporary Western laws (the hunting of the otter was deliberately left out of the 1975 Protection of Wildflowers and Creatures Act so that the Act would be approved; the otter was added to the list of protected animals three years later in 1978); negative Western corporate environmental policy (we aim to reduce the impact of our business on the environment…); and environmental taxation (to pay environmental taxes, to suffer penalties for environmental destruction) (see Beard, 2003).

So are there special or optimal places to learn? This important question remains largely unanswered in contemporary literature on learning, yet the place in which we learn, as we shall now show, is very significant to the learning experience. This is a two-way process: the place influences human behaviour and human learning. Interaction occurs with the human (social) world and a more-than-human world (MTHW) (Abram, 1997). In this chapter we explore a diverse range of outdoor and indoor places and spaces, both real and virtual, social or more than human, natural or artificial, private or public, formal or informal that can influence the experience of learning. These are the issues that are the concerns of the first cog in the Learning Combination Lock: the *belonging* dimension.

Often learning programmes focus on activities, with less focus on the needs of space or place. This can reduce learning effectiveness. Indeed there is a saying that if you were a fish the last thing you would discover is the water around you! As we shall now demonstrate, there is a close relationship between learning and working, learning activity design and the learning environment/s in which they take place.

What we are witnessing is the evolution of new spatial ecologies. The richness is exciting: spaces and places for human functioning are diversifying. Places and spaces are designed for or occupied for various functions or purposes: for meetings, for creativity, for sharing and constructing knowledge, for reading and quiet reflective work, just to name a few. A new city-wide ecology of spaces might also be emerging, as highlighted in the case examples described below.

The importance of space for reading, thinking and talking

An approach to reflective learning, referred to as 'Coffee and Papers' (see Beard, 2010), got its name from learning and development settings in hotel lounges where the learning experience was designed to be comparable to reading the Sunday newspapers, in a relaxed environment, with a relaxed but focused mind state. Essentially it consists of an invitation to individuals to read themed articles and to intentionally relax in an environment that is special for each individual. Coffee and Papers typically generates high levels of learner engagement and knowledge generation through the process of individual reading in a retreat simulation, followed by social conversational learning. The experience is designed to develop a specific sensory–cognition, or body–mind state of 'relaxed alertness'. Individuals experience comfort, with a degree of solitude, to enhance concentration and thinking. Coffees, teas, fruit juices, croissants and fruit add to the sensory experience. The quiet solo experience involves individual, internal conversations. After a period of solo reading the group reassemble and construct collective conversations, critically exploring the range of readings. The acquired collective knowledge can be substantial. One senior manager said of one such session:

> One of the more effective learning community development exercises, in my view, followed the Coffee and Papers sessions each morning. During these sessions, differing views concerning the same articles were discussed and new insights developed based on individual experience outside the articles. This led to a spin of ideas that spurred more new ideas, and reshaped some of my initial thoughts of the articles. It appeared that many of the participants shared this experience regarding the Coffee and Papers sessions.

The articles are themed, such as organizational development (OD), and taken from both scholarly and professional journals: *Harvard Business Review, People Management, Management Learning, Management Education and Development, Training and Development, Industrial and Commercial Training, Sloan Management Review*, and many others. Hardly Sunday morning reading! In the corporate world one chief executive sat in her stockinged feet on a stool in a hotel lounge, surrounded by strawberries coated in chocolate, and coffee and croissants and papers. She said: 'Colin, I am in heaven. I never have the time to read any more. I have lost the power to think or read with any depth these days… I am enjoying this experience so much!' Senior executives admit to the pleasure at effectively being given permission to experience an extended period of *thinking* and *concentrating*. The *place* signifies that *time* for concentration is important and a legitimate extension of work.

The UK National Health Service facilities managers and HRD managers concerned with new workplaces, and the various barriers to change thrown up by organizational culture (see Beard and Price, 2013), might find a Coffee and Papers approach a pragmatic means of gaining executive buy-in to the strategic possibilities inherent in new workplaces. The Coffee and Papers experience had a profound effect on a whole organization. Staff in the UK's National Health Service (NHS) have responsibilities to sustain professional development through reading of evidence-based clinical practice. Time to read about such clinical practice, however, had largely diminished due to the dominance of everyday activities; the *doing* dimension of learning. Concentrated reading and the subsequent collective sharing was not happening for a number of reasons, including that of guilt associated with relaxed reading at work. Reading might not be interpreted as *doing* work. However, the staff of one primary care trust (PCT), having experienced Coffee and Papers on a training programme, put forward what turned out eventually to be a successful proposal brought to senior managers under the workplace umbrella. The proposal, as part of an 'Inspiration Award' scheme in 2009, included some of the following required actions suggested in order to implement this idea:

- Encourage staff to write *reading time* into their objectives.
- Develop a marketing campaign across the PCT showing that it is okay to sit and read clinical material.
- Provide education for managers to help them understand how to enable staff to absorb current evidence.
- Understand the cost of allowing staff time to absorb evidence, but also calculating and understanding the cost, service and other benefits.
- Purchase resources to make reading easier.

The provision of, and the informal legitimization of, reflective space within working environments is underexplored. The importance of such experiences to the corporate progress is highlighted by Ray Anderson, the well-known CEO of the Georgia-based global company Interface Carpets: when he realized he had little understanding of the notion of sustainable development he started reading more widely, and more critically, about his role in it as a business leader in society. His reading changed his views, his business and his life. The company is widely recognized as leading the way globally in business sustainability, winning many international awards. Significantly, the dawning experience for Anderson, often referred to as an epiphany, was initiated through reading with an open yet critical mind.

Space for working and learning — ECHQ and GCHQ

In the knowledge economy, learning and working are converging phenomena. Pragmatism guided the redevelopment of a London headquarters of global property consultancy E C Harris. The head office or ECHQ, as it is labelled, was redesigned as a solution to several strategic challenges, notably differentiation and rejuvenation of their surveying practice, intent on projecting itself as 'the built asset consultancy'. Space utilization is their business. The developed design involved some 20 per cent of the available space as a semi-public front of house with clever but discreet security. Their workplace was reconfigured, tiered and layered with some 900 staff accommodated by 545 'work stations'. The project is credited with dramatic increases in profitability, staff satisfaction and knowledge generation, as well as a significant reduction in space requirement per head and CO_2 emissions.

The three key layers of the workplace were as follows: layer one created public areas available to anyone, including the practice's clients and collaborators. This area was welcome 'public' space, for staff and visitors, involving the cafe/social dynamic as a conversational form. Layer two was available though less formally recognized for 'friends' of ECH to have space to work, online, with a desk. Layer three was a restricted 'staff' hot desk and milieu of varied light office spaces, designed to achieve a richer range of spaces for different conversations, with efficient density without packing, and allowing for 'clusters' of mobile teams. The result was that the traditional desk is no longer the fixed space at which a worker is expected to sit. The ECHQ approach was significant for me in that if it were to be replicated in collaboration with other businesses in the City of London, then possibly, for the first time, there would be an ecology of spaces and places providing a network of home and 'away' spaces, for inner and outer conversations that mirror the understanding of the whole person spatial–functional awareness of management learning and knowledge creation in a rapidly changing world (Beard and Price, 2012).

GCHQ is a very different organization, concerned with, for example, anti-terrorism and cyberspace monitoring. The benefits from a significant workplace redesign were significant. Their new circular building looks rather like a football stadium from the air. The outer ring, however, is not seating as in a stadium but a circular area or walkway called The Street. The new building encourages new ways of working, reducing response times, and the outer circular ring of walking space is the modern equivalent of the peripatos. A work-anywhere culture was developed: more open-plan areas, greater desk and knowledge sharing, and agile team working.

Indoor learning: the new classroom

Indoor learning environments in schools, colleges, universities and training centres are undergoing a metamorphosis, and change of label from 'classrooms' to 'learning spaces'. The changing language is a signpost of the transformation. Future learning spaces will provide greater flexibility and mobility of people, knowledge, furniture and other artefacts. Physical issues such as furnishings, air quality and acoustics, lighting and colour clearly impact on learning. The box below suggests useful design principles for schools.

Twelve school design principles based on brain-based learning research (from Lackney and Fielding, 1998)

1 Rich, stimulating environments – colour, texture, 'teaching architecture', displays created by students (not teacher) so students have connection and ownership of the product.

2 Places for group learning – breakout spaces, alcoves, table groupings to facilitate social learning and stimulate the social brain; turning breakout spaces into living rooms for conversation.

3 Linking indoor and outdoor places – movement, engaging the motor cortex linked to the cerebral cortex for oxygenation.

4 Corridors and public places containing symbols of the school community's larger purpose to provide coherency and meaning that increases motivation (warning: go beyond slogans).

5 Safe places – reduce threat, especially in urban settings.

6 Variety of places – provide a variety of places of different shapes, colour, light, nooks and crannies.

7 Changing displays – changing the environment, interacting with the environment stimulates brain development. Provide display areas that

allow for stage-set-type constructions to further push the envelope with regard to environmental change.

8   Have all the resources available – provide educational, physical and a variety of settings in close proximity to encourage rapid development of ideas generated in a learning episode. This is an argument for wet areas/science, computer-rich workspaces all integrated and not segregated. Multiple functions and cross-fertilization of ideas are the primary goal.

9   Flexibility – a common principle in the past continues to be relevant. Many dimensions of flexibility of place are reflected in other principles.

10 Active/passive places – students need places for reflection and retreat away from others for interpersonal intelligence as well as places for active engagement for interpersonal intelligence.

11 Personalized space – the concept of home-base needs to be emphasized more than the metal locker or the desk; this speaks to the principle of uniqueness; the need to allow learners to express their self-identity, personalize their special places and places to express territorial behaviours.

12 The community-at-large as the optimal learning environment – the need to find ways to fully utilize all urban and natural environments as the primary learning setting, the school as the fortress of learning needs to be challenged and conceptualized more as a resource-rich learning centre that supplements lifelong learning. Technology, distance learning, community and business partnerships, home-based learning, all need to be explored as alternative organizational structures for educational institutions of the present and future.

It is said that students spend approximately 20,000 hours in classrooms by the time they graduate (Fraser, 2001). Despite this fact, little is known about designing learning space: the classroom has remained relatively unchanged over the past 100 years! Typically, indoor learning environments have been strongly associated with 'lecture theatres', 'classrooms' and 'textbooks'. The term 'learning space' embraces a somewhat contemporary and broader campus: including e-learning technology and virtual discussion groups; distance education; common informal areas such as halls and other social group spaces; informal furnishing such as sofas; outdoor green spaces such as woodlands, lakes and decking; and amphitheatres, atrium- and mall-style spaces. We call this a spatial 'ecology', consisting of many different spaces and places to experience learning. Individually tailored learning is currently in vogue, as is technological change. Experiential learning will increasingly reach out into local communities and the broader learning environment of the future will be considerably different.

Contemporary thinking about learning environments is reflected in a broad definition offered by Indiana University, who define a learning environment as:

> A physical, intellectual, psychological environment which facilitates learning through connectivity and community. (http://www.indiana.edu)

One substantial university research programme on learning environments in the United States notes that:

> Well-established research shows that students learn best when they are actively engaged rather than being passive observers... there are three avenues an institution can promote to foster active student learning. First, certain teaching methodologies, such as problem-based learning, promote active student involvement. Second, the classroom furnishings can either enhance or hinder active student learning. Thus, tables and moveable chairs enhance while fixed-row seating hinders active learning. Finally, technologies which require student initiative, such as interactive video-discs, promote active learning.
> (http://www.-lib.iupui.edu/itt/planlearn/execsumm.html)

Physical issues such as furnishings, air quality and acoustics, lighting and colour clearly impact on learning. The architectural mantra is that 'form should follow function'. Form has, however, traditionally dictated function: many learning spaces in schools and universities throughout the world are designed by facilities managers. In the UK, a Design Council report, *Kit for Purpose: Design to deliver creative learning* (2005), notes that current learning environments tend to:

- reduce the range of teaching and learning styles possible and affect the interaction between teacher and student;
- undermine the value placed on learning;
- not adapt to individual needs;
- hinder creativity;
- be inefficient, wasting time and effort;
- cost more in the long term.

The pedagogy of space remains underdeveloped. The design of learning spaces in formal education has traditionally been restricted by complex building regulations and procurement procedures. But new designs are now emerging, with a focus on the kinds of spaces required for modern learning activities: group learning, spaces for deep concentration, spaces for being innovative or creative, for being analytical, and spaces for quiet reading (see the 'Coffee and Papers' exercise earlier in this chapter). Architects use a range of terms for such spaces, such as *den* for team learning, *club* for knowledge interaction, *hive* for individual processing and *cell* for concentrated study.

Becher (1989) uses an 'ecological' approach to workplace design, and refers to the need to observe the movements of people or tribes and their creation of territoriality. This notion of 'territoriality' highlights power, politics and ownership in the use of learning spaces. Ideally, experiential learning might enable learners to be architects of their own space, with opportunities being provided to continually reshape and redesign psychological and physical space, as individuals and/or in collaboration with others.

Both indoor and outdoor learning spaces, whether real or virtual, are usually constructed spaces rather than 'natural', thus presenting opportunities to rethink and reconfigure space for learning. The ubiquitous garden shed, or its equivalent, has significance for individuals as a place of inventive learning. Research by Golding (2005) in Australia highlights gender issues in the use of learning spaces by rural communities. From a diverse sample of men in rural towns, around 95 per cent prefer to learn in practical situations, hands on, and outside wherever possible. For many rural Australian men with limited formal literacies, appropriate space may take the form of a fire shed or outside at an agricultural field day or demonstration. The existing literature on the effectiveness of situated learning supports such research observations (eg Lave and Wenger, 1991). People prefer to learn in situated contexts: often in practical situations akin to where they work or feel 'at home'. Ongoing research has also been conducted since the 1980s on a neighbourhood 'house'-type model that is attractive to women but not necessarily to men.

The outdoor elements of the learning 'campus' are increasingly important to the student choice of university, affecting the quality of the learning experience. Such spaces might include timber decking, amphitheatres and artificial lakes; these informal spaces are increasingly being used for more formal learning, with learning spilling out of the classroom into such spaces. Innovative relaxation 'lecture theatres' with seat hammocks slung from roof beams are to be found in Turku Polytechnic in Finland and such examples serve to illustrate how the learning environment can be specifically designed so as to enhance certain mood or mind states, such as relaxed alertness, a concept we explore later in the book.

Learning spaces also have micro-climates consisting of tiles, ceilings, walls, floors, desks, books, computers and many other objects, all of which can be used in creative ways to enhance the learner experience. The floor is ideal to create models and concepts with large groups of people, using masking tape, large pieces of coloured card and other training aids. The walls are places to create 'graffiti walls' using decorating lining paper, so that people might contribute thoughts or reactions to events through drawing or scribbling words or phrases. Walls can also be used to place and move stick-it labels, or to project colours or images to influence mood. It is likely that futuristic classrooms will have walls that become large functional working spaces, made of glass in the form of a touch screen that can be written on. In this way, handwritten material and electronic text, pictures, diagrams and other images can be interchangeable and moved by hand (rather than with a mouse), in a similar way to the functions found in interactive whiteboards. This is good news for the kinaesthetic learner who prefers not to sit behind a desk for long periods. Technological developments increasingly influence the design and use of learning space, with interactive whiteboards and large plasma screens emerging in classrooms, enabling the capture of 'live' intellectual property.

Educational designers such as Australian Truna Turner (2005), in examining the epistemologies of immersive video gaming, suggest that design principles of gaming offer potential for new forms of educational literacy within an interface of the virtual learning environment. Such video games engross players in complex and challenging activities and signpost potential future design for virtual experiential learning. E-learning is undergoing dramatic changes, becoming more experiential, and a new term *e^2-learning environments* has emerged (electronic-experiential learning) (Beard, Wilson and McCarter, 2006).

But US research suggests that there are concerns about space within educational learning environments, as public spaces are diversifying while private spaces are declining:

> Given the need for solitude, it is ironic that what most universities do is to create an environment in which students are rarely alone. Intent on forming a campus community, campus architecture creates communal spaces: classrooms, student living quarters, outdoor quads, dining halls, recreation centres, and now even libraries are places to be designed to be with others. Where, then, do they go to be alone… Where is the private space? (Behuniak, 2005: 11)

Paradoxically, contemporary educational thinking requires greater student reflection on personal and professional development within formal education. Reflection usually requires access to private thinking space, something that is well known by the outdoor learning profession.

Outdoor learning

In *Rethinking Outdoor, Experiential and Informal Education* (Jeffs and Ord, 2018), prominent writers explore a range of outdoor settings, from water environments, and mountains, to residential and informal outdoor experiences. Ord (2018: 108) offers a critical review of how we regard mountains, and comments that 'journeying through mountains and climbing to their summits is understandably viewed as a fundamental ingredient or a cornerstone of outdoor and adventure education'. The book also contains a significant chapter on the many socially and culturally constructed concepts of 'wilderness' or 'mountains'. No matter how we regard or intellectually analyse the notion of wilderness, the outer more-than-human world remains a powerful presence in the lives of many humans.

Outdoor learning environments are undergoing a transformation: outdoor locations for learning are much more than an outdoor classroom, or a vast recreational playground, or a battlefield of unpredictable wilderness elements. Outdoor environments have a long history of providing very special spaces for individuals to learn, in a profound way, about themselves and their social interaction with others, as we shall discuss throughout this book. There is clearly more to the outdoor learning environment than merely a utility location; it is an integral component of the learning experience. There is much to learn from the use of the outdoors for learning, especially in terms of working with nature and the seasons and the elements. The learning process is transactive, with learners interacting with other learners, with facilitators, and with place and space. However, a long-established question exists within the outdoor learning community concerning the extent to which facilitators should intervene when the learning space itself has a profound influence on the learner: the outdoor professionals ask '*to what extent can the mountains* (metaphor for place) *speak for themselves?*' Merely 'being' in nature can be a powerful experiential intervention in itself, and this theme is central to contemporary developments in therapy, including, for example, nature therapy, adventure therapy and horticultural therapy.

The Outer-World Learning Environment (The Belonging Dimension)

The 'outdoors' conjures up words such as 'natural', 'earth' and the 'environment', all of which are used interchangeably in the literature. Yet the extent to which the outdoor environment is contrived or natural is also worthy of further exploration. The natural surroundings of mountains, lakes and 'fresh air' energize and revitalize people, and beckon them back to their primitive roots. Consalvo (1995: 2) introduced her book of ready-made games for trainers with the following comment, which illustrates the immense sensory richness of the natural environment. Let the imagination flow and recall the sensations:

> Blue sky, red sunsets, white puffy clouds, green fields speckled with flowers, pine covered paths, moonlit meadows, crickets chirping, birds singing, snow crunching under foot, the smell of the spring thaw, summer sweetness, autumn decay, a salty breeze, burning leaves, the squish of mud, the sting of hot sand and the cold of snow are just a few among the plethora of sensory images we experience while outdoors. These sensations often tap emotionally and spiritually uplifting memories.

This quotation conjures up so many essential facets of experience, which some providers cherish while others take for granted. The outdoor environment is essential to creating pleasurable sensations and positive moods. The environment gives us natural ecstasy, and there are many elements or ingredients that can be used to increase sensitivity to learning:

- the changing seasons;
- heat and cold;
- ebb and flow of tides;
- wet, humid and dry;
- differences in day and night;
- natural rhythms of life;
- unpredictability of the elements;
- topography;
- dramatic landscapes;
- flora and fauna;
- natural art;
- spiritual awareness;
- remoteness;
- wild sounds.

These natural elements can be further divided into their subcomponents. 'Remoteness', for example, could include solitude, space, quietness and mental 'sorting-out time'. A cave is a good place to sit alone and listen to our inner voices as we experience total darkness, solitude or sensory deprivation for a short period. It is also a place to develop communication skills; talking in the dark with other colleagues provides no visual clues.

Disappearing boundaries: indoor–outdoor, natural–artificial

Indoor and outdoor places have much in common; they both have the word 'door' in them! The opening of doors, metaphorically speaking, presents people with new opportunities; to go through the door in order to arrive somewhere else. When we use the term 'outdoor learning' we tend to think of a place outside of the house, the space where the learning can occur; it is the so-called natural environment in which many experiential activities are conducted. The provision of experiential programmes is predominantly concentrated in two types of setting or environment: indoors, in rooms, and outdoors, usually but not exclusively in places of scenic beauty. The two differ greatly, but the boundaries blur as the outdoors meets the indoors and vice versa. Opportunities exist for experiential providers to diversify the use of the outdoor and indoor milieu, too.

The outdoors can be brought indoors through simulation, when people create the outdoors through fantasy. Saunders (1988) describes a number of examples of indoor 'simulation gaming' under the umbrella of experiential learning. He includes an example of a game called Island Escape, where participants are stuck on a volcanic island that is about to explode, and comments that 'whilst this is a fantasy game, participants rapidly introduce themselves to other people, and reveal their backgrounds, interests and skills' (1988: 136). Saunders argues that simulation gaming combines the features of games (rules, players, competition, cooperation) with those of simulation (incorporation of critical features of reality). He suggests that it can be used most effectively for encouraging communication, and as a diagnostic and prognostic instrument. 'Diagnostics' involves detective work to identify issues for people to work on, with case studies that replicate the essential features of a real-life situation, while the 'prognosis' involves predicting future performances of people. The simulation takes place indoors, in a classroom or hotel, for example, and uses a fantasy island for participants to escape from.

Other common examples are the well-known and well-used team decision-making exercises such as the NASA Moon Game and Desert Survival. There are now a whole range of resources using outdoor 'scenarios' for use indoors: stranded on an island, stuck in the jungle or marooned at sea, for example. In Chapter 5 we explored the 'Great Escape Game', offering, for example, an indoor competitive team-building activity in simulated submarines.

Greenaway (1999) offers an interesting, insightful view of the terms 'outdoors' and 'indoors'. On his website, he refers to 'indoor–outdoor management development'. Greenaway describes this indoor gaming as being in direct contrast to the outdoors, where metaphorical associations with work are provided by mountains becoming cashpoints, canoes becoming taxis and ropes becoming telephone cables. These interesting trends demonstrate how indoor trainers liven up sessions by bringing in the excitement of the 'simulated outdoors', while some outdoor trainers concern themselves with metaphoric links to the indoor world of work, ensuring transfer and justifying the use of outdoor management development. Greenaway goes on to look further at the similarities, not the differences, noting that the outdoors and the indoors have much in common:

- **Powerful images.** Both real and simulated outdoors evoke powerful images.
- **Neutral settings.** Real and simulated outdoors provide a neutral setting where participants will be equally disadvantaged.
- **Back to basics.** Without sophisticated technology to assist or blame, the demands and issues tend to be simple, basic and inescapable. Excuses and pretensions tend not to survive for long in 'survival' situations (whether real or imagined).
- **Novice learners.** The novelty of an outdoor scenario (real or simulated) instantly places managers in the role of the learner. This willingness to appear before peers as a 'learner' seems more likely in an outdoor setting than in a setting that more obviously resembles work and in which a manager is already supposed to be reasonably competent.
- **Span of relevance.** To bridge the gap between outdoor and work settings generally requires a wider span of relevance than bridging the gap between two work settings. Practice in making connections across wide

gaps increases the range of experiences that managers can bring to bear on any one problem.

- **Depth of learning.** Where learners do succeed in making connections between two very different settings, they tend to be at more profound levels. It is important to distinguish here between the relatively superficial connections that are designed into exercises, and the more profound connections made by individual managers when flashes of insight jump across the gap between 'outdoors' and 'work'.
- **Versatility.** Managers can more readily test, discover and demonstrate their potential and versatility (an important asset for managers facing change) in settings or simulations that are most different from their everyday work.
- **Enhanced realism.** Both approaches claim to make the training experience more realistic, but what could be further from reality than imagining that a neatly trimmed lawn is an alligator swamp or that a mountain top is a cashpoint (both outdoor training exercises), or imagining that an air-conditioned training room is a jungle or an Arctic wilderness (both indoor training exercises)? These would all be triumphs of the imagination over reality! What is surely meant by 'realism' in these contexts is more intense involvement – whatever the balance of fact and fiction, and however similar or different to work the experience may be.

In the latter point Greenaway explores the nature of reality and its relationship to the degree of engagement or involvement of the participants, a subject explored at length in Chapter 5. Scores of outdoor locations define and enhance experiential learning. The parameters of the term 'outdoors' are not limited to land-based activities. Some providers use sailing vessels to provide experiential learning. It is both outdoor and indoor learning.

Outdoor experiential development can of course take place on boats, outdoors or indoors, in the air, on water, in underground caves or on land. But all these locations can be still further divided. Land can include habitats or terrain such as jungle, forests, desert or mountains. Figure 4.1 illustrates a range of environments, and it is clear that the experience can be enhanced if there is an understanding of the opportunities that the places and spaces offer for learning.

Figure 4.1 The environmental grid

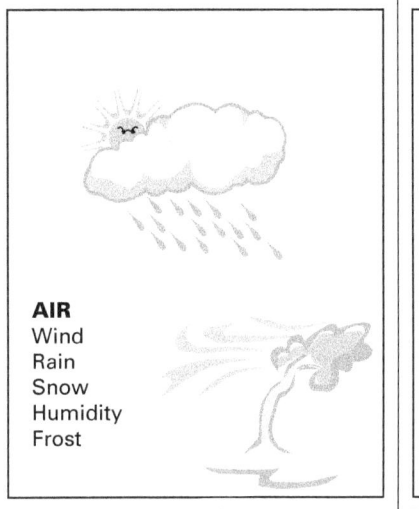

AIR
Wind
Rain
Snow
Humidity
Frost

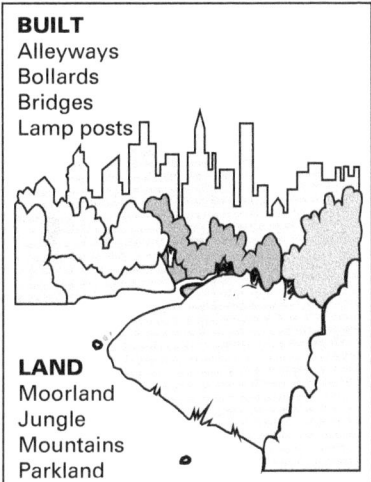

BUILT
Alleyways
Bollards
Bridges
Lamp posts

LAND
Moorland
Jungle
Mountains
Parkland

WATER
Lakes
Streams
Canals
Rivers
Ice
Puddles
Sea
Tides

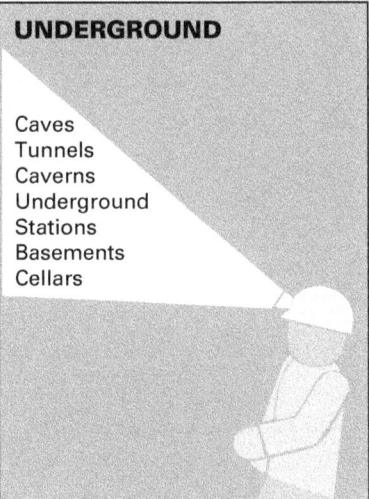

UNDERGROUND
Caves
Tunnels
Caverns
Underground
Stations
Basements
Cellars

Reaching out: learning in city space

The urban environment is attracting more interest from experiential providers for a number of reasons. The city environment can be closer to home for many people, and it is rich in social and cultural learning opportunities. Sometimes referred to as the 'concrete jungle', it can be exhilarating and exciting. Proudman (1999) suggests that there is a need to 're-mystify' the urban environment. The traditional powerful wilderness 'solo' as a meditative experience might also take place in an urban cathedral. It can also be frightening and intimidating, and can be seen in a negative light. Our own international outdoor management development work in places such as Kenya and Beirut has highlighted to us the real and very different risks associated with venturing outdoors to work in a city environment, as opposed to the comfort of the hotel or National Park. High levels of anxiety about venturing out into the city were expressed by many African and Arab participants on one development programme. That urban safety management should be taken seriously and offered as 'challenge by choice', addressed in Chapter 3, is an important rule.

Urban outdoor programmes can provide development opportunities that are similar to wilderness programmes. The recognition of the value of urban socio-ecology underpinned the development of the 'urban wildlife movement', emerging originally in the UK from the heart of Birmingham in 1979. There is a fantasy connection here too, as J R R Tolkien's *The Lord of the Rings* was based on wet woodland, known locally as Moseley Bog, and it was the protection of this site that became the inspirational force that mobilized the early pioneers of the urban wildlife movement. Urban wildlife projects can make ideal activities for people to undertake as the activities for experiential learning, a subject that we explore later in this chapter. Urban parks, woodlands and waterways can serve as places for adventure experiences. The urban canal system offers opportunities to journey on land and water, and the physical environment of buildings and walls provides ideal abseiling and climbing opportunities. In the United States, the term 'buildering' has been coined to describe this activity (Proudman, 1999: 331). The urban environment includes bollards, kerbs, lamp posts, pavements, trees, gutters and benches for innovative use in experiential programmes. Urban spoil heaps can provide for scrambling and biking. In the UK, one outdoor activity centre has benefited from funding from the Lottery and built a 'rock park'. The first of its kind in the UK, it consists of huge boulders lined by bridges, allowing climbers to cross from one to the next in continuous sequences. This leads us to consider the nature of artificially constructed learning environments, and where the boundaries of 'real' environments and 'artificial' environments interface, a subject of much debate. Many so-called natural landscapes are indeed created by human activity.

Experiential learning through the tall ship experience

Shabab Oman is the Tall Ship of Oman, which is the only Arab country to use sail training as an experiential learning platform. The ship, a 52-metre barquentine, was purchased secondhand in 1977 and had previously been the *Captain Scott*. It was built in Buckie, Scotland, by Herd and MacKenzie and commanded by Victor Clarke, who also skippered the Gordonstoun School vessel the *Prince Louis* and therefore has a lineage with the principles of Outward Bound and Kurt Hahn.

Shabab Oman commenced sail training in Oman in 1978, providing adventure training in groups of 24 from the armed forces of Oman. The ship has continued, steadfast in this role, for 27 years and to date some 600 trainees have passed through it. The basic concept is to provide sail and adventurous training, using the medium of the sea to develop personal skills, leadership potential and to foster teamwork. This in turn recalls Oman's long seafaring traditions and instils a link with history while pitting participants against the present-day challenges of the sea to deliver a powerful learning experience.

The Experiential Training Concept: trainees embark for a period of three weeks when the ship is operating on the coast of Oman and for up to four months when the ship deploys abroad. The trainee group consists of a mix of all branches of the armed forces, the police and occasionally civilians. The group work and live together within the confines of a sailing ship and they learn basic elements of seamanship and navigation while developing life skills of teamworking, problem solving and leadership. The idea of using the sea as a levelling medium from which to launch an experiential learning programme is not new and yet it possesses the potential to reveal quickly a person's inner strengths and weaknesses. The sea provides an ever-changing and challenging environment, which pits a person against an unrelenting, unforgiving and formidable opponent. Trainees develop self-confidence through the successful completion of previously inconceivable tasks, working at height and in atrocious weather conditions, which infuse an enduring sense of achievement and often greatly enhanced self-esteem.

The sea can provide some of the most difficult environmental living and working conditions known, and facing these challenges can result in a powerful emotional and spiritual experience: from a towering sensation of euphoria to possible moments of despair. Although these actual sensations may be short-lived, they carry a powerful memory capacity and one that is likely to remain for a lifetime. The resultant experience can be a personal watershed and deliver life-changing properties. Sail training in the Middle East with young members of Oman's armed forces has proved to be a highly successful enterprise and one that continues to provide a valuable Outward Bound learning experience, in the mould of Kurt Hahn's principles.

Chris Biggins, Commander, *Shabab Oman*

Artificially created learning spaces

An exceptional creation – a corner of the world that is immensely old, full of surprises, lovingly and sometimes miraculously well maintained, and nearly always pleasing to look at. It is one of the busiest, most picked over, most meticulously groomed, most conspicuously used, most sumptuously and relentlessly improved landscapes on the planet. (Bryson, 2000: 1–2)

The landscape in most countries is not particularly 'natural'; indeed 'naturalness' is very much a contentious term (Beard, 2003). While most landscapes are artificially created by human intervention, we are now witnessing new forms of artificial environments being created in cities for the purposes of adventure learning and play, and they often emerge in areas of industrial dereliction. In the UK, in Sheffield, many artificial recreational sites have developed in an ad hoc cluster, and have transformed urban decay and dereliction. It is here that Europe's largest dry-ski resort was located for many years, with ski slopes, snowboarding facilities, toboggan rides and ski waterjumps, and they have all been built on old spoil heaps. Nearby, converted out of semi-derelict buildings, 'The Foundry' was a first for Britain in that it was the start of a new breed of fully commercial indoor climbing walls, attracting 60,000 people at its peak in 1996. These artificial 'mountain-like' venues are prevalent now, and ropes courses remain popular throughout the globe. The Foundry was host to the first European indoor climbing championships. Interestingly however, it was young students who turned their undergraduate dissertation ideas into a reality, when 'The Foundry' climbing centre was created from their initial ideas.

Located nearby, a skateboarding and rollerblading building called 'The House' was created by unemployed young teenagers by transforming an old abandoned warehouse. They were initially just enthusiasts, wanting somewhere to stunt-play and have fun, and they seized upon an opportunity to rent a derelict warehouse. These young people now operate a successful business, providing skateboarding and rollerblading for many other young people. Their experience of 'business' is exciting and natural for them, and it has grown from their own indigenous experience and sense of adventure. They simply shifted from play to entrepreneurial activity, following their instincts. This illustrates experiential learning at its best. Their business brings with it a whole subculture of clothing, music and language, and 'The House' appears to be a replacement of the 'youth club' for some of their customers.

Attarian (1999: 345) defines an artificial environment as a 'man-made structure, device or environment that simulates a natural setting, which can be used specifically for teaching or participating in outdoor activities'. Such structures can take many forms. A climbing 'wall' can be located on the outside or inside of a building, or in an alleyway at home within an urban or in a rural environment. Artificial white-water rafting courses are now being used for firefighter rescue training of crash victims located in rivers, and complex aircraft flight simulators have long been used for pilot training. In the United States in Arizona in 1970, the first major artificial surfing environment called the 'Big Surf' was created on an island lagoon.

The use of artificial spaces for experiential learning is of greater significance than has hitherto been realized. The urban environment lends itself to urban community initiatives, with inner-city schools and other urban groups, and it is the environment where many of the 'at-risk' youth are growing up. Working with urban projects can provide opportunities for youth development and management development alike. It is also in the urban environment that many young people are using initiative, in a very entrepreneurial way, turning their experience of urban play into business ventures: experiential learning at its best?

In 1994 a company called Rockface in Birmingham in the UK created a much broader leisure experiential environment, again from a derelict warehouse in the city. While the climbing walls form the foundation of the centre experience, there are also bars and restaurants. The centre offers a range of experiences for different visitor groups, including programmes for people with disabilities, training for executives, children's activities, and family fun and adventure. The climbing walls are adorned with a range of artefacts, such as artificial drainpipes and toilets, which amuses many of the teenagers. The walls and ceilings house abseiling platforms, rope bridges, a Jacob's ladder, a tower game and an artificial cave. The cave has been created using wooden panels to form a box structure around the rear of the climbing walls. Painted black to create almost total darkness, the caves also house climbing holds, chimney breasts, ramps and circular tunnels of various dimensions, and the routes change levels using trapdoors in the floors or ceiling. In darkness, people experience many sensations, some 'natural' and some artificially stimulated. Masses of thin ropes dangle down from the ceiling in places on to people's backs, and some floor areas are crunchy natural gravel. Small bells tinkle to give delicate sounds, which the designers have built in especially for people with various levels of sensory disability. The site is continually evolving and it is difficult to classify it as a teaching classroom, a recreational site, a fun-fair or a leisure centre. It is this multiple perception that underlies its unique success as a place to experience.

Quite by chance, some cities are developing their 'adventure zones', replacing old industries and the world of production and traditional 'work' with rejuvenating businesses involved in the world of leisure, tourism, training, coaching, play, learning and adventure:

places of work	to	places of adventure, coaching, leisure and learning;
workers	to	business owners and managers;
mines/mechanical production	to	places for recreation and play;
derelict	to	regenerative in nature;
environmentally damaging	to	reducing recreational pressure on the natural;
old industries	to	new ones.

In time some will become institutionalized, moving from:

inventive fun	to	recreation;
recognized recreation	to	competitive sports;
sports	to	Olympic sports.

Pedagogy and personal development

Amid the urban factories and surrounding streets young people create their own challenges and rewrite the rules of education. They learn through play, fun and recreation. Although the overt goal might be the challenge of new stunts, pedagogy and personal development clearly underpin such experiences. Ironically, these skills often become institutionalized as 'qualifications' as governing bodies embrace the skill repertoire. Qualifications exist for sailing, swimming and gymnastics and are already well established, but new skills are emerging for skateboarding, stunt-biking and indoor climbing. The young climbers' Spider Club in the UK developed its own star ratings for young climbers, enabling them to progress systematically through stages of learning. This development grading was partly in recognition of the unsuitability of the adult international route classification system based on the 'degree of difficulty' (Arran, 1998). The young climbers start at a grade associated with recreational fun climbing, but opportunities are provided for the development of more serious competitive climbing if children want to.

> **Experiential learning: urban climbing and young people**
>
> The initial development of Levels of Climbing for young people: Spider Club awards – The Foundry, Sheffield, UK.
>
> There are five indoor levels of competence – leading to two outdoor levels:
>
> - **White Spider.** I can climb to the top of the basic vertical wall; I can belay using a stitch plate under close supervision; I can tie a figure-of-eight knot with help; etc.
> - **Yellow.** I can safely put on a safety harness; I can describe the differences between top roping, leading, bouldering, traversing and soloing; etc.
> - **Orange.** I can tie a bowline knot with a fisherman's knot as a stopper; I can belay a lead climber with close supervision; etc.
> - **Green.** I know how to tie off a stitch plate; I can tie a clove hitch knot; etc.
> - **Blue.** I can 'down-climb' a route of grade 15 on any Foundry walls; I can traverse both sides of the corridor using only features for feet, and red/blue handholds; etc.
> - **Purple Outdoor Spider.** I can climb a top-roped grade severe on limestone; I can climb a top-roped grade severe on gritstone; etc.
> - **Gold Outdoor Spider.** I can demonstrate how to protect a climb by placing cramming devices, wires and hexes as running belays; I can name and describe the characteristics of three types of rock; etc.
>
> **SOURCE** Arran (1998)

These urban adventure sites allow for competitions with carefully simulated routes being designed for coaching, training and development programmes. But the young climbers are also forming a new breed; some have not tasted so-called 'real' natural outdoor climbing at all. Artificial climbing walls are now used by 82 per cent of UK climbers, 42 per cent of them on a weekly basis.

Technological advancements have given rise to artificial ice walls that have the consistency of toffee and so return to their original shape ready for the next climber. All these artificial environments offer the advantage that they can easily be manipulated or altered.

Reconfiguration of the learning environment creates a new set of challenges, and new climbs or skate stunts are being sought by many young people as they search for their own adventure learning on the doorstep, after school and particularly in the winter months. Surface technology and route design are key to this thriving new business area of simulated indoor activity-based learning and play, and there are clear technical, social, environmental and commercial advantages. These sites also create new opportunities for providers of experiential learning, for corporate training or youth development programmes.

If nature is experienced as uncontrollable or inaccessible then the natural environment is likely to be increasingly copied, manipulated, simulated, altered, merged or upgraded with human-made components. Such manufactured environments suit many commercial outdoor ventures and such developments might provide opportunities for the design of new learning environments. The simple list below of outdoor activities illustrates the diversity and complexity of the term '*artificial*'. The term artificial can refer to:

- *a device* (such as a bolt, gadget, or equipment);
- *an activity* (canyoning, coasteering, rollerblading, indoor climbing);
- *the elements* (artificial snow, artificial lights, simulated wind, simulated waterfalls);
- *structure/location* (a climbing 'wall', rollerblade, rafting or slalom 'courses');
- *whole environments* ('resorts', adventure 'zones', adventure 'islands').

CASE STUDY *A consultation process involving: a) the six-dimensional modelling and b) human experience mapping, then c) the residential experience*

Sparks Consulting is located in the United States and it was founded to help secondary-school rowing athletes find the right university for them in relation to their academic, athletic and social goals. As our company grew we expanded into rowing 'camps' because we saw a need for camps to give athletes more substantive individual attention, and to challenge them to strive for more within their sport. After eight years our camps not only span the United States, they now include international camps in New Zealand and Holland. As we expand our offerings, we keep searching for new ways to enhance the *'camp experience'* so as to help our athletes get the most out of their time with us.

Our goal is to build greater self-awareness through sport on our camps: we want the young athletes to leave not only knowing more about rowing, but to be more aware of who they are, what they want, and how the sport can help them achieve their goals in school and beyond. We want our camps to be more than simple rowing camps. However, we sought advice after we hit a wall in the development of our camps. We got the rowing elements right but we needed fresh insight from an expert in experiential learning and design and so we approached Colin Beard for help. The first help he provided was to get us to understand the basic needs of our clients. Using a rope and six plastic lids, Colin gave us a visualization of the Learning Combination Lock model to help us to see and appreciate the connection between doing things, knowing things, sensing things and feelings. He then explored the more complex ideas about *belonging* and *being*. As we talked and worked our way around this visual and physical model, we considered numerous ways to help camp attendees develop their own sense of belonging and ways of being in our camps.

After this first phase we applied this model by exploring real data collected from six women who experienced sleeping on the streets of Sheffield for just one night in order to *experience* what it might be like to be homeless. We were given two sets of the same data, but each set was organized differently. We were asked to scribble out bits of data that we found interesting on a long, wide sheet of paper. There were three zones: what the people were experiencing before, during and after the awareness-raising, experiential charity sleepout event. Once we had mapped out as much as we had time for, we were asked to talk and walk Colin though the event as experienced by these six participants (spatially – before, during and after). We found it particularly useful to map out our understanding of what had happened, specifically when the data was organized based on experience, not by person.

The final task was to map out one of our domestic camps. We wrote down everything we thought the campers experienced before, during and after camp so we could have a visual of what was happening, or rather what we thought might be happening. We discussed and mapped out what the camp participants were experiencing on different levels (anxiety, the environment, the emotional roller-coasters, the role of technical knowledge, the sense of belonging, their identity and sense of self) and began generating a plan for how to enhance or minimize these to create a better overall experience for participants and staff. While we did not have enough time to completely map out a potential camp experience, we learnt what we needed to do and shortly thereafter began mapping out and altering our camp activities. One example is that we will ask all campers to use string and Post-it notes to outline their individual. We will then use a large rope to explore the collective experience. They will use the string and then rope to indicate their highs and lows, and with the Post-it labels they can add more detail to these major highs and lows. This will not only help the campers to understand better and reflect on what they did at camp and how they can use this information going forward, it will aid us in collecting more valuable data to map out their experiences and to explore the extent to which we are successful in achieving our goal of improving their awareness.

Sparks Consulting (www.sparksconsult.com)

The advantages of simulated recreation environments

- Social:
  - can take part regularly; high levels of accessibility, by walking or public transport; for the urban and rural population;
  - potential for greater social interaction: crowds, spectators, cafes, clothing, music, youth culture, etc;
  - reduced trespass, eg mountain bikes on footpaths;
  - reduced conflict with other users: public on streets, as in skateboarding, and in National Parks, as in mountain biking;
  - located off the streets.

- Commercial:
  - potential to increase the number of participants and beginners;
  - all-season participation possible;
  - suitability for experienced and beginners;
  - creates a new market of participants;
  - suited to experiential development programmes for managers, youth, children, etc;
  - equipment and clothing sale/provision at location;
  - cafe/bar and tourism functions;
  - time and space zoning.

- Environmental:
  - controlled environment: 'conditions';
  - less susceptibility to the unpredictable elements of the natural environment;
  - less travel: people and equipment;
  - potentially less environmental impact;
  - less direct physical environmental damage;
  - less pollution;
  - less ecological damage;
  - less environmental unpredictability;
  - less risk.

- Technical:
  - mimic the 'best bits': features and obstacles;
  - local natural environment may not contain the necessary features in one place;
  - a valuable training resource;
  - creating new champions, in sport and recreation;
  - added safety for training of pilots, schoolchildren/youth, managers, firefighters, etc;
  - artificial lighting provides winter opportunities in the UK: floodlit;
  - controllable conditions;
  - can create unique/unnatural challenges: totally new and not found in natural conditions – beyond the natural.

Figure 4.2 The four-stage support wave

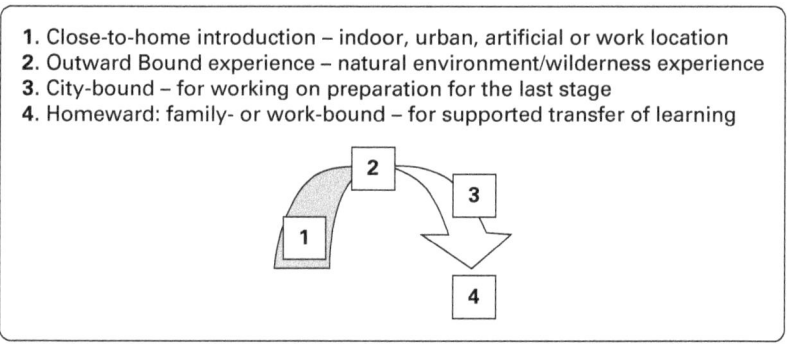

1. Close-to-home introduction – indoor, urban, artificial or work location
2. Outward Bound experience – natural environment/wilderness experience
3. City-bound – for working on preparation for the last stage
4. Homeward: family- or work-bound – for supported transfer of learning

Significantly, these artificial environments also offer locations for the four-step approach that is discussed in Chapter 3. Barrett and Greenaway (1995) offer ways to overcome the negative effects of youth returning from significant wilderness experiences. Urban locations can offer entry and exit stages for residential wilderness programmes, as shown in Figure 4.2. The urban location provides a step in the process for people to realign themselves, and so avoid the negative shock and consequence of a sudden dramatic return to start-point environments.

Empathetic strategies and the outdoor therapeutic 'effect'

Concern about the overusage of the wilderness by an ever-growing population escaping to the outdoors seeking a 'fresh air fix' has been expressed by Ogilvie (1993) and Cooper (1998). Ogilvie suggests that this degradation is now on a scale such that lip service to environmental issues is no longer enough, and that the traditional attitude of outdoor users to use the environment as a playground or testing place for the self can place them in the uncaring category. Ogilvie embraces this notion in his adapted version of John Adair's action-centred leadership model involving the *team*, the *individual* and the *task*. Ogilvie adds a fourth dimension, the *earth*, arguing that now it would make sense to construct this model with a fourth circle (see Figure 4.3). Likewise Mortlock (1984) warns against professional insensitivity towards the environment and suggests that there should be an awareness of, respect for and love of *self*, balanced against an awareness of, respect for and love of others, balanced against an awareness of, respect for and love of the *environment*.

Figure 4.3 The team, the task, the individual and the environment

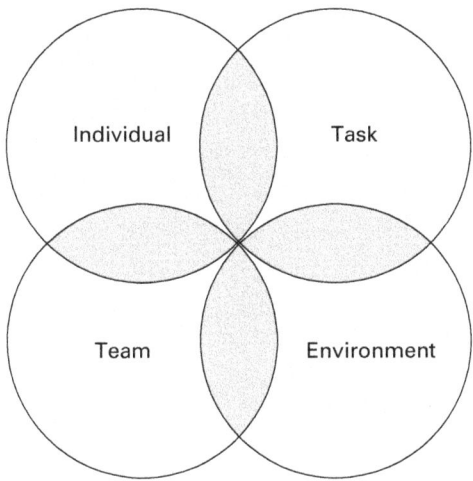

With the pressure to provide learners with novelty (Irvine and Wilson, 1994), some providers feel that adrenalin-raising activities or confrontational-type experiences will excite and motivate people (see, for example, Vanreusel, 1995). The requirement of challenge and risk can also create adversarial, aggressive approaches to the natural world, where some elements of nature are seen as providing a powerful negative force to be overcome.

The use of the outdoors as an educational 'resource' has a long history in Western culture. Charlton (1992) notes that there have been many protagonists of the view that there is not a single social ill or physical problem that would not respond to a course of treatment in the outdoors. Charlton also notes a prevalent dichotomy of approaches towards the outdoors, using terms such as 'combative' (conquering) towards the natural elements, or 'empathetic' (affinity). The historical perspective of the outdoors as a therapeutic environment is reflected upon by Charlton, who comments that in the scouting movement, it was long ago regarded that exposure to wilderness was a suggested cure for everything from flat-footedness to 'bad citizenship'!

The environment has long been regarded as an important place for healing, repair and personal development. Miles (1995) offers a US view on wilderness as a healing place, a place for programmes helping people 'at risk', renowned for its rehabilitating power, for recuperation, for developing management skills, for personal spiritual well-being and for youth work. Significant epistemological and ontological challenges face such research. 'Biophilia', for example, concerns the environmental effects on people such as the post-operative patient recovery rates when subjected to stimulation in the natural environment; the results are promising. The person–environment relationship is of course a two-way process, and the subtle impact of the natural environment on our health is now receiving more attention. Research that was carried out long ago by Ulrich (1974) set out to measure the attractive and aversive human physiological responses to natural phenomena. It suggests that combative strategies may operate against natural stimuli that are produced when we are in natural outdoor environments. Some early research was carried out on post-operative patients in hospital and early indications were that patients who overlooked natural green space had shorter post-operative stays and fewer post-surgery complications, and required less medication and analgesics.

More recently, Kellert (1993) suggests that spending time in green space has many positive physiological responses such as reduced heart rate, reduced blood pressure, and increased cognitive functioning, performance and creativity. These responses are said to come from a number of stimuli such as colours, textures, natural smells, decreased noise pollution or more interesting sounds, such as running water and exposure to the elements (wind, rain, heat, cold, etc). Doctors now advise 'countryside walks' as an alternative option to drug or medicine prescriptions.

The natural environment is a place for learning about self-healing, although many people remain sceptical about the claims made, doubting the power the natural environment has. The sceptics rely on others to prove it to them, yet the overwhelming evidence suggests that it is the very spiritual and emotional nature of the outdoor environment that underpins the reason for its power; perhaps it cannot be measured. This leads us towards a realization that indeed there might be something very, very magical 'out there'. The truth about nature and the nature of truth are elusively intertwined.

Outdoor environments: therapeutic experiential learning

Although healing and nature, and learning and change, are closely related, the role of the outdoors in the healing process is little understood. This is due partly to the dominant old paradigms of psychology and psychotherapy: Freud is said to have actively steered therapy away from the world of nature, thus driving a wedge between psychology and nature (Burns, 1998). However, with the emergence of family therapy there was a move away from the introspective analysis on the couch. Burns describes the early embryonic work of Milton Erickson, who often assigned clients tasks involving interactions with nature, thus replicating traditional healing practices of the past. This use of tasks in nature is of interest in experiential learning.

'*Adventure therapy*' and '*nature therapy*' are emerging outdoor initiatives that warrant closer examination in order to illustrate this point:

> Adventure therapy is said to be an active, experiential approach to group (and family) psychotherapy or counselling:
>
> - Utilizing an activity base (cooperative group games, ropes courses, outdoor pursuits or wilderness expeditions).
> - Employing real and/or perceived (physical or psychological) risk (distress/eustress) as a clinically significant agent to try to bring about desired change.
> - Making meaning(s) (through insights that are expressed verbally, non-verbally, or unconsciously that lead to behavioural change) from both verbal and non-verbal introductions prior to (eg frontloadings) and discussions following (eg debriefings) the activity experience.
> - Punctuating isomorphic connection(s) (how the structure of the activity matches the resolution of the problem) that significantly contribute to the transfer of lessons learnt into change behaviour.
>
> (Gillis and Thomsen, 1996; http://fdsa.gcsu.edu:6060/Igillis/AT/front.htm)

In this definition the healing process of nature is largely unacknowledged: nature is omitted and perceived as utilitarian, as a functional backdrop in adventure therapy. Conversely, *nature therapy* or *ecotherapy* presents a more integrative role for nature in the therapeutic process. *Ecotherapy*, for example, is said to be a healing process that seeks to enlarge and enhance people's body and mind–spirit perception through a greater connection to the wilderness; it deepens the sense of connectedness with nature, and helps overcome other forms of alienation in people's lives. Nature therapy can embrace a healing role for specific plants and animals: working with injured orphaned birds, for example, can result in a healing effect on young people facing a similar predicament (see www.naturetherapy.com).

Therapeutic applications seek to improve healthy behaviours and reduce unhealthy behaviours, and to develop mental and physical well-being. The plethora of emerging disciplines of nature therapy, ecotherapy, conservation therapy, adventure therapy and horticultural therapy all have much in common in that the environment, to a significant extent, acts as the therapist: professionals involved in such therapeutic work grapple with this and other issues that lie at the boundary of learning and therapy. Gilsdorf's enquiry (2003) into the professional identity of providers of these experience-based therapies notes that the field is relatively young, with more questions than answers. He attempts to shed light on the link between learning and therapy with reference to the work of Bateson (1981, in Gilsdorf, 2003) (see also Chapter 2), who refers to a number of levels of learning. Learning level 1 focuses on content learning, learning level 2 is the learning of strategies, structures of thinking and habits, and is clearly linked with personality traits. Gilsdorf suggests that learning level 3 goes further:

> in that it is basically concerned with the reassessment of established strategies, structures of thinking and habits. In other words learning 3 describes much of the process which, when explicitly put into a certain professional context, is called therapy. Education, at least in its institutional forms, has narrowed the scope of learning almost exclusively to teaching content and is also focusing heavily on cognitive learning, neglecting emotional as well as psychomotor aspects. Experiential and adventure education has mostly countered this tendency. Cultivating and increasing the therapeutic potential within adventure, instead of delegating it to the domain of therapy, could thus be an important step in the process of the establishment of a truly different learning culture. (Gilsdorf, 2003: 59)

One leading UK charity concerned with substance misuse challenges individuals to build self-esteem, self-confidence and motivation through the power of activity in wildlife-rich environments (Hall, 2004). The catalytic triangle used by the programme is that of nature, activity and relationships. One person describes how the programme of dry-stone walling in the National Parks changed his life, and how he went on to become a self-employed landscape designer as a result of the programme. The question of the role of the activity such as dry-stone walling and the healing power of the natural surrounding environment in the therapeutic process becomes interesting. Abbot (1987: 148) suggests that the activity should:

- require a group effort for their success, and therefore encourage interpersonal cooperation and trust among the group;
- consist of adventurous activities that involve some degree of risk;
- be physically demanding and therefore require or induce some physical fitness;
- be conducted in a natural environment;
- generate a sense of achievement, usually as a result of the individual's own efforts.

The role of the environment is explored in detail by Burns (1998), who suggests that there is some consensus among environmental psychologists that we are hardwired with powerful adaptive mechanisms as part of our psychological and biological make-up and that these are triggered by natural stimuli. The environment, particularly the outdoor natural environment, has much more to offer than just a 'location' for the delivery of experiential learning. The environment is an integral and powerful part of experience. This is significant in terms of the design and delivery of experiential programmes. A skill that is increasingly required of learning providers is the ability to provide a range of environmental experiences and, where necessary, to manipulate, in a positive and beneficial way, many of the environmental ingredients that make up a powerful learning experience.

Sustainable learning environments

Some organizations fail to respect the fact that they make direct profit out of the natural environment, regarding nature as a free resource. Encouraging people not to take the environment for granted, to take positive action and give something back to the environment can and should be promoted, in many different ways. Such action can help avoid environmental alienation and exploitation. Despite the fact that the earth is the bank upon which we draw all our cheques, the economic value of the environment remains misunderstood. The environment has an important role in any enterprise. The environment unfortunately provides a place where we deposit our waste, the arena for recreation and adventure, and the places to venture on holidays. If we harvest too many natural resources then the environment becomes degraded, and education, leisure and recreation are all adversely affected. But there are clearly difficulties associated with merely applying monetary values to nature.

Caring for and valuing the natural environment is more than just the design of low-impact activities. For many businesses going 'green', being empathetic towards the environment or being 'environmentally friendly' can unfortunately be perceived as a trade-off between profit and corporate citizenship. As a result, some organizations remain distanced from sustainable development, a process that meets the needs of the present generation without compromising the needs of future generations to meet their own needs (WCED, in Beard, 1997). Some outdoor educational institutions regard themselves as environmentally friendly and divest themselves of responsibility through their teaching of environmental education. Ultimately a preparedness for some form of environmental action is required other than 'education' in order to repair the environment: someone has to plant the trees and repair the erosion caused by footpaths. The four main impacts are:

- **physical impact** – of the structures, buildings, and damage to walls, property; damaging fires;
- **social impact** – on local community such as noise at night, drunkenness, litter;
- **psychological impact** – when one group spoils the experience of another;
- **ecological impacts** – disturbance to wildlife, collecting eggs, trampling on nests, having a picnic on a shingle seashore where terns nest.

We encourage many experiential learning providers to buy environmentally friendly equipment and clothing, and so support market trends in this direction. We also encourage facilitators to increase the levels of environmental awareness in clients by generally acknowledging the beauty of the environment they are working in, and by making their own personal contribution. This can be done in many different ways, for example procurement processes, such as the purchase of recyclable flooring, washable flipchart paper, pens and pencils made from recycled plastic vending-machine cups, or by those using the outdoors for learning by rebuilding dry-stone walls, by planting trees or by funding others to do the practical work. We can also make our activities carbon neutral, reduce energy consumption and resource depletion.

For people working in the outdoors the Learning Combination Lock model (see Figure 4.4) offers the potential to give attention to the design of experiences that embrace and respect the more-than-human world. This inclusion is rarely found in other experiential learning models, which focus on the social interactions of humans. In this way the model is balanced, consisting of three inner-world and three outer-world dimensions important for learning. Thus if we include the senses there are seven dimensions of learning in total, and in this model we deliberately separate the social (human) world experience from the more-than-human world (MTHW) experience and, in doing so, we emphasize the neglected complexity of the more-than-human world, including the 'natural' world, the spiritual world, and the 'artificial' and material world. Both the human and more-than-human world experiences are of course part of the human dimension of belonging in the world, so important in the understanding of human learning.

Figure 4.4 A seven-dimensional model that embraces the more-than-human world

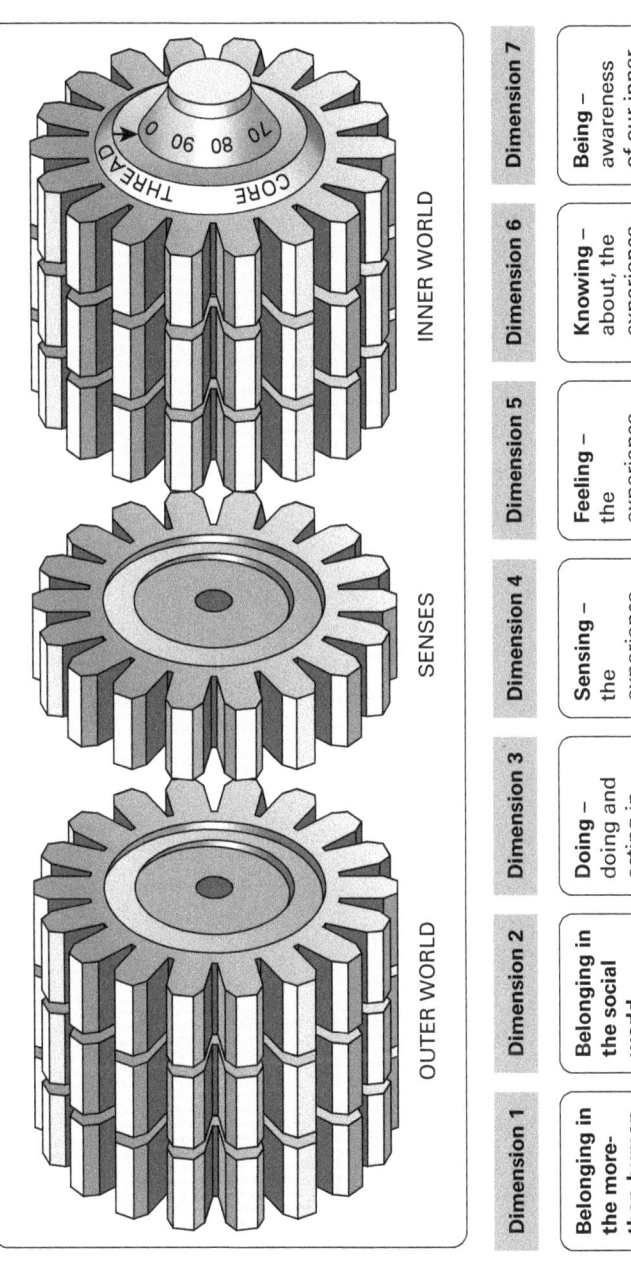

Conclusion

This chapter has highlighted a range of theory and practice relating to our sense of belonging in the world. We have explored how we interact with humans and the more-than-human world, and in doing so we have indicated the vast range of 'out there' experiences that can help us to learn from our external environment: from tall ships to sheds, caves, climbing walls and urban dereliction. In exploring this diverse range of environments for learning, we have taken a closer look at the emerging pedagogy of space and place. We considered how *signpost terminology* points us to the future, with contemporary defining parameters of 'learning environments' identifying a wave of global transformation. This signifies a break away, metaphorically and physically, from the restricted nature of the traditional classroom.

Multidisciplinary specialists are at last interacting: designers and managers are talking to learning specialists and significantly to the learners themselves. Much has been learnt from the outdoor learning community, and there exists a constant shift and blurring of boundaries of indoor–outdoor and natural–artificial. Artificial nature is growing and moving indoors. We believe that good learning environments will increasingly provide areas that maximize the flexibility and mobility of people, the mobility of information and the mobile nature of the very spaces and places we inhabit in order to learn and work.

Learning environments continue their journey of transformation. The 'classroom' boundaries are blurring, reaching out into communities. Technology is taking indoor learning out into the streets and beyond. The future is exciting but the global campus of experiential learning must be environmentally sustainable.

Experiential learning activities, behaviours and actions

05

(the doing dimension)

Many people mistake activity – the doing of things – with experiential education. Maxine Greene reminds us that experiential education is really an internal process by which people can 'wake up' and construct a coherent world for one's quest for freedom and transformation by integrating a variety of perspectives and vantage points. FRANK (2011: 64)

Introduction

As we outlined at the start of this book, experiential learning has a long history. The ancient but well-known Chinese Confucian philosophy '*I hear I forget, I see I remember, I do I understand*' laid the early foundations, the lineage, for subsequent Western interpretations concerning experiential learning. This Chinese aphorism gave rise to the 'Tell–Show–Do' cone of instructional techniques model by Edgar Dale (1969). But what do we mean by 'do', and what is meant by the 'real' thing? Dale's Cone of Experience (1969), shown in Figure 5.1, argues that learners retain more information when 'doing' purposeful experiences, as opposed to 'hearing' or just 'reading' about the experience. But what if a reading experience in a special location, with special circumstances, proves to be quite profound? Is this experiential learning? We believe it is.

Figure 5.1 An interpretation of Edgar Dale's Cone of Experience

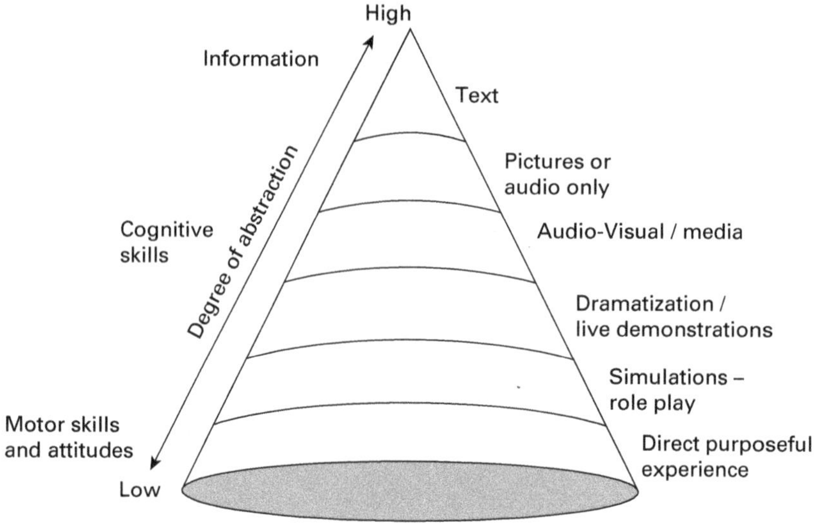

- High
- Information
- Text
- Cognitive skills
- Degree of abstraction
- Pictures or audio only
- Audio-Visual / media
- Dramatization / live demonstrations
- Simulations – role play
- Motor skills and attitudes
- Direct purposeful experience
- Low

'Doing' involves more than physical activity. Doing something involves the whole person, as a sensing, thinking, feeling human within an environment. To *do something* is to try it out, perhaps to practise it. In this way we *experience* it, for ourselves: we get to feel it, to sense it, to understand it and to *immerse* ourselves in 'doing'. This presents 'doing' as a richer conception, not the limited notion of doing as merely an 'activity', which has been criticized by Roberts (2012) in his book *Beyond Learning by Doing*. We not only learn by actively doing things, we also learn by interacting with others and so learn the art of interacting, we think to learn, and so learn to think, we learn with our feelings, and so learn to feel, we use our senses and our body to learn and so learn to observe and sense. Doing is also about our actions, our behaviours and our sense of agency: we can change and transform our selves and the world that we inhabit. The experiential learner is always part of this rich milieu of shifting experiences, both social and more-than-human; he or she also enriches it with his or her personal contribution (Boud and Walker, 1990). This reciprocity, this continuing complex and meaningful interaction with the world, both human and more than human, is of central concern to our understanding of the term *experience*. 'Doing', as merely 'physical activity', is fundamentally an erroneous interpretation of a central principle for experiential learning.

Some people say they are practically minded and they don't like theory. They say they like to be doing things and be active, and get hands-on experience. Yet Kurt Lewin (1951) suggests there is nothing so practical as a good theory! Too much activity-based 'doing' leads us into an activity trap, often involving uncritical doing, without thinking, and this can be risky. At the European Experiential Educators (EEE) conference in Greece in 2012 many delegates informally discussed the idea that less or not 'doing' might indeed result in more learning. There was a consensus that too much 'doing' can limit learning.

Experiential thinkers such as the Norwegian Fridtjof Nansen suggest that if we take to, or do, adventure, it should be in order to see the 'land beyond', explore what is hidden, and to respond to the call of the unknown including the *nature life* or the *friluftsliv*. Others like Maxine Greene take a similar view about what we purposefully do in life, but from a slightly different perspective. She suggests we learn to *wake up*, and in the act of doing things consider what might be and what is not yet. Her ideas are rooted in the concept of *freedom* and perspective change, a theme that is found in other great thinkers such as Mezirow. Similar views are adopted by Friere in his exploration of oppression, and Rogers in his exploration of freedom from a therapeutic perspective (see Smith and Knapp, 2011). 'Doing' in experiential learning terms is much more than just a physical activity: action linked to *purpose* and *will* present wider life options.

Many educators, therapists, adventure programmers and corporate learning and development specialists have developed specific types of experiential learning within their practice. Issues such as how we plan for experiences and choreograph them where required, how we discover opportunities for learning experiences, the sequencing and timing of learning experiences, the way any experience is discovered or introduced, its degree of perceived relevance and reality, and the combination of people, places, materials, rules and restrictions all present a potentiality infinite and rich experiential milieu. In this chapter we introduce these important fundamentals, and in doing so create a typology of activities along with the rationale or theory in use. This chapter will offer some innovative and pragmatic examples found within current experiential practice in order to demonstrate the application of the typology. The subject of the experiential of 'doing' things is the subject of the second cog of the Learning Combination Lock.

Planned or unplanned experiences?

The extent to which both experiential providers and learners plan to learn from experience, or whether it just happens, is an important consideration.

For many people life's journey, and the learning from it, is not at all planned. Life simply emerges and unfolds. Others are more proactive and plan many of their more meaningful life journeys. Significantly, the extent to which people learn from any journey or experience depends on many factors.

Educational psychologists define learning as a change in the individual caused by 'experience'. However, 20 years of experience in a job, for example, does not directly equate to 20 years of learning. How people create and manage their 'experience' is crucial to the process of learning. In order to help people to get the most from experience it is necessary to unleash curiosity so that people actively seek learning, so that they can plan to unveil something that was previously hidden. It is equally important that learners can respond to unanticipated and unplanned experiences as they occur. Megginson (1994) examines why people take different approaches to self-directed learning. He refers to these two basic approaches as planned and emergent learning, and created a grid, reproduced in Figure 5.2, to represent four types of learner. He researched these four different learner types, and classified people as those who have high or low pre-planning for experience, and those who are high or low in emergent, responsive learning strategies. Megginson noted that there are two fundamental challenges that face those who help others to learn. Some people, he suggests, do not take responsibility for the direction of their own learning and some people do not learn from the experiences they have. Planned learners take this responsibility for the direction of their learning, whilst emergent learners respond to and

Figure 5.2 Planned and emergent learning

PLANNED SCORE		
High		
	WARRIOR	**SAGE**
	Plans experiences but tends not to focus on the learning from them	Plans, responds to and learns from experience
	SLEEPER	**ADVENTURER**
	Shows little initiative to plan or respond to and learn from new experiences	Responds to and learns from opportunities that arise but tends not to plan new learning experiences
Low	EMERGENT SCORE	High

learn from experience. Adventurers are thus high on emergent learning and low on pre-planned learning strategies, whereas the sage is high on both. Warriors are low on emergent strategies, and so Megginson recommends activities to hold them in awareness of immediate experience. For adventurers he offers a set of goal-setting activities. The sages, he suggests, can find their own development directions. Sleepers can find any planned or emergent changes daunting and so techniques such as the use of written reflective logbooks can enhance emergent learning. The use of learning plans for the coming year or month or from a future project can develop proactive learning strategies. Gestalt verbal awareness sensitizing can help, such as the use of stream-of-conscious-thought talking. Here each statement is preceded with 'I am aware of...', eg 'I am aware of my feelings of anxiety at the moment.' This can be used during an experiential event when people can express the experience they are having in their terms, and thus first acknowledge and then develop their learning from their experience. This can help access the rich reservoir of thoughts, feelings and impulses about an experience that might otherwise lie dormant. Facilitation strategies require an understanding of sleepers, warriors, adventurers and sages; then different training methods can be applied so as to maximize their emergent and planned learning.

The evolving milieu

> Experience is created in the transaction between the learner and the milieu in which he or she operates – it is relational. An event can influence the learner, but only if the learner is predisposed to being influenced. Similarly, the learner can create a fruitful experience from a limited event, but only if there is something with which they can work. (Boud, Cohen and Walker, 1993: 11)

Fundamental to experiential learning is the establishment of experience/s for learning, and there are many approaches that facilitators can use in order to help people to learn from experience. A wide range of practical ideas are offered below.

The Great Escape

Many relatively new companies around the globe are now offering team-building indoor activities based on escaping from simulated situations. One commercial company located in northern England is called the Great Escape Game (https://thegreatescapegame.co.uk/our-escape-rooms/submerged/). The product range includes: *Abducted*, *Alcatraz*, *Submerged* and *Underworld Conspiracy*. The website entices clients, saying that the surroundings are eerily calm, and you cannot find a single member of your team, not a person, not even a body. You begin to ask yourself, what happened here? Where is the team? Suddenly, the doors air-lock behind you, trapping you in deep water with only 50 minutes left in the oxygen reserve tank. As lights flash and sirens soar, the intensity of your new surroundings become clear. You must work quickly to power up and communicate your emergency to the surface before your time runs out. This type of team-building activity is becoming increasingly popular with a wide range of clients. Some of the core ingredients to these escape-based scenarios are to be found in other outdoor adventure-based as well as online gaming activities, and so we will explore a range of other experiential programmes so as to build a picture of some of the more common ingredients used in choreographic approaches to experience design.

Outdoor adventure learning

In outdoor and adventure learning, outdoor pursuits such as canoeing, climbing, camping and raft building have traditionally been the experiential 'activity' for learning. Rodwell (1994: 133) describes traditional outdoor approaches that use recreational or adventure activities thus: 'Outdoor training usually requires the trainee to perform a series of tasks which incorporate outdoor pursuits such as… climbing, abseiling, caving, orienteering, canoeing, sailing… and they usually involve training for management skills, team-working skills, personal development and physical challenge.' Badger, Sadler-Smith and Michie (1997) confirm this relatively high level of outdoor-pursuit activities in their research into outdoor activities being used in management development programmes and noted that, in their sample of 100 firms, respondents said that they had participated in the following activities:

- Rock climbing – 79
- Orienteering – 47
- Sailing – 16

- Canoeing – 37
- Camping – 31
- Rafting – 16
- Caving – 16
- Others – 74

The last figure is the interesting one and it represents the tip of the iceberg of change in the design of learning activities used in outdoor programmes. The 74 per cent of 'other' forms of activity represents a very diverse array of experiences. One company brochure, Black Mountain (1996), demonstrates this movement away from traditional management development activities:

> This shift towards a wider spectrum of delivery techniques has attracted a dedicated professional team that can design and deliver indoor seminars, outdoor exercises, desktop simulations, experiential games, video projects or motivational events. Over the past five years we have moved away from the use of outdoor pursuits in response to our clients' needs, which have become more focused and sophisticated. As people become more exposed to development techniques, more effective and high-impact solutions are required.

Outdoor learning is moving away from an overemphasis on old paradigms, where the outdoor pursuits of 'canoeing, climbing and caving' are used to teach 'teamwork, communication and leadership'! The level of sophistication of provision parallels the deeper understanding of experiential learning. Provision now gives greater consideration to pre-activity interaction, review and transfer, and follow-up activities, and learners' needs are identified more carefully. Learning can be enhanced through the design of learning activities that embrace the milieu of adventure, fun, leisure and recreation.

Dramaturgy

The concept of planned and unplanned learning can be further explored in dramaturgy, which recognizes that learning design and learning outcomes can be both anticipated and unanticipated. Martin, Franc and Zounkova (2004) offer a holistic and creative approach to programme design and a large section of their book on outdoor experiential learning is devoted to very creative courses and games, game logistics and game descriptions.

CASE STUDY Dramaturgy in outdoor experiential course design

This case study focuses on a unique approach to outdoor experiential course design. It highlights how 'dramaturgy' (Martin, 2001; Martin, Leberman and Neill, 2002) is developed through crafting and recrafting a course programme in terms of how the learning experiences are co-designed. Course instructors place emphasis on dramaturgy, an holistic method of course design, characterized by the intertwining of a wide variety of social, physical, creative and reflective/emotional 'games in nature' using 'the dramaturgy wave' (Figure 5.3) (Martin, Franc and Zounkova, 2004).

The approach draws on pioneering work by the Czechs and Slovaks on experiential dramaturgy:

> Dramaturgy means 'the art of theatrical production', the main task of which is to examine the links between the world and the stage. The 'dramatist' chooses themes from society and a place that reflects these themes. Pieces of work and music are then chosen to reflect these themes. (Martin, Franc and Zounkova, 2004: 15)

There are five stages involved in developing dramaturgy:

1 Development of the main course theme.
2 Development of the scenario (first part).
3 The practical dramaturgy (activity/game creation and selection).
4 The completion of the scenario.
5 The dramaturgy on the course.

As the term dramaturgy originates from the sphere of theatre, film and TV, the drama principles of *script, production, performance, journey* and *stage* are utilized to maximize the impact and outcome of the course. Dramaturgy is a method of selection and time order of the activities with the aim to reach the maximal pedagogical effect. It integrates, within itself, the questions (and also answers) concerning the participants on the course (their age, mental and physical maturity...), time and space. The key thing for all dramaturgy considerations is to determine and realize the pedagogical, educational, recreational and other aims, which the course wants to reach.

In dramaturgy the programme is flexible and very holistic, and there are often continuous, reflective changes to the content as facilitators constantly

Figure 5.3 The dramaturgy wave

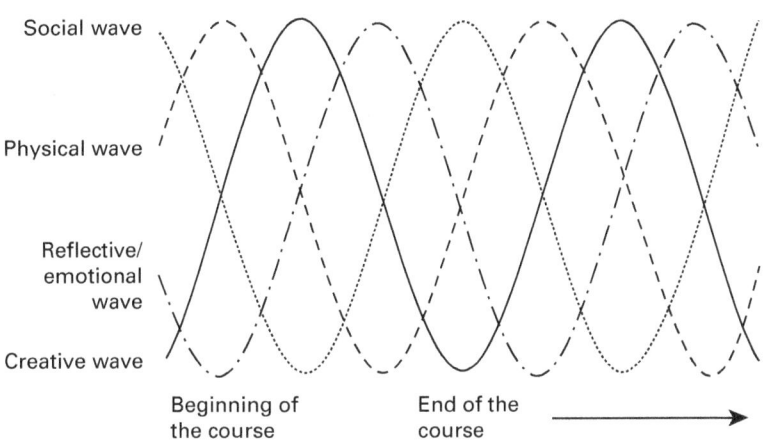

SOURCE Martin, Franc and Zounkova (2004: 25)

re-examine the goals or objectives. The activities are often rewritten and the programme reshaped (sometimes on a regular basis at nightly meetings) to match the learner's needs. Here, unanticipated learning is experienced and is central to the design. At each stage of the course instructors reflect upon the balance of the waves, so that one does not override another. A metaphor for this process comes from waves crashing on a beach, the bigger waves swamping the smaller ones; often, the physical activity 'wave' in traditional outdoor courses tends to dominate.

The holistic balance of the dramaturgy approach involves creating, developing and playing, art, music, drama, and adventure games and activities, which are mixed in order to challenge different dimensions of a person – physical, social, mental, creative, spiritual, and so on. The course design is monitored by instructors to provide both pace and rhythm and is further adapted according to the group needs arising during the course. This experiential approach has enriched programmes internationally, reflecting different unique cultures and style (Martin, 2011; Leberman and Martin, 2005).

Martin, Franc and Zounkova (2004) describe in detail over 30 games under four sections: creative, social, physical and psychological (reflective/emotional). Such a classification is useful and our own experiential learning masterclasses help facilitators to create a folder of activities under such headings in order to carry out a detailed analysis of the essential ingredients.

Professor Andrew J Martin, Massey University, New Zealand

Designing experiences: a simple experiential typology

The purposive nature of learning means that in some programmes it is often necessary to determine the 'wants' of the learner, ie what the learner perceives to be his or her need; and the 'needs' of the learner, ie what the facilitator perceives the learner needs. The combination of the determined needs and wants can then be expressed in terms of learning outcomes. This requires in addition an understanding of the culture of the people and the organization, the resources available and practical considerations, such as whether the programme can be residential. In each experience the choice of combination of these variables is the underpinning precept of the educative process that is experiential learning.

Restaurants offer a diverse menu for takeaway meals, offering a great deal of choice. Up to 150 options adorn such menus; this is only possible because common to many options are a few central ingredients. Likewise in experiential development programmes there are often common activities, but the outward manifestation of the experience is different. Determining, for example, issues of theme, place, objects, activities and rules is a function of the milieu necessary to create the learning outcomes. For example, an organization whose internal culture is competitive may require competition to be reflected in the learning experience. In contrast, an organization that operates by consensus may find a competitive milieu a counter-productive experience. However, exposure to experiences outside the cultural norm of the organization may be a catalyst to stimulate creativity and innovation. It is a question of effectively determining what outcomes are required for the individuals, groups or organization, while recognizing that the learning is a continuous, long journey.

The need for learning often reflects a gap, or imbalance, in skills, knowledge or attitudes, and the learner is helped, to varying degrees, to move from his or her current way of operating to a preferred way of operating through the learning experience, as shown in Figure 5.4. The journey away from the norm of 'sameness' often helps people to see this gap more clearly. Sometimes, however, there is also a need for 'metaphorical space' to escape, to 'sense' release and feel free.

Journeying over periods of time and through physical and metaphorical space is an important component of any learning. The journey from where the learner is to where the learner needs to be is fundamental to the experiential process. Knowing the needs can determine the focus and end point.

Experiential Learning Activities, Behaviours and Actions (The Doing Dimension)

Figure 5.4 The learning gaps: altering time and place to increase learning

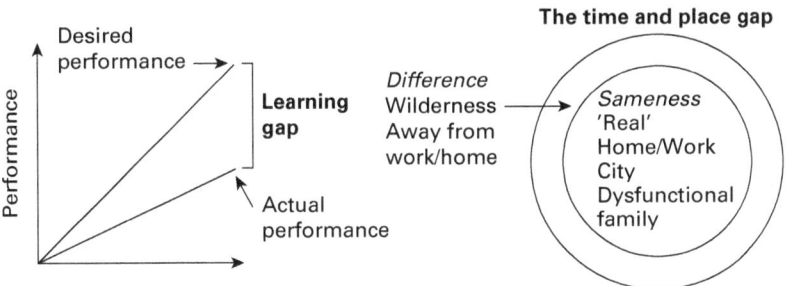

Knowing the participants can determine the start point, distance to be travelled, and the number of steps necessary to achieve the destination. Lifelong learning means that the end point of the learning journey is, however, little more than a staging post that, once achieved, enables learners to embrace a new set of challenges. A journey might venture into another place, away from the everyday environment, so as to gain a different view or perspective. Creating the right medium or milieu for a learning journey is thus a function of a number of considerations. To assist the planning of creative experiential learning programmes we offer a typology, shown below.

A basic experiential learning programme typology:

- Set a **target,** goal or objective, where goals create an underlying 'state of mind'.
- Create a sense of a **journey or destination** – physical movement and exercise; people, information and objects are moved from A to B.
- Allow participants to **exercise many forms of intelligence.**
- Create and sequence a **theme** of **social, mental, psychological and physical activities** – mind, feelings, spirit and body.
- Adjust the **elements of reality.**
- Stimulate the **senses.**
- Use **construction or deconstruction in activity design**: a physical object (eg a bike, a wall or a raft) or a non-physical item (eg a clue, a phrase or a poem).
- Design social **collaborative or competitive strategies, possibly with reward mechanisms.**
- Create **combative and/or empathetic** approaches to the environment.
- Create **restrictions:**

- obstacles;
- sensory blocking, eg blindfolds;
- rules;
- procedures.
- Provide elements of real or perceived challenge, problem solving and/or risk.
- Set time constraints.
- Allow people to deal with change, risk, success and failure – and the stretching of personal boundaries.
- Design sorting and/or organization skills – a mass of data, information to sort or activities to do or consider.
- Include functional skills such as surveying, juggling, map reading, knot tying, etc.
- Design quiet time for reflection – physical or mental space.
- Allow the story of the experience to be told.

(adapted from Beard, 1998)

Adventurous journeys

Underpinning all of these ingredients is the learner journey, and a physical journey or activity can be an isomorphic representation of a wider life journey. The physical journey can be orienteering, a short walk in the hotel grounds or distance travelled in kayaks. 'Outward Bound' is a nautical term referring to the outward journey of a ship: Outward Bound schools had a strong focus on sea expeditions. This is partly because Kurt Hahn in his early days collaborated with a businessman in shipping, Lawrence Holt, to develop his ideas and schools.

Many outdoor and indoor experiential programmes design into the experience a journey and movement, often involving the building or construction of things: physical objects, such as canisters or bikes; and non-physical objects, such as theories, poems or art. Physical exercise on such a journey impacts on learners' energy–tension balance, as physical exercise is known to be one of the most powerful positive regulators of mood, a subject we examine in Chapter 7. Rules and restrictions, whether real or perceived, can impede or speed progress. Likewise, problem solving can include collaboration or competition. Many things can influence a learning experience.

Experiential Learning Activities, Behaviours and Actions (The Doing Dimension)

Adventure, whether indoor or outdoor, requires an element of real or perceived risk to which the participant is exposed through their engagement in an activity. This risk can be physical, emotional, intellectual or material. 'Adventure' embraces many facets of people's lives and it forms the basis of the experiential milieu. The dictionary suggests that adventure is a 'remarkable incident', 'an enterprise or commercial speculation', 'an exciting experience' or 'the spirit of enterprise', and an adventurer is 'one who engages in hazardous enterprise'. 'To be an adventure an experience must have an element of uncertainty about it. Either the outcome should be unknown or the setting unfamiliar' (Priest and Ballie, 1995: 307). The 'venture' part of the word adventure implies the element of travel, with or without a purpose. The many dictionary definitions of the term 'expedition' are that of *a journey with a definite purpose*. In expeditions there is also a target or goal, and a time constraint.

A plethora of activities are currently offered in locations around the world offering adventurous travel as experiential learning. Eco-adventure travel is an area that has increased rapidly over the past decade to become one of the leading areas of income for the tourism industry today (Swarbrooke *et al*, 2003). Greenforce, Frontier and Earthwatch are three such organizations that offer an unusual and new combination of learning journeys that I have termed *edventure*. These organizations construct a new form of multilearning experience for young people, containing a subtle mix of educative features for self-development: adventure, travel, environmental or community development work and skills in scientific wildlife monitoring. These organizations are usually charities recruiting paying volunteers to support wildlife projects around the world. Coral Cay is a not-for-profit organization at the cutting edge of eco-tourism that recruits volunteers to gather information about some of the world's most endangered coral reefs and rainforests. Volunteers are trained in a range of skills including scuba diving, coral-fish identification and survey techniques. What is particularly interesting is that research by Nolan (2004) highlights the 'learning' element as a key motivational driver for people joining as volunteers, but some such experiential projects remain almost exclusively for those who have, or are able to raise, the necessary funds.

Greenforce was inspired by the commitments made at the Earth Summit in Rio in 1992 to identify and protect the biodiversity of the planet. One brochure is titled 'Work on the wild side! Conservation expeditions'. Volunteers are offered an 'experience of a lifetime'. These and many other practical environmental organizations grew out of the great demand for an educational 'experience'. Frontier is a non-profit organization promoted by the Society for Environmental Exploration, and has the following in its 2000 brochure:

> Taking part in a *Frontier* expedition is a once-in-a-lifetime experience... Future employers will be impressed with your achievements both in getting there and in succeeding in your project. Many former volunteers have used their expeditions as the basis for project and dissertation work for bachelor's degrees and master's degrees. Frontier is also a 'Sponsoring Establishment' for research degrees through the Open University, the ONLY volunteer conservation organization to have achieved the status of a field university. If you want a career in conservation and overseas development work, *Frontier* is the only option. With all volunteers eligible for a level 3 BTEC qualification in Tropical Habitat Conservation just on the strength of 10 weeks of training and work on a *Frontier* expedition, becoming a volunteer gives you a chance to kick-start a career in this highly competitive field. A recent survey found that 62 per cent of former *Frontier* volunteers have achieved such careers thanks to their experience with *Frontier*.

Operation Raleigh selects young people to take on major expeditions around the world, and they too offer such projects in the international dimension of their development programmes:

> Challenges in the outdoors, and involvement in community or environmental projects, are well established as a successful means of developing staff. Combining these with intensive international work in remote areas, Raleigh creates a framework within which learning can be transferred to the workplace. Working and living with people from different backgrounds for an extended period helps equip employees for today's fast-changing and demanding business environment. Working in real time, generating solutions to real problems, the experience proves sustainable and effective at developing the following qualities: teamworking, leadership, interpersonal skills, confidence, motivation and assertiveness, initiative, flexibility and resilience, adaptability, maturity, awareness of self and others.

Expeditions

Wilderness programmes in the United States and Australia use expeditions that last as long as 100 days, and these are oftentimes to reappraise life. They often result in powerful life-impacting learning and, as such, expeditions are still used by many organizations to offer development opportunities for young people in growth, self-development and active citizenship. In the United States there are Family Expedition Programmes to assist dysfunctional families to cope with, for example, at-risk youth. The expedition thus becomes the opportunity to construct a microcosm of the family life journey so that it can be reappraised and renavigated in real life. Other forms of adventurous journeys are also used for youth and adult development programmes. In 1978 Operation Drake was launched in the UK. With the success of Operation Drake, Operation Raleigh followed in its footsteps in 1984. Its aim was to develop leadership potential in young people through their experience of expeditions. Operation Raleigh, renamed Raleigh International, sends 'venturers' between the ages of 17 and 25 years on a 10-week expedition. Expeditions are being increasingly used in many other ways, from management development to adventure tourism. The UK Institute of Management suggests that:

> There is growing evidence that expeditions are gaining an emerging prominence and profile within the realms of human resource development (HRD). Arising from this evidence is a suggestion that expeditions contribute to personal growth or development of desirable capabilities that are relevant to work contexts. (Surtees, 1998: 25–26)

Advertising for expeditions is increasingly found in management journals. More adults are engaging in such life-enhancing journeys; even virtual expeditions can now be found on websites! Surtees (1998) completed an interesting comparison with our learning activity typology and found that expeditions have remarkably similar ingredients. Allison (2000b), in his research on post-expedition adjustment, discusses some of the possible themes emerging from an extensive empirical study of young people returning from an expedition, and addresses the need to re-examine epistemological and ontological perspectives used for research into experiential learning. His study focuses on the now widely recognized phenomenon of post-expedition readjustment into everyday life, and Allison argues that this can be seen in a positive light (rather than being likened to a form of post-traumatic stress disorder). Allison suggests that the loss of expedition friends, community and the expedition environment might simply indicate the adjustment pains of positive personal growth brought about by such powerful experiential learning. Among the personal growth themes emerging were:

- increased tolerance and patience;
- increased awareness and appreciation of more basic things in life;
- a change in environmental values, eg recognizing how people use their cars to travel very short journeys that are easy to walk;

- an understanding of the intensity and nature of the new friendships and the comparison of those with friendships at home;
- better relationships with siblings;
- a greater sense of personal and spiritual perspectives on life;
- a sense of service and giving;
- a change of self-concept.

(adapted from Allison, 2000b: 71–77)

Allison was able to draw out these themes that relate to the individual sense of being, where young people clearly see the world in a very different light when they return home following this powerful experiential learning event.

Journeys can take the form of smaller detailed micro-hikes over a few metres of the floor of a forest or the circumference of a tree! Journeys can involve an orienteering exercise, or they can involve simply getting objects or people from A to B. They can be metaphorical, in thought only, and mind journeys form the basis of guided fantasy work in therapy, a subject that we also cover in later chapters:

> A typical guided fantasy would engage the client in envisioning himself or herself as undertaking a hazardous journey, overcoming obstacles, meeting a wise person, and returning with a gift or message. In such a scenario, the therapist intentionally engages the client in constructing a 'self-as-hero-on-journey-of-liberation' story, as a means of empowering the client and helping him or her to celebrate his or her own powers and capabilities.
> (McLeod, 1997: 81)

Planning the journey and the learning from it is one of the key skills of the experiential provider, and it is of immense significance to the learner.

Sequencing learning activities

Another key consideration in the 17-point typology set out above is the sequence of activities. Primer activities often include ice-breakers and acquaintance exercises to reduce inhibitions or to create trust, empathy and teamwork (see, for example, Schoel, Prouty and Radcliffe, 1988). Experiential activities also develop skill, knowledge or awareness, and often start with specific narrow skills and then move on to aggregate or 'broad' skills such as teamwork, communication, time management, emotional

Figure 5.5 The experiential wave

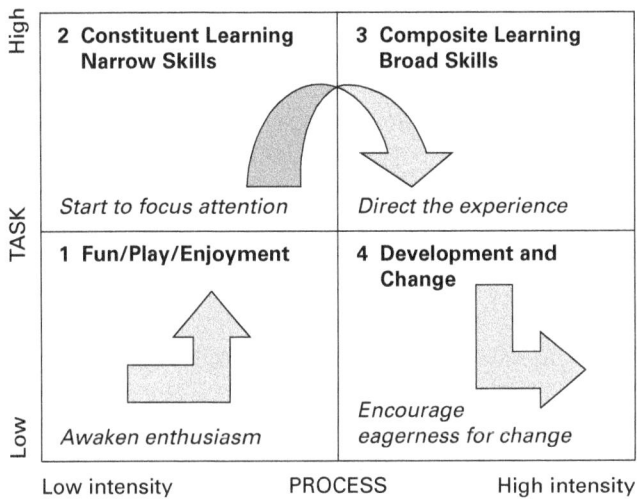

intelligence or leadership. This use of narrow 'activities' has to be examined in the light of their function. Broader and more complex activities provide depth to the experiential learning process, as is seen from the framework in Figure 5.5. Adapting the model of Dainty and Lucas (1992), this simple framework can be created both to classify outdoor and indoor experiential learning programmes and to show the sequencing of activities from play to intense self-development over the period of a programme.

Narrow skills such as listening or questioning can be focused on first. These might be built on later, as they are a subset of skills for teamwork or communication, which are very broad skills. Narrow skills can also be less developmental and more functional, for example knot tying, map reading or juggling skills, and they may be included to build up to complex functional skills for a journey such as orienteering.

By combining Cornell's flow learning (1989) with a model by Dainty and Lucas (1992) we have created the following four-stage sequence or activity wave:

1 Awaken participant enthusiasm with ice-breakers and energizers.
2 Start to focus attention with medium-sized activities and narrow skills.
3 Direct the personal experience with larger, broader skills.
4 Share participant enthusiasm using regular reviewing activities.

Mind and body

So far in this chapter we have been discussing physical activity predominantly in the outdoors. It is important to remember that experiential learning involves a linking of the mind and body. In this section we now consider some aspects of addressing adventures of the mind. We discuss the mind–body links in more detail in Chapter 6 about the senses, and in Chapter 8 on knowing and intelligence.

In athletics, computing and city finance, it is the young who dominate: they are fast off the blocks. But other professions, such as wine tasters, judges and prime ministers, seem to be dominated by older people. Why is this? When people are young they have the advantage of speed of mind and body, yet as they get older they retain a distinct advantage, and it is called 'experience'. Both young and old have different advantages. The brain shrinks with old age (Robertson, 1999) and it is crucial to keep the brain fit. The brain is a very powerful machine, requiring 'attentive' rather than passive stimulation. Brains need stimulation and it is crucial for the shaping and remoulding of the electrode 'muscles' of the mind (Robertson, 1999). Some outdoor experiential programmes do not engage the brain sufficiently and the mind–body balance is a consideration, as is the affective–cognitive balance. Books on brainteasers for trainers are now available as off-the-shelf learning activities.

The left side of the brain works on logical, linear processing and is also concerned with language, reading, writing and analysis. The right side of the brain is concerned with intuition, parallel processing, images and metaphors, patterns and visual recognition. Left-brain stimulation can be created by designing appropriate elements of problem solving into development activities, and, significantly, examples of daily mind stretchers are to be found in nearly all daily newspapers.

Challenging the mind: mental olympics – cognitive, mathematical–logical examples

1 Challenging cognitive exercises can be added to other exercises, eg the coded game: 12 M (months) in a Y (year)

    365 D in a Y
    4 W on a C and so on…

Or more complex:

Experiential Learning Activities, Behaviours and Actions (The Doing Dimension)

2 Explain the reason for the distribution of the following letters above and below the line:

$$\frac{A\ldots\ldots\ldots EF\ldots HI\ldots}{\ldots BCD\ldots\ldots G\ldots\ldots}$$

(See base of box for solution)

Or:

3 This urban exercise utilizes three street bollards in the city centre, labelled as a, b and c. Tyres are numbered 1, 2, 3, 4 and 5. They are placed one on top of the other in order with 1 at the top of the pile at bollard a. The tyres must be relocated on to bollard c in the same order but the following rules apply: only one tyre may be carried at any one time and it must be placed in a pile before any other tyre can be picked up; a smaller number must always be placed on top of a larger number.

Some people might need to be started off, ie 1 to c; 2 to b; 1 to b; 3 to c; etc.

This session can be used with time limits with certain allocated members carrying the tyres, whilst coordinators, who can be restrained in any way by rules or restrictions, tell the carriers what to do. An example is that the coordinators might be some distance away and operate their instructions by walkie-talkie, or in a coded language. Printed T-shirts with numbers, symbols or letters are ideal for many of these exercises. T-shirts can have + or ÷ or × printed on the backs for people to complete calculations.

Or:

4 Build mathematical challenges into other activities, eg physical, recreational or navigational activities. The 'bike it' exercise (see Beard, 2010) involves constructing or assembling a bike – exercising the many forms of intelligence. Here participants are provided with a set of accounts, and activities to carry out for money, including the solving of cryptic clues, mathematical problems, theoretical models to create, journeys to undertake, team skills to decide, jobs to divide – all to build a bike, through earning money to buy the parts, or expertise. But the frame and the handlebars are hidden in the city or the wilderness of the National Park, and clever problem solving will find them – but that requires brainpower.

(Solution = straight and round letters)

Rules and obstacles

Many other simple rules, obstacles or procedures can influence the degree of adventure, challenge or difficulty of any experiential activity. In digital games, rules are important and they need to be clearly understood by designers and the players: 'rules are fundamental to every game, without rules a game cannot exist' (Whitton, 2014: 90). Rules provide structure and in some ways they represent the defining characteristics.

Rules and obstacles can also allow greater flexibility in programme design so that the experience can be altered and levels of challenge can be reduced or increased. Time constraints, for example, might mean that items such as bike parts can only be purchased during specific times. Two-way radios can be used on certain frequencies; battery life can be measured or curtailed. Solar panels can be used to charge batteries or equipment so that people can only carry out some tasks when the sun is shining. Items can be placed in the way of routes and the journey might only be allowed at night or through certain territory. Instructions can be given on a tape recording through earplugs so that only one person can hear them at any one time. Communication might be restricted to coded whistles or translated into another language.

Obstacles can include sensory deprivation or sensory adjustment, and might include blindfolds, earplugs, glasses to improve or remove vision, nose pegs or gloves to remove feeling or to create clumsiness. Tarpaulins can be used to separate teams and they might be allowed to pass items only through a narrow aperture. Sorting and organization skills are also important: a mass of data, a mass of information to sort and make sense of, or activities to decide who does what and when. Why? Because knowledge is one thing; organized knowledge is a million things! The range of combinations within the milieu increases the level of challenge. While the milieu is endless, it does need a degree of focus, structure and reason.

The following rules and restrictions apply!

1 The time limit to complete the activities is just 220 minutes.
2 Each activity can be completed only once and will earn you money.
3 Each activity requires you to estimate your projected earnings and to submit it to the facilitator before commencing.
4 Physical activities will be paid in dollars; mental tasks will be paid in euros.

5 The four teams will have radio contact for 10 minutes only during each half-hour.
 6 One team member must be blindfolded at all times. One person must wear gloves at all times. For blindfold and glove wearing, rotation of the wearers is allowed.
 7 A sum of 10 dollars will be paid for each digital picture of the team 'completing' an activity.
 8 An up-to-date set of accounts must be ready for inspection at any time.
 9 Teams A and B will submit a mind-map plan of their proposals to the facilitators before commencing.
10 Teams C and D will not be required to produce a plan.

Constructing and deconstructing

Construction and deconstruction is a core concept in learning. It can be applied to physical objects, from bikes to rafts to dry-stone walls and bridges, and has been an essential component of many outdoor experiential programmes. Other options include the construction of something that is non-physical, such as a diagram or a theoretical construct. This can be done with the aid of navigational tools, a topic we covered in Chapter 3.

Plastic toy kits like giant Lego blocks, or trucks that can be built from components, are off-the-shelf devices used to create artificial 'tasks' and often specialist kit is sold on training websites: they can easily be assembled and disassembled. The plastic kits do not create real tasks – their reality is metaphoric. 'Ready-made kit' used to take the form of traditional planks and drums, used in raft building in outdoor teamwork development, but these are increasingly being replaced by a plethora of new manufactured artefacts. Everything from tank driving to juggling is being used by some providers in the search for novel forms of learning activities, as the increasingly sophisticated and discerning audience may get bored if they have 'done it before'. Irvine and Wilson (1994) challenge some of the mystique about some outdoor experiential events, and argue that 'novelty' might form the basis of such a rationale. They also quote Long and Galagan who suggest that the outdoors is where educational and organizational norms do not exist for people to hide behind.

The core experiences can also be deconstructed: rafts- and planks- and drums-type experiences involve building something, getting wet, testing and then racing the product in a competitive sense. These experiences can then be re-engineered into alternative projects. The advantage is that the client can be given choices, and alternatives: corporate buy-in and involvement can be increased.

Handling physical objects

A number of research papers and case studies highlight the pedagogical value of the use of object-based learning (OBL) in higher education. Objects can facilitate the transition from handling/discussing through to collation, analysis and the development of abstract ideas. Museums are particularly familiar with the use of objects for teaching. The bodily kinaesthetic handling experience, and subsequent thinking aloud through conversation, appear to be key.

In experiential learning a range of inanimate and 'unreal' objects are also used for people to project thoughts and feelings on to. Assagioli (1980) developed the idea of psychosynthesis, which partly uses a whole range of imaginative techniques so that people can project their inner thoughts and emotions on to images or symbols. This can enable expression of issues that lie deeper in their inner self, including emotional issues. Projection onto objects appears to remove some of the embarrassment that occurs in traditional face-to-face talking; deeper forays into the 'personal' become possible. For example, discussions or reviews can use 'natural stones', selected by participants to enable them to talk about themselves, say, in terms of why they chose that stone. By talking about the colour of the stone, its shape and size, personal meanings and values can be vocalized, and feelings and values can be *projected* on to the stone. People also talk about their *inner* self as being different: the stone only represents what people see on the outside. It is much harder to talk about these things candidly, person to person, or person to group. The position of the stones in relation to the others can also be significant in terms of the way groups or teams see themselves. Group difficulties can be broached more easily. In the case of natural stones, the objects become the metaphor to transfer meaning.

Russian dolls can be used to symbolize people, power and position of other people. Playing cards can be used: diamonds represent hard *facts*, hearts explore *feelings*, spades dig deeper – *findings*, and clubs explore possible *futures* (Greenaway, 1996). One technique devised to control either excessive dominance or shyness by young people in a group is called 'having the bottle to speak'. It has a double meaning. It involves using a plastic bottle, and people wanting to speak must wait for an opportunity to take it from someone else. If a person with the bottle has finished, he or she holds it out for others to take it, and as a sign of friendship people help to create discussion by sharing the talking, and taking and holding the bottle. For some it is hard to *have the bottle to try it*. The technique can also be used to ensure silence to those not holding the object, and the technique can illustrate fairness and balance of talk time.

Learning activities: exploring reality

> Hanging by a single rope 80 feet from the ground, controlled by a colleague whose previous knowledge of ropes was tying his shoelaces, could not under any circumstances be described as a game. (Butcher, 1991: 28)

In order to help people learn from experience, learning providers use a combination of activities and draw on drama, sculpting, role-play, art, stories and metaphors. They encourage learners to express thoughts and ideas about their experience. However, the degree to which these activities are perceived as 'real' or 'relevant' can have a significant effect on the learning experience. We have previously described a range of learning activities and offered a simple typology. We now consider these learning activities in terms of dimensions of 'reality', exploring how 'reality manipulation' can offer opportunities to unlock learning potential. While levels of reality can be reduced or increased to influence learning, making the right choices requires a clear understanding of the processes involved. In this section we offer a range of examples of 'real' and 'simulated' activities, and give guidance on the raising and lowering of reality in experiential learning. We now focus on a deeper understanding of the second cog in the Learning Combination Lock.

What is a real experience?

Item four in the learning typology was 'adjust elements of reality'. What is this term *reality*, and how might providers work with it for the benefit of learners? Harwood (2005: 224), in her work on storytelling as an organizational development tool in the health-care sector, refers to Bohm, an eminent physicist, who created the notion of 'presented' reality and 'represented' reality:

> Presented reality is viewed by Bohm as the classical Newtonian physical universe comprised of 'objects' or 'things' that are observable through the five senses, and about which there is common consensus, for example the price of a loaf of bread or how many part-time workers there are in the organization. In contrast, 'represented reality' then ascribes meanings to presented reality, for example 'that supermarket charges too much for its bread' or 'part-time workers tend to be women'. These realities are not 'in' the data itself but are interpretations of what the data means, and thus open to alternative readings.

In digital gaming the 'reality gap' is an important concept, and it includes anything in the design gap of the learning experience and the real world that might prevent engagement (Whitton, 2014). Some games continually shift between simulation and the real world. In higher education the degree of subject *relevance* is an important consideration for students, and pedagogic research into affective motivational states reports that a significant number of students, when asked to comment on what lecturers might do more of or less of in lectures, called for an increase in the degree of 'relevance' and 'reality' of the material they present (Beard, 2005). Outdoor learning providers claim high levels of reality in their programmes, and Krouwel and Goodwill (1994: 220) argue that reality is the key advantage to using the natural outdoors for learning, as 'reality is perhaps the greatest asset of all in management development programmes that use the outdoors. There is no artificiality in the exercises outdoors; the problems are real, the issues are dynamic, the constraints are felt. There is no need to act – it is the real world.' This implies that the learning activities are very 'real activities' as opposed to artificial 'games'. We argue that such a concept of 'real' requires greater scrutiny.

Martin, Franc and Zounkova (2004: 58) argue that dramaturgy games are: '"life as if" or "a draft for life". Games create a model world, allowing people to enter various life situations that are otherwise not accessed by them, to experiment with various situations or roles and to explore their reactions to their new situation.' In digital games there is much written about the nature of reality, and 'whether the game is shown in two or three dimensions, the degree of professionalism of design and the levels of realism' (Whitton, 2014: 174). Realism, according to Whitton, is significant and relevant to the learner and their learning. There are many levels to the experience and perception of reality, including visual reality (whether a game, for example, is photo real, or cartoon style), the degree to which the simulated mechanics are real and real time (for example, a flight simulator). There are also mixed-reality digital games, moving between the real world and, for example, an avatar world.

The games are said to connect with normality as the emotions, processes and interactions during the game are 'real'. Likewise, Price says that in outdoor development work, 'It is important that it be totally real because then you get real emotions, real fear, high anxiety, high or low morale, real aggression and real learning' (Price, cited in Bank, 1994: 10). Butcher (1991: 26) stresses the need to reproduce the work environment during company training sessions, to make learning more 'realistic': 'It is essential that training programmes have included in their designs, components that reproduce these problems, in a more tangible and realistic form than has been employed by many training consultants in the past.'

Holman, Pavlica and Thorpe (1997) consider this 'vague and indeterminate nature of reality' that results in the meanings of experiences being contested. In our view, understanding the impact of construction, deconstruction and orchestration of all the elements of 'reality' is a key requisite for experiential learning.

High levels of reality do not always present the best option for learning. What does Butcher actually mean when he refers to 'tangible and realistic'? Reality appears to have many different interpretations for different people. 'Real' might equate to the 'workplace-like' space, the degree of 'relevance' of the activity, or the extent to which the outdoors is seen as a real place. In Chapter 4 we explored how the notion of a journey might involve venturing away from the routines of the real home or real community environments in order to learn. Reality might refer to real tasks or activities, to the real people involved (eg negotiators), the real skills developed, the real objects used, the real learning outcomes or the real place in which the learning is undertaken. The notion of 'reality' is a much more complex phenomenon than is often realized, and, as we shall now argue, it requires greater exploration in terms of its impact on learners.

Butcher, a former army training officer, avoids a deeper exploration of 'reality' in suggesting that 'hanging by a single rope 80 feet from the ground, controlled by a colleague whose previous knowledge of ropes was tying his shoelaces, could not under any circumstances be described as a game' (1991: 28). Reality, in this situation, is not located with the activities, but rather in the form of real emotions that can emerge from such a situation, and which can heavily influence learning (we investigate emotions in Chapter 7). Perhaps Butcher views reality through the influence of his background in the armed services, where trainers 'use experience-based training to prepare people for the discomfort, depersonalization, and emotional strain encountered in combat' (Walter and Marks, 1981: 3). These combative styles from the armed forces often intentionally use 'in-your-face' techniques that push and prod as a form of 'distressed learning' designed to increase anxiety levels and so stimulate learning (Yerkes and Dodson, 1980). Distressed learning works for some people but such methods can be rather crude, creating a superficial confrontation of emotions such as fear and trepidation, thus teaching people to tame, combat and suppress their fear as if in preparation for real warfare. Rightly, this interpretation of reality and of experiential learning is not a panacea for all learning.

If learners cannot experience the 'real thing' they can of course experience something that is perceived as real, in a physical sense or an emotional sense. Learning environments can also be seen as unreal, bearing no resemblance to the learner's customary environment. The military use a combative approach to the outdoor environment and it was the military that first used artificial climbing blocks for training. This manipulation of facets of the learning environment might suggest that the space for learning is simply another element to be artificially choreographed as a 'bag of tricks'. Space for learning, as we explore in detail in Chapter 4, is an important consideration. Steve Van Matre (1978, 1979) helps children to understand how photosynthesis occurs, by getting them inside a leaf-shaped tent, with ping-pong balls, where the children pretend to manufacture sugars. At a higher-education level, learning can spill out of the classroom into the wider community, as seen in the case study below on law clinics.

CASE STUDY Law clinics: using high-reality strategies in experiential learning

Law clinics have their roots in the United States, where Law is normally a postgraduate course. They remain a widespread method of legal teaching, often having the dual purpose of meeting the massive unmet need for legal advice in a jurisdiction without a comprehensive legal aid system, as well as maximizing the student learning to make up for the general lack of a later work-based stage of learning.

There has been a substantial growth in law clinics in many countries – including Australia, South America and South Africa – but in the United Kingdom they remain uncommon. Clinics may take a number of different forms – including placement-based (or extern-ship) clinics; clinics that offer a pure representation service (such as the Free Representation Unit in London); and full casework and representation models (such as Northumbria University's Student Law Office), which are effectively full in-house law centres.

The Northumbria Student Law Office is a compulsory element in the undergraduate law degree, with about 130 undergraduate students working for a full year under the supervision of 15 practitioner members of staff. In any given year the programme will take on 500–600 clients, with problems ranging from employment to divorce, from consumer disputes to top-level criminal appeals, and from housing cases to human rights applications.

Case study 1

'A' was convicted of involvement in armed robbery and given a substantial prison sentence. He contacted the Student Law Office and over a period of four years various groups of students worked on his case, identifying potential grounds of appeal against the conviction. The students then helped 'A' with his application to the Criminal Cases Review Commission, who referred the matter back to the Court of Appeal. The students then briefed a leading Queen's Counsel to represent 'A' at the appeal, and they helped to prepare the case for its hearing. The conviction was overturned as being unsafe, and further groups of students then helped 'A' with his application for compensation for his wrongful conviction. Running such long-running cases is obviously a major challenge, but the case provided a number of generations of students with valuable learning in analysing criminal law – and in rectifying a serious miscarriage of justice.

Case study 2

'N's mother died in a nursing home after some months of severe neglect. There was a substantial delay while the prosecuting agencies decided whether to bring criminal proceedings against the owners of the home. When they decided not to prosecute, N decided he wished to sue the home on behalf of his deceased mother. However, to do this the executors of the will would have to bring the action. They did not wish to do so as they had only agreed to act as executors as a favour to the family. The students helped N to draft the documents to the High Court to replace the executors, and they briefed a supervisor in the Law Office to represent the client at court as they lacked the right to appear in court at that level. With this case the students not only learnt a huge amount about an area of law that they had only studied in brief, they also had the opportunity to draft documents for the High Court, to advise and assist their client and to brief counsel and attend court.

In management training Kirk (1986: 87) suggests that there are three main dimensions of reality to consider: participant reality, theoretical reality and resource reality. Participant reality involves the extent to which the design and content of the learning event relates to the learners and their jobs, organizational environments, personal abilities and expectations. Theoretical reality is the extent to which the content of the learning event relates to the existing body of knowledge concerning the nature of management and management learning. The nature of reality lies in questioning the theoretical models or concepts that are being applied and whether these are 'real' or 'true'. Resource reality is the extent and cost of resources that go into staging and running the learning events and whether the expenditure can be justified. If learners do not relate their 'experience' on a programme to their experience in real life, then the experience is likely to be criticized as having little relevance and this can affect the transfer of learning. Binstead and Stuart (1979) focus on three other dimensions of reality and offer reasoning and guidance for adjusting the degree of reality. They elaborate on the reality of the process of learning, the reality of the tasks that people complete and the reality of the environment in which people are learning.

High levels of reality do not always result in more significant learning. Although it is hard to tap into past, present and potential future experiences of learners so as to create high perceived reality, high-reality strategies can:

- integrate learning and work role activities;
- take the learning event to the job;
- bring the job to the learning event (tutor-led);
- bring the job to the learning event (participant-led);
- provide a range of alternative activities within the learning event;
- change the work situation to match the learning event.

(Binstead and Stuart, 1979)

There are situations where lowering reality permits a different kind of learning. Low reality may be appropriate, for example, when more radical alternatives need to be considered, so that new horizons can be opened up. We can use fantasy to reduce inhibitions, and role play to allow a feeling to be expressed or to create a feeling that 'This is not really me; I am just playing a part.' This kind of learning involves moving out of the reality of self in order to see something different. High-reality events would appear to be inappropriate and often dysfunctional when: 1) there is a need for

Experiential Learning Activities, Behaviours and Actions (The Doing Dimension)

growth- rather than maintenance-orientated learning, eg to allow a learner to consider radical alternative behaviour, ideas, etc; or 2) there is sufficient threat invoked in high-reality situations for it to be a barrier to learning.

Managers building and sailing a raft might experience a low reality in terms of environment (they don't usually work outside) and of task (they don't usually build and sail rafts). There is high reality in terms of process (they do use teamwork, communication skills, etc in their work – but then, who doesn't?). The process skills practised on a mountain do not always get 'transferred' back to everyday behaviours. High-transfer techniques might allow the learner to progress slowly to high reality, as in the negotiating case study below.

A practical case study: altering reality
Negotiating public access to the UK countryside: skills development

The early part of the course uses 'narrow skills' practice. Negotiating is a 'broad skill', involving many narrow skills such as listening, questioning, diplomacy and so on. On this course we thus deconstructed 'negotiating' into its many narrow subskills such as influencing, persuasion, listening, tactics, entry, developing rapport, closing and so on. The latter part of the course then used broad skills practice, but with varying levels of reality or simulation. The exercises were as follows:

From: LOW CONTENT REALITY

- **Exercise A: redecorating the office**

    The material was taken from a standard loose-leaf package on negotiating. It is a paper exercise. There is no incentive. It concerns a contract price to decorate an office suite. Content reality is low. The written case material on decorating contains a review sheet that looks at the forces in use in negotiating and the approaches that can be used by the two sides. People are asked to identify opening gambits and write their answers on paper.

- **Exercise B: driving a bargain**

    A written exercise about cars – people are told that this is a warm-up for a real car exercise when people can pit their wits against real negotiators! This adds to the incentive to concentrate on all exercises. Here the content reality is again low – the people involved do not negotiate car prices in their jobs.

- **Exercise C: buying a new car**

    Real cars are used. Real logbooks are used. Real car prices are offered. Car book prices are available. Cars can be inspected and faults found, both inside and outside, as they are located in the car park. The keys are made available. One is an uncleaned four-wheel drive and the other is a nicely valeted VW Polo. The brief informs people, 'You have moved to the National Park and need a four-wheel drive for bad weather and to tow your new caravan.' False money is used but a prize is offered. The people that the participants negotiate with are real trained negotiators and they are located in an office where the deals will take place. Final agreements are written in sealed envelopes so that the winners can be decided later. Content reality is again low; process reality is high.

To: HIGH CONTENT REALITY

- **Exercise D: negotiating access to UK land on behalf of the public**

    Here we use high-content reality and high-process reality. Real negotiators are again present. Real information is provided – facts and figures on sheep headage payments, ranger support offered, wall damage payments and litter arrangements. Participants are real access officers or public-rights-of-way officers. They are observed on video by the rest of the group. The incentive is to try to do a good job in front of their peers, to try to put all the skills and knowledge acquired on the course into practice, and they try to meet their own pre-set prices and subsidy targets decided in their negotiating plans. They argue their case with real negotiators and are debriefed afterwards. The video is then replayed with self- and peer-assessment taking place.

Fantasy

Fantasy is a form of psychic play, suspending reality. It is not just for children and the technique is frequently used to frame the mental state. In *101 of the Best Corporate Team-Building Activities We Know!*, Priest and Rohnke (2000: 5) offer fantasy as one type of 'framing' the way an experiential activity is introduced. They make reference to the popular 'fantasy or fairy tale introductions that include such items as spiders, sharks, alligators, poison peanut butter, radioactive yoghurt, nitroglycerine, TNT, corrosive acid, floods and forest fires'. One UK company offers many innovative theatrical-based training techniques, including *animating ideas* where people can 'Extend the boundaries of experience and realize your dreams and themes, through your own fantastic animated creations. You select the style, develop the characters, devise the stories and provide the voices... Hours of endeavour. Seconds of footage. Years of satisfaction' (Experience Creative Development, 2000).

Fantasy 'kits' for use in training offer many set scenarios: stranded on an island, capsizing on a lake or being stuck in a jungle. Brochures suggest that reality can be enhanced 'with a set of 20 slides that will make your participants glad they are warm and dry'. Participants are even given 'I survived the rainforest badges' after completion of the programme! Learning activities deliberately move from fantasy to reality. In *The Handbook of Management Games*, Elgood (1984), although not entirely satisfied with the term 'game' because its use may detract from the seriousness of purpose, discusses the nature and value of games, simulations and exercises. Elgood (1984: 8) identified four criteria that a game should satisfy:

1. It has a sufficiently clear framework to ensure that it is recognizably the same exercise whenever it is used.

2. It confronts the players with a changing situation, the changes being wholly or in part a consequence of their own actions.

3. It allows the identification beforehand (if desired) of some criterion by which it can be won or lost.

4. It requires for its operation a certain level of documentation, physical material, computation or administrative/behavioural skill.

Three models of games were identified by Elgood. The first are *definitive models* in which there is a clear answer and desired result to the game. This reflects the creator's view of the world in which, if certain behaviour occurs, there will be a specific result. The second type of game involves *probabilistic models*. This type of game is not as rigid and predictable, and allows for individual behaviour. It helps to create awareness of alternatives and the fact that people are prone to misunderstand what are thought to be common concepts, eg workers negotiating a wage structure with managers. The third type of game is concerned with *individual models*. These involve exploring and comparing the individual solutions to the game in a non-judgemental way that recognizes the value of differences. Elgood (1984: 12–13) categorized games as follows:

- Games based on a definitive model:
  - traditional model-based games;
  - puzzles;
  - in-basket exercises;
  - mazes;
  - programmed simulations;
  - enquiry studies;
  - encounter games;
  - adult role-playing games.
- Games based on a probabilistic model:
  - structured experiences;
  - organization games;
  - organizational simulations;
  - practical simulations.
- Games based on individual models:
  - in-basket exercises;
  - exploratory games.

Fantasy can create a sense of atmosphere, excitement and adventure, involving suspending disbelief, and the use of magic and mystery. Some adventures tend to be completely set in a fantasy world, or they might involve moving from the real world to the fantasy world and back again. This often requires some form of trigger between the fantasy world and the real world; for example, in *The Lion, the Witch and the Wardrobe* (Lewis, 1980), people walk into the wardrobe and into the land of Narnia. A secret code might be hidden in a cave, and there might be a 'quest'. Many of the characters in children's fantasy go through rites of passage, with helpers 'guiding them' into maturity: they learn to believe in themselves, and their lives are enriched from the experience of the quest.

Guided fantasy is a journey of the mind involving images with a deep symbolic meaning. Fantasy and guided imagery can be used to develop more awareness of thoughts and emotions, leading to the creation of greater self-awareness and personal growth. Relaxation techniques also use guided fantasy to take people on a mind journey to favourite places and imaginary environments that lower the heart rate and stimulate positive feelings. *The Temple of Silence* (Ferrucci, 1982) can be adapted: set in an imaginary world, a story we tell concerns a journey up a cold, snowy mountain, where we arrive at a cave. Sitting by a fire in the cave is a wise old man – the sage. We had opened the door of the training room to let in some fresh air, and as we lay on the floor in the dark the wind got up and it started to snow heavily and the snow actually came into the room! The atmosphere was beginning to change as the reality blurred with our fantasies: two participants from Outward Bound Singapore had never seen snow before! Workshop participants were later asked to go out into the surrounding fields and woods and find somewhere to be alone with their thoughts, somewhere they could not be seen and where they could not see anyone else. This was to let their imagination develop even further.

Play and reality

As observed in a variety of mammals, it would appear that play serves to *rehearse and exercise skills* in a safe environment. This can be seen in kittens playing together, stalking and pouncing. Recognition of the value of play is not a recent phenomenon. Games have been played for thousands of years and there is clear evidence from the Egyptians of 'acrobatics, gymnastic games, tug-of-war, hoop and kicking games, ball and stick games, juggling, knife throwing, club throwing, wrestling, swimming, guessing games, games of chance, and board games' (Booth and Moss, 1994: 5). Plato (1953) advised that any builder must first play at building. It is clear from general observation how successful children are with learning where play forms a key role. By age three children have learnt to walk, speak, handle a variety of objects, control their limbs and bodily functions, and operate in social environments. They learn in a 'natural' way and, it would appear, often carry out an activity just for fun; more importantly, they appear to enjoy themselves. It is normally non-threatening and usually conducted in a safe environment for themselves and for other children. Significantly, 'their involvement with the learning process is total. There is no separation between learning, play, work and leisure. Life is all of these at once and its process is spontaneous' (Heap, 1993: 16).

Play offers a powerful mind state for learning. Play is culturally and politically defined. Adults may require permission to play because attention is focused on 'ought to be' doing or 'could be' doing: worries and concerns, regrets and mistakes – about things in the future and of the past – can present inner barriers, preventing the states needed for learning (Carlson, 1998; Mallinger and De Wyze, 1993). Mallinger and De Wyze (1993: 171) comment that:

A workaholic parent may be physically present but non-existent as a nurturing parent... Each stage of [child] development lasts for only a very brief time, and once completed, will never be repeated. Miss out on enough such experiences, and you will end up with only a pale, vitiated sense of ever having had children.

In contrast, children experience play as just 'being', naturally living 'the moment', the 'here and now'. Piaget (1927), who studied his own three children and other children, identified three types of play:

- **sensorimotor play** – involves the practice of behaviours and exploratory learning often seen in young infants;
- **pretend or symbolic play** – found in children from two to six years;
- **games with rules** – played from the ages of six or seven years upwards.

Children often seem to enjoy free play with materials such as sand, paints, water and clay. They frequently become totally absorbed in this creative process and the materials provide an opportunity for learning about the nature of materials, conservation of material, spatial, textural and other dimensions.

Play is difficult to define, and it is said that within the literature associated with research on digital games the most neglected area is that of games for play (Whitton, 2014). Play can remove us from the reality of everyday life, and shift us into a timeless or subconscious state. Furthermore, play can generate those natural pleasure drugs of the brain we talk about in Chapter 8. Games can also be fun – and fun influences our mental state. Genuine and authentic fun involving a teacher or facilitator will often generate engagement, rapport, a feeling of a safe environment with stronger social relationships. Fun, as an emotional state, also enhances memory. In interviews of 39 students the vast majority felt that learning should be fun and 'four key elements' emerged:

1 Lecturer attitude, enthusiasm and relationship with students.
2 Active, novel and experiential learning.
3 Social and collaborative aspects of learning.
4 A pressure-free learning environment.

(Whitton, 2014: 121)

In the years 1890–1920, $100 million was used to build playgrounds in the United States (Cohen, 1987). These playgrounds were formed in order to minimize delinquency and improve morals and health. The first adventure playground was built in Copenhagen in 1943, and its director Bertelson stated, 'There can be no doubt that in the case of so-called difficult children, free play presents a solution to their problem' (Cohen, 1987: 32). This initiative led to the establishment of the International Playground Association, with Bertelson defining an adventure playground 'as a place where children are free to do many things that they cannot do elsewhere in our crowded urban society' (Cohen, 1987: 32). The assault courses that are used by adults in management training exercises are a sophisticated form of playground.

Unfortunately, not all children play. The father of economist John Stuart Mill would not allow his son to play; he wanted his son educated from birth. Similarly, Froebel, born in Thuringia, Germany in 1782, had an unhappy childhood and, influenced by the writings of Rousseau, developed a kindergarten (garden of children) where children could, like flowers, 'blossom'. This was a reaction to the drilling methods used in schools, and in the kindergarten children were allowed to play and were encouraged by adults. Also, play in children is not always undertaken in a light-hearted and pretend manner, as can be seen in Golding's *Lord of the Flies*. Play has the potential to have a negative influence.

So how do we experience play as adults? It is difficult to draw boundaries that clearly define play from other forms of activity, and Smith *et al* (1986) described how it is also difficult to categorize the various types of play. However, they identified five main characteristics of play:

- **intrinsic motivation** – the child plays for the sake of play and not for other external reasons;
- **positive effect** – the child enjoys and finds satisfaction in the play;
- **non-literal** – play is pretend and is not taken seriously;
- **means/ends** – the child is more focused on the process and behaviour than on the actual outcome;
- **flexibility** – there can be a variation in the context or form of behaviour.

Play for adults includes not just sporting activities and board games at Christmas but, according to Cohen (1987: 15), psychological games in which he included 'encounter groups, growth movements, self-help groups of some sorts, following the guru, self-therapies, and all kinds of ego-fests. Obviously, many people take these activities very seriously and some need help. But for many people, going to groups has become a form of "deep" play.' Furthermore, the playing of games would appear to be an activity that is conducted by children of all ages. Berne's (1973) *Games People Play* proposes that we all possess within us the ability to play the role of parent, adult and child in our interactions with others.

What is all too apparent in this discussion about games is that they are an essential learning process for young people to develop the skills necessary to survive in later life. Games develop cognitive, affective and behavioural skills that can be used in both personal and work lives. For adults, involving oneself with certain types of play activity, with the exception of formalized games, is often frowned upon. It is assumed that as adults we are mature and have passed through the stage of playing games.

Suspending reality: drama and role playing

> Generally, there is felt to be a very sharp distinction between learning and amusing oneself. The first may be useful, but only the second is pleasant.
> (Brecht, quoted in Willett, 1977: 72)

The quotation above creates a cynical juxtaposition of amusement and learning: Pollock (2000) coins the term 'infotainment', reporting that 'companies are turning to music, storytelling, visual art and even comedy in order to develop their people, engender creativity in the workplace and enhance the corporate image'.

We now explore role *play*. Drama is defined as: 'The enactment of real and imagined events through roles and situations. Drama enables both individuals and groups to explore, shape and symbolically represent ideas and feelings and their consequences. Drama stimulates and shapes aesthetic development and enjoyment through valuing both affective and cognitive responses to the world' (Curriculum Corporation, 1994: 16, in Attard, 2001).

Role-playing techniques have been roughly classified as:

- performed or imagined (passive or active) (Hamilton, 1976, in Attard, 2001);
- scripted or improvised (Hamilton, 1976, in Attard, 2001);
- involving one individual or many;
- participants required to play themselves or someone else;
- participants required to play themselves under a familiar or unfamiliar set of circumstances;
- stooges may or may not be used in role plays – and sometimes are used as *agent provocateurs*;
- subject may be pre-briefed and deceived, or pre-briefed and not deceived, or not pre-briefed at all;

- scenario inductions can involve one-line prompts or several;
- participants may be constrained into a highly structured-response format or, alternatively, be given a free-response format.

(adapted from Yardley-Matwiejczuk, 1999: 36)

The above list provides innovative facilitation ideas. Role play can facilitate problem solving and enable people to enhance awareness and understanding. It can have a degree of spontaneity. However:

> In reports of such role-play activities there is an overwhelming assumption that we all know what we are talking about when we mention role play. Occasionally hints emerge, about aspects of induction or technique, that suggest the authors might know a thing or two about good practice, but these are rarely articulated fully or made explicit. Moreover, there is no evidence of a critical stance towards the question of whether role play is being appropriately or inappropriately utilized. (Yardley-Matwiejczuk, 1999: 34)

Playwrights from Sophocles to Brecht have used their 'plays' to teach, and convey facts and political attitudes to their audiences, but variations from the traditional play now exist. The term 'spectactors' is used to describe a technique that involves people moving from observation as 'watchers' to being involved as 'actors'. *Invisible theatre*, for example, might involve two people walking into a shop where they start to argue about something. The real people eventually take sides and then join in! But there are ethical issues here, which we examined in Chapter 3.

Drama is potentially attractive to many adult learners as many people watch plays, films or soap operas and become affected by the experience. There is a distinction between using dramatic techniques as a teaching method and teaching theatre. Theatre is an art form that focuses on a product: a play or production for an audience. Drama used in experiential learning is more informal and focuses on the process of dramatic enactment for the sake of the learner, not an audience. This teaching technique is referred to as 'creative dramatics' in order to distinguish it from theatre arts. Classroom drama is not learning about drama, but learning through drama. Drama's goals are based in pedagogical, developmental and learning theory as much as or more than being arts-based. Significantly, the focus is on the growth and development of the learner rather than the entertainment or stimulation of the observer.

By means of dramatic activities students use and examine their present knowledge in order to induce new knowledge. Bolton (1985) argues that while school learning is an accruing of facts, drama can help students reframe their knowledge into new perspectives. Therefore, this teaching technique places the learner at the centre of the programme design and encourages reflection and the development of greater understanding of self and others. Facilitators, too, can utilize the reflective dimension of drama in training programmes. This will help participants to make a personal commitment to training and develop greater knowledge about themselves and others and their role in the workplace. Drama works on the theory of raising a dilemma. A facilitator stops the action, and the learners offer possible methods of resolving the situation. The actors play out the various suggestions in context, and debate can follow concerning the outcomes.

According to van Ments (1994), the idea of role play, in its simplest form, is that of asking people to imagine that they are either themselves or another person in a particular situation. Learners are asked to behave exactly as they feel that the other person would and, as a result, they and/or the rest of the class will learn something about the person and/or situation. Role play, then, is a form of imaginization and communication that can be used for different purposes. Different types of role play demand different approaches – the way in which the role play is introduced, the description of roles, the facilitation and the post-play analysis will vary according to the type of role play that is being used. It can be used, for example, to describe or demonstrate events, to practise skills, to give feedback or to sensitize people to reflect upon events.

CASE STUDY Circus and radio

OLS Unique Solutions is a small business based in the UK, and prides itself on its creative approach to finding training solutions for the commercial sector.

Case study 1

OLS was asked to help energize and motivate an HR department after they had been through a major organizational change. The client requested that the end result could only be achieved through team cooperation and, second, that there needed to be scope to see colleagues 'in a new light'. OLS designed a workshop where the delegates had 48 hours to devise, rehearse, resource and perform a circus show lasting 45 minutes for an audience of 300 schoolchildren. Specific skills varied from erecting the big top and learning clowning performance and trapeze to top-quality sound production. After the workshop, the HR manager described the event as 'the most effective team build I've ever been involved in'.

Case study 2

OLS was involved in a key strategy meeting for a national public-service provider. The senior team was facing a major piece of strategy development work that required a positive mindset to ensure success. OLS set the team the challenge of producing a professional-quality 30-minute radio play. This involved designing, scripting, recording and the post-production of the piece. The initial reaction of the team was of disbelief, as they did not feel they could accomplish such a task in the time frame. However, by the end of the day, all the individuals were amazed and felt enormous pride at what they were able to achieve. As a result of this newfound confidence, the business meeting the following day was highly positive and effective. On completion of any delivery, the evaluation phase focuses on the outcomes. Feedback is vital.

The case studies explain why many leading-edge outdoor experiential providers, such as Brathay in the UK, possess drama studios and art labs as well as kayaks and climbing equipment.

CASE STUDY Leadership competencies in Malaysia

When it comes to our leadership development programmes first we understand competencies. Competency is a combination of skills, job attitude and knowledge, which is reflected in job behaviour that can be observed, measured and evaluated. Competency is a determining factor for successful performance. The focus of competency is *behaviour*, which is an application of skills, job attitude and knowledge. Competencies are the set of behaviour patterns that the person needs to bring to their role or position in order to perform its tasks and functions with competence. How we approach leadership development programmes is to focus on the development or improvement of the required competencies of leadership in order to be more effective. One of the ways we measure/assess the competencies of a leader is through their behaviours. One of the most frequent methods used is Assessment Centre.

So what has this got to do with experiential learning-based leadership training? When it comes to our leadership training workshop one of our objectives as trainers/learning facilitators is the creation of *greater self-awareness* of behaviours (whether they are effective, or ineffective) so that leaders are able to realize the gaps they need to bridge. This way people learn through experiencing the process of leading via experiential activities, and at the same time they observe one another's behaviours. Training can be more effective when leaders are being exposed to their own behaviours (which leads to competencies), and from these behaviours observed and competencies assessed through psychometric tools, we are able to more effectively pinpoint the areas that might need improvement.

So how do we bring out the 'behaviours' in training? We do this by using experiential learning activities known as business simulations, or role play. Competencies are clusters of observable behaviours and actions made up of components including knowledge, skill, self-image and traits. Whilst knowledge and skills are readily understood, we add to this the issues of self-image or how people see themselves. We include identity and self-worth. For traits we include habits and enduring characteristics such as self-control, trust and listening. So, if we look at this in terms of experiential learning, the impact will be greater if we provide experiential learning activities that bring out the competencies mentioned above relating to 'behaviours' or 'traits'.

Two examples of some of the experiential learning activities we use are as follows:

- **Paper Plane Inc business simulation**
  Working in a team, operating as a company called Paper Plane Inc, the team needs to design and produce a plane and sell it to customers. Each member will play a different role such as wing engineer, plane fabricator, plane constructor, flight tester, inspector, etc. We then observe the behaviours of the team, how the team leader leads the team and also to measure their results/performance at the end of the time given to see whether they have managed the cost well, earned a profit, produced quality planes and met customers' expectations.

- **Pandemic board game**
  Pandemic 2 is a free online game based on the spread of disease. The game allows flexibility in creating a 'plague', including whether you want to be a bacteria, parasite or virus. Each disease has its own strengths and weaknesses. This is a cooperative management board game where the team needs to manage two concurrent priorities: to find cures and save the world, and to treat diseases from outbreak to a critical level until even a cure found will be too late to save planet earth. There are five different role players, each with different sets of skills/strengths and the team needs to strategically plan every move, manage crisis (epidemic), stay focused, share knowledge and ideas, be able to listen and negotiate, as well as problem solving and decision making, and so on.

In short, any training or learning workshop, in my view, without experiential learning activities or business simulations, will not be as effective and impactful. Humans learn best by experience: engaging all the senses, emotions, and mental and psychological faculties. Also, the main objective of training is that leaders or learners will have a change of behaviour (improvement, growth, acquiring of new habits or discipline). With activities that surface behaviours of individuals for observation, assessment and awareness, it helps us to support individuals to realize and recognize their own behaviours (and therefore competencies) and so identify gaps to change, improve, learn, unlearn or relearn.

Theophilus Wong, CEO Fishcamp Training; Petaling Jaya, Selangor, Malaysia

Rafts and planks... or real projects?

Many experiential learning providers are working closely with National Parks, NGOs and other organizations to set up and use 'real' environmental or community projects for the purpose of experiential learning events (Beard, 1996). Such programmes, while being more empathetic to the environment, can have a real sense of purpose. As a result they can be very productive, in many ways, such as for the learners, the organizations involved and the natural environments. These real experiences that make a positive contribution to society and the environment can replace simulation activities, such as computer-based scenarios, or pack away kit that is rebuilt by the next clients such as raft building with planks, drums and rope. More significantly, real projects may have a positive motivational impact on learning, affecting the way participants engage in the learning experience. Corporate facilitators report high levels of motivational energy towards projects that are 'perceived' as doing *good work* of a charitable nature: they have altruistic appeal. This phenomenon requires more research, but this connecting with community and earth appears to have high value and is increasingly important in holistic experiential learning.

Popular community projects include the building of playgrounds for children, and delivering hospital radio programmes or theatre performances. The options are indeed endless and with creativity the benefits can be considerable to all parties concerned. Charities such as the Royal Society for the Protection of Birds (RSPB) and the National Trust in the UK offer 'team challenges' in their brochures, and have specialist staff to help to coordinate such projects. These tasks are suitable for learning activities. This also has management development benefits in terms of social accountability, social auditing and the notion of business as a positive social force.

Metaphors and storytelling

There is a traditional saying, in 'metaphorical speak', which is, 'Let the mountain (the experience) speak for itself.' There is a school of thought, however, that the experience, in the form of stories, needs to be told.

The *story* is one of the basic tools invented by human beings for the purpose of gaining understanding. Indeed, stories solidify our memories, and everyone looks for opportunities to tell their stories in one way or another (Schank, 1992). Collison and Mackenzie (1999) assert that there have been great societies that have not used the wheel, but none that have not used stories to generate ideas, morality and values. The earliest stories were probably chants or songs and contained epics, myths, parables, fables, fairy tales and folk tales:

> Asked to name the most powerful communication tools, few business people would be likely to list storytelling amongst them. That, however, may be changing, as organizations are reawakening to the potential of one of the oldest forms known to humankind of passing on knowledge. In the UK, organizations ranging from large retailing firms to government agencies are finding that working with story is a highly effective way to facilitate internal and external communication, develop teams and leadership skills, and to engage the attention of clients and customers. (Collison and Mackenzie, 1999: 38)

Parkin (1998), in *Tales for Trainers*, describes the use of stories and metaphors to facilitate learning. She refers to the use of sets of cards that ask people to describe themselves as birthday presents or cartoon characters, or smells, or drinks. People might respond, she illustrates, by saying they are teddy bears because they are soft and cuddly, or that they are like water because it is pure, it flows and it supports life. In personal development, facilitators can create fantasy metaphors, and Parkin describes how the inexpressible can be explored by speaking in a non-prosaic language. The tale of the 'ugly duckling', for example, is a classic story relating to self-esteem. Parkin offers examples of stories aimed at personal development, business development and a wider world context. They can help people to 'analyse and maybe change their views about themselves and their levels of self-esteem' (Parkin, 1998: 18).

Storytelling and conversation analysis have also been used extensively in social-science research and in conference work where management development issues and concerns need to be brought to the forefront (Gold, 1996; Gabriel, 1998; Samra-Fredericks, 1998). The core of all psychotherapy is also based on storytelling, as clients tell and retell their stories as individual life-story or personal narrative. McLeod (1997: back cover) argues that 'all therapies are, therefore, narrative therapies, and that the counselling experience can be understood in terms of telling and retelling stories. If the story is not heard, then the therapist and the client are deprived of the most effective and mutually involving mode of discourse open to them.'

The *survival note* is an example of the use of story to help surface and explore organizational culture. Teams are asked to agree and write a basic survival story of the key things that a replacement team would need to know about working in the organization. They are asked to focus on and describe to the newcomers the key to maintaining their existing 'way of doing things' in order to minimize the impact on existing customers or clients. Facilitators can also use stories to lessen participant anxiety, by creating stories that contain elements of self-disclosure, as seen below.

A short self-disclosure story
Learning from mistakes: interviews – an unfortunate incident on a Scilly island

The Scillies are known as the Fortunate Islands. Colin Beard tells a true short story of one unfortunate experience on the way to this island for an interview. He caught the wrong train, got off the train, tried to get a taxi to catch up with the right train – an intercity express – but… no money, he went to the bank, oh no… queues, eventually in the taxi he was back on track, arrival at the heliport… oh no… he was booked on the helicopter the previous day… strange but he thought it was today! It was the wrong day for the interview… what a silly mistake… he met the local vicar waiting in the queue… he was supposed to be on the interview panel! Was delayed by fog the previous day… he invited Colin to stay… then more fog and delays, arrived eventually on the Scillies… oh no… they gave the job to someone else the previous day…! Back home to lots of 'How did you get on?'

A note left by father-in-law (the moral of the story): 'S/he who never makes a mistake never makes anything!'

Below is a second specific case study on the use of images and stories, through the use of cartoons.

CASE STUDY Adjusting reality – art and images

The use of cartoon images as a reflective tool embraces a mixture of art, humour and storytelling and, as Janni of the Royal Academy of Arts comments, 'arts-based learning is all about using different parts of your brain' (in Pollock, 2000: 19–23). Artists can be employed to create such images. Back in the early 1980s Colin Beard used an artist to assist in a training programme for Shell executives in their prestigious Lensbury Club on the River Thames. The delegates were people who were close to retirement, and to help them to move into semi-retirement they were asked to work with a Shell initiative, designed to help environmental projects. It was called the Shell Better Britain Campaign. Coming to terms with some of the difficulties of facing retirement, as well as working with environmentalists and environmental charities, was difficult for the people concerned. The culture of the organizations that they were likely to meet was probably going to be very different from their own. In their new role as officers for the Shell Better Britain Campaign, their job was to help advise groups and offer grants. By the end of each day the artist had many of their fears and concerns sketched on to huge sheets of paper in the form of cartoon images. It was cathartic to smile and laugh together at the images of Shell executives in Batman capes, abseiling down the Shell HQ in London, armed with rucksacks of information on the environment! Bulges of cheques filled the side pockets, and some were falling out, slowly floating down to the ground. The drawings also showed Inland Revenue letters about their tax, pensions, expenses and other issues hanging out of their back pockets, reflecting some of the other more personal concerns!

The cartoons were great fun and they helped in the 'seeing' and 'airing' of difficult subjects. The funny, depersonalized neutrality is a strength in cartoon work. The 1980s were the time when adult comics boomed (Mallia, 1997: 93), and our inspiration to use this medium came from more established superhero characters such as Bob Kane's Batman in Gotham City and from *Peanuts*, created by the great Charles Schulz.

Management development and cartoons

Comics or newspapers can present cartoon strips to convey important messages in both adult work and youth work. We have also used stereotypical cartoon images to explore issues. One is of a woman sitting knitting on the sofa and a man reading the paper and ignoring comments from his wife, 'It's not what you say, it's what you don't say... and the way you don't say it!' Messages lie within the humour, in the script or image, and the events and actions, as well as in the physical characters of the people portrayed. An interesting account of the use of comic strips we came across, by Mallia (1997), refers to pioneering experiments with an ongoing soap-opera-style comic to aid the development of total quality management programmes (Kaizen) in a Maltese microelectronics industry. Comics, Mallia suggests, are capable of inducing interest in young and old alike, and yet have the potential to be a powerful reflective tool. One of the earliest definitions of this genre is by Waugh, who suggested in 1947 that a comic is a form that must include these following elements: 'A narrative told by way of a sequence of pictures, a continuing cast of characters from one sequence to the next, and the inclusion of dialogue and/or text within the pictures' (Mallia, 1997: 96).

Here, then, we see the close link between cartoons and the art of storytelling and journeying. Parkin (1998: 3) comments that storytellers would typically be travellers or minstrels, passing on important information from town to town:

> Storytelling was seen as a vocation requiring many skills, such as powerful communication, appropriate use of language, insight, sensitivity and accuracy, and in order to do the job well, the storytellers had to develop their own minds in ways that other people at that time did not. They had to develop their memory and visualization skills, and using these skills, be able to trigger memorable pictures in the minds of their listeners, for it was in this way that the information would be best understood and remembered.

Parkin suggests that the ingredients for a good story are characters, a good plot, some sort of conflict and a resolution. Experiential providers might also consider becoming adept at storytelling, as 'scenarios' often form the backcloth to experiential activities. Consalvo (1995) suggests that scenarios that are fantasy or patently artificial require the internal consistency of a 'good story' to facilitate the suspension of disbelief, 'buy-in' and active engagement of the trainees. Harrison is quoted in Mallia (1997) as saying that 'the cartoon is a drawing which (a) simplifies, and/or (b) exaggerates'. Some cartoons, however, are intrinsically complex.

Comics, Mallia suggests, are next in line for acceptance within the world of experiential learning and, as a unique form of entertainment, 'comic strips have become a social phenomenon. Their ability to capture contemporary economic and social events with remarkable accuracy and finesse means they are preferred areas of study for… educationalists, who at one time were apt to moralize about comic strips, [and] now use them as a teaching aid' (Schetter, 1992: 35). Mallia suggests that the use of comics for instructional purposes is infinite. For example, he suggests that they can be used to act as ice-breakers at strategic points in the lessons, or to create interest in a subject being discussed. They can aesthetically elevate traditional instructional text, inspire emulation, generate tools for a new channel of communication for the learners and project an atmosphere of informality.

In a cognitive capacity, comics can:

- communicate information;
- simplify instructions;
- be used to illustrate a point being made;
- be a tool in linguistic instruction;
- stimulate discussions;
- be a source of visual culture;
- be a mnemonic tool of cognitive retention.

(Mallia, 1997: 103)

Cartoons can be used to explore the outcome of learning, to compare different perspectives of the same event, to reflect upon emotions, or tell something about the people involved. There is a tendency to think cartoons are concerned with jokes and that humour must pervade. Humour might, however, provide clues to underlying issues or feelings. Cartoons can allow difficult issues to surface in a non-threatening way. Stories can be created using speech bubbles or thought bubbles and captions (see Figures 5.6 and 5.7) and unfinished statements or speech prompts can also be used to lead the storylines in a certain direction: useful in the development of reflection or review.

If cartoons are to be drawn then warm-up exercises are needed and hints and tips can be provided on facial expression and movement. The sequence of pictures and speech bubbles go from left to right, ie whoever speaks first should be on the left of the picture, and it is necessary to start drawing any sequence from front to back, ie first draw whatever is nearest to you.

Figure 5.6 Simple line-drawing practice and reflection bubbles

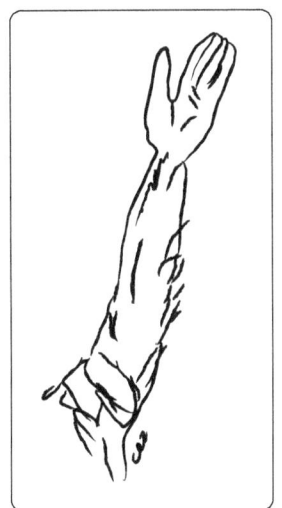

Using photographic images and computer software

Digital camera images can be used for cartoons or newspapers. These images can be simply brought together and reduced into a cartoon strip by importing them into presentation or drawing packages (such as MS PowerPoint). Speech and thought bubbles can be inserted and filled in by learners (see Figure 5.7). Learners can select and sequence images. Similarly, instamatic cameras can be used to record images, and the photos can be sequenced (and rearranged) on a flipchart, allowing captions and speech bubbles to be added by hand on to the flipchart paper.

Cartoons and comic strips offer powerful reflective tools. Combining art, dialogue, situations and outcomes, they can tell the story succinctly and humorously. Cartoons capture the essence of what is going on; rather than attempting to be an exact record, cartoons can help us dig deeper emotionally. *Cartoon cards* are available for trainers to purchase (see Terrell, 2000). Each has statements and images about characteristics of people in teams. Another technique is *photo snapshots*, a photo-in-the-mind method that can be used through pretending the learner is a camera, creating snapshot images in his or her mind between blindfolded periods. This can be used to create flashbacks of, for example, special events or moments, or to revisit special places through imagination. They can be described to others by the 'camera' person.

Figure 5.7 Reflective tools – digital camera images and speech and thought bubbles

Reflections on reality: reading and writing

Finally we consider the use of reading and writing as a powerful reflective tool in experiential learning, as 'biographical' work. Writing techniques are recognized and valued as important in facilitating experiential learning, and there are many techniques and formats that can be used. One technique is *lifelines*, a method involving people using rope or string to create a sequence of waves representing highs and lows in life. A knot is tied along the line to delineate the point in life where people are now and so reflective thoughts and discussion can then focus on 'What next?' A second technique, *Life Stages*, involves writing about events in life as if they were chapters of a book. McLeod (1997: 62) describes psychodynamic narrative and structured life-story interviews, where he begins by asking people to think about their life as if it were an unfinished book, with chapters representing major parts of a person's life. It is suggested that there should be between three and eight chapters, and each chapter requires a name and an overall content description. The links between each chapter are also discussed in his work. Other techniques might include:

- **writing lists and mind maps** – clusters of ideas on the topic;
- **guided imagery** – involves free writing stimulated by an image such as 'being on a journey';

- **stepping stones** – reviewing formative life experiences from the vantage point of the present;
- **the daily log** – to record the day's events;
- **the period log** – to record a current period in the writer's life;
- **dialogue** – creating a dialogue with a person, event or object from the writer's life;
- **altered point of view** – writing about oneself in the third person, or about someone else in the first person.

(from Lukinsky, 1990, in McLeod, 1997: 77)

Another technique is writing one's own obituary, or that of a colleague through the process of interviewing. *Critical incident techniques*, *good practice audits* and *journal keeping* are all explored by Hunt (1999) in an excellent chapter on reflective practice.

Reading is something that many development trainers might incorporate more in programmes. Reading clearly provides opportunities for adventures in the mind, although it is perhaps seen as an academic thing to do, associated with school, university or college. We provide details of a reading experiment in Chapter 4. In the experiment we create a relaxed ambience and use a 'coffee and newspaper' approach to reading, exploring and encouraging indigenous thinking and modelling without any pressure. Tony Buzan (2000), in his book on speed reading, refers to Vanda North, who is ranked as one of the world's fastest readers. After speed-reading training, she realized that: 'For 21 years she could have been reading twice the amount, with better comprehension, or she could have read exactly the same amount and had nearly a year extra to be with friends, to travel, to explore and to have even more fun!' This is a good investment strategy under anyone's terms.

Doing and reviewing

Learning can of course be enhanced, or diminished, by reviewing activities that support reflection. Whether it is called reflection, debrief or reviewing, there are similarities in that they all have a potential role in supporting learning. Reviewing ideally should be an engaging experience in itself and we offer some guidance in the case study below, produced by Roger Greenaway. His website is full of creative ideas (reviewing.co.uk). Returning to the metaphor of a film, it is interesting that one of his early popular books (Greenaway and Hilditch, 1993) was called *Playback*.

How active reviewing supports learning and change

Active and creative approaches to reviewing create good opportunities for reflection, communication, learning and development because they can readily:

- engage and develop a wide range of learning-style preferences;
- connect the worlds of thinking, talking and doing;
- produce holistic, dynamic and focused learning;
- access intuitive and tacit knowledge;
- enrich the experience of learning from experience;
- enable some testing of ideas within the learning process;
- increase the range of strategies for the effective transfer of learning.

Whenever people get stuck in rituals and clichés encountered in verbal modes of review, introducing active and creative modes can help to free up the process: the opportunity to think and communicate in *pictures* or *patterns* or through *mime*, *movement* or *drama* or through *verse* or *music* provides alternative modes that help people get *unstuck*. Participants discover new ways of thinking, new ways of expressing themselves and new ways of understanding and explaining things. It is true that new angles can be discovered through astute questioning in all-talk reviews, but new angles can often be more readily produced by changing the ways in which people create, tell and compare their stories about their experiences. For example:

- **For sharing an experience:** the storyteller (learner) reflects on their experience by making a storyline showing their ups and downs. The storyline becomes a visual aid that allows the audience a glimpse of the big picture before hearing the detail of the ups and downs.
- **For talking about group dynamics:** the storyteller arranges and rearranges objects into patterns showing how roles, relationships and group performance have been changing.
- **For examining critical moments:** the storyteller re-creates critical moments through action replay. Typically, participants replay themselves. New information emerges when the replay is paused and people are interviewed about what they were doing, feeling and thinking at the time. This restaging of key moments tends to bring out greater honesty and understanding.

- **For exploring future scenarios:** the storyteller walks through a large map of past journeys and new possibilities, tries different choices, explores new routes and discovers various consequences.

It is difficult to achieve this quality of reflection when following the more passive traditions of private reflection or group discussion. Fruitful private reflection requires a high level of mental discipline that includes sustained curiosity, accurate recall, high self-awareness, the ability to see other perspectives and plenty of imagination. More perspectives are clearly available in group discussions, but when people sit in the same chair all the time, it can look and feel as if everyone is stuck in the same place – both physically and mentally. Whether reflecting alone or in groups, active and creative methods increase engagement and movement and sustain the dynamics from which change is more likely to arise.

Successful transfer of learning will also be more likely if the review process has been engaging and holistic. Not only is such learning more reliable, it is also more aligned, more integrated and more ready to use.

Roger Greenaway, an international specialist in Reviewing Skills Training (http://reviewing.co.uk)

Conclusion

Mumford (1991: 31) suggests that 'if we provide individuals with a greater capacity to learn from the widest possible variety of opportunities, we are empowering that individual to be in greater command of his or her destiny'. Experiencing rich learning opportunities is the essence of experiential learning, and this chapter has outlined the basic ingredients used in the design process. The 17-point typology set out in this chapter acts as a general guide to the learning activity design process, and serves to highlight the importance of design skills in experiential learning. Together with the Learning Combination Lock model this typology is useful to create a development needs analysis for clients.

In this chapter we examined the creative use of activity sequencing, planned and unplanned learning, and the use of journeys, large and small, from life journeys and expeditions to orienteering and micro-hikes. Sensory blocking, fantasy and play, the provision of rules and obstacles, problem solving, and the use of objects for a variety of purposes were all briefly explored so as to set the scene for detailed work in later chapters. This milieu provides a multiplicity of innovative ideas to select from so as to enrich the learning experience; however, good practice and a sound theoretical understanding must always underpin the choices made.

Also in this chapter we investigated in some detail the effect of altering the nature of perceived or actual 'realness', and how it influences the experience of learning. The use of activities that include training kits, traditional outdoor recreation, circus, radio production, cartoons, theatre, drama, art, storytelling and writing all received attention. We clarified the many facets of 'reality' and we explored how altering these facets provides opportunities to unlock more learning potential.

Training is sometimes conducted as part of staff 'away' days. Being away from the daily working environments can result in everyday cultural norms and expectations being shed. Away days remove some work distractions and the sense of play can reduce inhibition, suspend reality, increase enjoyment and stimulate relaxed alertness. Different perspectives surface, status and egos can fade into the background. However, as we have shown, much will depend on the quality and care with design and delivery; but no matter how thorough the planning, important outcomes can derive from unexpected experiences.

Sensory experience and sensory intelligence (SI)

06

(the sensing dimension)

The perfume of a loved one inhaled by one of our 23,000 daily breaths is scanned by 10 million olfactory receptors capable of detecting approximately 10,000 different odours. BURNS (1988: 55)

Introduction

This chapter highlights the importance of our senses, sensory awareness and our sensory intelligence in the experience of learning. The human senses receive a great deal of information about the outside world. The human inner world also generates considerable sensory data both from the body surface, and also from sensors inside the body. Perception works well when objects are appreciated by a variety of senses. The senses are important for experiential learning as they play a key role in connecting these inner and outer worlds.

It is the sensory experience – what we see, hear, smell, touch and so forth – that, in simple terms, results in observations, followed by varied reactions. Sensory awareness is an underestimated phenomenon: sensory data coming in influences our thinking, feeling and judging, therefore it might be said that *sensory intelligence* (SI) is potentially more significant than emotional intelligence (EQ). SI might be considered to be a more advanced self-awareness state. But of course these component elements of an experience are not divided or sequenced in such a simplistic way.

Amplification and habituation

Sensory awareness can enrich the human life experience. We can of course learn to amplify sensory experiences that bring more positive feelings: fresh-baked bread, the morning air, crisp snow, buzzing bees in the warm sun, fresh coffee. The downside is that these experiences can habituate, if experienced too often! SI and sensory awareness can similarly enhance learning. Whether it be the spoken word, handling an object, or watching the demonstration of a particular skill, the senses are the means of contact and communication with the outer world: between people and the non-human or more-than-human world. This basic fact that we communicate through our human senses can be so easily forgotten by trainers and facilitators. Equally important is the realization that we regularly need to experience changes in sensory stimulation to avoid habituation, or sensory dulling through overuse of one sense mode. This is why whole-person experiential learning strategies recognize the important role of the human senses, a role that should not be underestimated.

The senses, six, seven, or as many as 20 or more, are central to the way we receive, perceive and experience, and judge the human and the more-than-human world. Although sound, smell, sight, touch and taste are five commonly quoted senses there are many others: interoceptors sense blood pressure and oxygen content, while others monitor temperature and pain. Mechanoreceptors aid balance and speed, acting in a way like a human GPS system, tracking and interpreting time and spatial form. This human GPS monitoring system, as we will show in this chapter, is extremely important in experiential learning; bodily and kinaesthetic spatial awareness is a fundamental component of *sensory intelligence*. Indeed the body as a whole plays an important role in the human understanding of very 'complex' things, particularly as the mind has a tendency to categorize and classify. Also significant in terms of the human sensory capacity is the notion of gut feeling or intuition, transcendental or 'out of body' experiences, and 'sublime' and 'spiritual' feelings: these are 'sensed'.

How many senses?

1 Visual.
2 Auditory: inner outer dialogue/voices.
3 Kinaesthetic/bodily/touch – muscles and other parts of the body send signals.

4 Smell – chemoreceptors.
5 Taste – chemoreceptors.
6 Sixth sense?
7 Temperature receptors.
8 Pain receptors.
9 Others.

These can be further divided: eg number 3 above, kinaesthetic experiences, consist of:

- **Interoceptors**: detect internal bodily reactions – blood pressure, heart rate, hunger, mood, arousal, etc.
- **Tactile**: touch primarily through skin.
- **Vestibular sense**: balance, gravity and acceleration.
- **Proprioceptors**: processing balance and body position through muscles, ligaments and joints.

The human senses: untapped potential?

The following highlights the great potential for using the senses to enhance learning from experience, by allowing subconscious knowledge to be accessed and developed:

- **Sight:** the rods in the eye detect colours in shades of grey and they can sense shape and movement. We have about 120 million rods. Amazingly, our eyes react in emergency situations and we can see much better: we see details we normally cannot see!
- **Smell:** the nose, at its best, can tell the difference between 4,000 to 10,000 smells.
- **Touch:** people who are blind use their fingertips to read Braille by feeling the patterns of raised dots on their paper, as there are about 100 touch receptors in each of the fingertips.
- **Hearing:** the auditory nerve carries messages from 25,000 receptors in your ear to your brain.
- **Taste:** we have 10,000 taste buds inside our mouths; even on the roofs of our mouths.

These facts highlight the potential for sensory experiences to increase human capacity/functioning.

External and internal signals, received through our sense receptors, are said to act as raw material for learning 'experiences' to be 'constructed', through the process of perception (Gross, 2001). The human experience is, of course, much greater than the sum of the individual bits of sensory data. Perception or processing moves the experience beyond sensation, and involves the memory bank of experiences, and higher processing levels, including the subconscious. Consider the following quotation by Peter Jarvis:

> All of our experiences of our life-world begin with bodily sensations that occur at the intersection of the person and the lifeworld. These sensations initially have no meaning for us as this is the beginning of the learning process… Thereafter we transform these sensations into the language of our brains and minds and learn to make them meaningful to ourselves – this is the first stage in human learning. (Peter Jarvis, 1999, writing on adult education)

The importance of this sensorial world to experiential learning appears, at least in this account, as not particularly significant. Jarvis suggests that the senses initially have 'no meaning', until they are 'processed' and 'transformed'. Now consider a contrary view, presented by Robert Kull in his book about his year in Patagonia, called *Solitude: Seeking wisdom in extremes*. Kull lived in remote Patagonia so as to study for a PhD the experience of solitude:

> In conceptualizing, organizing and thinking about these sensory impressions, the immediacy of experience can easily be lost. It requires patience and practice to soften this habitual activity by over and over letting go of thought and analysis to simply stay with the swirl of sound just as it is without trying to do anything with it. (Kull, 2008: 279)

Here we see that Robert Kull suggests a contrary position; that the act of processing raw sense data, essentially thinking about it, can spoil the complex 'immediacy' of the experience. Similarly Sheets-Johnstone (2009: 380) describes such events as 'Instances in which we are at a loss for words, so stunned by something we cannot speak': partly due to the inadequacy of speech when it comes to describing movement or emotionally laden events that move us. This subject will be of concern to the experiential coach, educator or facilitator, and so in this chapter we explore this core issue, concerning processed versus raw sense appreciation, particularly in connection with their role in experiential learning. The chapter also offers guiding thoughts for facilitation on a range of sensory dynamics: the notion of sensory intelligence, sensory arousal, sensory reduction, sensory stepping, sensory overload, solitude and silence. The chapter will also consider how the written and spoken language has a negative side effect that is not well known, namely its role in distancing us humans from nature, and the beauty of the more-than-human world.

So what is sensory intelligence?

Sensory intelligence is the degree to which we develop our ability to be aware of, and work with, our own sensory states. It is also about how we learn to read our sensorial pleasures and displeasures, to work with both positive and negative sensory experiences, within ourselves, and within others to develop individual, community and organizational creative energy and collaborative effort so as to improve life and planet balance (Beard, 2012). The regular commuter going to work often looks bored and tired of the journey. Sat next to the commuter is a visitor to the town or city. The tourist is excited by the experience, and the pleasurable sensory stimulation makes them alert for more. Why is there this difference when the stimuli are potentially the same? Can the stimulation awareness button be reset? These are fundamental questions that affect the processes of learning.

Sensory intelligence involves developing our awareness, and to practise:

1 being aware of our *sensorial* relationship with the world, particularly the immediacy of the here and now and its impact on the self;
2 tuning into, working with and managing immediate *sensory experiences*, particularly pleasurable ones that have zero cost;
3 reconnecting our senses with the positive and negative, natural and spiritual elements of the self, through guided sensorial experiences, particularly in uplifting social and/or outdoor natural environments;
4 developing an ability to motivate the self through life-enriching, *sensory experiences*;
5 developing an ability to recognize and tune into the *sensory needs and experiences* of others;
6 working with *sensorial experiences* typically found within our important relationships.

Let's give some simple examples to guide practice. Reawakening the senses of a whole community:

People had to walk to their jobs, and to whatever shops were still open. We began encountering each other on the streets, 'in person' instead of by telephone. In the absence of automobiles, and their loud engines, the rhythms of crickets and birdsong became clearly audible. Flocks were migrating south for the winter, and many of us found ourselves simply listening with new and childlike curiosity, to the ripples of song in the still-standing trees and the fields. And at night the sky was studded with stars! Many children, their eyes no longer blocked by the glare of house lights and street lamps, saw the Milky Way for the first time, and were astonished. For those few days and nights our town became a community aware of its place… The breakdown of our technologies had forced us to return to our senses, and hence to the natural landscape in which those senses are so profoundly embedded. We suddenly found ourselves inhabiting a sensuous world that had been waiting, for years, at the very fringe of our awareness, an intimate terrain. (Abram, 1997: 62)

The quotation above, from *The Spell of the Sensuous* by the philosopher David Abram, describes the effect of an experience that triggered a sensory reawakening in a local population. Following the impact of this hurricane on their town, people experienced the world around them very differently. Sensory awareness returned to them. Ordinarily for many people, everyday experiences incorporate an avalanche of stimuli, arising from the sounds and sights of cars, from televisions and street lights, and added to by other consumptive data, all appealing to our senses through advertising media. This sensory world continually attempts to sell us goods, images, services and formulated experiences. This can easily create a human world that becomes sensorially dulled, a world that has blocked out many pleasurable, naturally occurring sensory phenomena. Technology in this story clearly added to the estrangement.

However, technology can also work in conjunction with the bodily experience: the continuing development of gesture-based technologies (GBT) for example, where fingers, hands and arms are now used to manipulate information – eg in the iPod, iPad and iWall – heralds a potential return to the use of the bodily movement to aid mental processing (Beard and Price, 2012). When we present statistics or graphs these forms can often seem unintelligible to non-scientists, yet new and very creative research (Gwilt, Yoxall and Sano, 2012; Gwilt, 2013) aims to translate such traditional complex scientific data into sensual physical objects, where contours, texture and colour of the physical form allow the data to be sensorially read or interrogated. This is a very different way of experiencing scientific data! Ironically the distancing of the human from the more sensorial world was even more profound as a result of the evolution of the human written and spoken language.

Language and the human sensorial experience

Language is sensorial, emanating from the body: complex sounds use the air of our breath, whereas written language takes the form of a kinetic dance across the page. It is what makes us uniquely human. Language can surprisingly have both a positive and a negative effect on the experience of learning, particularly in relation to how language shapes our experience of the sensuous outer world. Good communication involves language that appeals to the senses: a study of Shakespeare reveals a language that powerfully communicates to the eyes, ears and to our human feelings: to 'gaze an eagle blind', to 'hear the lowest sound' and so 'gross in taste' (Knight, 2002: 83). Language, particularly in this poetic form, generates rich sensory pictures for a world created inside our heads. Yet language is also problematic: language is spoken one word at a time, and the written language is read one page at a time, line by line. Thus both the written and spoken word are essentially linear in format, which can limit human understanding of complex, multidimensional, interrelated issues. Sheets-Johnstone (2009) in a chapter titled 'On the challenge of languaging experience' notes how the brain and body essentially work with our three-dimensional world: up/down, right/left and front/back.

Facilitator briefing

The briefing involved about 20 of the 40 staff involved in a very complex activity. The meeting was about the delivery of The Great Langkawi Race for 90 very senior and talented clients at the Westin, Langkawi Island, Malaysia, in late 2012. The delivery had to go to plan. A lot was at stake, and a very professional delivery was expected by the client HR department. What they required was perfectionism: nothing must go wrong and safety must not be compromised. For the water activity alone the local fire brigade were to be on standby on a jet ski, and two instructors were to be in kayaks, with several staff on the beach.

> In a small hotel nearby, the senior and experienced facilitator stood up and spoke. She carefully explained: *There are 90 senior clients involved. There are three groups of 30 with three subgroup teams in each. There are three major activities: 1) Fast and Furious; 2) Slow and Steady; and 3) Hybrid. Within these there are many smaller activities. Each group will have 30 people doing each of the major activities. Each group will select 10 people to allocate to each of the three major activities.* More detail followed. *This group will be based at...* I looked around. There were facial expressions that suggested to me that more than a few people were not getting this. It was hot and they were tired. Written briefings of this complex experience had taken me several readings to sort it all out in my head when I received it over the internet some weeks before, back in the UK.
>
> One of the activity facilitators in the audience who was not so afraid to speak said: *Let me get this straight, so there are...?* Following yet more verbal detail there were more puzzled faces. However, the facilitator then got up and took hold of a whiteboard pen. She drew the three teams in boxes along the top axis of the board and colour-coded them: the blue team, the green team and the red team. Below these she then drew big boxes down the left side axis: 'Fast and Furious', then 'Slow and Steady', then 'Hybrid'. She had created a 3×3 grid. Then the number 10 was written in each grid space... it all became clear. The group frowns disappeared. A new visual–spatial form had clarified things alongside the verbal brief. The insufficiency of the linear nature of speech had been overcome.

Sheets-Johnstone (2009) and others (Lakoff and Johnson, 1999; Gallagher, 2005) also note that the period before written and spoken language is often referred to as *pre-linguistic*. Gestures, noises and facial expressions would have naturally played an important role, although *pre-linguistic* implies a language vacuum, as if no language existed. These authors reject such an idea, and instead they suggest that language might have evolved from a basic sound-gesture phenomenon, very much linked to the sensual more-than-human surrounding world. This sound-gesture sensorial evolutionary precursor to the spoken and written word might be better acknowledged if the term '*post-kinetic*' phenomenon were used (Sheets-Johnstone, 2009: 5). Humans continue to furnish everyday language with these bodily-spatial metaphors in order to aid mental processing. For example, we say: to *support* our case, to use *step-by-step* logic, to *grasp* a concept, and to feel a bit *down* every now and then. *Further*more, we study *higher* or *further* education (see, for example, the work of Lakoff and Johnson, 1999). Our mental reasoning is thus underpinned by a rich language of spatial-bodily metaphors; clearly learning is not a purely cognitive process, as somehow disembodied as tradition has largely held.

The body and the brain are also connected to the senses. The work of Nina Bull in the 1950s is particularly illuminating in this respect and it is described in Sheets-Johnstone (2009). Nina Bull hypnotized people into one of six emotional states and they would later describe these emotional states in neuromuscular or bodily terms. In later experiments participants were read a selected description from one of their own reports and they were then locked into that emotional state by hypnosis, and told they would not experience other emotional states until they were unlocked. When asked to get into another emotional state they reported how they were unable to access these new feelings or emotional states because they were stuck in the previous specific postural or bodily attitude: 'I feel light – (so) I can't feel depression' (Bull, 1951: 84, 85, in Sheets-Johnstone, 2009: 200). The locked-body muscular posture had prevented access to the new feelings: the body–mind synergy couldn't function.

Reasoning and learning also arises from the integration and interaction of our brains with our bodies as an *embodied* experience, and this occurs within a particular environment, as *embedded*. The connected relationship of the brain, body and environment should not be underestimated in experiential learning. It is illustrated in practice by the 'Walk the Talk' pedagogy described later in this chapter.

The separation of the human from the more-than-human sensorial world is linked to the evolution of language. In very simplistic terms, the shift occurred from early sounds anchored in the onomatopoeic, a long word relating to speech rooted, for example, in the sounds of the natural world (a name or word mimicking the sound of a particular bird, for example). Such sounds were aided by bodily gestures also. This language was further developed by the use of pictographic and ideagraphic language (picture-based and idea-based). This use of the sounds developed into more complex form with the use of the rebus. The rebus used words that have natural meaning on their own to create a new word with no root natural meaning, such as *bee* and *leaf* to create a new word *belief*. Ultimately this gave birth to the sounds and shapes of the simpler aleph-beth, or early alphabet, which once linked the spoken and written word with the sensorial earth: the letter Q, for example, was a pictorial representation of a monkey with a tail in the original Hebrew *aleph bet*, which predates the English alphabet. The work of David Abram (1997) skilfully shows how the sensorial more-than-human world has thus been intercepted and distanced by the development of the alphabet, and the written language. However, pictographic languages such as Chinese still retain their original connectivity with the earth. What appear to the Western eye as complex Chinese symbols are relatively simple if the original pictorial form is understood: the word for 'rest', for example, has pen strokes or lines that are derived from a picture of a person sitting under a tree. Gestures were and still are also important for language: it is said, for example, that the Italian dictionary has a supplement of important gestures. The inadequacy of human language, and its sensorial distancing effect, is illustrated in recent research in remote Patagonia by Robert Kull (2008). His frustration with the inability of the written English language as he struggles to make notes for his PhD about *solitude* is expressed with a stark honesty:

> I drop the notebook and feel myself sink more deeply into the world. All desire to write disappears. What has happened to my flow of language? I fall mute before such wonder and beauty. I try to describe the delicate shades and patterns of shifting colour as wind swirls water around immovable rock, but my images feel dull and trite. There is no dance between word and world. What I see and feel begs a sensuous tango, but my words march static and stiff in lines across the page. (2008: 184)

It appears the mountains certainly do speak for themselves! The traditional Outward Bound approach to facilitation in the 1940s may have been more significant than hitherto recognized:

Six generations of facilitation techniques

1 1940s: let the experience (mountain) speak for itself.
2 1950s: speak on behalf of the experience.
3 1960s: debrief the experience.
4 1970s: frontload the experience.
5 1980s: isomorphically frame the experience.
6 1990s: indirectly frontload the experience.

SOURCE Priest, Gass and Fitzpatrick (1999)

Written and spoken words fell silent: the sensorial experience, in its raw state, spoke instead very directly and personally to Robert Kull. Processing such experiences onto paper became almost impossible for him. Mental processing and subsequent attempts to capture the experience in writing failed. Kull notes that:

> Coming into Wilderness Solitude is like studying where everyone speaks a language you have forgotten so long ago now it seems completely foreign. You know you have something important to learn, but you don't understand. I take time to keep listening and listening. I hear the voices of nature and try to translate what I hear into conceptual thought language so I will know I understand in my mind. But the language of nature cannot be translated into human concepts. It is deeper and different. I realize I have heard and understood when my heart softens and opens to love and peace and beauty around and within me. (Kull, 2008: 279)

Kull avoids a glorification of his special solo adventure: his writing does not become the stuff of gendered heroics. His deep, quasi-meditative experiences are often preceded by a significant sensory awareness: of his breathing, and of the awareness of simple objects or sounds around him. This is often referred to as a *mindless* state (see, for example, Tolle, 2006), where little or no mental processing occurs. The experience just is; it is raw and unprocessed, it possesses a magic quality. Related notions include spiritual intelligence, centring and presence, and these are covered in more depth later and also in the chapter on knowing. Meditative experiences take us beyond our three-dimensional world mentioned earlier. In listening to our breathing we also access the fourth bodily inside/outside dimension – and possibly even the fifth life and death dimension:

> At rest or in meditative experiences, insides are commonly present only in the form of breath and the silence that rings in our ears. All is quiet. But it is also warm and alive. (Sheets-Johnstone, 2009: 373)

Interpreting and misinterpreting words

Natural and *wilderness* are difficult words to characterize or interpret: language can be clumsy and inadequate at times. Many words in everyday use that have been taken for granted as understood increasingly come under critical examination, particularly in academic journals, through deconstruction narratives. Let us give an example of what we mean. The creation of an urban-wilderness opposite or duality is seen by some as being particularly unhelpful. For some writers this duality is typical of dominant Western narratives. It is in this vein that Willis (2011: 95) cautions the use of the language word *wilderness*, as being somehow special and elite, or superior, and usually as somehow *sublime*. In a US context, with reference to the work of Cronon (1995), Willis offers a critical interpretation of this word *wilderness*. She cites the US national parks as a 'gendered privilege', preserved so that the nation's men could retreat there and forge themselves anew. Recent work (Norris, 2011) also challenges the basis of many outdoor education practices, suggesting they have been uncritically adopted, as experiences originally derived from indigenous peoples. These include the solo, vision quest and other phenomena associated with rites of passage. These deconstructionist narratives are critical, enlightening, opening up new vistas, questioning the taken-for-granted. Yet this genre of adversarial academic writing, where key words in use have to undergo a meaning deconstruction test in the quest for a milieu of alternative interpretations, can potentially be unhelpful, as Jay Griffiths suggests:

> Literacy is an epistemology of the built world, physically, in libraries in towns, but metaphorically too, the constructed artifice of our written culture, book-bound, which encourages our philosophies and values to move even farther away from nature – to say nothing of the constructs of deconstructionism and post-deconstructionism. (Griffiths, 2006: 19)

This quotation from Griffiths (2006) comes from her book *Wild: An elemental journey*. Here she offers an alternative to the term wilderness.

Going 'away': outdoor sensory-awakening experiences

It is with these critiques in mind that we want to consider the importance of the sensory experience in nature and wilderness. Outward Bound has long embraced a particular form of sensory awareness, through the form of the 'solo', where people venture into wilderness alone, for several days, finding space to ponder life and self, and be at one with nature. Kurt Hahn's educational vision insisted that true learning required periods of silence and solitude as well as directed activity. These and other core ideas served as the driving force behind the establishment of many prominent institutions of the time such as the Duke of Edinburgh Scheme, United World Colleges and Outward Bound.

Interestingly, the majority of outdoor development providers in the UK are clustered in the places that are designated as Areas of Outstanding Natural Beauty or National Parks. It is said that the Lake District National Park in the UK contains the largest cluster of development training organizations in the world. Within this vast range of special outdoor environments, rich sensations connected with the more-than-human world are experienced that can take learning into the realm of an exciting adventure. Outward Bound Singapore (OBS) is located on the beautiful island of Pulau Ubin, sometimes referred to as the Adventure Island. The location was specially selected for outdoor development activities that use the local rainforests, mangrove swamps, a quarry and the surrounding seas and offshore islands. OBS also has a swimming pool in the tropical jungle, and a gymnasium and many climbing walls and towers. The climate in Singapore is humid and warm, and some 'classrooms' for learning are covered but not completely walled, and a cool breeze replaces air conditioning. These rooms are neither indoor nor outdoor: words give rise to definitional and descriptive dilemmas. *Indoor* and *outdoor* and *rooms* are difficult to clearly define.

Sensory acuity can be heightened when the everyday sensory overload is reduced or eliminated. When total darkness and silence exist inside a cave the conditions are ideal. Sight is redundant, so other sensations become enhanced. We listen out for any noise and it is accentuated by the acoustic echo, we smell the damp air and feel the creeping cold. We learn about the intricacies of communication in a cave where visual cues are eliminated. This can have interesting results, including enhanced listening behaviours. Other experiences might reduce or enhance visual communication: blindfolds are often used in outdoor education (see, for example, Priest and Rohnke, 2000; Martin, Franc and Zounkova, 2004; Neuman, 2004). Gloves can be used to reduce tactile sensations of the fingers. Bare feet sensorially increases the body connection with the earth. Contrasting sensations provide a change in stimulation.

Sensory experiences can raise awareness of our flow with, or against, the natural rhythms and energy levels of the body in relation to our human and more-than-human surroundings. In outdoor learning, common divergent sensory stimulations include, for example, light and dark, noise and silence, shelter and exposure, calm and energized, food satiation and hunger, loneliness and gregariousness, solitude and crowdedness, hot and cold air, wet and dry clothing. The combinations are endless, and on a grander scale, fire, water, earth, mountains and rivers are just some of the many sensory features of the natural or urban environment that can be used to influence learning, a subject we cover in Chapter 5. Chris Reed (1999) refers to the five basic elements in the outdoor environment: earth, air, fire, water and spirit – and suggests that they are symbolically important. Fire, he suggests, is a symbol of action and creativity, and of destruction and new life. Fire can send people into simple, meditative, reflective states simply by being watched. Water can symbolize feelings, emotion and dark undercurrents. Air symbolizes ideas and intellectual pursuits but also insubstantial dreaming and lofty idealism. The fifth element, spirit, pervaded all that Reed's group did over a weekend but he noted that 'the ether is invisible, insubstantial but ubiquitous'. Higgins (1996, 1997) refers to other elements by adding weather, shelter, food, darkness and silence.

Our human senses often remain in tune with the natural rhythms in the environment. Sensory channels can be pre-sensitized prior to an experiential activity or event. Such sensitizing is a vital part of our ability to create a good experiential learning climate that enables the doors of our mind, body or spirit to be opened up. Tuning-in with learners to sensory experiences can be supported using *continuous stream talking* (inside-the-head talking or vocalized/spoken to the outside) generating responses to immediate sensations and feelings: 'right now I sense the…'

Silence is powerful in helping to raise sensory awareness, as is meditation. Rainforests offer extremes of sensory stimulation: numerous animals continuously send out signals, such as warning signals of an encroaching predator. Animals can sense a storm coming well before the rains, and much earlier than humans. Humans learn to *read* natural signs in this way. Our senses can be alerted to read other changes: in light, humidity, wind, colour and shadows. Experiential learning is as much about observing and reflecting as it is about *doing*: the outdoors is a good place to sharpen observational and sensing skills.

In 'Fire in the sky', Walker (1999) explores the three dimensions of 'self, others and nature', as used by Colin Mortlock. He proposes some activities that he suggests can improve participants' interconnectedness to the earth and to awaken the human senses:

- self-introductions (respect for diversity of individual stories, how you got there);
- sitting on the ground or natural materials (simple contact with the earth);
- sitting to talk in circles not lines (cyclic nature of life processes and natural things);

- being inactive and alone (quietening down, going inwards, inviting nature in);
- walking differently from in the city (eg slowly, silently, blindfolded – unfamiliarity);
- walking barefoot (direct contact with dewy grass, rock, wood, earth, leaves);
- walking in unfamiliar places (gorges, undergrowth, logs, snow);
- leading, giving help (risking, reaching out, human care and contact);
- being led, receiving help (expecting understanding human care and contact);
- focusing on natural rhythms (tide, wind, sunset/rise, stars, moonrise/set, night sky);
- focusing where possible on wood fire (natural processes, history of life, universe);
- telling, inventing and listening to stories, legends of the earth (images of other ways of life);
- sleeping on the ground, if possible outside (expanding awareness, dreaming);
- sitting silently observing together (sharing different perceptions of the world).

(Walker, 1999)

Experiential learning in the natural outdoors can also provide ways of reframing our thinking about the natural environment, by altering our inner scripts, changing the 'metaphors', 'images' and 'labels'. Using the natural environment for corporate environmental awareness training could be a powerful awakening, yet ironically, environmental training rarely uses the environment as a teaching medium (see Beard, 2003).

The senses in higher-education teaching

Susan Behuniak (2005), US professor of political science, in developing a 'pedagogy of solitude', is exploring how digital sounds and technological devices (iPods, computers, e-mails, televisions) can threaten the very silence and space needed for contemplation. Behuniak argues that in the fast-food-like stream of contemporary education, the incursion of these portable technologies into private space appears to create environments in which the learners cannot hear themselves think. Behuniak refers to the research by David Strayer, a professor of psychology, who argues that when aural flooding occurs the eyes will go to a place or thing but that place or thing will not actually be seen or registered. Tuning in and out of sense registration is an important concept to consider in the experience of learning.

In contrast, a substantial range of contemporary techniques exist for stimulating the senses: PowerPoint presentations, interactive whiteboards, video clips, sound bites, blindfolds, masks, drums, whistles, coloured cards, special-effects lighting. Yet language can inhibit in other ways. If a lecture experience is dominated by excessive periods of unskilled oration, poor artificial light, stale air, and the immobilizing effects of rows of uncomfortable seats, the senses become dulled. The experience is deprived of the beauty and richness of learning because of the limited sensory experience. The same might be said for textbooks, and researchers have recorded paradigm shifts from all-text-based design to visual language representation, thus building a dynamic relationship between text and graphics using multigraphical representation. Graphical interpretations become a vehicle for useful communication that harbours the potential to convey concepts in various ways. The relationship between textual and visual representations in the design of multifaceted graphics can be enterprisingly and influentially integrated, with technology developing a new generation of texts that offer a new form of 'visual language' (Lin, 2005).

Neurolinguistic programming (NLP) acknowledges the clear link between thinking, language and behaviour: neuro is thinking, linguistic is language and programming refers to behaviour/actions. NLP research reveals that we think in patterns. Think of hot chocolate and it might be that we smell it, see it, or feel its warmth on a cold morning. These represent the dominant three thinking patterns of pictures, sounds and feelings and give rise to what is termed VAK analysis (referring to visual, auditory and kinaesthetic representational or 'rep' systems), often used by facilitators and trainers. The way we use mental maps relates to sensory perception, and research shows that people tend to concentrate on one or two senses. People find it easier to remember things when associated with sensory recall, and NLP practitioners call these 'accessing cues', involving eye movements and speech categories. Examples include 'I see what you mean', 'I hear what you say'. These cues offer insight into the sensory associations and the preferred thinking mode of learners, helping facilitators to read the learner and modify communication to be in tune with learners and not just the sender.

Higher-education lectures increasingly use PowerPoint presentations: but they can so easily dull the senses. Such presentations can be made more stimulating using a variety of sensory techniques. In the business and the environment lecture the lecturer might tell students about the possibility of making a lot of things from recycled plastic (auditory dimension). This can be stepped up a sensory level by also holding up a fleece made of recycled bottles, and a carpet made out of corn (visual dimension). Samples might be passed around so that students can feel (tactile dimension) the softness of the plastic fleece. This sensory stepping has the tendency to gradually raise levels of interest and engagement. Video clips can be added, to emerge out of one of the photographs on screen: an internationally renowned speaker, Ray Anderson, for example, with a powerful presence, speaking to the US senate about greening business and sustainability. Traditional lectures can be transformed from a predominantly oratory experience to a multimedia (multisensory) experience, offering a richer experience in order to help a broader range of learners to engage and understand.

However, there are potential problems associated with the increased stimulation by the use of technologies. A counter-argument is that although technology enables us to influence people's senses, with ultraviolet light, strobes, the internet, computer presentations, iPods, large screen images and quadraphonic sounds, the overusage of multimedia can also create sensory flooding or sensory overload. Increasingly it might be that there is little or no space for thinking.

A single medium, rather than 'multimedia', can result in stimuli focus. An example of this in an educational setting is the use of 'digital learning objects': small bites of animation, audio recordings, assessment items, movie clips, still images and diagrams. With these 'learning objects' the educational content is broken down into constituent components, and these 'free-standing' components typically focus on a single educational objective or concept. Tutors are able to select learning objects on an individual basis and construct teaching materials from them as required. In the UK the learning networks of the Higher Education Academy are building cooperative banks of such learning objects for exchange.

Embodied learning in practice: walking and talking the learning

HE postgraduate students researching the history of the development of the environmental movement are given a 300-year database of important dates and other key information. This document has been developed over many years by previous professional environmental staff and in recent times by university students. This embraces the notion of 'inheritance' – whereby the materials developed by participants are passed on and further developed by the next generation of participants. Different groups of people research different issues starting with these inherited materials: environmental law, the voluntary sector, government departments and reports, and other significant events. The sheer volume of information and the sense of not knowing can be overwhelming, giving rise to anxiety. Over the weeks the whole group initially produce basic fact-sheets and folders (or Wikipedia) on voluntary-sector organizations, laws and other issues. These materials are also passed on to the next cohorts.

After several weeks of seminars, research sessions and discussion groups, a large integrative spatial map is constructed showing the history of UK environmentalism, either on the floor or a large table using a base template of laminated coloured cards given to each specialist research group: blue for laws such as the National Parks Act, yellow for NGOs, grey for quangos such as the Countryside Agency or Natural England, orange for key events in history such as the Second World War or the Mass Trespass. Colour coding can be a powerful learning tool or trigger. In addition, they use numerous other blank cards that they furnish with dates and other information. All the essential kit is presented to the students in a plastic video case.

The map, created by the students, reveals the extent of their knowledge of the subject and when finished students walk the talk (talk through the history while actually walking the time lines), right up to the present day. The students defend their case orally (viva) as they move physically through time offering a milieu of critical narratives, depending on their perspective and context. There are no 'right' answers. In addition, the walking and gesturing means that a kind of 'kinetic melody' is composed, as the embodiment of the journeyed narratives supports the learning. This walking and talking kinaesthetically aids learning, and reinforces the complexity of the scenarios, creating a kinaesthetic imprint, as understanding is tested in a visual–oral way. The experience thus consists of individual and group research, as they construct the historical map, and offer oral defence and further explanation.

The same process can be used for literature reviewing, or the examination of business products (see Beard, 2010). Texts are spread out in a large space and debated and discussed as people move around them – the spatial reorganization and debate is key. Students explore similarities and differences, creating multiple interpretations.

For a full account see Beard (2010)

Digital games and the design of multisensory experiences

Rather interestingly de Freitas and Maharg (2011) note that the adoption of game-based technologies has broadly followed an uptake curve associated with first the military, then medical, then business and later – and rather slowly – education. Gaming is an arena where the sensory interface is significant: gaming is multisensory by its very nature. Augmented and virtual reality are growing areas where the sensory enhancement is becoming particularly specialized. Whitton (2014: 168) notes that 'most modern digital games employ an array of media types, including visual elements, animations, cut scenes, and video, text, speech, sound effects and music'. Sometimes sensory augmentation can create sensorial overload and split attention, particularly if the senses compete in the engagement processes, such as a voice conflicting with what is being visualized in text on the screen. The tone and nature of the voice is also significant.

Sensory stimulation in learning and therapy

The only book titled *Sensory Intelligence* has been produced by Annemarie Lombard from South Africa (2007). The text is based on her experiences as a therapist and her work explores the impact of people experiencing positive and negative effects resulting from their differing sensory thresholds.

Purpose-built, multisensory spaces have been created for therapeutic work with children and adults with special needs. Using primary sensory stimulation and relaxation techniques, carers and patients share the sensory 'experience' together (see www.snoezelen or www.spacekraft). This sensory therapy is designed to allow individuals time, space and opportunity to enjoy the sensory components of the environment at their own pace and free from the demands of other thinking activities. The sensory environment provides pleasant sounds and music, light displays, appealing aromas and contrasting textures to stimulate the senses and improve the quality of life for persons with a variety of learning difficulties and physical problems. Pinkney (1999) states that the aims of this sensory therapy are:

- to provide a stimulating environment to heighten awareness;
- to provide an interesting atmosphere to encourage participants to explore their environment;
- to provide an environment offering security, allowing participants mental and physical relaxation;
- to provide an unrestrained atmosphere where participants feel able to enjoy themselves;
- to stimulate the senses in order to create a sensory picture;
- to stimulate the sensory building blocks that make up perception.

This list appears to offer a useful set of underlying conditions for any experiential learning activity. The company SpaceKraft manufactures white and black rooms:

> The white room uses light and sound and is accompanied with white furniture and walls to create an environment that can help relax, calm and stimulate individuals. This therapeutic environment has a proven record with clients with various difficulties, from profound and multiple to moderate needs. Mainstream schools are now recognizing the value of such a resource. Imagine the white room as a blank canvas where a colourful palette of lights is projected to give a stunning world of colour and imagery. Relaxing music gently plays in the background whilst the vibro acoustic seat resonates deep bass sounds through the body. All these combine to provide a powerful sensory experience and valuable tool for carers and teachers. The black room… black helps with particular visual problems; brightly coloured items against a black surface are easier to identify because the black does not reflect the light… UV paints,

shapes, bubbles and fabrics along with UV fun tubs are very popular... Ultra violet is also used extensively along with UV reactive equipment. Imagine the black room as a darkened theatre where occasionally a glowing hand-held object appears as if by magic. (www.spacekraft.co.uk)

Sensory stimulation, emotions and mood

Colours change our emotions: warmer colours have faster impulse or wavelength frequency. Room colours alter moods and can be adjusted using projection: coloured glass or plastic, or coloured light bulbs or overhead transparencies or electronic software. Red stimulates blood and is good for activity areas. Violet is good for sleep, calms the body and balances the mind. Blue lowers blood pressure and reduces stress, whereas green balances the body and is a spirit colour. Negative ions are known to produce good moods and these negative ion concentrations are found after rainstorms and around bodies of circulating water such as waterfalls, seashores and rivers. They may even be associated with shower water. Positive ion concentrations produce bad moods and are associated with smog or warm, dry winds (Thayer, 1996). Watching fire, listening to the flowing water and noticing the silence are powerful experiences. Breathing the clean morning air, savouring and appreciating basic shelter and food, and experiencing darkness are less common everyday experiences for increasing numbers of people. For stressed people these can be very welcome experiences. However, they must be treated like the volume control when listening to your favourite music: too loud and the stimulus can be painful, too low and it has little impact. The ideal stimulus solutions for learning lie somewhere in-between, and they can vary according to our needs and moods.

Nature-guided therapy

Rehabilitative strategies, using sensory stimulation, also occur in 'nature-guided therapy'. Burns (1998) explores the evolutionary connectedness of people and place and offers sensory stimulation as a central approach for therapeutic interventions. Significantly, he quotes the work of historian Roszak who lays responsibility for psyche–environment detachment in psychological theory and practice squarely at the feet of Freud, who, he says, actively steered therapy away from the outer world of nature: 'As much as any other Positivist philosopher of his day, Freud toiled under the influence of one of the most commonplace images in our language: the spatial metaphor that locates the psyche "within" and the real world "outside"' (cited in Burns, 1998: 4).

In bringing nature back into the work of therapy, Burns uses a sensate-focusing process involving nine stages:

1 Define the problem that needs addressing.
2 Define the desired outcome.
3 Assess whether ecotherapy is appropriate.
4 Formulate the therapeutic programme.
5 Select a relevant sense modality.
6 Create a sensate-focusing task.
7 Commit the client to the task.
8 Explore the post-task experience and learnings.
9 Teach ongoing sensate-focusing tasks.

CASE STUDY The exploration of self

Visual manipulation: using masks for self-development

Masks can serve as useful metaphors, particularly during times of change. Masks can assist in getting into the hidden and unknown (Johari Window, Luft, 1961). Masks can help to unlock ideas that normally remain hidden in the subconscious, and can provide a vehicle for the expression of these new insights (Johnstone, 1981). Creating masks can accelerate learning in a number of ways. Masks can:

- Deepen our understanding of ourselves as we surface and explore our unconscious or unacknowledged assumptions, which have been taken for granted (Schein, 1992).
- Focus on the uniqueness of each individual's situation; this is not a simple puzzle with a right answer but a complex issue with a range of possible solutions (Revans, 1982).

Sensory Experience and Intelligence (The Sensing Dimension)

- Use metaphor to assist us to identify (or clarify) our sense of self, our strengths and our 'overstrengths'.
- Access the creative side of our brain, which uses images, shape, colour and takes a holistic view.
- Take us beyond aesthetics and art – we are not creating pleasing objects that are gentle to the eye but are identifying strong statements that help us to explore within and express ourselves more fully.
- Provide the opportunity to work with others, gain feedback and support and have fun.
- Offer a hands-on, kinaesthetic activity.

Example: using masks in coaching and mentoring

Making masks engages the right creative side of the brain, using metaphor, symbolism and thinking holistically, using imagery. For many mentees, accelerating their learning through using both sides of their brain simultaneously is an unfamiliar and challenging process. Their typical work demands much of the left logical side of their brain, which engages in linear processes and language. Working in a kinaesthetic way can stimulate creativity, leading to unexpected insights and 'ah-ha' moments. These may not emerge through more usual mentoring processes that rely on only visual or auditory communication. Masks can be part of a process of expressing how you perceive yourself (Goffman, 1971). They can also provide an opportunity for gaining feedback on how you are perceived by others. This kinaesthetic process, involving feedback from others, can also help to unlock aspects of our subconscious mind. This technique can be used as a reflective tool to explore where one is, and also as a visionary tool for expressing how one wants to be, either in our career, or our whole life plan. Such processes form the core of coaching and mentoring practice. As mentors, we also need to constantly reflect on our practice and strive for self-development. Masks can also be valuable tools in our development: as mentors we should consider our shadow side or overstrengths. Do you recognize any of the following images in your mentoring practice?

- Mr Fix-it (always looking to deliver solutions);
- a mirror (merely reflecting back our mentee's concerns);
- a waiter (offering a menu of choices);
- a crow (pecking at certain issues);
- a wise old owl (dispensing wisdom).

In experimenting with processes such as mask making on ourselves, we will gain greater insight not only into our own professional practice but also into the processes we might suggest or employ with our mentees.

Vivien Whitaker and Toby Rhodes (for a full account see Beard, 2010)

Inner sensory work: presence and anchoring

In order to develop deeper sensing, the traditional view of reality, as perceived through our everyday stimuli of the senses, is best suspended. This facilitates entry into forms of unconscious learning. How can we do this? Senge *et al* (2005: 88) refer to three stages that can support deeper 'knowing': sensing (observe, observe, observe), presence (retreat and reflect and allow inner knowledge to emerge) and realizing (acting with natural 'flow'). Presence requires sensing from a deeper source, sensing the subtlety of the experience. This, they say, can result in a heightened awareness and a panoramic sense of knowing (Senge *et al*, 2005: 89). It is at this point we see the delineating boundaries of the Learning Combination Lock model disappear: in reality there are no boundaries between the senses, no boundaries between the mind, body and spirit, no boundaries between the inner world and the outer world, between self and others (including other fellow species). In Chapter 8 you can read a number of life experiences that illustrate and explain these phenomena and are found in the sections on naturalistic and spiritual intelligence.

Gardner (1993), in his work on multiple intelligence, makes reference to higher-level cognitive operations that go beyond 'an intelligence'. The '*sense of self*' placed the greatest strain on his multiple intelligence or MI theory, and this was a prime candidate for higher- or second-order ability. Intuition, presence, anchoring, flow experiences, peak experiences, and other similar phenomena all involve the engagement of higher mind states, and such states all appear to involve, to a varying degree, the engagement of the subconscious mind.

Sensory anchoring is a technique used to enter the subconscious mind, and involves a process of developing and holding on to the right mind state through conscious choice. An 'anchor' is a sensory stimulus such as an image, a piece of music, a perfume, or a smell that triggers a certain response in us, such as the ability to access certain mind states, to access certain feeling states, replace unwanted feeling states, or to experience an event or day in a different way. Anchoring develops an ability to tap into inner potential.

In a similar vein, the principles of accelerated learning also suggest that people learn faster when the mind–body–cell balance is in good condition. A mind state known as the *memletic state* concerns the balance of: environment–nature (natural rhythms, living things, sense of 'being'), physical (health and fitness, sleep and body rhythms), mental (relaxation, meditation, energy, calm, attention, concentration, sensing, intuitive), and the cellular (food, oxygen, water, toxins). Sensory work at this level is remarkably hard to describe and define but Gladwell (2005: 182), in his book titled *Blink*, offers an exciting array of everyday experiences and research experiments that describe unconscious phenomena of the mind. They are examples of how we *think without thinking*. He offers the example of expert food tasters who have developed a very specific sensory vocabulary, allowing them to describe precisely their reactions to specific foods. The following example from his book highlights the great potential for developing all of our senses to enhance learning from experience, by allowing subconscious knowledge to be accessed and developed:

> Mayonnaise, for example, is supposed to be evaluated along six dimensions of appearance (colour, colour intensity, chroma, shine, lumpiness and bubbles), 10 dimensions of texture (adhesiveness to lips, firmness, denseness, and so on), and 14 dimensions of flavour, split among three subgroups – aromatics (eggy, mustardy, and so forth); basic tastes (salty, sour and sweet); and chemical-feeling factors (burn, pungent, astringent). Each of these factors, in turn, is evaluated on a 15-point scale.

Conclusion

The senses significantly affect the learning experience and there is a need for more research into the role of the senses in learning. While the senses act as information conduits, perception plays an important role in the complex interpretation of incoming sensory data. In this chapter we have offered a number of examples where the senses can be used to enhance or reduce the experience of learning. The chapter has explored a range of indoor and outdoor activities that awaken the senses, as well as ideas for sensory enhancement and reduction, sensory flooding and solitude, the use of masks, and the applications of sensory work to higher mind states, learning difficulties and therapy. We have also explored sensory intelligence, the difficulties of the human language and the development of visual language.

A number of other chapters in this book also contain information on sensory stimulation and deprivation. The practical technique of developing a relaxed alertness as a mind state for study, for example, is covered in Chapter 7, as is the use of music or smell or other forms of mood-altering methods. Sensory reduction can also be used to create challenging obstacles, and these are discussed in sections on learning activities. Our senses also provide us with a mass of information that in turn can trigger certain emotional responses, and it is these emotional responses to experience that are the subject of the next chapter.

Experience and emotions   07

(the feeling dimension)

Emotions and feelings are the key pointers both to possibilities for, and barriers to, learning. MILLER AND BOUD (1996: 10)

Introduction

Historically, the expression of emotion has been associated with weakness and irrationality, and frowned upon in many institutions, yet emotions are inextricably linked to learning and development. Boud, Cohen and Walker (1993: 14) emphasized this perspective noting that 'Of all the features that we have mentioned, emotions and feelings are the ones that are most neglected in our society: there is almost a taboo about them intruding into our education institutions, particularly at higher levels.' John Dewey wrestled with the nature of 'experience' and 'experiential learning', and he expressed concern that the emphasis on the intellectual or cognitive side of people alienated them from their immediate environment, and thus from their emotional, affective self (Crosby, 1995). At the heart of this concern lies the question: 'To what degree is learning an emotional experience as much as it is an intellectual one?' What we do know is that memory is enhanced when there is an emotional element attached to a learning experience.

Emotions are of course connected to all aspects of our experiences, and life's emotional roller-coaster can be difficult to navigate at times. Earlier we described how in many therapeutic approaches emotions act as a compass for the therapist who reads the emotional compass, and act as an *emotional-experiential guide* for people to access their emotional self that sometimes is lurking in the subconscious. So it is with learning and life in general. Emotions are crucial to a stimulating and satisfying life, but people do not necessarily experience the right emotional waves at the right time, or place, size or frequency. Emotional aptitude can help access and surface unconscious feelings, to control negative thoughts and anger, and to reduce conflict. This can facilitate more understanding of feelings and emotions, allowing progress towards more productive behaviours that positively enhance learning and life: increased calm, the ability to challenge a belief set, or the development of increased sensitivity to self and others. Few people find sufficient time to step back into calm periods to reflect upon life and its ups and downs, and to learn from what has gone before. Emotional intelligence (EQ), it is said, can contribute to an improved life: through improved communication, increased team morale at work, more collaborative working, less energy wasted on politicking and game play, thus reducing poor attitude or indifference. Understanding and managing emotional intelligence might represent a good investment.

Eckhart Tolle (2006) suggests that emotions are the body's reaction to the mind, or a reflection of the mind in the body. Emotions arise at the place where mind and body meet: bodily emotions will give a truthful reflection of the mind. This helps to make clear links with our holistic model. In the previous chapter we made reference to the ground-breaking work of Nina Bull, who used hypnosis to explore body–emotion connectivity, showing that 'postural attitude' is vital to the ability to feel emotions.

Becoming aware of and understanding emotions, and the shifting emotional dynamics of learners, is a difficult but necessary skill for coaching or facilitating. Many emotions are perceived in simple terms as either positive or negative, but this can be unhelpful as negative emotions can take people out of their comfort zone and lead into deep transformational experiences, as we shall mention in Chapter 9. In this chapter, we focus on these roots of human emotions, how we can discover feelings and needs, and develop practical approaches to create space for people to consider their emotional response to an experience. We also explore some of the emotional underpinnings to experiential learning, and examine some of the subcomponents of emotions; for example, learning states, humour, fear, pain, identity and anxiety. We take a brief look at a range of new and old ideas that enhance positive change in people, such as mind fitness, imagination, sculpturing, rewiring, mapping, sensory awareness, emotional catharsis and release, the use of rituals, and spiritual feelings and sacred places. In the six-dimensional experiential learning model this is the foremost dimension of the internal state.

Fast thinking

The emotional response to incoming sensory data is subject to long-established neuronal connections in the brain. When people see, hear, smell or feel something, the sensory information is doubled up. One set of information is speedily sent along a short circuit to the amygdala of the brain, through split-second responses. This is *fast thinking*, System 1. The other set of information is logically analysed and reflected upon elsewhere, sent down by the slower route to the area known as the neocortex. This is System 2, or *slow thinking*. If a stimulus has been linked to danger in the past, then the region of the brain called the amygdala will spring into action. This amygdala is in fact the storehouse for emotional memories, and so is a major source of instant reactions and gut feelings, which are hard to ignore (Robertson, 1999). This quick response is mostly for survival, helping people to avoid anything from snakebites or bumping into people to car crashes. However, some fast responses are not always up to date and can be inappropriate in the fluid social world we humans now inhabit (Goleman, 1996). The sight of a dentist or the words 'merger' or 'corporate change' can instil fear and panic in some people, giving a strong irrational reaction in them. Rewiring or reprogramming some of these instant emotional responses to overcome negative feelings and create more positive feelings is a challenge many experiential providers face when providing appropriate training and development. We believe all facilitation requires a sound understanding of emotional intelligence.

Another way to understand these issues is to consider that there are essentially three brains in the human. The old brain is found at the base area where the spinal cord ends. It is reptilian-like, managing the automatic functions such as heartbeat, breathing and temperature regulation. This we will call the *functioning brain*. The middle brain is higher up and responsible for engaging fast emotional reactions, and this we will call the *feeling brain*. The new brain is advanced and particularly developed in humans, consisting of cerebral frontal lobes that do more complex, slower processing. This part is divided into left and right hemispheres. This we will call the *thinking brain*. Nobel Prize-winner in economics Daniel Kahneman has written a book called *Thinking Fast and Slow* (2011); by fast he is referring to the feeling brain, and he also calls it System 1 thinking. By thinking slow he is referring to the work of the *thinking brain*. His book examines some of the myths associated with the supposed primacy of these slow and fast thinking functions. One of the book's main themes is the author's description of how little control we actually have over our own System 1 responses and the degree to which our subconscious intuition, and human biases, affect System 1 choices. Much of our life operates on System 1 autopilot. One of the best pieces of advice he gives is to act calm and kind, regardless of how you feel.

The rational–emotional debate continues to attract attention from many disciplines; it has a protracted and contentious history. Over 2,500 years ago fundamental modifications of teaching occurred when the old 'reciting' of the Sophists was transformed to embrace a broader 'teaching of the soul' by the use of questioning by Socrates (Crosby, 1995). For Plato, however, emotions were inappropriate territory, as irrational urges that needed controlling, and for Kant emotions were regarded as an illness. Jay Griffiths (2006: 6), commenting on her school experience, remarks that 'emotions came only disinfected. The furies of grief and joy were somehow considered unhygienic, passion a nasty germ.'

Research work on emotions in higher education confirms the significance of emotions in student engagement in learning in higher education (Beard, 2005). The research data shows that students experience a very real emotional journey: one that affects their whole being, containing many significant events that influence their disposition to learn. The roller-coaster experience of 'flourishing or distress' states has adaptive tendencies operating to 'balance' the extremes of energy and tension, acceptance and rejection, pleasantness and unpleasantness, success and failure, solidarity and rejection. These emotions are undoubtedly private and personal but they are also strongly and inextricably linked to the social. Many emotional scenarios appear to contribute to the establishment and maintenance of student identity, and are grounded in significant social relationships. These social bonds with peers, family and lecturers create differentiation, an inherent sense of belonging, and they appear to be influential in the construction and development of self-esteem. Yet students find few spaces to challenge and express their feelings about their learning experience, and Mortiboys (2002: 7) comments that it would be disturbing if universities were emotion-free zones, but noted that 'curiously, so much of the culture in higher education implies that they are'. These deliberations continue to inform the extent to which thinking and feeling are connected.

Communicating with feeling

Marshall Rosenberg (2003), who studied and worked with Carl Rogers, suggests we can improve relationships and create more harmony if we learn to separate observing from judging by using non-violent communication (NVC). To align our lives with our core values he recommends we apply a four-stage model: first *observing* (without evaluating); second, understanding how we *feel* in relation to what we observe; third, to understand the deeper underlying *needs, values and desires* that underlie our and others' feelings; and fourth, the ability to make *requests* that might enrich our lives. At the core of this work is the fact that the human mind naturally classifies and analyses, and in doing so we so easily fall into the trap of giving bad or good judging 'labels' when we observe the behaviour of others. This in turn so easily leads to unproductive and/or destructive communication and interaction. Rosenburg suggests we learn to observe without moralistic judging, and to get to the heart of our feelings about others or self through understanding our unmet needs and the unmet needs of others.

Compassionate communication and compassion-focused therapy
Powerful theory and practice systems for education in the emotions

> Love and compassion are necessities, not luxuries. Without them, humanity cannot survive. (H H Dalai Lama XIV)

There exist today a fairly broad array of curricula and approaches for education in the area of emotional mastery. However, I will present here what I consider to be two complementary and uniquely powerful, research-based theory and practice systems for both understanding and teaching emotional awareness and mastery – Compassionate/Non-Violent Communication (CC), developed by Marshall Rosenberg, and Compassion-Focused Therapy (CFT), developed by Paul Gilbert. As will be summarized below, through both CC and CFT, we learn to apply a concept that is key to learning emotional balance: that our thoughts underlie our emotions, and that we can learn to transform 'thought habits', and thereby increase our emotional resilience. With CC and CFT, then, we learn to transform from blame and judgement thinking (a key contributor to most difficult emotional states), towards understanding and compassion, which are actually some of our deepest needs as human beings. We then become more able to access and express our higher (and happier, as CFT research shows) selves.

According to Rosenberg, our learned language of blame and judgement can lead to unconstructive and often damaging emotional states. Below is a simplified summary:

- Self-judgement thinking leads to… anxiety, shame and depression.
- Other-judgement thinking leads to… fear and anger.

The practice of the CC process, with time, facilitates an internal shift – as we learn to translate learnt (anger-inducing) blame and 'should' thinking to increased self-awareness, through looking at our underlying feelings and needs. We thus move from a sense of alienation (from ourselves and others), to a greater understanding and connectedness, through four main steps/processes:

- Learning to think and speak based on direct observations, versus biased evaluations.
- Acknowledging and taking responsibility for our feelings, by realizing that outer circumstances are just the trigger for our feelings; the cause is our blame-based thinking, and our attempt to fill needs is at the root. This leads to deeper self-understanding, and we are able to move from passive or aggressive communication to honest, assertive self-expression.
- Building an awareness of our (and others') underlying universal human needs (such as for well-being, connection/compassion and meaning). This creates true self-empowerment – by building an awareness of our underlying needs, as well as constructive thinking to help realize them.
- Learning to make requests versus demands.

Through the CC process, then, we learn to look and listen within. The CC 'needs-consciousness' facilitates an ever-growing process towards a more honest self-understanding: we become deeply self-connected, which Rosenberg says is perhaps the greatest use of NVC, and which then allows us to more compassionately connect with others. In the process, we build a sense of shared humanity and acceptance, with a realization that all human behaviour is an attempt to meet needs.

Both CFT and CC provide uniquely effective processes for working with one of the most challenging emotions of all – anger. Rosenberg uses the term 'anger transformation', for the process (described above) through which we learn to translate our blame thinking, to awareness of underlying feelings and unmet needs. The critical link between blame thinking and anger is well-documented by social psychologist Timothy Wilson, who reveals that blame thinking is significantly higher than average in parents who are physically abusive, and that interventions designed to teach new belief systems are effective in decreasing abusive behaviour.

CFT's founder, Paul Gilbert, has developed a three-pronged model of 'Emotional-Regulation Systems', which not only has powerful applications in emotional education work, but also highlights the benefits of CC (and CFT) practice. This meaningful, applicable and research-based therapeutic model is summarized below:

- The 'Threat System'– associated with anger and fear (or 'fight or flight') states.
- 'The Drive and Resource-Acquisition System' – associated with pursuits and 'wanting'.
- The 'Soothing and Safeness System' – associated with kindness, connection and 'non-wanting'.

CFT brain research has highlighted the power of this approach related to emotional resilience: among its core findings is that teaching people to shift from judgemental and unconstructive self-talk, to more compassionate, self-soothing internal dialogue, reduces depression and anxiety and increases happiness ratings. As Russell Kolts (a CFT practitioner) describes, teaching and practising compassion (for ourselves and others) develops the pre-frontal cortex associated with the 'Soothing and Safeness System' (where we are happiest), and at the same time weakens the amygdala area, associated with the Threat System. So CC and CFT both serve as an antidote to fear-based thinking; both systems help us dwell increasingly in the 'Soothing and Safeness System'. It should be noted that 'Mindful Self-Compassion Training' is a CFT-related approach, with similar practices (in an educational context), but was beyond the scope of this illustrative piece.

It is worth pointing out that the skills taught through CC and CFT systems incorporate the core areas of emotional intelligence, as defined by Daniel Goleman, primarily: self-awareness, emotional regulation (self-soothing) and interpersonal skills, such as compassion and assertive communication. It should also be noted that a key (proven) aspect in the effectiveness of both CC and CFT is mindfulness – *the ability (and commitment) to detach from our emotions through self-awareness.* As for educational applications, CC-based educational approaches include a broad array of exercises, centred on practising mindfulness in the four key areas of: observations, feelings-awareness, needs consciousness and requesting versus demanding. An example is the anger transformation process briefly mentioned above; another type of exercise that is foundational to CC work is empathetic listening practice. Two core CFT training approaches are compassionate imagery (towards self and others), and compassionate self-talk and self-coaching practice.

Based on deeply meaningful (research-based) theories and practices then, CC and CFT processes can provide a powerful foundation for educational work in the area of emotional mastery. CC and CFT theory and work can help us contribute towards, in the words of the late educator Paulo Freire, 'the creation of a world in which it is easier to love' – where we are better able to understand and connect compassionately with ourselves and one another.

Diana Kubilos, MPH, trainer, facilitator and programme developer, Malaysia (dkubilos@yahoo.com)

Emotion and experiential learning

Crosby (1995: 11) suggests that 'we find ourselves in continual transaction with the physical, psychological, mental, spiritual world, and philosophy should be a systematic investigation into the nature of this experience'. It is frequently the case with traditional education and training that emphasis is placed upon cognitive and intellectual considerations. In order for any experience to be interpreted as positive, learners require a number of constructive attributes, including confidence in their abilities and self-esteem in order to recognize the validity of their own views and those of others. Other attributes include support from others whom we work with and bounce ideas off, and trust to generate confidence in the validity of the views of others and be able to incorporate them with our own where necessary. It would therefore appear that, for learning to occur and an opportunity for learning not to be rejected, there has to be an attitudinal disposition towards the event.

In essence, the affective domain can be seen to provide the underlying foundation for all learning. Postle (1993: 34), in support of this perspective, quotes Heron as saying: 'Valid knowledge – knowledge that is well grounded – depends upon its emergence out of openness to feeling.' He continues by drawing on the work of Langer: 'the entire psychological field, including conception, responsible action, rationality and knowledge is a vast and branching development of feeling'.

Here it is important to explore briefly the notion of emotional intelligence (EQ), particularly given that more holistic approaches to human understanding are adopted in experiential learning. Emotional intelligence is defined by Bagshaw (2000) as 'the ability to use your understanding of emotions, in yourself and others, to deal effectively with people and problems in a way which reduces anger and hostility, develops collaborative effort, enhances life balance and produces creative energy'. The notion of emotional intelligence as 'EQ' was popularized by Goleman (1996) by building on the ideas of social intelligence as developed by Howard Gardner and others in the development of multiple intelligence (MI) theory. Goleman argued that having a high EQ was a different way of being smart, and his focus was on the emotional competence required to be a star performer. Some authors, such as Woodruffe (2001: 26), are more sceptical about such claims, arguing that it is not new territory. Woodruffe refers to emotional intelligence, in an article titled 'Promotional intelligence', as simply a new brand name for a set of long-established competencies. Woodruffe quotes one company making great claims that emotional intelligence can 'identify and develop better internal leaders, maximize productivity, create more effective teams, improve the selection process, reduce turnover, boost sales, improve organizational culture and morale, stimulate creativity and cooperation, and outperform the competition'. If only success in business were that easy to achieve.

Goleman also based much of his thinking on research by Salovey, who classified emotional intelligence into five main categories: 'handling one's emotions, managing emotions, motivating oneself, recognizing emotions in others, handling relationships' (Goleman, 1996: 46). To be able to understand this as an emotional basis to learning is of primary significance to experiential providers, who are increasingly called on to understand, manage and contain the emotional climate of their learners or clients. Fineman (1997) lists the work of many influential writers on the subject of the debilitating nature that anxiety, fear and stress have in interfering with learning, but notes that emotions are seen as 'unwanted' and 'undesirable' in the rational, logical workplace. The rules of emotional expression are corporately defined and there can be significant differences, as between individuals' privately held feelings and the emotion they display at work. These are some of the emotional issues addressed in high-ropes courses. The 'leap of faith' involves climbing to the top of a telegraph pole, releasing one handhold then another and standing upright, and then building up courage to leap towards a trapeze. Inability to reach the trapeze results in the safety harness kicking in; grabbing the trapeze results in an emotional high. Success, however, is about sensing and handling the fear and later transferring the learning to other life situations; these are key learning outcomes.

Managers learn to survive, learn how to avoid blame, learn how to operate in their organization and learn when to be deferential. These, according to Salaman and Butler (1990), are emotional behaviours that can help to avoid the painful experience of being singled out or blamed, and because we need allies. It is suggested that such fear-based management strategies in the workplace are likely to be ineffective and undesirable (Applebaum, Bregman and Moroz, 1998). Also emerging is popular literature on the negative aspects of fear-based parenting, citing evidence that young people, in these climates, are likely to self-destruct (Gray, 1999). Fineman (1997: 21) also comments that, in virtual working, networking and teleworking, 'managers will need to learn new ways of defining and expressing their feelings, status and identities, while developing alternative approaches to managing others' emotional lives under these working conditions'.

We experience an array of emotions, although researchers continue to debate which emotions might be of a primary nature. Goleman (1996) reports primary candidates as anger, fear, shame, sadness, enjoyment, surprise, love and disgust. Some primary emotions, such as fear, have an important impact on learning. Moods can be regarded as a subset of emotions, but they are said to be different from emotion in that:

> We can think of mood as a background of feeling that persists over time. Usually our moods are subtle, but sometimes they can be intense and overwhelm us. Moods are not the same as emotions, but they do have a great deal in common with them. Moods are sometimes defined as less intense and longer lasting than emotions, although this lower intensity isn't true in the case of serious depression. Unlike most emotions, moods don't seem to have an identifiable cause. That is, there usually isn't an obvious cause-and-effect relationship between our moods and events. This isn't true of emotions. (Thayer, 1996: 5)

Thayer regards the central dimensions of mood as a balance of energy and tension, and he says that mood indicates a greater tendency to do certain things. A person often says 'I am in the mood to…'. The experiential provider is expected to manage the mood and emotional climate of learners to varying degrees, but it is this energy–tension balance that is of significance, as a reduction in tension, for example, can increase energy levels. Moods are also heavily influenced by rhythms, and chronobiologists call these 'endogenous' biological rhythms, as they are governed by our internal biological clock. This internal clock becomes more apparent to us when we fly across time zones and the disrupted internal clock then makes us feel less alert or more energized in time with the old time zone, a phenomenon known as jet lag.

Thayer notes that energy levels rise to their highest levels in the first third of the day, until around noon. They then drop in the mid- to late afternoon, reach a sub-peak in the early evening and decline until sleep, thus creating the rhythmical wave of daily energy. Larger waves are created by seasonal variations such as the reduction of light in winter, and these too are of significance to mood. Moods are also influenced by exercise, food, drink and fresh air, and the daily energy wave underpins many of the basic strategies for the active management of moods. 'Positive, optimistic thoughts accompany positive moods: in other words moods and thoughts are congruent' (Thayer, 1996: 35). Thayer discusses state dependency, a phenomenon whereby, if we learn something in a particular mood state, we remember it better when we are in that same mood state, and Thayer, using a banking metaphor, suggests that there are separate mood memory banks for particular positive and negative moods.

The power of the emotional state

Morris (1969: 158) suggests that the object of any struggle is to experience 'optimum stimulation':

> When a man is reaching retirement age he often dreams of sitting quietly in the sun. By relaxing and 'taking it easy' he hopes to stretch out an enjoyable old age. If he manages to fulfil his 'sun-sit' dream, one thing is certain; he will not lengthen his life, he will shorten it. The reason is simple – he will give up the Stimulus Struggle.

Although this 'struggle' for balance in life, for optimum experience, is largely an emotional one, it can take on many dimensions. Megginson

(1994), now a retired HRD professor, writes down 10 goals each year. These are goals that he wants to achieve to create balance in four main areas of his life: his mind, his body, his emotions and his spirit. To ensure a consistent focus each day he sets specific 'SPICE' goals: spiritual, physical, intellectual, career and *emotional*: these help him either to stay on course or to change direction. Adler (2000: 6) in offering a 'Life Content Model' suggests that:

> 'Being' is the ultimate goal type. To be 'happy', 'content', or 'fulfilled' is as near as we get to understanding human desire… Quite simply doing, knowing and getting is with a view to being happy rather than sad. Some people, however, are 'being' people even on a day-to-day basis. They experience the 'now' rather than putting off being to some future time, which may never be. They take time to stop and smell the roses.

Deferment is a common way that reduces the value of life experience. The 'being' is always delayed until later: 'When I get this, then I will…' This presents a basic underlying life tension, an emotional imbalance of 'being' versus 'getting'. The phenomenon of 'being' emerges in many forms in the literature on experiential learning, psychology, adventure and sport. Yaffey (1993: 10) describes this emotional phenomenon of 'pure perception, uncontaminated thought and freedom to Be' as the key ingredients in the state of mind known as 'peak experience', a term originally coined by Maslow (1971).

We now examine more closely the nature of 'being', and we look at experiential opportunities that can create stimulation for optimum learning (see Figures 7.1 and 7.2).

Figure 7.1 Catching waves and finding calm

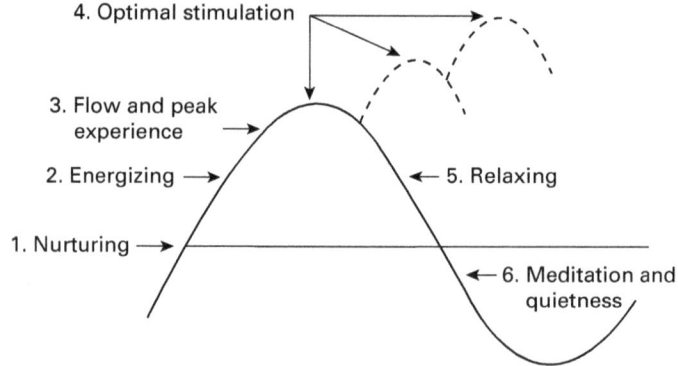

Emotional waves

The idea that life experience is a continuous stimulus struggle was a topic examined in *New Scientist* in an article called 'Thrill or chill' (Schueller, 2000), with photographs of white-water rafting, surfing, paragliding and other extreme sports. The article describes how some people will do anything for high levels of stimulation, to get an adrenalin rush, while others prefer the quiet life. People can of course get an adrenalin surge without jumping off a building or hang-gliding. Farley, a former president of the American Psychological Association, described how those who push the frontiers of the mind rather than the body could get an adrenalin rush through other means. He said, 'Einstein was way beyond the handrails. He was literally creating his own vision of the Universe. What sustained his mental life was the "thrill of it"' (Schueller, 2000: 23). Significantly, this adrenalin rush can also come during mentally demanding learning. As with any adventure, the pleasure comes once you have landed safely and the relaxing opiates called endorphins gush through the body; the natural ecstasy is produced from the learning, creating strong positive emotions. Experiencing a high can be exhilarating, a form of peak experience, and it can come in many guises. But providing learners with repeated high-energy activity may produce low returns for the learners if their optimal stimulation levels are exceeded (see Figures 7.1 and 7.2). High-energy seeking can also be overplayed. The troughs shown in Figure 7.1 represent emotional relaxation – calm waters, the lulls between the waves, the time to smell the flowers – and they are as important as the high-energy waves. Balancing the energy and the emotional waves is significant to the experiential provider's role.

Experiencing emotional calm

Finding emotional calm is essential sorting time. It is also time just to 'be', and involves stepping back and finding mental and physical space to think. A practical exercise in experiencing calm is given later in this chapter; it is an example of getting inner calm and stimulating the senses. Experience has to be reflected upon so as to make sense of it, by making connections to other experiences. So-called 'mindless' activities appear to have a clear function in that they allow the everyday sensory bombardment to cease for a while, allowing the mind to sort things out and take stock:

> The same sort of spontaneous sorting through of existing information occurs during certain mindless, rhythmic physical activities like jogging, swimming laps or mowing the lawn; or during habitual routines that no longer need the conscious brain's full attention, such as showering or commuting on the same route each day. Just as it does during sleep, this spontaneous process of reflection allows one to momentarily suspend the intense flow of new information to the brain. This enhances the processing of existing information, thereby preparing the person to handle the demands of the rapidly changing environment. (Daudelin, 1996: 39)

Daudelin (1996) offers some fascinating thinking on the process of reflection, and refers to the work of J Allen Hobson, professor of psychiatry at Harvard. Hobson's book, simply called *Sleep*, explains how sleep reduces the level of incoming sensory data and allows for the reorganization and storage of information already in the brain, thus better preparing people to handle the demands of the working day. This same sorting and filing also occurs during waking time, through activities that appear to be of a mindless nature. This is often what is happening in some adventure programmes when people plod the mountains or drift over water in Canadian canoes. Other activities include meditation, prayer or journal writing. Similarly, the garden shed or greenhouse is a place for people to potter, find space to be alone or to plan the day; there are classic everyday thinking alone times. We have already mentioned that the Outward Bound solo involves people being alone in wilderness. Voluntary castaways left alone on islands have provided unique television footage of personal interactions and relationships. Significantly, such programmes often contain interviews of people describing their unique and special place to be alone, whether it be a hilltop, a rock outcrop, a sandy beach or an old barn. They are personal places to think and sort things out, and the provision of this space is essential in experiential programmes.

Meditative experiences, for example, can generate more intense states of mind:

> There are many words for the extreme forms of joy. In the Buddhist tradition, it is called bliss and is considered to be a natural state arising from non-attachment and compassion. Meditation is a way of attaining it. When a person is no longer bound by his desires or emotional needs, then life can be experienced as bliss. Many other religious practices bring about ecstasy, literally standing outside oneself. In ecstasy we transcend time and space. (Wilkes, 1999: 256–57)

It is useful to explore these emotional states prior to, during and after experiential activities (for example, see the practical case study on flow learning through relaxed alertness later in this chapter). Fox (1999) offers three ingredients at the top of a list of 32 recommendations to experiential providers to encourage spiritual experiences: 1) allow time for relaxation; 2) allow time for solitude and personal reflection; 3) allow time to explore and interrelate with nature alone.

By combining the 'adventure waves' of Mortlock (1984) with the flow learning of Cornell (1989) and the work of Dainty and Lucas (1992) we can create a six-stage emotional wave (see Figure 7.2):

1 Create conditions for pre-contemplation – reading, thinking, imagining.

2 Awaken participant enthusiasm – ice-breakers and energizers.

3 Start to focus attention and concentration – medium-sized activities, narrow skills.

4 Direct and challenge the personal experience – larger, broader skills.

5 Share participant enthusiasm – using reviewing activities.

6 Encourage quiet personal reflection.

Energy waves are implicit in many other development models, such as the four stages of nurturing, energizing, peak activity and relaxing developed by Randall and Southgate (1980) and the gestalt cycle (see Figure 7.3). A six-stage programme developed by Porter (1999) can also represent a wave of change, and consists of entry, pre-contemplation, preparation, action, maintenance and relapse or integrated change. Throughout this book we focus on numerous 'waves' that form the holistic learning experience. Ice-breakers stimulate the first wave, and energizers add stimulation to subsequent waves.

Figure 7.2 Learning waves

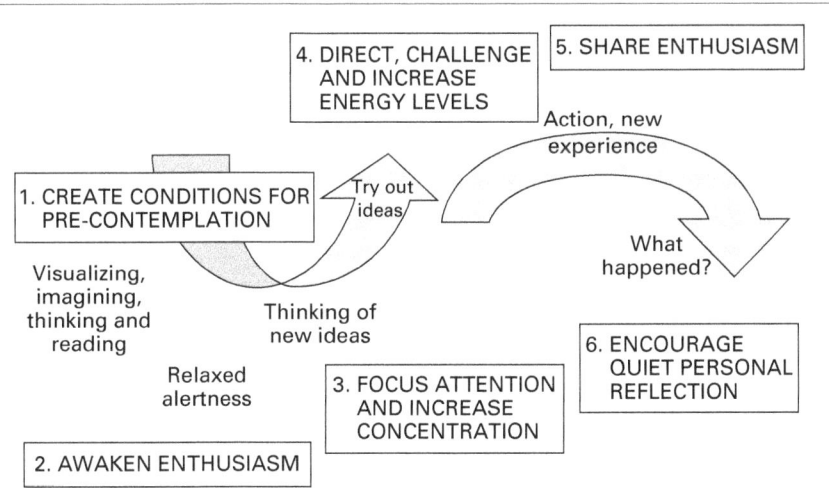

Providers encourage six stages (Upper case)
Learners complete six stages (Lower case)

Figure 7.3 The gestalt wave

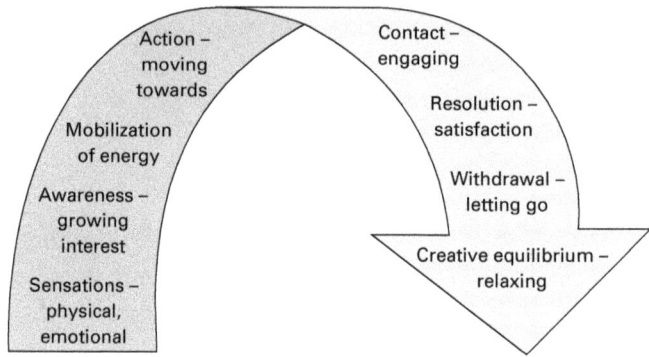

Pre-sensitizing exercises can increase the awareness of sensory systems and hence the experience itself, prior to a wave. The pacing of energy waves, and the sequencing of physical or mental activity, is equally important; rising waves can be full of adrenalin, whilst the subsiding wave can induce endorphins and cause calm and relaxation, important to reflection time. Too many waves of any one kind may result in habituation and reduced responsiveness and so monitoring energy levels is important.

Heron (1999: 233) refers to the ability of facilitator pace to influence energy and mood levels: speech modes *clock time* and *charismatic time* are two such examples. Clock time is 'verbally dense, fast, loaded with information, somewhat urgent and in a subtle way over-tense'. Speech in charismatic time is warm and slow, and tends to contain pauses and silent moments. The voice mode here is deeper, has clear, rhythmic inflections and sounds almost poetic. Clock speech waves are staccato in form, whereas charismatic speech waves are gentle and rolling. The voice is a powerful tool that can be used to create a range of effects.

Flow learning

'Flow experience' is considered by Macaloon and Csikszentmihalyi (Boniface, 2000: 66) and it is suggested that activities 'must be finely calibrated to a person's skills – including his physical, intellectual, emotional and social abilities'. The idea of matching activities to these four criteria within learners is clearly an important skill for learning providers in the design of enhanced learning. Getting people to focus and concentrate on a specific task, or to focus on an object in an almost meditative way, reduces or removes many other external stimuli, and removes attention from self-centred emotional needs; it is the basis of a powerfully positive experiential state of mind. It is a state of mind that leaves behind boredom and worry. In much of the literature relating to this subject, reference is made to these and other special and spiritual environments in the emotional, intellectual, physiological or physical sense. In literature on adventure, for example, Miles and Priest (1990) say that personal transcendence is also experienced when risk is courted and met, when we invite adventure into our lives.

Boniface (2000) offers an excellent analysis of these and other positive experiences, and refers to the work of Csikszentmihalyi, who suggests that people who are deemed 'beginners' do not experience the much-sought-after socio-psychological condition of flow, because beginners find the activity demanding, and conscious thought and/or anxiety are present in high levels: a form of conscious incompetence. In order to attain flow states, certain levels of experience, skill and conditioning appropriate to the level of challenge must first be attained, moving through levels of conscious (deliberate/clumsy) competence to unconscious (automatic/without thought) competence (Strangaard, 1981).

Opportunities for flow experience lie somewhere between tasks that are too simple and those that are too challenging. The relationship between perceived risk, level of challenge and personal competence thus appears to be a central factor in the flow-state experience. Such powerful experiences have also been referred to as 'peak experience' or 'peak performance'. These terms are used interchangeably, but there are some essential differences. Wilkes (1999) suggests that a flow state is a form of extreme joy: it is characterized by extreme concentration, a loss of self-consciousness and an altered perception of the passage of time. Athletes and artists experience it; indeed, she suggests that all activities that are perceived as highly meaningful can yield flow states. In competitive swimming some people are able to swim fast in a focused state yet see their own hands in slow motion flowing along the glistening water, and enjoy the experience with an almost out-of-body sensation. Jazz musicians, comedians and teams report achieving these flow states (Hopfl and Linstead, 1997). In intense creative artwork some people almost enter the picture and lose track of time. Csikszentmihalyi made specific reference to artists, and concluded that painters must want to paint, and that it was the students who were able to savour the emotional 'sheer joy of it' who went on to succeed as serious painters (Goleman, 1996: 107).

Flow or 'optimal experience' can be broken down to its constitutive parts. Csikszentmihalyi identifies them as 'conditions of flow':

- challenging activity requiring skills;
- clear goals and immediate feedback;
- merging of action and awareness;
- concentration on the task at hand;
- the paradox of control;
- loss of self-consciousness;
- the experience is autotelic.

To create these characteristics in learners would be ideal, as peak performance is associated with superior functioning, often described in athletes as having an underlying state of clear mental focus, combined with a highly energized state, relaxed yet adrenalin-ready, and in control and confident. Wilkes (1999: 250) argues about the design of programmes: 'we cannot make flow and joy happen, but we can provide the interior situations where they are most likely'. In Chapter 4 there is a very simple yet natural and practical example of how to encourage a form of relaxed alertness through reading, develop a playful approach to intellect and create powerful productive learning. Deep reading and deep thinking can be powerful parts of an experiential programme, and can give rise to original, indigenous learning.

Experience, learning and 'identity'

All learning is grounded in prior experience. The past consists of banked emotional 'experiences', and these can both drive forward and restrict new learning from experience. Elements of change represent the unknown, and can cause concern about the future: the comfort zone becomes overstretched. Why is it, however, that some people adapt to challenging experiences sometimes whereas at other times it is difficult? Risk can be high or perceived as high, but it is usually fear that underpins the deeper feelings of worry and concern. These fears become strong barriers for some; for others it is a powerful drive presenting an adventure. Martin, Franc and Zounkova (2004: 82) offer extensive coverage of psychological and emotional safety in outdoor learning, and they explore facilitator and participant psychological risk. What is suggested is that clear strategies are needed to predict problems, to reduce the intensity of activities when required, and to develop sensitivity to culturally mixed groups. The concept of 'challenge by choice' is often a foundation principle in outdoor learning, and the authors suggest that facilitators avoid pushing people to open up. It is also suggested that psychologically oriented activities are not presented one after another.

Fear is in essence the body's reaction to the mind, more particularly the egoic mind. The fragile ego is frequently under threat. Fear, often in a subconscious way, involves the identification with the mind projection to a threat of a future or past event, resulting in tension, worry and anxiety. The mind often seems to compulsively seek to avoid or escape from the immediate experience of the now, of the present moment. Yet being present in the moment shifts the self into a state of no worry or anxiety (Tolle, 2006). The need to attain the future, trying to get somewhere else as if the present is an obstacle, can result in a poor life experience as the present is in essence all we ever have. Elsewhere we refer to this as a deferring life habit as people focus on getting something, knowing something or having something that will give supposed meaning to life. This can so easily negate the immediate life experience.

Postle (1993: 34) addresses barriers on a more personal level:

> As I see it, we often cling, with the intensity of addiction, to the comfort that comes from staying with our preferred mode and keeping away from the other modes. I remain convinced that this is usually because at some point in our history, one or another – or all – of the four modes of learning may have become debilitated or ruined. If this debilitation or damage was severe, whether locally or generally, then staying with the preferred mode may also successfully defend us against the feelings associated with that early hurt. If so, then our interest in action, or dreaming up futures, or caring, or arguing, whichever most keeps quiet our painful history, can indeed come to have the intensity of addiction.

Attributing an experience with a positive or negative emotional interpretation may influence the degree and type of learning. Postle (1993: 37) describes three kinds of learning that inhibit us:

- omitted learning – lack of love in an upbringing, which results in a person being unable to receive or give love;
- distorted learning – can occur when a person is told that he or she is hopeless, not talented, etc;
- distressed learning – learning that occurs with distress in the form of forced learning and compliance.

These are significant issues to learning providers. Negative learning experiences significantly influence our outlook on life, how we interact with others and with our experiences, and even the extent to which we are prepared to venture into new learning experiences. Postle (1993: 38) emphasized the vast importance of previous experiences in the shaping or avoiding of future experiences:

> Distorted, omitted and distressed learning have vast power. They can drive people into the most bizarre forms of 'I have to' or 'I can't' behaviour. They compel us to devise and install incredible personal and social behaviour rules with the purpose of supposedly keeping us safely in our familiar 'comfort zone'. We may then go too often to the same parts of life's landscape and rarely or never to other districts.

Negative emotions and feelings can inhibit present and future learning. This may lead to the conclusion that a negative experience will also lead to negative interpretations about the experience. This need not be the case, and many of life's most powerful learning opportunities occur as a result of painful experience. People hate work when there is too much to do, and often dream of not having to work at all. Yet people fear being unemployed and celebrate finding employment. More significantly, what we do at work is often a significant element of the description of our identity, 'what we do for a living'. This point is also illustrated by Parr (2000). In her book on education and identity, she describes her research with mature women returning to education and how, on the face of it, their reason for entering education later in life is the wish to gain the qualifications they did not gain at the 'conventional age'. Digging below the surface, however, she uncovers more complex reasons. She declares that the reason to return to education was:

> as much about identity as it was about paper qualifications. It could have been described as a 'life-raft' for some students – as one of them said 'it's saved my sanity'. What emerged very clearly from what they said, was the desire to redefine at least part of their identity, to see themselves in a different way and exert a degree of control over some aspects of their lives. (Parr, 2000: 1)

Parr goes on to describe how, when people are questioned about their education and learning, superficial responses can be misleading. Many women, when a trusting climate was developed, talked readily of trauma in their lives. Some questioned the way in which they had been defined by others, and talked of the social pressures on women to conform to a particular identity. Some told of psychological, physical or sexual abuse, overbearing parents, alcoholism or the death of a child or other family member. For many there was an inner drive that steered their return to education, and it was associated with power and control, confidence building, independence, self-image or a desire to prove their ability. Despite the fact that a number of women had experienced their early school educational experience as largely negative, many saw their return to (adult) education as positive and therapeutic, as a form of cathartic leisure activity, by doing something for themselves for enjoyment. This presents an interesting juxtaposition of leisure and learning. Perceiving their learning as a 'leisure experience' and paying to learn made it more enjoyable and increased their motivation.

Practical ways to access feelings

> The razor blades are in a safe place (but I can't help noticing that length of rope in the garage!!!!)... I will phone you soon for some quality psychotherapy. Regards. (from a master's-degree student to her tutor)

In this section we further explore humour, metaphors, trilogies and storytelling as navigational tools to access and influence the emotional connections to the experience of learning. We offer additional ways to work with emotions in experiential learning, including techniques to surface feelings and challenge emotions.

Sensing, surfacing and expressing both positive and negative feelings require skill and care. Difficult feelings do not go away by being denied or censored: to deny feelings is to deny learning. Good practice allows the richness of the emotions of learning to be expressed in a way that maximizes understanding of learning processes. To access deep emotions in learning can be difficult, as there is associated risk. Emotions are often perceived as dangerous, unknown territory.

The emotional climate: mood setting and relaxed alertness

Learning is more effective if people are in the right frame of mind. In Chapter 6 we explored the psychological state known as 'relaxed alertness' as an optimum inner state for learning. Such a mind state requires the development of a certain ambience and mood, with the associated stimulation of certain senses. New tools continually enter the marketplace that are designed to stimulate senses and affect mood, and these include 'relaxation glasses' and 'mind-lab' audiotapes. Adverts exist for 'progressive accelerated learning', using state-of-the-art sound technology to create and encourage particular types of brainwave patterns. These apparently enable people to experience a focused state of consciousness and, because the brain gives messages to the body, sounds and light pulses can influence the physical condition. Music and stories, for example, can generate special moods or mind states: police advice to pubs is to play music from children's programmes to reduce aggression on the streets at closing time. Music affects the rate of breathing, blood pressure, pulse rate and muscle activity, and specific types of music can be played to correspond to brainwave activity. Music wavelength can correspond to welcoming, or the raising of energy levels, reflective mood induction or preparation for departure. Pulses of flashing light and sound vibrations are known to influence brainwaves and therefore mental and emotional states. Many writers comment on the power of music in facilitation and, in particular, in the importance of setting the atmosphere or learning climate (Benson, 1987; Robertson, 1999; Heron, 1999). Four main types of brainwave can be stimulated: alpha waves indicate alert relaxation, when the brain is open to new information and thought processes are clear and calm; beta waves are present in the state when we are most able to use critical faculties, solve problems and make decisions; theta waves are slower still and support creative thinking; delta waves indicate deep sleep.

Olfactory sensations are also important (Wilson, 1997: 282):

- Orange improves communication.
- Basil and lemon increase mental clarity.
- Pine is refreshing and inspirational.
- Ylang-ylang relieves anger.
- Bergamot is calming, and found in Earl Grey tea.

Many smells are now available as canned products, and they allow for experimentation with sensory stimulation to influence the mood and ambience.

A practical exercise: experiencing calm

Use before sorting time or solo time:

- Make yourself comfortable: find your own place to lie or sit relaxed with your hands down by your side or clasped on your lap.
- Read these instructions once and then proceed.
- Concentrate on the enlarged circle, below.
- First take three minutes to listen to your own breathing.
- Now concentrate on the exact middle of this circle

Use only your peripheral vision, and slowly stimulate your senses:

- see three objects around you;
- hear three sounds;
- smell three things;
- feel three things.

(You might have a slight feeling of an out-of-body experience.)

Robertson (1999: 240) describes how volunteers were easily tipped from sadness to elation by simple techniques. He describes some simple experiments he conducted, such as how simply pulling eyebrows upwards for a few seconds can change people's mood. Moment by moment the brain is changed by experience: by what people think, see, hear or remember. By using a variety of relaxation exercises and brain gymnastics, Robertson suggests that people can make their experience more effective.

Overcoming fear

Emotions influence everyday behaviour, and they can have a distorting effect on learning. Johnson (1996: 185) describes in detail a case study where he changed powerful, fear-based blockages in a person in a maximum-security prison, a rich context in which to explore ideas about working with experience on such emotional issues. Johnson reports that he 'tapped into his emotions... unblocked an emotional dam, unfroze his major emotional plumbing and facilitated his renaissance'. Some of the basic issues addressed in this and the previous chapter are that anger and aggression are often based on fear, and that trust is a strong antidote to fear. Fear is one of the strongest primary emotions, which can be both conducive to improved learning and toxic to learning. Fear is the result of powerful emotional circuitry embedded in the brain resulting in a conditioned response. Mallinger and De Wyze (1993) describe these fears as being present in many people and they describe people who pride themselves on being reliable, hard-working and self-disciplined; they are indeed regarded as perfectionists. Their offices and homes are neat and organized, and they are always in control. They are successful and financially secure. The downside is that although they may be confident and poised on the outside, they may be hurting inside, for their standards are so high that they constantly set themselves up for disappointment, and such perfection may prevent them from enjoying life and even forming relationships. Being too much in control can result in being out of control. Such fears need managing so as to create balance. Learners with signs of being 'too perfect' might have:

- a fear of making errors;
- a fear of making the wrong decision or choice;
- a strong devotion to work;
- a need for order and a firm routine;
- emotional guardedness;
- a tendency to be stubborn or oppositional;
- a heightened sensitivity to being pressured or controlled by others;
- a need to know and follow the rules;
- an inclination to worry, ruminate or doubt;
- a need to be above criticism – moral, professional or personal;
- a chronic inner pressure to use every minute productively.

(adapted from Mallinger and De Wyze, 1993)

The research that produced Mallinger and De Wyze's book, *Too Perfect*, was initially conducted on neurosis, but many of the doctors professionally associated with the authors commented that the findings were close to many of their own behaviours. The book describes how being overly in control can get completely out of control, encouraging people to look at their own mental scars produced as a result of fear. The suppression of fear, a fear of the truth, of how it actually is, is a reason for much misguided behaviour, especially managerial actions at work when there is reluctance to be honest, with other people and one's self. People often fail to see that there is something fundamentally wrong. Harvard professor Chris Argyris describes how this phenomenon affects communication at work. His article, 'Good communication that blocks learning' (1994: 77), says:

> What I have observed is that the methods these executives use to tackle relatively simple problems actually prevents them from getting the kind of deep information, insightful behaviour, and productive change they need to cope with the much more complex problem of organizational renewal... and they do not surface the kinds of deep and potentially threatening or embarrassing information that can motivate learning and produce real change.

The communication blockage can be further illustrated by reference to the communication model in Figure 7.4. People are experts at rituals and cliché, gossip, fact, solutions and judgements at work. It is the 'functional communication' of work, for some managers. The communication triangle has significance for experiential learning providers, in reviewing and reflection

Figure 7.4 The communication iceberg

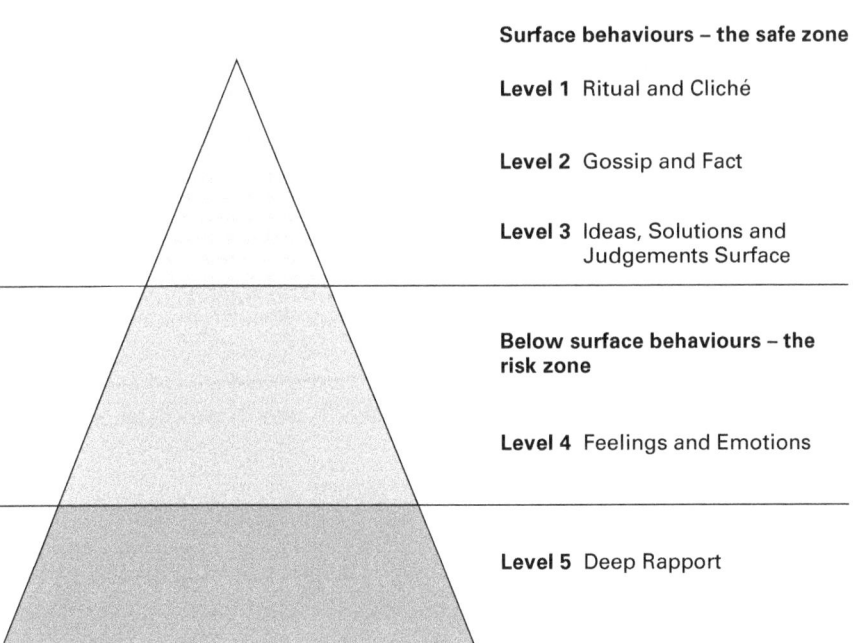

skills. If learners are not in touch with their own fears, emotions and feelings, then a priority need is to help them to access the right levels of inner communication through deeper levels of rapport, to move beyond the superficial haze of rituals and cliché, facts and solutions.

Argyris (1994) argues that logical, robust, solutions-focused behaviour is not always appropriate and that in the name of positive thinking managers often suppress what everyone needs to say or hear. In a self-protective haze of defence, single-loop responses provide single-loop solutions. The fix-it hat is donned and the same old fix gets the same old responses. Trusting others to make mistakes is part of the process of letting people learn, yet managers when coached to let go of being in control describe feelings similar to having had addictive cigarettes taken away. There is a sense of redundancy in not being able to fix:

> It is not difficult for people to identify with the notion that work life is 'emotional'. Fear, worry, contempt, envy, anger, infatuation, loneliness, pride, joy, guilt, tedium and so forth are embedded in working experiences – to a greater or lesser degree. The extent to which they are overtly expressed, or publicly admitted, depends on the nature of the individual and the openness of the organization's culture. Emotions can be seen to shape, and be shaped by, myriad work actions, such as decision making, training, selling, persuading, hiring. Learning – creating, retaining and reproducing new knowledge or behaviour – can be regarded as implicit or explicit to these activities. (Fineman, 1997: 13–14)

Learners do tend to talk more easily about any emotional elements of experience in the past tense rather than the 'here and now' but experiential providers can encourage learners to speak about their experience in the 'here and now', in continuous dialogue. Sometimes a range of questions, such as 'How are you feeling right now?' when a person is on a high-ropes course, can be the simple trigger required to surface the inner feelings. Similarly the question, 'Has anyone else had these feelings?', can encourage other members of the group to become aware of and express their feelings. Observation of body language by providers, especially facial expressions, and carefully and gently feeding back what is seen, can also be a trigger for learners to express feelings.

Mapping and accessing emotions

Experiential learning providers use techniques to help participants map out fears. By revisiting past experiences some of the unwanted circuitry in the brain can be rewired. 'Fear maps' can be created – and then rewritten.

Asking people when they have been sad, bad or glad in their life can be a very productive start to this process. Recent research in higher education used emotional maps to highlight the roller-coaster of felt emotions, and the importance of identity and relationships over the student year (Beard, 2005). Maps can also be used to help people see where they have been or want to go to. Take the London Underground map. The real rail lines do not travel in straight lines as the map would have us believe, but if the map showed reality it would be far harder to use.

In a critique of Kolb's theory of experiential learning, Holman, Pavlica and Thorpe (1997) argue that this learning theory is placed within the cognitive psychological tradition and tries to explain social, historical and cultural phenomena in a very mechanical way. However, far from 'functioning systematically and mechanically, a person's inner life reflects interpersonal transactions, for example conversations and dialogues. In this way, thinking, even when alone, always remains quasi-social' (1997: 140). What they are saying is that people talk to themselves; we all have our inner dialogue. Before a difficult or undesirable event this inner talk can be destructive or positive. Thinking and reflecting through the inner talk is a quasi-social phenomenon, because we have inner conversations with ourselves through these other inner people. In Chapter 9 we refer to this in *The Inner Game of Tennis* by Gallwey (1986). Wilkes (1999) in *Intelligent Emotion* has a chapter devoted to 'The people who live within us', and recommends that people train and develop their own inner family. She suggests that 'our culture encourages us to think of ourselves as one person and no more' (1999: 39).

Psychologists have called the main personality the ego, which is Latin for 'I'. It is usually the leader of the family but if it becomes too dominant all the rest of the family are silenced. Using positive affirming language can overcome some self-destruct language of this inner family of the self, as sometimes just one inner person takes control of the others. However, there are ways to take back control. One voice inside the mind is the critic, talking all day long, and seemingly setting many of the rules by which we live. Challenging these rules can be very useful: these rules create many negative and destructive thoughts. Characteristic 'critic conversation' is 'I must never make mistakes', 'I must never look foolish'.

These same rules underpin everyday fears. They have a powerful effect on people, and experiential learning providers can encourage people to re-examine them: underlying these rules is the fear of losing control. Many people do not change behaviours due to fear of what might happen. Fear of losing control or fear of finding something out that cannot be faced, about self or others, can give rise to hesitation and apprehension. The inner voice

Figure 7.5 The Johari Window

	Known to self	Not known to self
Known to others	Arena	Blind spot
Not known to others	Façade	Unknown

says it is safer to do it the way we have always done it, resulting in compelling passion to control oneself and others. The Johari Window (Figure 7.5) is useful in exploring these issues. The Johari Window is used regularly by experiential providers to examine how people approach others. It was created by Joseph Luft, a psychologist, and Harry Ingram, a psychiatrist (hence the origin of the name – the Joe and Harry window!). The window shows four panes. The top left-hand window, for example, contains the aspects of self that are known to self and are evident to others. The façade covers aspects that are known to self but hidden from others.

Control brings more apparent safety, comfort and security, in a world surrounded by machines and computers that control the environment. Getting away from mobile phones, satellite systems and predictable, regulated environments might explain why some people stretch themselves by seeking rescue-free wilderness. High-ropes courses are now commonly used in many countries to demonstrate a range of basic emotional responses to challenges. These techniques focus on the emotional base to learning. One development centre we visited had pictures on all the walls showing exciting images that represented many of the basic emotions in life, such as fear and challenge. One image of a sailing boat had a caption that said that a boat was safe when it was in the harbour but that was not what it was designed for.

Learning providers can also help people to address fear with less dramatic methods, asking people to spring-clean – with three steps – the inner rules that sit in their unconscious mind. Learners can rewrite their own rules and realize that it is okay and human to make mistakes. Learners can learn to value themselves, warts and all, loosening the grip of perfectionism:

1 The rule (the left-hand column):
   I must never show my nerves in public.

2 Which really means (the right-hand column):
   I couldn't stand the embarrassment if people saw me looking flushed and nervous.

3 So we revise the rule:
   I prefer not to show my nervous feelings in public… but if I do people will understand. Importantly it would not be the end of the world. Most people feel nervous about these things at one time or another. I might not like it but I can cope with it.

Using trilogies in emotional work

Benson (1987: 203) makes reference to the *I Ching* (Book of Changes) and suggests that the clever experiential group worker should 'use allegories, figures, wondrous speech or other hidden, round-about ways, to convey meaning and resolve difficult situations'. Popular, well-known trilogies are also used to help resolve difficult emotions.

They help people to get in touch with the unconscious inner environment, helping them to read and interpret what is happening, especially cause-and-effect thinking, and so enable them to move towards positive change and transformation. Breaking down the mind processes into simple steps and grasping what is generating external actions and behaviours can be a powerful experiential event for people. Frank (in McLeod, 1997: 25) notes that 'it can be demonstrated that in all human societies people experience "problems in living" that are dealt with through a combination of listening, reframing, catharsis, interpretation and behaviour change'. Many writers have recommended a variety of basic steps for iterative change, which are commonly used in development training. They have a gestalt feel to them in that the steps help concentrate on the 'here and now' of feelings and so paradoxically result in change.

Calmly speaking the inner feelings is a vital step. Anger as an expression of emotion is alright, but the direction in which anger is sent is more significant: how it is sent and to whom it is sent are key concerns. In dealing with our anger and other emotions we see the usefulness of these trilogies. Anger is actually designed to protect people from a perceived threat, and so they cannot be angry unless they are also afraid. Fear then can induce anger but, when people want to try alternatives, an anger-management relaxation technique can be used, as shown in trilogy two, below. What is so interesting is that there are many such trilogies and they are all so similar. Assertiveness, negotiating, giving and receiving feedback, and criticism training all have common roots in three-step trilogies (see trilogy four). Significantly, all of these trilogies, according to Wilkes (1999), are based on trilogy six, which is the basic trilogy.

Altering the mind: six trilogies for change

Trilogy one: the emotional intelligence

1 **Red light.** Stop; calm down; think.
2 **Amber light.** Say the problem and how you feel.
3 **Green light.** Go ahead and try your best plan.

(Goleman, 1996)

Trilogy two: the self-anger control trilogy

1 First, say **stop**; I don't like this.
2 Second, take a **deep breath**; during exhalation, relax face, mouth, jaw, etc; take a deep breath in; during exhalation, relax hands, shoulders, arms.
3 Lastly, continue with a **slower, more controlled pace**, trying new, less angry behaviours.

(Lamplugh, 1991)

Trilogy three: the calming trilogy for use on others

1 **Calming** the person. Focus on calming his or her emotions, not logic.
2 **Reaching.** 'Uh huh, I see…' (nodding). 'We can sort this out by…' All of this is to develop gradually a less emotional base to the talking, with open-ended questions.
3 **Controlling.** Break down the issues into their basic components and move towards solutions.

(Lamplugh, 1991)

Trilogy four: used in assertiveness, feedback and negotiating

1 **Listen** to what is being said and show that you understand – don't deny, defend or justify.

> 2 **Focus** on the issues and facts, and seek clarification.
>
> 3 **Move** towards a solution and agreement on the solution.
>
> (Fritchie, 1988)
>
> Trilogy five: to dispute the internal voice of defeat – the critic
>
> 1 **Thought stopping.** As soon as you hear it, say 'Stop it' to yourself.
>
> 2 **Challenging accuracy.** For example, 'Would I really like myself if I were so perfect?'
>
> 3 **Making the negative purposeful.** Replace 'I cannot do it' with 'This is a real challenge for me.'
>
> (Wilkes, 1999)
>
> Trilogy six: the basic trilogy map
>
> 1 **Revise** the past.
>
> 2 **Revitalize** the present.
>
> 3 **Redirect** the future.
>
> **SOURCE** Wilkes (1999)

Using humour and other positive emotions

People can also release excess emotions such as anxiety through relaxation and fun, and the function of ice-breakers and energizers is to do just that. We often ask new university postgraduate students if they think it is possible to have intense experiences that create a state of ecstasy while studying! We are of course referring to flow experience, but they still laugh. However, endorphins are generated by certain physical and mental activities. A sense of humour can be a powerful influence on learning, and studying can become a form of play.

Humour can be a way of facing, making light of and communicating to others the stress that is being experienced. Cognitive and affective learning are not separately lived phenomena.

One reason for being interested in the role of humour, as an emotion in learning, was that we wanted to encourage students to 'let go' of their obsession with grades, and instead to access and gain a greater understanding of the underlying emotions and feelings that influenced their ability to learn. We wanted them consciously to experience flow, take more risks, make learning more fulfilling and let the grades take care of themselves. Some people can connect to their feelings through humour. Real student–lecturer correspondence on distance learning programmes is shown in the four examples below.

Humour in learning

1 'This presentation is a vast improvement on your first assignment, from which my optic nerves are still recovering', said my tutor on reading my attempt as a student at using a draft standard dot-matrix printout.

'Positively my last fling! You asked for "lots of comments" – and I have surpassed myself, and I am now off to immerse myself in an extremely large gin and tonic. Not to drown my sorrows but merely to recuperate', said my tutor on reading the last edition of my 'draft' dissertation!

2 Some student humour during the stressful last leg in the period of doing a dissertation: 'Would it be better to lump the data together? What do you think? Does it make sense? (Sounds like a song!) The razor blades are in a safe place (but I can't help noticing that length of rope in the garage!!!!)… I will phone you soon for some quality psychotherapy. Regards. PS Someone told me you can buy these [dissertations] on the world wide web?'
(Extracts from a letter to me as a tutor, sent from a Senior Training and Development Officer at a major UK hospital studying for a master's degree)

3 'Well, it's now 12.30 in the morning and I think I should go to bed. This has been a useful exercise for me, even if tedious for you. I look forward to any pearls of wisdom you may wish to cast in my direction. Goodnight!'
(Senior Training Manager, London Underground)

4 'Dear Colin, I have added to my draft in the past two weeks but still feel frustrated by a lack of real headway, combined with a growing feeling that I'm not really sure what I'm doing!!'
(Training Manager, Magistrates' Courts)

SOURCE Beard and McPherson (1999)

When people look up to the sky, put on a happy face and smile, it can make them feel good (Robertson, 1999: 241). People can be encouraged to experience sad feelings by slouching with their shoulders low, with head bowed and eyes looking down at the floor. Holding the eyebrows up high for a minute can make people feel more positive. Adopting positive physical postures does work and, for example, it is worth doing before dealing with difficult issues.

Accessing emotions through popular metaphors

Metaphors present a powerful tool to access and explore feelings. A single word can possess multiple meanings; yet as the common saying goes, one picture can be worth a thousand words. And if one picture can be worth a thousand words, then one experience can be worth a thousand pictures. And if an experience can be worth a thousand pictures, then one metaphor can be worth a thousand experiences. But in the end, a metaphor only possesses value when:

- it is able to interpret the experience;
- in a manner that provides a picture;
- that produces words;
- that have meaning;
- for that particular person.

(Gass, 1995)

Metaphors can be used to help people to understand that which might otherwise remain misunderstood or unobserved. Visual–spatial intelligence, for example, can be stimulated by metaphoric interpretations, by developing the ability to learn directly through images and thinking intuitively without the use of verbal language. Heron (1999: 102) suggests that in facilitation, theoretical inputs can be enriched by interweaving them with a variety of imaginal inputs. He offers seven examples:

- **metaphor** – the imaginative use of myth, allegory, fable and story to convey meaning;
- **instance** – describing an illustrative incident, or dramatic case study, from real life;

- **resonance** – recounting associations and memories evoked by what is going on, in order to find meaning through resonance with the form of the other situation, which may be from some quite different field;
- **presentation** – presenting non-verbal analogies in the form of graphics, paintings, music, mime or movement;
- **dramaturgy** – combining metaphor with presentation in a creative piece of theatre;
- **demonstration** – showing in your own behaviour, both verbal and non-verbal, what it is you mean; modelling a skill in action, positively showing it well done, and negatively showing how it can degenerate;
- **caricature** – giving feedback to someone by mimicking his or her behaviour and caricaturing, in a kind way, the salient features to which you wish to draw attention.

The imaginative use of myth, metaphor, allegory, fable and story to convey meaning is the focus of this next section. In the 1960s and 1970s environmental campaigners helped people to 'see' concerns about the earth, using titles like *Silent Spring*, *The Population Bomb* and *Only One Earth*. In 1993 a popular book about communication between men and women hit the headlines. It was called *Men are from Mars – Women are from Venus* (Gray, 1993). On the back of this book the promotional piece said:

> Once upon a time Martians and Venusians met, fell in love, and had happy relationships together because they respected and accepted their differences. Then they came to Earth and amnesia set in: they forgot they were from different planets. Using this metaphor to illustrate the commonly occurring conflicts between men and women, Dr John Gray explains how these differences can come between the sexes and prohibit mutually fulfilling loving relationships.

A metaphor can provide another way of reflecting and focusing on a particular experience, so allowing us to gain new insights. A metaphor is a figure of speech that transfers meaning. The word itself is derived from the Greek *meta* (trans) and *pherein* (to carry). According to Parkin (1998), a metaphor is a comparison, a parallel between two, sometimes seemingly unrelated, terms. Metaphors tend to be used to help people to 'see' or 'connect' in their minds, to and from real or imagined inner and outer worlds. Providers of experiential learning often consider the activities as being more of a medium for learning, a means to an end, and see the value in the process of learning rather than in the nature of the activities per se. The activities employed are important though, as, in theory, they often serve as metaphors in themselves and so strengthen the potential connection between the programme and the workplace (Gass, 1992; Gass and Priest, 1998), ie metaphor is the analysis of experience.

Morgan (1997a), in his book about organizations, offers a unique and original mechanism to help us to see, understand and manage organizations. He does it through a series of different metaphors. However, he also offers a word of caution and suggests that insightful learning through the use of seductive metaphors has its limitations: 'Any given metaphor can be incredibly persuasive, but it can also be blinding and block our ability to gain an overall view' (1997a: 347). In other words, metaphors can create ways of seeing and ways of not seeing. Using many different metaphors can thus help us to overcome the limitations of others. Morgan offers 'Bibliographic notes' towards the end of the book, and explains in some detail the historical use of metaphors. He describes how Aristotle suggested that the metaphor was midway between the unintelligible and the commonplace. In a similar vein Black (1979) developed an 'interaction theory' of metaphor and suggests that metaphorical statements have a primary subject and a secondary subject, and that the metaphor works by projecting the characteristics or implications of the secondary subject on to the primary subject, with effectiveness due to the degree of resonance between the two.

Feelings about work are so often expressed in metaphorical terms: 'I am just a small cog in a big machine'; 'I'm in a new team creating a work of art!' Picture-based metaphors help with a way of seeing, thought-based metaphors illustrate a way of thinking, sound metaphors guide a way of hearing, emotional metaphors access a way of feeling and activity metaphors can illustrate a way of doing things. Parkin (1998: 10) in her book on storytelling explains the use of several ingredients in a personal metaphor, using a common saying, 'My head is as heavy as lead', where:

- The **topic** is head.
- The **vehicle** is lead.
- The **ground** is the feeling of heaviness.
- The **tension** is dissimilarity between the two domains, ie lead is metal and the other is head or flesh.

In therapeutic work metaphors help people to surface unconscious thoughts and feelings. The metaphors connect the conscious mind with the unconscious mind. 'Trust' and 'fear' in participants might, for example, equal loss and exposure. In dealing with addictions, trauma or abuse, much of people's sense of existence or personality is beyond their awareness, and the therapist helps to apply the metaphor based on a client's behaviour (Stouffer, 1999). The client creates this self-metaphor with the help and guidance of the therapist, to help access his or her sense of being.

Corporate metaphors are likely to be very different. Metaphors can be used, for example, as concept-forming in a corporate event designed to connect an experiential activity to workplace production issues. High-rope challenges can represent the challenges of real life. Cliffs can represent the challenges of a giant project or that daunting change in life that an individual might have to face. Finding good metaphors that enable us to see things differently requires skilled experiential providers. Benson (1987: 204) suggests that instead of coming at problems from rational deliberation and logic, which can lead to protectionism and defence, metaphors can be more intuitive and spontaneous:

> Every method, exercise, or technique then as I use it, is a metaphor: a way of shifting perception and creating meaning. I am not interested in any medium or technique as an end in itself but as a means of engaging people and providing a context for work, which is directly related to the members' level of ability and willingness to act. From this perspective the value of any technique lies not in its skill or knowledge base but in what it points to, its ability to act as a signpost, open up dialogue, and encapsulate meaning.

A metaphor can also be introduced through storytelling, or through cartoon images. These can be powerful ways to reinforce learning from experience, in both the unconscious and conscious. Cartoons, art, drama, models and conceptual frameworks are all enabling media that allow us to readjust our perceptual field, our ways of seeing and understanding the world. They can be powerful cathartic tools, simplifying and reducing complexity on the one hand, but also making emotional issues easier to grasp and comprehend. Many of these techniques were discussed in Chapter 5, where we explored the adjustment of experiential reality. In this chapter we explored the possibility of accessing, in a metaphoric sense, the 'inner family' of people within our minds. This requires careful listening and the construction of metaphors of the person, or 'self-metaphors'.

In the global Outward Bound movement there has long been a debate about letting the experience speak for itself. Rustie Baillie, back in the 1960s, then a course director at Colorado Outward Bound in the United States, first coined the phrase, 'Let the mountains speak for themselves' (Bacon, 1987; James, 2000). Later, Outward Bound included the 'Metaphoric Model' to raise awareness of the metaphoric nature of the activities (Hovelynck, 2000). Gass (1995) in his *Book of Metaphors* offers a clear and concise approach to the use of metaphors in adventure programmes, where the matter of letting the experience speak for itself is located alongside many other techniques. He examines the pragmatic use of metaphors in development work, building on his background in therapy, and argues that metaphoric transfer of learning takes place when parallels exist between two learning environments. A metaphor is an idea, object, process, environment, task or description that is used in place of another different idea, object, process, environment, task or description to help people to see or make a connection to reality. If the connection is through an idea, object, process, environment, task or description that is actually identical, and 'real', then the connection is said to be isomorphic (see Gass and Priest, 1998 for a description of examples). The classification offered by Gass is fashioned from the work of Bacon and Kimball in 1989 (in Gass, 1995). Gass created different facilitation techniques, based on six generations of facilitation skills that have evolved over time. In order to demonstrate the purpose and function of the six techniques, Gass uses the internationally well-known outdoor exercise called the Spider's Web. The Spider's Web is an exercise that uses a descriptive metaphor, and involves people trying to get through but not touch a mass of cord usually tied between two trees to create the spider's web. We have rearranged the six examples so that techniques that can be used prior to the event are presented first. Thus:

- *Prior to the activity* taking place the facilitator would ask questions that focus the learning that might occur. The facilitator **directly frontloads** the experience.
- *Prior to the activity* the facilitator would set the scene or context of the activity so as to relate it to the specific learning, eg to the work conditions of participants such as the problems of loading in a warehouse environment, or to the reception desk team, etc. The facilitator **frames** the experience.
- *Prior to the activity* the facilitator might deliberately but indirectly make reference to fictitious events to try to prevent certain behaviours occurring, eg 'We had a group last week that did this and failed because everyone put their "fix-it hats" on and moved straight into solutions mode, preventing discussion from...' The facilitator can **indirectly frontload** the experience.

As we remarked earlier, experiential learning programmes move from *introduction* to *action*, to *reflection* and *transfer*. These four stages all offer opportunities for various interventions and non-intervention, but choosing not to intervene can be powerful, requiring trust in the process, letting the experience or event speak for itself. There are other options to consider after the event:

- *After the activity* the facilitator might not make any insightful comment about the experience. The **experience speaks for itself.**
- *After the activity* the facilitator might provide the group with feedback about their general behaviour after the experience, such as what they did well, what they might need to work on, what they learnt, etc. The **facilitator speaks for the experience.**
- *After the activity* the facilitator would use questions to foster a group discussion about the above. The **facilitator debriefs the experience.**

Frontloading, framing and other techniques can be developed much further. Providers can include appropriate famous film clips, video footage of previous groups, TV soap extracts or cartoon images to send powerful messages. They often work well with young people. These media can reinforce key points, especially if they are seen as coming from other known or respected sources. Such media can be potent when the medium and message speaks for itself, thus providing excellent techniques that remove the scepticism associated with the facilitator who provides instant expert solutions. In contrast to letting the experience speak for itself, or speaking on behalf of the experience, some researchers such as Greenaway (1993) suggest that learners can be facilitators of their own ideas, and self-facilitation is very much a learner-centred approach.

Conclusion

Learning is enhanced when people discover things for themselves through their experiences. There is always a degree of emotional engagement and people often remember their experiences, and then in turn remember what they learnt from these experiences. This requires a commitment to the wider discovery of 'self', and a preparedness to experiment and review personal values and beliefs. Although experience is flowing like a river all around people every day, many people do not make the most of experiential opportunities, and it is often an emotional state that prevents maximum learning from experience. Emotional intelligence underpins learning as a basic building block. Yet many experiential learning providers, whether teachers, or trainers, do not give sufficient attention to emotional issues for many reasons, despite emotional competency being at the core of achievement in learning. Knowledge has been divorced from emotional reasoning because of a long-held belief that learning is purely a cognitive function, associated with outmoded notions of 'intelligence'. In this chapter we have explored the notion of emotional intelligence, and increasingly there is evidence of the introduction of 21st-century competencies, crafted by nations that recognize that schooling should develop such intelligence in our children and young people (see, for example, https://www.moe.gov.sg/education/education-system/21st-century-competencies).

There are many signposts that point to a range of emotional states that underpin learning, and so in the facilitation of experiential learning the ability to read, navigate and work with the underlying feelings that can restrict or enhance learning is important. All experience, and all adventures, are essentially an emotional experience; they are experienced in the mind, and the emotional hub is located in specific parts of the brain.

In this chapter we have offered ideas as to the role and function of emotion in experiential learning. We offered insight into ways of reading the signs and working with emotions as part of the experience, and we examined ways of accessing the roots of emotion in experiential learning. We also examine other aspects of emotion work in Chapter 8, 'Experience, knowing and intelligence'. This chapter explored more ways to access the feelings and emotions dimensions of learning, representing the fourth tumbler of the Learning Combination Lock model. The chapter explored the states of relaxed alertness and the energy–tension balance, as well as mood-influencing techniques, including stimulating scents and body-language adjustment. Identity, fear of failure, pride and success, and perfection were seen to play important roles in experiential learning. Accessing techniques included the use of 'mapping' to gain entry to the deeper levels of dialogue of the 'inner voices'. Rewriting our inner rules using trilogies, humour and metaphors were all investigated as means to access emotions.

Experience, knowing and intelligence

08

(the knowing dimension)

At school he struggled with foreign languages and teachers were exasperated by his ponderous way of thinking for a long time before answering questions, and even more by quietly talking to himself under his breath. The boy seemed happiest on his own... The teacher had said that the school would be a better place if he weren't in it... So what was different about Albert Einstein – what enabled him to turn from a difficult boy into a world-famous genius? WINSTON (2003: 311–12)

Introduction

The above question was posed by Lord Winston in a book called *The Human Mind*. At the core of this comment is the interesting subject of thinking slowly. Einstein was clearly a slow but deep thinker, and even from an early age it took time for him to do his careful processing. How do we know, how do we think and what is intelligence? These are important issues to understand in learning from experience. Here we build on issues such as thinking too little, or too much, thinking in patterns, and thinking with emotion, and with the body, making clear links with other dimensions of the Learning Combination Lock model. We explore multiple intelligence (MI) theory and offer ideas for working with these dimensions of intelligence, including a more detailed look at some of the neglected forms of intelligence, namely creative, spiritual, naturalistic and emotional intelligence. The chapter concludes with a very brief consideration of the experience of higher mind states, including wisdom.

Human learning: is it really all in the mind?

The human brain weighs 1,300 to 1,400 grammes, and they are hungry organs, consuming about 20 per cent of our body's energy resources. Our brains are powerful processing organs, and we have been studying the brain for many years in order to understand how it works. One of the most reported brain accidents occurred in September 1848, and it has been mentioned in 60 per cent of all books on neuroscience. Much has been learnt from this accident and, in particular, how Phineas Gage at first seemed to survive the penetration of a metal rod through his brain, but how it was discovered that his personality eventually completely changed. He suffered from bouts of anger and showed an inability to hold down a job. In a number of ways the exploration of his brain damage initiated considerable interest in the idea of mapping damaged brains, and today this mapping is now at a very advanced stage, thanks to the understanding of medical research on damage and illness, and the invention of brain-scanning technologies.

Our brains are continually being influenced by our outer-world experiences; in Chapter 3 we noted that London taxi drivers appear to have enlarged areas of the brain known as the hippocampus, due to their work in comprehending, memorizing and navigating the spatial layout of thousands of roads and streets (Woollett and Maguire, 2011). The hippocampus, and the adjacent areas, are important for both emotions and memory. The hippocampus and the adjacent areas are where long-term memory is stored like a filing cabinet in the brain. These areas receive sensory data from our senses and integrate them into a single experience. Important memories grow stronger while the less important ones grow weaker. The connections with the hippocampus break down during the human ageing process. The brain promotes forgetting in another way, and this is a good thing; when neurones grow through frequent, repeat experiences they overwrite old neurones.

The brain reacts to external experiences by the release of numerous internal chemicals, as we explored in Chapter 1, when we considered how business is using this knowledge to create habit-forming products, and pleasurable experiences. When a need is created this can evolve into a habit, compulsion or addiction (Eyal, 2014), and much of our daily behaviours occur with little or no conscious thought, and arguably many of these behaviours fall into the realm of habit. Dopamine is our internal reward (pleasure) hormone, and it is just as addictive for us as it is for rats! These neurotransmitters are generated by neurones within the brain, whereas hormones are released by glands in the body and distributed to the blood, and they have an effect on the brain. Neurotransmitters tend to act very quickly and more directly compared to hormones, although the effect of hormones tends to be longer lasting, sometimes several days. Dopamine activates our reward or pleasure systems, controlling arousal levels in the brain; it is vital for motivation and appears to be released when we are curious, so it is useful for learning. It is also, however, implicated in addiction. Serotonin is a 'feel good', inhibitory neurotransmitter and affects our mood; high levels are associated with optimism. It is important for sleep, and reduced levels are implicated in depression. Endorphins are hormones sometimes referred to as our natural opiates. This is because they modulate pain, reduce stress and can produce a feeling of calm and relaxation and, like dopamine, they can also become addictive. The two pleasure drugs of dopamine and endorphin operate differently in that the former gives us the high (ups), whereas the latter, endorphine, is pleasurable in that it calms (downs). The latest findings from neuroscience can be useful for learning, evident by a new book produced by Collins called *Neuroscience for Learning and Development: How to apply neuroscience and psychology for improved learning and training*. The neuroscience behind our habits, our levels of attention, our sense of belonging, and our memory is particularly useful.

Theorizing about how humans learn, and the potential role of the brain, has been subject to continuous reassessment over many years. The sense of incomplete understanding about human learning continues to plague prevailing dominant thinking on the subject. This has led to an unremitting quest for more 'complete' ideas about how we humans learn. This work of course is crucial to the theory and practice underpinning experiential learning. In Chapter 2 we introduced a quick and simplistic history that can be remembered in the form of a code: BCHSE. In Figure 8.1 we again reproduce this chart, albeit in a slightly simpler form.

Figure 8.1 shows how notions about human learning have shifted considerably over time, from exploring animal learning (*ethology*) to inform us how humans might learn, towards a 21st-century understanding that is a complex '*ecology*' of ideas, embracing all the dimensions that we cover in our Learning Combination Lock model of the seven core dimensions of learning. Cognitivist theories (C) began to surface in the late 1950s. The cognitive focus saw the 'human' as unique, intelligent and rational, and so computational brain processing involving thinking, remembering, analysing and seeking ways to explain and make sense of the world was suggested. Major contributors included Lewin (1951) and Gagne (1974), but perhaps the most well-known was Bloom (1956), who developed a spatial hierarchy

Figure 8.1 BCHSE: a very simple history of human learning

Time period	1900–1940s	1950s	1960s	1970s	1980s	1990s	2000–
Human learning theories (BCHSE)	B Behavioural (ethology, animal focus)						
		C Cognitive (computational brain)					
			H Humanist (empathetic/nurturing)				
				S Social construction of knowledge (social interaction)			
						E Rich ecological complexity	

SOURCE Adapted from Beard and Price (2012)

of cognition (higher/lower forms of knowing). Hierarchical models are problematic, particularly when some writers relegate experiential learning as a basic *lower* level of *practical* learning (see, for example, Young, 2008). This chapter explores human thinking, and human intelligence, and we suggest many practical ideas for working with this experiential dimension of learning.

Although social constructivist theories remain influential they are now positioned among a milieu of views about human learning, and this multidisciplinary interpretation that we are calling the new *ecological* view (E), presents a richer picture of how humans learn. These more complex ideas are similar to the understanding of the ecology of a rainforest.

Thinking with the body and thinking with feeling

Here are two more key terms. The study of how we can know the world is called *epistemology*, and it is linked to the study of 'being' in the world, known as *ontology*. While *knowing* is the focus of this chapter, *being* is the subject of our next chapter, representing the last dimension or cog in the model: they are of course connected as our being influences our way of knowing the world around us and our knowing influences our way of being in the world.

We have suggested elsewhere that knowing involves more than just mental processing. Knowing also involves *bodily knowing* (this view is known as *embodied cognition*). For now we will simply call this *thinking with the body*. Bodily knowing is also covered in Chapter 6 (the *sensing* chapter). Knowing is also strongly linked to our environmental surroundings (this view of knowing is known as *embedded cognition*). A simple way to understand the way the brain works is to work with a slightly more complex idea beyond the 'three brains' we put forward in Chapter 7. Imagine now there are four operational zones of the brain, as follows. The old brain at the top of the spinal column is reptilian-like, managing the automatic functions such as heartbeat, breathing and temperature regulation. This we will call the *functioning brain*. The middle brain, slightly higher up, is responsible for the *sensing brain*, engaging fast emotional reactions to the incoming sensing data, and this we will call the *feeling brain*. The newer brain is more advanced and particularly developed in humans, consisting of cerebral frontal lobes that do more complex, slower processing. This part is divided into left and right hemispheres and reference is often made to left-brain and right-brain dominant people. This big frontal part we will call the *thinking brain*. Thus we have the functioning brain, the sensing brain, the feeling brain and the thinking brain. Nobel Prize-winner in economics Daniel Kahneman has written a book called *Thinking Fast and Slow* (2011) and by fast he is referring to the feeling brain, as feeling tags are sent rapidly to the brain for fast-survival decision making. He also calls this System 1 thinking. By *thinking slow* he is referring to the work of the *thinking brain*: here, slower, more rational processing takes place. His book examines some of the myths associated with the supposed benefits of slow rational thinking or fast feeling-thinking. One of the main themes we present here in this book is just how little control we actually have over our own System 1 feeling-thinking responses, and the degree to which the subconscious mind, including our human biases, also affects fast thinking. Much of our life operates on System 1 autopilot.

The organizing mind: patterns and creative thinking

As we noted at the very start of this fourth edition, a key characteristic of the human mind is that it has a tendency to organize, sequence, differentiate, classify and to generally explore and find patterns of relational connectivity. Every living being tends to categorize (Lakoff and Johnson, 1999): this is important in understanding how the embodied mind works in learning experiences. Lakoff and Johnson give a simple explanation by way of the fact that the eye has 100 million light-sensing cells but there are only about 1 million fibres leading to the brain, therefore the clustering of information is necessary. This necessary reducing down of information involves data clustering, underpinning why we tend to categorize. It occurs because so many neural connections of the brain cluster information in this way. Such categorization continually occurs in everyday life, in both conscious and subconscious ways: we first observe things in the world then classify them as bad or good, right or wrong, as scary or friendly, as simple or complex, beautiful or ugly. In this way the idea of separating the brain, and our thoughts about intelligence, from our sensing, feeling, bodies is clearly a mistake: there is no separation in reality, and this has practical implications for experiential approaches to learning.

Complex things are usually regarded as complex because, for many people, difficult-to-'see'-and-understand topics involve the bits of the subject or problem having a complicated spatial–relational connectedness. Furthermore, complexity is made difficult because our human spoken language, whilst an astonishing development, is also problematic in that when it is spoken it is limited to one word at a time and therefore linear in format. Spoken language thus struggles to describe complicated things; however, the bodily GPS system helps overcome such language limitations (see Chapter 6 on sensory intelligence). Spatial metaphors are found, for example, deeply embedded in our everyday speech; the brain often sees things in this spatial way. In order to add richness our linear spoken and written language is enhanced with spatial–bodily metaphors that aid the brain in thinking and processing: *step-by-step* logic, to *support* an argument, to *grasp* an idea, how time *flies*, to feel *on top of the world*, *lifelong* and *lifewide* of learning.

Let's explore this a bit further in terms of more practical implications for experiential learning. We now give some examples of how the human tendency to categorize can help learning. We will illustrate these ideas by reference to the development of creative, critical and conceptual thinking. We will return again to the subject of creative intelligence (CQ) later in this chapter.

CASE STUDY Industrial ecology and The Market Place

The Market Place is an experiential approach described along with many other practical experiences in *The Experiential Learning Toolkit* by Beard (2010). A detailed account of this experience, with a focus on the role of pattern detection for creative thinking, is also given in a paper by Beard and Goode (2013). Both accounts describe an approach to the exploration of a relatively new concept of industrial ecology (IE). The idea of industrial systems evolving to mimic the quasi-cyclical systems of natural ecosystems in terms of energy and material flows is a difficult topic to teach. The concept embraces the systematic recovery of so-called 'waste', the dematerialization of the economy, and the need for the development of management systems that encourage collaboration, networks and interconnectivity.

The experience uses 60 or so commercial products that all have some element of both creative design and sustainable environmental design built into them.

They have first been separated into four different bags labelled: 1) materials, (carpets made from natural corn, recycled materials, new types of materials); 2) domestic products such as toothbrushes, razors, washing-up brushes, nail brushes, etc; 3) technology (solar panels that charge phones and laptops); and 4) artistic approaches (earrings made from waste bottle tops/necklaces made from old magazines). A few business products can first be selected and used by the facilitator to illustrate and show basic patterns, or the development of interesting trends. They are then emptied out on a large table for four groups to work with, and the groups get to swap over bags/tables. Participants initiate a discussion by handling the products. This is followed by a process of organizing the materials into spatial patterns. Participants are encouraged to make sense of what they see by journeying from simply touching and describing in the first instance, to an organization and categorization processing as 'higher' levels of thinking develop. The code is HDOAC, which represents handling, discussing, organizing, analysing and conceptualizing. Within these categories participants then move objects on the tables and try to make further sense of what they see using laminated black arrows: these tend to really enhance the thinking processes. Participants move, sort and order the products in any particular way so that they can illustrate any trends or patterns. Other prompt cards are used to facilitate spatial-relational pattern detection. Kinaesthetic and sensory experiences, along with group discussion and interaction, embed the learning (touching, handling, testing out, winding-up radios, powering mobile phones, iPods and laptops from a solar panel, feeling soft clothing fabrics made from plastic bottles). Bodily movement is thus an essential principle in this learning experience, and the session allows for the physical movement of people to different tables, and the movement of information and objects. The session also has a strong focus on the social construction of knowledge.

In this approach there is a clear shift from messy 'practice' to conceptual, 'higher' levels of thinking using spatial-relational pattern detection, real business products and creative-collaborative conversational work. The session concludes with a plenary session exploring how the principles of industrial ecology (IE) are now exhibited and laid out in the patterns detected in all four tables. IE is thus typified, for example, by the number of products that have used waste material from another business to create their products; how LED technology has resulted in a breakthrough that has reduced material and energy usage whilst providing more powerful lighting; or how smartphones are multifunctional, therefore reducing material consumption.

With this kind of experience we must ask where the boundary of experiential learning is in this activity. Many people erroneously think that experiential learning is practical learning – this experiential approach clearly demonstrates that this is not the case. We should also ask: if higher education is concerned with 'higher level' thinking skills, is higher thinking related to human intelligence? Let us consider this important question. A further significant question concerns how we might work with more up-to-date concepts of intelligence to help people learn in an experiential way.

Supporting critical, conceptual and creative thinking: using laminated prompt cards to facilitate pattern detection

- **First-level** describing. Descriptor cards: eg WIND-UP RADIO.
- **Second-level** laminated flow/arrows: highlighting relational flows.
- **Third-level** basic conceptual analysis cards: eg BUSINESS TO WASTE. BUSINESS TO BUSINESS. PRODUCT DIVERSITY. MATERIAL FLOWS.
- **Fourth-level** higher conceptual analysis cards: eg DE-MATERIALIZATION (minute yet powerful torch developed as a result of LED bulbs/swipe cards, not keys. Less material).

What is intelligence?

In a book titled *Psychology: The science of mind and behaviour*, Gross (2001: 589) comments on the difficult subject of intelligence by saying that 'perhaps nowhere else in psychology does so much… research and theory attempt to define the concept under investigation'. Old and outmoded views on intelligence considered a potential link between brain size and intelligence, and ideas existed that people with prominent eyes had good memories (Gardner, 1993: 12)! In 2005 the *Times Higher Education Supplement* in the UK carried a front-page story titled 'IQ claim will fuel gender row', reporting a paper in the *British Journal of Psychology* where two prominent psychologists argue that men have larger brains than women, apparently making them capable of tasks of higher complexity!

Intelligence testing was first commissioned by the French government, who wished to test and classify persons of lower intelligence for special-needs education. These early tests measured children's verbal, memory and mathematical skills and were devised by Alfred Binet, and it is from these that modern psychometric testing instruments grew. Testing is concerned with measuring individual differences in intellect or abilities, and Gross rightly notes that, in one form or another, controversial quantitative testing of intelligence has impinged on the lives of most people. While intelligence might be interpreted as that which only tests measure, it is clear that our understanding of intelligence has played a central role in the development of the theory and practice of teaching and learning. Much contemporary thinking about intelligence has advanced due to neuroscience research on brain disorders and brain scanning.

Within higher education, intellectual ability is construed as a cognitive benchmark (see Figure 8.2), and wrongly thought to be the same as 'intelligence'. In education, intelligence has been strongly linked to cognitive skills such as problem solving, reasoning, critical analysis, judgement, initiative and comprehension. Contemporary academic experiential approaches to assessment, however, are now applying many different measurements (see 'Fair assessment', below)

The standard intelligent quotient (IQ) tests have often excluded many of the contextual or experiential subtheories, including the world outside school or vocational work, which requires many kinds of abilities. Some tests offer a broad assessment: one contemporary online service offered a broad-spectrum IQ test, and scored for the following abilities: arithmetic, spatial skill, logic, spelling, short-term memory, rote utilization, algebraic, general knowledge, visual apprehension, geometrics, vocabulary, intuition and computational speed. Rather interesting was the inclusion of intuition, which was defined as an ability to develop answers without consciously dealing with the problem at hand. Terms such as 'out of the blue' or 'it just struck me' were said to be associated with intuition. Some scientists believe that intuition is an innate ability to sense what is going on, that this is partly due to the presence of vast archives of experience and that 'intuition is not some paranormal ability to see the future, but a technique of learning what to look for in a given environment, and of doing so without the conscious brain getting in the way' (Winston, 2003: 349). It is intriguing that at times the so-called higher 'thinking' brain is not required for fast execution of certain activities. The subconscious should not be underestimated: it appears it can operate at very high levels.

The Learning Combination Lock Model

Figure 8.2 Levels of cognitive development in education

MASTERY

Evaluation – judge, evaluate, support, comfort, avoid, select, recognize, criticize.
Synthesis – summarize, argue, relate, précis, organize, generalize, conclude.
Analysis – select, compare, differentiate, contrast, break down.
Application – predict, select, assess, find, show, use, construct, compute.
Comprehension – identify, illustrate, represent, formulate, explain, contrast.
Knowledge – write, state, recall, recognize, select, reproduce, measure.

Drawn from Bass, B S (1956) *Taxonomy of Education: The Classification of Educational Goals*, Longman, London

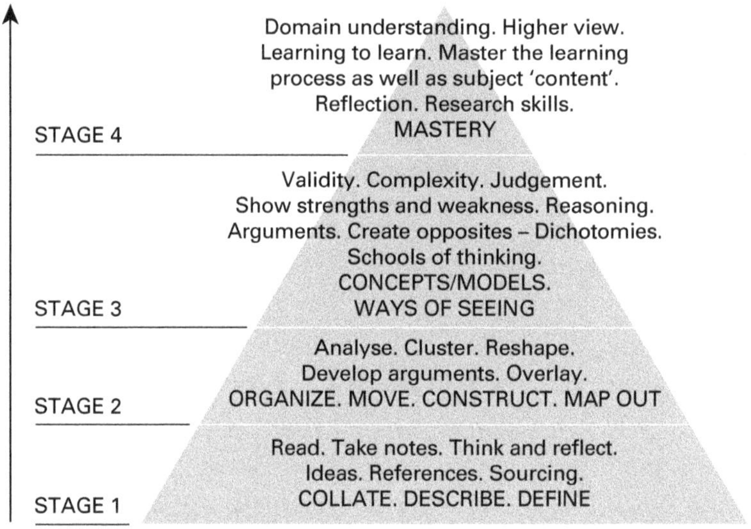

STAGE 4 — Domain understanding. Higher view. Learning to learn. Master the learning process as well as subject 'content'. Reflection. Research skills. **MASTERY**

STAGE 3 — Validity. Complexity. Judgement. Show strengths and weakness. Reasoning. Arguments. Create opposites – Dichotomies. Schools of thinking. **CONCEPTS/MODELS. WAYS OF SEEING**

STAGE 2 — Analyse. Cluster. Reshape. Develop arguments. Overlay. **ORGANIZE. MOVE. CONSTRUCT. MAP OUT**

STAGE 1 — Read. Take notes. Think and reflect. Ideas. References. Sourcing. **COLLATE. DESCRIBE. DEFINE**

Drawn from a multi-media CD ROM 'Mastering University', available from Gower Publications (2005) and produced by Colin Beard

---

1. Gathering information and utilizing resources
2. Developing flexibility in form and style
3. Asking high-quality questions
4. Weighing evidence before drawing conclusions
5. Utilizing metaphors and models
6. Conceptualizing strategies (mind mapping, pros and cons lists, outlines etc)
7. Dealing productively with ambiguity, differences and novelty
8. Creating possibilities and probabilities (brainstorming, formulas surveys, cause and effect)
9. Debate and discussion skills
10. Identifying mistakes, discrepancies, and illogic
11. Examining alternative approaches (shifting frame of reference, thinking out of the box etc)
12. Hypothesis testing strategies
13. Developing objectivity
14. Generalization and pattern detection (identifying and organizing information, translating information, cross-over applications)
15. Sequencing events

Drawn from Jensen, E (2000) *Brain-based Learning: The New Science of Teaching and Training*

The many forms of intelligence

A qualitative, biological view of intelligence, of particular significance to experiential learning, is that intelligence is an adaptation to the environment in which we live. Such a qualitative view is reflected in the early work of Piaget in the 1950s, who regarded intelligence as 'essentially a system of living and acting operations, ie a state of balance or equilibrium achieved by the person when he is able to deal adequately with the data before him. But it is not a static state, it is dynamic in that it continually adapts itself to new environmental stimuli' (quoted in Gross, 2001: 590).

New insights about intelligence continue to emerge, creating greater breadth and depth to this complex subject. Harvard professor of cognition and education Howard Gardner published many books and articles on neuropsychology and cognitive development before focusing on his seventh book in 1983, *Frames of Mind: The theory of multiple intelligences (MI)*. It was this book in particular that placed his research at the centre of educational theory. Gardner proposes a qualitative view of 'an intelligence' as the psychobiological ability to solve problems, or to fashion products that are valued within one or more cultural settings. He also states quite clearly that 'there is not, and there can never be, a single irrefutable and universally accepted list of human intelligences' (1993: 59). MI theory is based on three fundamental principles (Gross, 2001):

- Intelligence is *not* a single unitary thing, but a collection of multiple intelligences.
- Each intelligence is *independent* of all others.
- The intelligences *interact*, otherwise nothing could be achieved.

It would appear that people have differing intelligence profiles and, significantly, there are few limits to the development of these intelligences. Gardner describes a number of categories of intelligence in detail and although he eventually settled on eight, he acknowledges that there may be more. Indeed Gardner created some 20 varieties of intelligence at one stage in his research. Gardner narrowed these down to seven intelligences then added another, naturalistic intelligence. There are numerous reasons why the concept of multiple intelligence has taken hold in education:

> Among these are that the theory validates educators' everyday experience: students think and learn in many different ways. It also provides educators

with a conceptual framework for organizing and reflecting on the curriculum, assessment and pedagogical practices. In turn, this reflection has led many educators to develop new approaches that might better suit the needs of the range of learners in the classroom. (Gardner, in Palmer, 2001: 276)

Gardner also comments on so-called higher-level cognitive operations that go beyond a straightforward notion of 'an intelligence' and remarked that it was the 'sense of self' that placed the greatest strain on his multiple intelligence or MI theory. The sense of self, he suggests, is a prime candidate for higher- or second-order ability.

Several areas of intelligence that form our fifth tumbler

1. **Mathematical–logical:** the ability to organize thoughts sequentially and logically.
2. **Verbal–linguistic:** the ability to understand and express ideas through language.
3. **Bodily–kinaesthetic:** the gaining of knowledge through feedback from physical activity.
4. **Musical:** sensitivity to tone, pitch and rhythm, and the ability to reproduce them.
5. **Visual–spatial:** the ability to learn directly through images and to think intuitively without the use of language.
6. **Interpersonal:** the ability to notice and make discriminations regarding the moods, temperaments, motivations and intentions of others.
7. **Intra-personal:** the ability to access one's own feelings.
8. **Naturalistic:** the ability to understand and be in tune with one's relationship with the natural environment.
9. **Creative intelligence:** the ability to be creative and innovative.
10. **Spiritual intelligence:** interconnectedness with the inner and outer world and the ability to sense the higher self.
11. **Moral intelligence:** the ability to act for the wider benefit of society, to have good principles and values.

Gardner, Csikszentmihalyi (who developed the concept of flow experience) and Damon (2001) embarked on the 'Good Work Project' in 1994 to identify how individuals at the cutting edge of their professions can produce work that is both exemplary and contributes to the good of our wider society. Their work continues into the new millennium and they continue to grapple with broader societal issues, analogous in some ways to the articulation of and commitment to active citizenship by educators such as John Dewey 100 years earlier. Dewey was concerned with both morality and spirituality in education, as was Kurt Hahn, the founder of the Outward Bound philosophy who emphasized the four pillars of *service*, *craftmanship*, *physical fitness* and *self-discipline*.

Learning experiences should allow people to reveal, explore and develop their own particular life gifts, which might include: an ability to be word smart (linguistic intelligence), to be number smart (logical/mathematical/scientific intelligence), to be spatially smart (visual/spatial intelligence), to be sound smart (musical intelligence), to be body smart (bodily/physical/kinaesthetic intelligence), to be people smart (interpersonal intelligence), to be self-smart (intra-personal intelligence), to be emotionally smart (emotional intelligence), to be nature smart (naturalistic intelligence), to be innovative and creative (creatively smart) and to be life smart (spiritual/moral/existential intelligence).

Given below is a detailed practical example of an assessment technique in higher education that provides a rich, experiential way to assess a broad notion of intelligence:

Fair assessment

This undergraduate module was designed to develop students' understanding of nutrition in health and disease with a focus on epidemiology and the role and impact of nutrition in health and disease, including intervention and prevention strategies. The specific assessment criteria were as follows:

- the ability to discuss appropriately the role of epidemiology in nutritional science;
- the ability to evaluate, accurately, specific issues of nutrition in health and disease;
- critical appraisal of nutritional research;

- the ability to prepare and design an effective nutritional intervention strategy to promote the health of a specific group;
- appropriate selection of ICT in the analysis and presentation of information;
- effective communication using established conventions in scientific reporting.

The creative way to assess this work through an experiential technique was that:

1 Students will be required to present and submit a **business plan** (20 per cent) for their **nutrition fair stall** to the panel in practical two. Each student will be allocated an eight-minute slot to deliver (10 per cent) their business plan. Students will be asked to deliver no more than five PowerPoint slides outlining their proposals. These slides should be comparable to their formal business plan. Each student will then be questioned by the panel regarding their proposal.

2 Students will be required to **prepare and run a stall** (20 per cent) at the Applied Nutrition Fair. This fair will be held in the main hall on floor six and will be open to other students, visitors, university staff and other academics. All stalls are expected to be of a professional standard. Students should consider the following when designing and running their stalls:

   - All information should be correct! You will be advising the public.
   - All stalls should be appropriately presented and professionally run.
   - Students are advised to provide a variety of materials for the public.
   - Each student will be allocated one table on which to hold their stall.
   - All students must create and sign a risk assessment in order to be allowed to take part in the event. These risk assessments should be countersigned by a member of the module teaching team prior to the event.
   - All students must adhere to appropriate health-and-safety regulations and risk management strategies.
   - The teaching team will be marking the stalls using the attached mark sheet (15 per cent).
   - Academic and technical guests will be asked to award each stall a mark out of five for 'impact and professionalism'. These marks will be averaged in order to give a final mark (5 per cent).

Jenny Williams, Sheffield Hallam University, UK

Neglected forms of intelligence

A central principle for us that underlies experiential learning is the integration of mind and matter (including the body and environment) and theory and practice. Rather than separating mind and body, emotion and reason, rational and intuitive, people and nature, there is now a growing recognition of the ecological, holistic fusion of these traditional dualities. For this reason we now explore some of the more integrative dimensions of intelligence that remain controversial and marginalized in the traditional literature about human learning. These are: 1) sensory intelligence; 2) emotional intelligence; 3) spiritual intelligence; 4) naturalistic intelligence; and 5) creative intelligence. In these areas thinking remains embryonic, with a developing language emerging that creates new space for the exploration and expression of these aspects and ideas about human learning. Naturalistic intelligence and spiritual intelligence are less neglected by outdoor learning practitioners.

Sensory intelligence – SI

Sensory intelligence (SI) has been covered in Chapter 6 in great detail and we argue that SI might indeed be more important than EQ. Although we do not cover the subject in detail here we do highlight some of the basic links of SI to thinking, remembering and forgetting. In Chapter 6 we also looked at the problems of thinking too much, a subject also covered in Chapter 9, the *Being* dimension of learning, where we discuss the advantages of being able to just 'be' in the here and now.

The role of the senses arises in many ways in experiential learning. In a review of the activities and learning that took place on a training programme with senior trainers in a health-care organization, all was going well until the review got to lunchtime on the first day. 'What did we do after lunch?' someone said. But no one could remember. There was a long silence. Everyone was thinking hard. Then someone got up and said: 'I remember we were sat over here, sitting in a circle.' Then almost in unison, everyone remembered the activity, the memory was released, triggered by the sensorial moving bodily (physically) or imagining so in the mind (mentally) to the very space where the activity took place. This can also happen when memory is triggered by other sensory associations. While working with Outward Bound Singapore we happened to find a yellow circle painted on a concrete outdoor training area. We used it to demonstrate the Learning Combination Lock model. The yellow circle on this programme became the senses, with the inside of the circle representing the inner world of the learner, whilst outside the circle represented the outer world. Coloured plastic hoops were placed on the ground to represent the other key dimensions of learning within and outside the yellow sensory interface. These colours, of the main circle and smaller hoops, became very significant to our memories over the next few days of the experiential programme. Yellow became the constant collective group code for the senses every time any sensory issues cropped up; this was of course a simple form of conditioning (code B), in that yellow highlighter pens were regularly held up to highlight emerging sensory issues. This memory trigger was linked to the yellow-lined model outside. This became a type of *sensory learning signature* (after Lindstrom, 2005). Likewise other senses trigger memories, which can enhance and support learning. This is particularly the case with simple icons (eg fast-forward arrows), bodily movement, memorable stories and smells. The senses are also recognized as having a memory *association* role in the development of corporate brands: Intel, for example, is a classic iconic sound. Martin Lindstrom has researched the phenomena of *sensory signatures* in commercial products and produced a book called *Brand Sense* (Lindstrom, 2005).

Emotional intelligence – EQ

In Chapter 7 we explored in detail the role that emotions play in learning, offering many practical ideas about working with emotions. Here we briefly explore emotions in terms of their specific role in thinking and in relation to whole-person notions of experiential learning. Emotions are the body's reaction to the mind, and emotions are played out in the theatre of the body, particularly in neuromuscular acts: fear and the tightening of the jaw; anger and the clenching of the fists; relaxation and lightness of the body when joyful; the expansion of the chest in triumph (Sheets-Johnstone, 2009). Movement and emotion go hand in hand: we are moved by emotion. This highlights the artificial nature of the cogs in the model; the separated boundaries of the model do not exist in reality.

There has been a rise in interest in the notion of emotional intelligence, or EQ as it has become known. Its popularization was brought about by Daniel Goleman with his best-selling book *Emotional Intelligence* (1996). Goleman drew on the work of Salovey and Mayer in 1990 and created a classification of emotional intelligence as five major domains: knowing one's emotions, managing emotions, motivating oneself, recognizing emotions in others, and handling relationships. These contemporary defining parameters of 'emotional intelligence' thus stress the importance of being able to manage both the 'inner world' (of self) and 'outer world' (of interactions with others, and the environment). The emerging language of intelligence in learning thus considers the complex 'whole-person', and acknowledges the milieu of social interactions and social relationships, recognizing perception, feelings, arousal states, expressive gestures/postures, moods and emotional cues. Our definition of emotional intelligence (EQ) that we offered in an earlier chapter is: 'the ability to understand the emotions in a given learning environment, in yourself (inner world) and others (outer world), to use this understanding to deal effectively with yourself and others, in a way that improves personal and professional development, reduces anger and hostility, generates collaborative effort, enhances life balance and produces creative energy'.

This elevated status of emotions as a measure or quotient of intelligence is rooted in the work of Howard Gardner (1983) on social intelligence. His work is acknowledged as playing a historical role in broadening and redefining intelligence, producing a shift away from the monolithic 'intelligence quotient' (IQ). Gardner influenced educational thinking by highlighting the complex multiple nature of intelligence, and in particular the notion of inter- and intra-personal aspects within social intelligence, which currently underpin thinking on emotional intelligence (EQ). Prior to Goleman's publication it was Salovey and Mayer (1990) who, drawing on psychological and cultural literature, proposed what is said to be the 'first formal definition of emotional intelligence' (Feldman Barrett and Salovey, 2002: xiii).

Emotions have been pitched as contradictory to rational thinking, and a protracted and contentious history exists as to the role of emotions in learning. The oppositional relationship is said to be located within the Western Cartesian dualism (Damasio, 1996), being 'traced from Plato to Descartes, and from Kant to the Logical Positivists' (Barbalet, 1998: 30). For Plato, emotions were inappropriate territory, as irrational urges that needed controlling, and for Kant emotions were regarded as an illness! Mortiboys, in *The Emotionally Intelligent Lecturer* (2002), has many interesting experiential activities for learning but he specifically notes that it would be disturbing if universities were emotion-free zones; yet 'curiously, so much of the culture in higher education implies that they are' (2002: 7). Mortiboys references many educational commentators who over many years have regarded the emotions as 'inappropriate territory'. Interestingly, emotions and emotional safety have always been a core concern of the outdoor learning community, and a significant literature base exists on the subject.

At the heart of concern over 'appropriateness' lies the question we address here: to what degree is learning an emotional activity as much as it is an intellectual one? The role of emotions in learning generates considerable moral and political debate; Boler (1999) in *Feeling Power: Emotions and education* offers a feminist critique of the politics of emotions in learning – she suggests that emotion is a notoriously difficult subject to define and that students find few spaces to express, resist and challenge. She (1999: 109) remarks that in higher education and scholarship, 'to address emotions is risky business' as it opens up a debate about public and private spaces. Emotional dimensions of the learning experience are often denied. Boler explores the taboos of emotions in education, and considers its roots in social control through the 'mental hygiene movement' centred on emotional engineering (girls were taught patience, self-denial, silence, love). Her work is particularly critical of the measurement and intelligence-testing movement, and of the self-help, consumer approach to 'emotional intelligence' by Goleman (1996) as a recipe for 'success'.

Boler suggests casting the gaze away from the term emotions; that we call it something else. Our view is that this something else begins to surface as part of the learning space, a new form of 'pedagogical space', where the experience of a physical, psychological and social space permits the development of language and activities that explore, express and accept emotions and feelings of self and others. This is an area we also explore in Chapter 4 on learning environments. In contrast, Furedi (2004) is strongly critical of the link between therapy and emotions. Furedi argues that the current 'therapy culture' generates a psychology of 'vulnerability' and warns that this imposes a new conformity through the management of people's emotions. Furedi argues that 'self-esteem advocates argue that it is not intellectual abilities, but how you feel that really matters' (2004: 160): thus 'the promotion of emotional intelligence is symptomatic of a climate of intellectual pessimism' (2004: 161).

Identifying and classifying emotions is problematic. Biologist Charles Darwin (1872) identified a comprehensive range of 30 emotions, which he classified into several categories, and argued that they essentially represented adaptation and survival mechanisms. More recent attempts to categorize complex emotions can also be found: proposals for 'master', 'basic', 'primary' (sadness, happiness, fear, anger, joy) or 'secondary emotions' (subtle variations of primary emotions such as euphoria, ecstasy, melancholy and wistfulness) as found in the work of Damasio (1996) and others. Plutchik (1980), however, concluded that there are endless possibilities of 'emotional classes', which can be determined to some extent by the sociocultural context or situation. 'Master emotions' such as shame frequently appear in the literature, as in recent work by Frijda and Mesquita (1994) and the shame–pride dichotomy of Kitayama and Markus (1994).

These emotions of pride and shame are said to be related to success and failure in learning and these in turn all play a key role in establishment and maintenance of identity, with the associated sense of belonging, differentiation and self-esteem (Scheff, 1997). A number of sociologists argue that the disposition to learn is grounded in social relationships, and in the construction of identity and self-esteem, and that these occur within the context of success/pride and failure/shame (eg Barbalet, 1998; Scheff, 1997). Ingleton (1999: 9) remarks that:

> By theorizing emotion as being formed in social relationships and significant in the development and maintenance of identity, its role in learning is constructed at a much deeper level. As such, emotion is seen to be constitutive of the activity of learning... Emotions shape learning and teaching experiences for both teachers and students, and the recognition of their significance merits further consideration in both learning theory and pedagogical practice.

Spiritual intelligence – SQ

In a chapter called 'The forgetting and remembering of the air', Abram (1997) beautifully describes the great significance of the air to past generations. He notes, for example, that the term 'psyche' is derived from an ancient Greek word that signified not only the 'soul' or 'mind', but also a 'breath' or a 'gust of wind'. The air is wind, breath, spirit and language; and the Latin *spiritus* means breath:

> The Navajo identification of awareness with the air – their intuition that the psyche is not an immaterial power that resides inside us, but is rather the invisible yet thoroughly palpable medium in which we (along with the trees, the squirrels and the clouds) are immersed – must seem at first bizarre... to persons of European ancestry. (Abram, 1997: 237)

Returning to an earlier definition of intelligence as an adaptation to the environment in which we live, others, in contrast, suggest that 'detachment' from our immediate environment and its sensory buzz can enable access to superior creative powers. Stewart (in Walter and Marks, 1981) notes that people discover their deepest self and reveal their greatest creative powers at times when the psychic processes are most free from immediate involvement with the environment and most under the control of inner balancing. This often requires *not thinking too much*. This is what we learn to do in the meditative state. Fox (1999: 455–57) in 'Enhancing spiritual experience in adventure programmes' describes many emotions and feelings associated with spiritual experiences in the outdoors, offers an analysis of anecdotal accounts of spirituality, and clusters the accounts under the following headings:

- spirituality as a fundamental aspect of human nature;
- spirituality as a sense of mystery;
- spirituality as a sense of awe and wonderment;
- spirituality as a belief in the connectedness or sense of oneness towards people, self and all things;
- spirituality as aesthetic beauty;
- spirituality as transcendent;
- spirituality as peak experience;
- spirituality as creating a sense of inner peace, oneness and strength;
- wilderness as a spiritual attraction.

Maslow developed a hierarchy of needs and described the base layers as need for food, shelter, physical health, family, education, social integration and intellectual, social and material accomplishments. But it is only when these needs are met that people reach their ultimate stage of human development: a positive state of self-actualization and the realization of one's potential. In this state people pour out playfulness, creativity, joyousness, a sense of purpose, with a mission to help others and with great tolerance, and these are accomplished in an environment of love and compassion. Maslow was perhaps describing a form of spiritual intelligence?

Stringer and McAvoy (1995) in *The Theory of Experiential Education* comment that the following attributes of spirituality were reported by participants of a wilderness experience:

Awareness	Human interconnectedness
Attunement	Inner feelings
Connection or relation to a greater power/deity	Inner or self-knowledge
	Sense of wholeness, oneness,
Inner strength	peace and/or tranquillity
Values	Intangibility
Shared or common spirit	

These lists offer a striking resemblance to the ingredients of wisdom and there is clearly much common ground. A practical example of experiential trainers explicitly using spirituality is found in the box below:

> ### Using spiritual intelligence
>
> The Findhorn Foundation is an organization that was started in 1962 in a caravan park in Scotland. Currently this successful organization seeks to demonstrate the links between the spiritual, social, economic and environmental aspects of life. Cooperation and co-creation with nature are major aspects of the foundation's work, and they declare that they are 'at the heart of the UK's largest international community based on spiritual values'.
>
> The Earth Centre in Doncaster in the UK was, from its inception, said to be the world's first environmental theme park. The Findhorn Foundation sent their staff to help in the training of the newly appointed workforce. Indeed, The Earth Centre later won a national tourism award as a result of the help that visitors received from on-site staff, who came largely from the ranks of unemployed former miners. The staff's special training lasted six weeks, by which time they had to be ready to launch the centre. Some were unable to read or write very well. Most knew little about the environment and most had few if any educational qualifications. What is significant about the training of the local people, however, is that the first stage of the three-part programme was specially designed by the trainers of the Findhorn Foundation. They developed the group, working first with feelings and needs, and nurturing their sense of belonging. Using many of the spiritual principles offered by Deepak Chopra (see the box below, 'Seven spiritual laws'), they examined and explored the important spiritual values associated with this mining community and their 'special place', a place that, like themselves, was undergoing a new and significant transformation. The local environment was shifting from being a coal-mining area to an internationally known green 'theme park'. The men and women were a close community, and hardship had beset them at the time of the closure of the coal mine. Their experiences in the dying days of the industry had been negative, and there was a sense of mistrust.
>
> The people all sat, arms folded, looking in disbelief at the strange trainers from Scotland when they first arrived. There was strong initial

resistance, mixed with a strange fascination. Eventually this fascination got the better of the local people; they succumbed to the charm of their experience, and many ended their training by participating in quite challenging events. Many created and read out their own poetry. Many unexpectedly shed tears with other local people as they unearthed some of their deeper feelings about their community and their sense of loss. Their emotional bedrock was not only exposed at times but was strengthened in their resolve to prepare for the next phase of their environmental training. Whilst the local people might have been seen as having low levels of formal education for their role as environmental guides, they eventually proved to be highly capable and well trained. The prestigious tourism award given to them derived largely from the spiritual experiential base that formed a central part of their training.

SOURCE Hartmann and Beard (2000)

Recognizing spiritual intelligence

The emotions associated with spiritual experiences are often difficult to describe. This is illustrated by two very interesting stories in Greg Child's book about mountain explorers, *Mixed Emotions* (1993). The stories focus on the spirit world, death, superstition and unexplainable phenomena. One story is about Roger Marshall on the treacherous mountain Kanchenjunga. He was stumbling down the mountainside with his strength slipping away. He was perilously close to falling down precipitous slopes when he heard a Japanese voice; he moved towards the voice, found a rope left by a previous Japanese expedition and descended to safety. But there were no Japanese people present on the slopes that day. Science leads us to seek rational, logical explanations for this: a physiological phenomenon, oxygen deprivation or distorted perceptions maybe? But science and myth are said by some to be one and the same, says Davies (1997) in his remarkable book exploring the botanical findings of important medicinal and hallucinogenic plants; *One River: Science, adventure and hallucinogenics in the Amazon Basin*. Spiritual intelligence locates itself in a person's 'life energy', and Chopra (1996) offers seven active spiritual steps and their appropriate law:

> **Seven spiritual laws**
>
> 1 Experience higher, spiritual self; list unique talents and three ways of expressing them; ask daily, how may I help serve humanity? *Law of dharma.*
>
> 2 Experience silence; commune with nature; practise non-judgement. *Law of pure potentiality.*
>
> 3 Offer a gift for everyone; receive gifts from life; wish everyone happiness, joy and laughter. *Law of giving.*
>
> 4 Witness choices in the moment; ask, will it bring fulfilment and happiness to me and others; ask heart for spontaneous right action. *Law of karma.*
>
> 5 Accept people and situations as they are; take responsibility for my situation without blame; defencelessness – no need to convince or persuade. *Law of least effort.*
>
> 6 Make a list of desires and release the list to the universe; remain established in self-referral. *Law of intention and desire.*
>
> 7 Allow self and others to be as they are; factor uncertainty into my experience; step into the field of all possibilities. *Law of detachment.*
>
> **SOURCE** Chopra (1996)

Naturalistic intelligence – NQ

Feeling a deep sense of closeness to nature and having a fascination with all things natural is part of this intelligence.

> I have it in myself. Early in my life I wanted to work with the Royal Society for the Protection of Birds (RSPB). As a boy I had had many special experiences in nature, sometimes feeling 'alone' in its strict sense, but also for me, connected with and close to the species around me. After graduating as a zoologist, I lived in the Amazon rainforests in the 1970s and the experience deeply changed my life. Twenty years later I became lost in a large tract of Malaysian rainforest. While this

> was potentially a very frightening experience, it became indescribably powerful. A strong sense of connection again emerged: the monkeys were watching me. I sat to observe the beetles and ants going about their everyday business. I was immersed in the intense sounds of cicadas and frogs. It was a beautiful experience that created a very extraordinary sense of 'self' for me.
>
> Later in life two more profound experiences occurred. I lived in a small wooden hut in the mountains in Wales protecting birds for the RSPB, and I lived alone with nature. I knew the birds and their calls. I knew the plants and their Latin names. A few years later I worked again with the RSPB, in an estuary with my own boat and outboard motor. I remember well the night when the full-moon spring tides created real danger for the birds. I went out in the semi-darkness of the night in my boat in strong winds and fast-flowing tides, rescuing baby chicks that had been separated from their nests and parents. There were many chicks washed into the tidal waters. Drowning and scared, they were pulled out into the boat and I took them back to dry land. Again I was out there all 'alone', surrounded by natural beauty and driven by some existential force, concerned for my fellow species.

Words alone cannot do justice to these kinds of experiences. Words are very problematic anyway. *Nature* and *naturalness* are considered contested terms. We are not going to cover these contested issues about words in detail here, although we cover some of these issues in Chapter 6, on sensing. For further reading about these contested terms such as *natural* and *wilderness* see, for example, Jay Griffiths (2006), *Wild: An elemental journey*, and William Cronon (1996), *Uncommon Ground*.

Cooper (1998), an outdoor education specialist, refers to special experiences of spirituality in the natural environment and suggests that such experiences result in a connectedness to the earth, and a heightened sense of being alive. They are located within what are called existential or transcendental phenomena. These experiences, he suggests, can be very powerful and spiritual for some people, and may present a turning point in life. Cooper goes on to recall the experience of a Professor Knowles who, when leading a night-time kayaking session, had an experience that changed his life. He was out with a group of 15-year-olds from the city as they set off into the night under a myriad of stars. They were then faced with an amazing sight of thousands of glow-worms:

> They were breathtaking. Each tiny glow came from a single phosphorescent light-emitting creature. Suspended like delicate jewels, the larvae of the fungus gnat had emerged to feed, their diffused glow reflecting on the faces of the exuberant students... we listened intently to the night and to each other. I was silent, allowing nature to speak... many students marvelled at the power of beauty and the place's serenity... In my mind, and in the minds of several students, a sacred place was established. It was the site of a special event, a place, if you will, at which individuals united with the powers of nature.
> (Cooper, 1998: 65)

Knowles returned to the same lake later with other groups but the experience wasn't the same. Leaders cannot predict such events, but they can set the scene, pre-sensitize people and make use of opportunities as they arise – if they themselves are sensitized to such things. Few people actually experience real darkness or a dawn chorus of birds awakening in the forest. Few people experience the strange silence when surfing waves. At the heart of naturalistic intelligence is an understanding of the human *reciprocity* with the more-than-human world. Abram discusses how, for many indigenous, oral cultures, a feeling of being truly alone when moving through nature, no matter how desolate or remote, is an alien concept. In order to understand this notion of *reciprocity*, try touching the fingers of another human. What is remarkable is that it not only allows you to feel the fingers of the other, but the sensuous feeling of your own fingers becomes possible. This is so with the surrounding more-than-human world. Sensing and feeling at one with nature is part of this naturalistic intelligence. More and more people are attempting to make sense of such experiences in their lives. Peter Senge and his co-writers (Senge *et al*, 2005: 63) beautifully describe a wildlife encounter of a colleague. He experienced a sense of oneness, a dismantling of the animal–human boundary:

> As I began to meditate, I looked to my left and saw two huge whales spouting water simultaneously. Then the whales put on the most unbelievable show... My heart was pounding, and I sat there in awe... Then directly in front of me, about 100 yards out, a lone whale gave me four spouts. Silence. A minute afterwards, off to my left, a whale rolled over four times. And then there was nothing... I felt as if I was bleeding from an open wound. I felt my heart was completely open and had merged with those of the whales. There was no separation between us. I remained in that open state of intense compassion for a long time, feeling as if I were on holy ground, as if I were in a great cathedral. I knew that I would never be the same again.

Sensing and spiritual intelligence

Much of this heightened sense of awareness is a learning experience of a higher order: it is learning beyond the simplicity of the experiential learning cycle. It is more than doing and reflecting. It is deeper. Mind and world are not separate. But often the associated sadness is due to the realization of our separation with nature. Senge and his colleagues refer to a three-stage sequence of sensing, presencing and realizing as part of a powerful experiencing process associated with the transformation of self and organizations:

- *Sensing* requires people to observe, observe, observe and to become at one with the world.
- *Presencing* requires one to retreat and reflect and to allow inner knowledge to emerge.
- *Realizing* is to create a new reality and to act swiftly with a natural flow.

Of interest here is the fact that many mystifying descriptions of moral, spiritual and naturalistic intelligence overlap so strongly. The development of such deep intelligence appears central to authentic change.

Creative intelligence – CQ

The concept of a creative quotient (CQ) is similarly perplexing and scientists have for some time tried to find out why some people experience inspiration and innovation so easily whilst others struggle. Intellect is not suggested as the critical ingredient of creative intelligence. The exact nature of creativity and innovation remains elusive. Interestingly, children seem much more adept at being creative, yet many adults appear to lose this ability more readily.

In the late 1940s Guildford, a psychologist, developed a model of human intellect and founded the idea of convergent and divergent thinking that formed the basis of contemporary research on creativity. IQ tests have primarily focused on convergent thinking but creative people seem able to free themselves from these thought patterns. Characteristics of divergent thinkers include ideas fluency, variety and flexibility, originality, elaboration, problem sensitivity and redefinition. Guildford failed to find a measure for CQ, as indeed have all researchers in their subsequent attempts.

Henry (1991) suggests that there are five schools of thought on creativity: grace, accident, association, cognition and personality. Other writers in the same book examine creativity in terms of metaphors (Morgan, 1997a), problem solving, lateral and vertical thinking (de Bono, 1991), intuition (Agor, 1991) and higher sense of 'self' (Ray and Myers, 1986). To be creative often means disturbing the status quo, and as a result innovators are said to be difficult to manage (Kirton, 1976; Belbin, 1981; Sinetar, 1992; Pinchot, 1991; Amabile, 1983). Innovators are said to be easily bored yet often regard their work as a form of play, and Henry (1991) and other writers support the notion that creativity arises through a playfulness of mind. Martin, Franc and Zounkova (2004) in *Outdoor and Experiential Learning* offer many interesting practical ideas on creative play, arguing that such mind states are encouraged in dramaturgy (which we explore in Chapter 5).

Kraft, in the journal *Scientific American Mind* (2005), builds on the work of Nobel Peace Prize-winner Roger Sperry, who researched left and right brain functions, and suggests that there are four steps to a creative mind: wonderment, motivation, intellectual courage and relaxation. Modern society, he noted, discriminates against the right hemisphere, yet it is responsible for divergent thinking, holistic and intuitive thinking, processing images, melodies, complex patterns such as face recognition, and being responsible for spatial organization of the body. Kraft notes that underlying creative ability is 'curiosity, love of experimentation, playfulness, risk taking, mental flexibility, metaphorical thinking, aesthetics – all these qualities play a central role' (2005: 20).

It is a long-held belief that play enhances the development of creativity. Neulinger (1974) produced a Paradigm of Leisure categorizing mind states that produce leisure and non-leisure conditions. 'Pure leisure' and 'pure job' are presented at polar extremes of a continuum. The variations are 'leisure-work' and 'leisure-job'. This mind-state concept underpins products of The British Trust for Conservation Volunteers: it sells work-as-leisure conservation 'working holidays'; the landowner pays for the work to be done, as do the holidaymakers: the work contributes to environmental improvement, and is paid for twice and sold as leisure (Beard, 1996)!

Creative people often experience their work as a calling or dedicated vocation: 'Creative people are happy with solitude, and they are less in need of discipline or order. Their dominant need may be to use their brains on complex problems, and this often overshadows their dependency on the approval or opinions of others' (Sinetar, 1992: 113).

Likewise Osborne (1963) argues that a major block to creativity is the tendency for others to evaluate ideas prematurely, and that it is useful to separate idea generation from idea evaluation. Others suggest that managers habitually damage creativity by finding reasons not to use a new idea, because 'people believe that they will appear smarter to their bosses if they are more critical – and it often works. In many organizations, it is professionally rewarding to react critically to new ideas' (Amabile, 1983).

Mind state certainly appears to be an important influence in learning to be creative. Falconar (2000: 48) describes these states in *Creative Intelligence and Self Liberation* as:

1 *Detachment*, in which there is a feeling of being cut off, as though the view of the problem is from far away.

2 *Involvement*, so that you become like a spring, feeling the body twisting as the spring tensions.

3 *Deferment*, avoiding a premature solution, which would probably become a poor one.

4 *Meditation*, reverie and free thinking, in which the mind is allowed to run free.

5 An *indescribable feeling* in which the solution appears to be on its own.

Falconar notes the sense of joy present in creative people, and says it is an emotion to be cultivated. Creative people, he says, are very aware of this and use it, and he refers to Eysenck's book *Genius*, which alluded to similar mind states. Likewise Maslow also wrote about such mind states in *Motivation and Personality*:

> The feeling of being simultaneously more powerful and also more helpless than one had ever been before, the feeling of great ecstasy and wonder and awe, the loss of placing in time and space with, finally, the conviction that something extremely important had happened, so that the subject is to some extent transformed and strengthened even in his daily life by such experiences. (Falconar, 2000: 53)

Creativity is concerned with doing things differently. In *Psychology for Trainers*, Hardingham (1998) examines the concept of reframing by using material from the work of Bandler and Grinder (1990) on neurolinguistic programming (NLP), who offered the following:

> An old Chinese Taoist story describes a farmer in a poor country village. He was considered very well-to-do because he owned a horse that he used for ploughing, for riding around, and for carrying things. One day his horse ran away. All his neighbours exclaimed how terrible this was, but the farmer simply said, 'Maybe'.

> A few days later the horse returned and brought two wild horses with it. The neighbours all rejoiced at his good fortune, but the farmer just said, 'Maybe'.
> The next day the farmer's son tried to ride one of the wild horses; the horse threw him and broke the boy's leg. The neighbours all offered their sympathy for his misfortune, but the farmer again said, 'Maybe'.
> The next week, conscription officers came to the village to take young men for the army. They rejected the farmer's son because of his broken leg. When the neighbours told him how lucky he was, the farmer replied, 'Maybe'.

Reframing inner scripts can generate significant mind states for creative thought. 'The meaning that any event has depends upon the "frame" in which we perceive it. When we change the frame we change the meaning. When the meaning changes the response changes also. The more reframing we do the more choices we have' (Hardingham, 1998: 116).

Falconar (2000) suggests that Eastern meditative mind states help creativity and he suggests two different ways of thinking. The verbal way, he remarks, is uncreative, while the other, consisting of visual images, feelings and intuition, constitutes creative thought. This polemic interpretation is, however, problematic: verbal expressive creativity is clearly a powerful medium for generating self-expression and creativity, as highlighted in the case study below. One might argue that without such verbal creativity we would not have 'fiction, theatre, and movie scripts, poetry, spoken word, slam poetry, etc' (Trules, 2005). Trules (2005), author of the case study below, suggests that while there are many forms that creativity can take, the term is socially and culturally relative: all human beings are capable of being self-expressive and creative (painter, writer, potter, plumber, teacher, or simply a human being living life). It is, he suggests, not just the province of Einsteins (introverted) and Picassos and Dalis (extroverted).

If, then, state of mind is significant for creative work, this has clear implications for the learning environment. People also utilize numerous techniques to create mind states such as the use of rituals, like showering and getting smartly dressed; using strong caffeine, alcohol or other drugs; and by the denial of sleep or food.

CASE STUDY Developing creativity and self-expression using storytelling and solo performance, by Professor Eric Trules

I believe that uncovering the personal story within and finding one's own 'personal voice' is an empowering and freeing art form. This kind of self-expression connects human beings across cultures. I am an artist-educator who wants to take this storytelling, film and theatre monologue work around the world, changing it one story at a time.

In 1985, I began directing, then writing and performing solo performance monologues. Two of them were shown at the Edinburgh Fringe Festival. I have taught 'Solo Performance' at the University of Southern California since 1994. From 1991 to 1998, I wrote, produced and directed an autobiographical 'personal voice' feature-length documentary film, 'The Poet and the Con', about my complicated relationship with my uncle, a career criminal and a confessed murderer. This kind of 'personal voice' filmmaking is the filmic equivalent to 'solo performance' in the theatre.

Later, as part of my Fulbright Scholar work for the University of Malaysia Sabah on the island of Borneo, I taught 'Solo Performance' to Chinese, Muslim and Malay college-age students – in English and in their native language. I had to find new techniques to teach storytelling because many of my students didn't speak English as their primary language. But with the help of one talented Chinese-Malay student, we found a way to communicate – and to discover the stories that lay hidden within each student. It took time. And trust. And an intuitive process of osmosis for the students to understand what I was looking for, what made a good story for an audience. After working with them for weeks orally, I finally had the students write their stories in Bahasa, their native language. I had them e-mail me the stories. Then I had them translated to English. I worked on them dramaturgically (the craft of developing and rewriting work in the theatre), and I had them retranslated to Bahasa. We went back and forth many times to get the stories as clear and effective as possible. Then we rehearsed for many more weeks. The same kind of language barriers and problems happened all over again. But again, the few who spoke English well were able to help me, and also help the others who didn't speak English well. At the end of the term, all the students performed their pieces in front of a full audience; all except one, in Bahasa. The audience cheered.

Original stories are honest, revealing, emotional, heart-warming, hilarious, and effective for a theatre audience. The stories were about sex, love, parents, childhood, ethnicity, death, fear, self-image, friendship, and many other intimate and personal subjects. They were stories for a multicultural tapestry of performers: white, black, Latino, Asian, Indian, all the colours of the rainbow that find themselves at the challenging and confusing time of adolescence and young adulthood. College-age stories – by real kids, real people, who are becoming, and are, real writers and artists. In the real, poetic, fractured, eloquent and profane language that they speak.

I can't say how many times students have told me that this kind of transformational self-discovery and intimate, personal writing work was the most powerful, memorable and important work they had done during their entire college careers. We all have stories within us. Secrets. Stories that we are too ashamed or embarrassed to bring to light. Who would want to hear these stories? Your horrible relationship with your mother or father? Your tortured, convoluted but triumphant coming-out story? Learning what trust and betrayal between friends means in life? Countless, unbelievable and unpredictable variations. What one comes to learn is that in the most neurotic, idiosyncratic and detailed personal story, when well told and well crafted, lies the universal. The story of my relationship with my mother, my father, my uncle, my friend, my lover, my enemy – the story of my fear, my triumph, my failure – is also your story. That's why stories are creative and cathartic.

What place does this personal storytelling work have in the field of education and in the field of learning? It is my opinion that too much time is spent in university on vocational training, on theoretical and academic issues, and/or on the mere acquisition and accumulation of knowledge. I know that this is what my college education was about. It was not until I graduated from university that I started to look at and discover myself. I think I started too late, and that discovering who one is and what one wants to do in life is an essential part of anyone's education. Certainly the two can coexist: academic and/or vocational training along with self-discovery. However, finding the latter of the two sorely neglected in both my own university education as well as in my observation of decades of students in my role as an educator, I have chosen my path to be that of educator of the 'self', ie how to look within oneself, discover one's own voice, and how to follow one's own unique path in life. It is what I teach in all my courses – self-expression and creativity. It's a crucial and essential part of 'learning'. Students are hungry for it.

Professor Eric Trules is an award-winning artist-educator and lecturer at the School of Theatre, University of Southern California, United States. He was a 2002 American Fulbright Scholar and spent eight months in Malaysia. He is an

Allen Ginsberg Poetry Award winner, and in over 30 years as a professional artist he has been a modern dancer, actor, clown, screenwriter, theatre and film director, arts festival producer, poet, documentary filmmaker, and solo performer. He offers international workshops in self-expression and creativity.

Contact: trules@usc.edu (www.erictrules.com)

Wisdom

Gardner (1993: 291), in his book on multiple intelligence, refers to four higher levels of cognitive work that go beyond a straightforward notion of 'an intelligence'. These are common sense, originality, metaphoric capacity and wisdom. Wisdom requires life experience and high levels of learning, considerable insight and experience, and a maturity that gives a strong ability to refuse to let the ego affect decision making and life choices.

Egan (2002: 19), referring to wisdom in the art of facilitation, remarks that 'helpers need to be wise, and part of their job is to impart some of their wisdom, however indirectly, to their clients'. He refers to two authors who define wisdom as 'an expertise in the conduct and meaning of life' or 'an expert knowledge system concerning the fundamental pragmatics of life'. Egan explores key characteristics that might usefully be developed in facilitator wisdom:

- self-knowledge and maturity;
- knowledge of life's obligations and goals;
- an understanding of cultural conditioning;
- the guts to admit mistakes and the sense to learn from them;
- a psychological and a human understanding of others; insight into human interactions;
- the ability to 'see through' situations; the ability to understand the meaning of events;
- tolerance for ambiguity and the ability to work with it;
- being comfortable with messy and ill-structured cases;
- an understanding of the messiness of human beings;
- openness to events that don't fit comfortably into logical or traditional categories;

- the ability to frame a problem so that it is workable; the ability to reframe information;
- avoidance of stereotypes;
- holistic thinking; open mindedness; open-endedness; contextual thinking;
- meta-thinking, or the ability to think about thinking and become aware about being aware;
- the ability to see relationships among diverse factors; the ability to spot flaws in reasoning; intuition, the ability to synthesize;
- the refusal to let experience become a liability through the creation of blind spots;
- the ability to take a long view of the problem;
- the ability to blend seemingly antithetical helping roles – being one who cares and understands while being also the one who challenges and 'frustrates';
- an understanding of the spiritual dimensions of life.

Conclusion

What does this knowledge about the nature of thinking, knowing and intelligence actually contribute to the practice of experiential learning? While the exact nature of intelligence remains controversial, it is clear that intelligence is more than just a range of cognitive abilities such as reasoning and problem solving. It is important to acknowledge the breadth of processes involved in thinking with the mind such as thinking with feelings, thinking with our bodies, deep thinking and shallow thinking, fast and slow thinking. Such knowledge can support the development of deeper forms of experiential learning.

In order to understand experiential learning this broad ecology of thinking, knowing and intelligence must be explored in practice. All influence how we experience the world. Learning is not separated from the landscape of the body, of gut feelings or intuition, of emotions and spiritual feelings, nor is it separated from the outer landscape of our surroundings. There is still so much to learn about knowing and intelligence. What we discover will undoubtedly affect the future development of experiential learning. In considering the nature of intelligences in people, there is a further dimension of intelligence that is worthy of a brief mention in a final spirit of provocation. In Senge *et al*'s book *Presence* (2005), the authors note that 'the blind spot' of contemporary science is experience. They comment that David Bohm, a former colleague of Albert Einstein, said that 'the most important thing going forward is to break the boundaries between people so we can operate as a "single intelligence". Bell's theorem implies that this is the natural state of the human world, separation without separateness. The task is to find ways to break these boundaries, so we can be in our natural state' (Senge *et al*, 2005: 189).

Deeper learning 09
(the being dimension)

Realize deeply that the present moment is all you ever have. Make the Now the primary focus of your life. ECKHART TOLLE

Introduction

The final cog in the learning combination lock is that of 'Being' – developing an awareness of our inner self and our relationship to the outside world. The question: 'Who are we?' has been asked by humankind for millennia and a proverb from the Inner Temple in Luxor, Egypt, exhorts: 'Man, know thyself, and you are going to know the gods' (De Lubicz and Lamy, 1978). This aphorism also may have influenced the Greek philosophers, resulting in 'know thyself' being carved into the Temple of Apollo at Delphi in ancient Greece, and prompting Socrates to declare that: 'The unexamined life is not worth living.'

This examination of life and being has absorbed philosophers without them ever providing a fully satisfactory answer. For example, the Roman Stoic philosopher Seneca proposed that a human was: 'A reasoning animal', which resonates with the scientific name 'homo sapien' meaning 'wise man'. This perspective also echoes 'the naked ape', which is how zoologist Desmond Morris (1967) described, analysed and interpreted the behaviour of humans.

Yet, surely we are more than animals? One suggested distinction is that only humans use tools but there are numerous examples from the animal kingdom in which tools are used, including chimpanzees using stones to crack nuts and manipulating grass straws to extract termites from their mounds (Goodall, 1971). Another distinction is that only humans have a theory of mind, yet, research into scrub jays suggests that when they cache food to eat at a future date they also pay attention to other creatures that may be observing them. If the jays feel the food might be stolen they often go back later and rehide the food in another place (Thom and Clayton, 2013).

Does this mean they have a theory of how other creatures might think, or are we, as humans, just projecting how we reason on to the shrub jays?

Neuroscience investigations into the operations of the brain provide more insights on the mind to add to those garnered from philosophy, zoology, sociology, etc. Yet, there is still a lack of clarity on what we mean by the concept of mind and where it might be located. Is there a 'ghost in the machine' with the separation of mind and body as proposed by Descartes or are we an holistic entity of an integrated mind and body as Dewey (1916) and Koestler (1967) proposed?

Previous chapters have focused on doing, sensing, feeling and thinking as experiencing. They all contribute to our becoming and our being. In this chapter we examine the nature of being and becoming and how they relate to experience. To do this we explore the following areas:

- The experience of being human.
- The importance of well-being.
- The nature of mindfulness.
- Reflecting on our past and present experiences.
- The practice of action learning.
- The experience economy.

Who are you?

Some of the most rewarding learning for course delegates often emerges from the unwinding process at the end of the day when they are relaxing or, perhaps, debriefing around a campfire. Conversations sometimes gravitate to deeper philosophical explorations about fundamental issues that can be built upon by educators and trainers. One constructive approach is to ask one or more of the following questions:

'Who are you?'

'Why are you here?'

'Where are you going?

These questions can also be applied in a more pragmatic organizational sense. For example:

'Who are you?' What is your organizational role?

'Why are you here?' What are you doing on this course?

> 'Where are you going?' What direction is the organization going in and is this one that you buy into and which supports the direction of your career?
>
> It is important to allocate sufficient time to this exercise, particularly if you are approaching it from a philosophical perspective. There is the potential to surface existential anxieties and people may need to be supported with care and understanding.

The experience of being human

Collins English Dictionary defines 'human being' as: 'a member of any of the races of *Homo sapiens*; person; man, woman, or child', and the study of being, existence and reality is called ontology, which belongs to a branch of philosophy called metaphysics.

One of the central considerations of metaphysics is the extent to which our experiences are the same as other people's. We can never fully transpose ourselves into their minds and bodies and therefore can never be completely sure that what we experience is exactly the same for them. In other words, is our understanding of the world the same as another person's? Probably not, given that we interpret the world based on our knowledge, experiences and emotions, which are unique to ourselves. Nietzsche observed that: 'Man has no ears for that to which experience has given him no access', thereby suggesting that to understand a concept we need to have had contact with it first. The following discussion of human being and human experience from Plato illustrates some of the considerations and challenges faced when trying to educate people.

Plato's allegory of the cave

In *The Republic*, Plato presents an allegory of how our experience of the world might not fully represent reality or may even be misleading. He describes a cave in which people have been chained since birth so that they can only look straight ahead at the wall of the cave. A fire, behind the prisoners, casts shadows of the jailers and puppets onto the cave wall and the voices of the jailers are interpreted as coming from the shadows. The prisoners, never having experienced anything else, consider the shadows to be reality.

Plato suggests that if someone drags a released prisoner out of the cave and into the daylight the intensity of the sunlight would be very painful. Gradually, however, the prisoner's eyes adjust to the brightness of the sun and, first, he see shadows, then reflections of people and objects on water, and next real people and objects themselves. After this, he is able to look at the moon and stars at night and, finally, to look at the sun and understand the impact its light causes.

With his newly enlightened insight, the freed prisoner begins to pity the still-chained prisoners and returns to the cave. He once again experiences a form of blindness due to the low levels of light in the cave, and the other prisoners assume that he has been made blind by his journey out of the cave and believe they should not repeat his journey. Indeed, if someone were to try to drag them outside the prisoners might try to kill them.

This allegory has been interpreted in numerous ways by philosophers, who suggest that the cave is the world and the prisoners are inhabitants of the world. Moreover, the chains represent people's ignorance and the shadows represent the way they see the world. What 'chains' of ignorance do you possess and what are the 'shadows' that limit your understanding of the world?

Well-being

For much of the 20th century, governments followed the principle of driving increases in gross domestic product (GDP) because this wealth in a population normally leads to improved health, a key foundation of well-being. However, focusing on GDP may also have negative effects, which became very evident following the 2008 financial crisis. As a result, President Sarkozy of France established a Commission on the Measurement of Economic Performance and Social Progress, which reported:

> It has long been clear that GDP is an inadequate metric to gauge well-being over time particularly in its economic, environmental and social dimensions, some aspects of which are often referred to as *sustainability*.
> (Stiglitz, Sen and Fitoussi, 2009: 8)

> The time is ripe for our measurement systems to *shift emphasis from measuring economic production to measuring people's well-being*.
> (Stiglitz, Sen and Fitoussi, 2009: 12)

In response to the limitations of a focus on GDP, the commission identified eight key dimensions of well-being for attention:

- material living standards (income, consumption and wealth);
- health;
- education;
- personal activities, including work;
- political voice and governance;
- social connections and relationships;
- environment (present and future conditions);
- insecurity, of an economic as well as a physical nature.

(Stiglitz, Sen and Fitoussi, 2009: 14–15)

The recommendations of the commission are welcome although not entirely new. In 1971 the state of Bhutan decided that well-being should take precedence over material advancement or GDP. It incorporated a number of principles into a Gross National Happiness measure and this strategy has since been adopted by many other countries, including the UK.

Another measure of well-being is the United Nations Human Development Index, which described human development as: 'the expansion of people's freedoms to live long, healthy lives; to advance other goals they have reason to value; and to engage actively in shaping development equitably and sustainably on a shared planet' (UNDP, 2010: 2). The index comprises three main dimensions: health, education and living standards – and the leading countries in the 2015 index were: Norway, Australia, Switzerland, Denmark and The Netherlands. The bottom five were: Burundi, Chad, Eritrea, Central African Republic and Niger. Given that education has a major influence on earning potential and 'greater satisfaction with life' (OECD, 2011: 193) it follows that the deeper the learning and education a person experiences the better the personal outcomes and well-being.

Mindfulness

An awareness of who we are, how we experience, and how we might improve our well-being has become much more visible with the growth of mindfulness, a form of meditation and reflection. The practice of meditation is believed to date back to around the 5th century BC in Buddhist India and Taoist China (Everly and Lating, 2002) and, over the centuries, has gradually spread across the world. During the 1970s, some of these meditation practices were disentangled from their religious dimensions, by Dr Jon Kabat-Zinn (1990) at the University of Massachusetts Medical School, and developed as a psychological tool in clinics to manage anxiety, stress and pain.

It is very easy to be caught up in our thoughts and to live our lives in our heads with little awareness of what is happening around us. This can also lead to thinking obsessively about particular problems in the past or the future and which seem to go round and round without ever being satisfactorily resolved. This rumination can affect people's well-being and result in stress and depression. To bring people into the present moment Kabat-Zinn encouraged them to focus their attention on the immediate internal and/or external stimuli they were experiencing, thus distracting their attention away from their problems.

In more recent years, the practice of mindfulness has rapidly increased as a means of managing stress, depression and other conditions. Much of this can be attributed to the success of Eckhart Tolle's (1997: 35) *The Power of Now: A guide to spiritual enlightenment*, in which he encouraged people to: 'Realize deeply that the present moment is all you ever have. Make the Now the primary focus of your life.'

Mindfulness has been defined in numerous ways to describe the importance of focusing and experiencing on the now:

> Bringing one's complete attention to the present experience on a moment-to-moment basis. (Marlatt and Kristeller, 1999: 68)

> The first component involves the self-regulation of attention so that it is maintained on immediate experience, thereby allowing for increased recognition of mental events in the present moment. The second component involves adopting a particular orientation towards one's experiences in the present moment, an orientation that is characterized by curiosity, openness and acceptance. (Bishop *et al*, 2004: 233)

Mindfulness involves directing one's attention to internal experiences, eg bodily feelings and sensations, emotions and thoughts; also paying attention to external experiences, eg sights, sounds and touch (Kabat-Zinn, 1994; Linehan, 1993). In our chapter on sensory intelligence (Chapter 6) we also touched upon this point. Guidance on how to practise mindfulness recommends the avoidance of judgemental evaluation of the internal or external stimuli. Instead of considering the stimuli to be good or bad, important or trivial, true or false, people are advised to just observe them (Marlatt and Kristeller, 1999).

In essence, there are three main skills involved with developing mindfulness:

1 Deliberately paying attention to moment-by-moment events as they develop either internally or externally.
2 Noticing how we habitually respond to these events.
3 Developing our ability to understand how we react to these events and carefully determining how we want to respond to the events.

One of the challenges of practising mindfulness is that when people stop mentally or physically chasing around, and slow down to meditate on internal and external stimuli, all sorts of thoughts and worries may surface and overwhelm them. In these circumstances, it is important to return to just being aware of the stimuli without being caught up in the emotions that can arise from disturbing thoughts.

Another of the key mindfulness practices to note is that thoughts are not us. What makes a thought seem real is the attention that we give to it, and if we divert our attention to something else then that original thought and the associated feelings disappear, at least while we are concentrating on other things. Williams (2017), former director of the Oxford Mindfulness Centre, recommends: 'Imagine standing at a bus station and seeing "thought buses" coming and going without having to get on them and be taken away. This can be very hard at first, but with gentle persistence it is possible.'

This observation of our thoughts as a neutral spectator distances and separates us from them and helps us understand that our thoughts are not necessarily us. A practical way to recognize this is to pay attention to the endless range of thoughts that pass through our head and how we make conscious and unconscious decisions about which ones to focus upon. For example, multiple images come into view when we look across a room or landscape – some elements attract our attention more than others: perhaps it is a moving image on a television screen, or a lone tree standing on top of a hill. But, we don't have to blindly follow our thoughts; instead we might choose to focus on the pattern on the curtains or a flower growing among the blades of grass. A mindfulness exercise can be found in our chapter on emotions (Chapter 7).

CASE STUDY The emergence of the three Cs concept

> For centuries we have been conditioned by nationality, caste, class, tradition, religion, language, education, literature, art, custom, convention, propaganda of all kinds, economic pressure, the food we eat, the climate we live in, our family, our friends, our experiences – every influence you can think of – and, therefore, our responses to every problem are conditioned. Are you aware that you are conditioned? That is the first thing to ask yourself, not how to be free of your conditioning. You may never be free of it, and if you say, 'I must be free of it', you may fall into another trap of another form of conditioning. So are you aware that you are conditioned? (Jiddu Krishnamurti)

A while ago when working with Colin Beard in Singapore I had to deliver a session with outdoor educators on the topic of 'professionalism'. It's not a word I have been fond of because of my own past associations with it, often along with the word 'maturity'. The image of a suited, cold, expressionless person is what I see. It means different things in different cultures too.

When I was able to let go of that image consciously, I realized I had no other idea about what 'professionalism' meant. I decided to redefine it in my mind as a map. What words do I associate with it? The mind map grew to confusing proportions before clarity began to appear in the form of patterns! This is so similar to what happens when I say I am confused. It's an unmanageable state of ambiguity with random unconnected thoughts.

Let me try to describe what emerged. I stayed with it a while, without forcing a solution, long enough for patterns and clarity to appear. I loved that moment. I also notice that this is applicable in every moment and aspect of living. It isn't new by any means. It is just another way of looking at our lives. I realized that there are three things that have an influence on everything we do. The Past we come from, the Present moment, and the Future or what we want to see happen. Most times we are either in the past or the future. This is beautifully put by Ugway in the film *Kung Fu Panda* in a play on words – *'Yesterday is history, tomorrow is a mystery, today is a gift, which is why we call it the present.'*
The past and the future affect our present emotional state, and therefore our behaviour. So it makes perfect sense that we need to be aware of what from our past is influencing our present actions, because that is certainly going to inform our conduct.

This is certainly true when we are in the role of an educator, attempting to enable another's learning. We carry our past and conditioning with us at all

Figure 9.1 The three Cs model: conditioning, consciousness and conduct

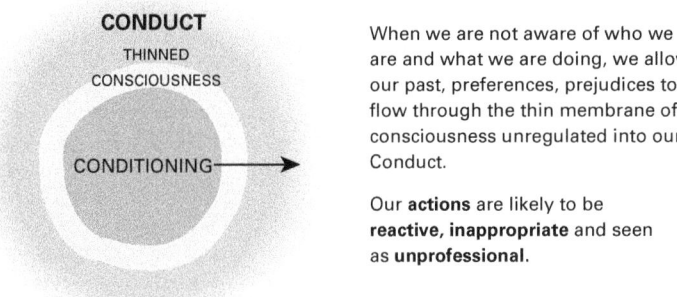

times. These three elements and their relationship is what this is all about. Conditioning, Consciousness and Conduct (Figure 9.1).

This relationship between the three Cs has become a centrepiece of almost everything I have done since. It just makes a lot of sense to me, and it appears a far easier way for me to understand why I do what I do. Let's take a dive into what Conditioning means. My partial list included the following:

- Upbringing – the way I have been brought up, the things that people told me are right, wrong, good, bad, things to stay away from, things to reach out for, definitions of success and failure.
- Schooling, training – the way I was taught may become the way I teach.
- Personal preferences – an idea about the way things MUST be (dress sense, eat with the right hand, don't use bad words, silence is a good thing in the classroom, respect means not challenging what you have been told).
- Morals and values – they have strong cultural influences. In some cultures, couples living together before marriage is unacceptable.
- Beliefs.

As facilitators, our role is to enable the learning of our participants. With a major part of our attention outside us, we forget that we also need to enable our own learning. We know that when we become better at what we do, we offer a richer environment to our learners. What prevents us from risking new things in a session is a fear of failure – what if it doesn't work the way I imagined? Yet, the battlegrounds for everything we do ARE the sessions we conduct (Figure 9.2). It is practice time, as well as delivery time! When we hold back from this risk taking, we play out old, tested, tried ways to a point where they become the same over time. We wonder when our work became so boring!

Figure 9.2 Heightened consciousness

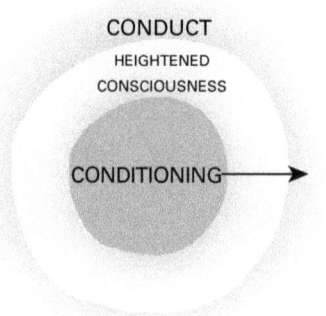

When we take time to think about where we are, who our audience is and our response to what we sense in the present, we are more mindful about our Conduct.
Due respect is given to our past, conditioning, training and education, yet decisions are informed by what is real now.

Our **actions** are more **appropriate and sensitive** to what is needed in the moment.

The idea of consciousness changes that. It can make our work exciting, progressive and more effective. This is my list of what consciousness could be or look like while facilitating:

- I have prepared, I have thought through why and what I am going to do. I have planned to death! Now is the time to throw it away – that's what will help me be alive to the present.
- I walk into that space, intensely aware that the audience I met yesterday is not the same I am meeting today. Life and time have happened to them in-between, and they are in some way different. Don't deal with them as though nothing happened in-between. Find out what is different if you want to know. Respond to who and how they are in the present – start from where they are. It's being respectful of change!
- Life happened to me as well. How has anything changed for me? How am I feeling right now? Am I carrying any anger, frustration, resentment into the learning space? Can I leave it on a hanger while I engage in the next few moments?
- Do I know how they are feeling in the moment? Do they want to be there, or somewhere else? Do I have a plan for dealing with that reality, or should I just go ahead with my agenda?
- I have prepared, but I am nervous because I have planned on doing something new. Shall I wear a mask of the 'know-all', or shall I open myself to the 'not knowing'? Can I stand there and allow myself to be playful and vulnerable?
- I walk into the learning environment, knowing that even if I have met them before, the environment itself will influence them. Whether they are in

a conference room in their own office, in a hotel, at an outdoor site, on a boat in the sea, or on top of a mountain – is going to affect receptivity and outcome.

- There will always be people to whom what I am saying does not make sense. They might challenge everything I say or do. How will I manage dissenters? What is the spirit with which I shall talk to them? What principles and values will come into play?
- How shall I deal with my own anger or resentment in case I feel it about something on the programme or in the classroom?
- How shall I deal with having to respond when I really don't know the answer?
- I know judgement (good/bad, right/wrong, etc) prevents exploration and discovery. How will I stay awake to its arrival in my thinking and language?
- What am I stuck to? What are my non-negotiables? Things that I think MUST happen?
- I want to keep people engaged and participating. I cannot do it for everyone and all the time! There will be moments when groups of people disengage because the style I use does not work for them, while it works for others. Am I varying my styles for inviting engagement enough to give everyone in the group a chance to learn something? Am I delivering to different styles?
- I am aware that learning is a life-long process. What they experience today may not result in a change of any kind tomorrow! The understanding may come 10 years from now. All I need to have from them is their attention today! Don't get attached to seeing change.
- Where is the group at in their understanding of the topic we are about to engage in? I would like to start from where they are, not where I am (assuming I am more well-read than them!). There is little value in completing what I came to do, if I don't begin with them in mind.
- Once the process has begun, and I am aware of all these different things, I want to be able to stay open to outcome. There is nothing to be gained by taking people where they don't want to go. For that I must be prepared (Read! Read! Read!) to go anywhere (almost!) they want to go that day. It may change tomorrow.
- Pause after listening to them. Pause after saying something. Breathe! Let the blood go to parts of the brain that can respond in the best manner in the moment. Quick reactions often come from practised, conditioned, old and little understood ways from the past. This is here and now! It needs to be responded to in the present, here and now! Ask – 'What is real NOW?'

- I do not want to exercise power over anyone. I am not here to change anyone. I am here to help someone see what they can't on this day. If I keep the power, they are likely to do what I want them to. If I give away the power, they are likely to do what they want to do. So ask at all times – 'Who has the power?', and if the answer isn't working for the group, change the conditions.
- Are my intentions behind what I am doing, clear to myself? Do I know why I am doing what I am doing? If not, get an answer!
- Stay calm. Stay happy. 'This is not about me!'

I'm sure there is lots more to be aware and conscious about. Think about what your list looks like, and sounds like. Keep it with you on cards as a reminder. Look at them occasionally, when you are in engagement with the group. I'm guessing it will change the way things are!

Vishwas Parchure, Pune, India (www.experiential.institute)

Awareness through the development of reflective practice

This natural introspection into our being and existence described above has been adopted and applied in organizational settings by many writers, and the practical considerations for active reviewing were explored in Chapter 5, in the *doing* dimension of experience.

Human beings have reflected on their actions for as long as we know; the circumstances described next are drawn from Kolb's writings about Lewin, and led to the formalization of the process of reflective practice. In 1946, Lewin and a number of colleagues worked on the development of training approaches in leadership and group dynamics for the Connecticut State Interracial Commission. Group discussion was encouraged between the participants and the staff, and records of the meetings were kept and later discussed by the staff without the involvement of the participants. However, the participants were concerned that they were not involved with this discussion and approached Lewin requesting permission to attend, and he agreed. Lippit, who was present, observed that a remark made by an observer was challenged by one of the participants who disagreed with the interpretation of events:

> At the end of the evening the trainees asked if they could come back for the next meeting at which their behaviour would be evaluated. Kurt [Lewin], feeling that

it had been a valuable contribution rather than an intrusion, enthusiastically agreed to their return. The next night at least half of the 50 or 60 participants were there as a result of the grapevine reporting of the activity by the three delegates. The evening session from then on became the significant learning experience of the day, with focus on actual behavioural events and with active dialogue about differences of interpretation and observation of the events by those who participated in them. (Lippit, in Kolb, 1984: 9)

Kolb (1984: 9) stated that this incident demonstrated that 'learning is best facilitated in an environment where there is dialectic tension and conflict between immediate concrete experience and analytic detachment'. To put it rather less academically, the learner was freed to think about events that happened in order to make sense of them.

This leads us to the question, what do we mean by reflection? Dewey (1938: 9) defined reflective thought as, 'Active, persistent and careful consideration of any belief or supposed form of knowledge in the light of the grounds that support it and further conclusions to which it leads... it includes a conscious and voluntary effort to establish belief upon a firm basis of evidence and rationality.'

Reflection-in-action and reflection-on-action

One of the main books on the subject of reflection is *The Reflective Practitioner* by Donald Schön (1983). He distinguished between what he termed reflection-in-action and reflection-on-action as a means of investigating how people used their experience to analyse and frame problems, propose action and then re-evaluate the experience as a result of the action.

Reflection-in-action considers the consequences of action while one is within the process. This is what we term concurrent learning. Reflection-on-action (Schön, 1987) involves thinking about previous personal experiences, analysing them and then developing personal theories of action; and this we call retrospective learning. The final chronological form of learning is prospective learning, ie exploring future possibilities, which is discussed in the next and final chapter.

Not only can reflection occur in a structured environment with formal support from the organization; it can also occur as a form of unstructured reflection where people gather together when they meet a challenging experience. This reflection occurs as managers attempt to make sense of the circumstances in which they find themselves.

Table 9.1 Reflection-on-action and reflection-in-action

Coached reflection (reflection-on-action)	Reflection-in-action
Planned intervention to support learning from an experience.	Spontaneous reflection that occurs as a result of a need to understand and respond to experience.
Learner(s) supported by a facilitator.	Learner(s) organize reflection themselves.
Is planned for specific times.	Can occur at any time but usually when understanding of the circumstances is necessary and when time is available.
Usually happens with learner(s) away from the immediate workplace.	Usually happens in the workplace.
Involves contemplation.	Reflection is an active process.

SOURCE Adapted from Seibert (1999)

Making sense of what is happening to themselves by professionals has been termed reflection-in-action by Schön (1983). This form of reflection occurs particularly where people face unusual and different experiences that they find difficult to structure and make sense of. Reflection-in-action does not necessarily require support or coaching because it happens spontaneously. However, for deep learning to occur there is a danger in relying on reflection-in-action happening, especially when time constraints put a premium on people making time to analyse what is happening. It is for this reason that many organizations have coaching, counselling and mentoring structures to support the development of their employees. Seibert (1999) called reflection-on-action coached reflection and illustrated the differences between the two (see Table 9.1).

Encouraging conditions for reflection

Although reflection-in-action can occur spontaneously within an organization, the possibility of it happening is conditional upon the variety of factors occurring at the time, eg work pressures may minimize the opportunity for reflection. In the research conducted by Seibert (1999), one manager described how, owing to a heavy workload, his reflection was momentary. This does not necessarily minimize the potential for reflective learning from the experience, since there may still be potential for profound insights.

However, constraining the opportunities for reflection may also severely limit the degree and quality of the reflection and therefore the degree of learning. It is hard both to do and to reflect at the same time when the issues are complex and may not be related.

Five main factors that encourage reflection were identified by Seibert (1999) and are described below:

1 **Autonomy.** Where people work autonomously they are personally responsible for their actions and therefore must think things through and decide for themselves. Where people operate within the responsibility of others there is a danger that they will abdicate the responsibility for thinking and just follow instructions. The degree of autonomy is the responsibility of the organization. Seibert described a manager, Ted, who was given a considerable degree of autonomy while working on the launch of a new frozen-food product. On his return from the assignment he experienced a very directive environment that allowed little opportunity for autonomy and reflection. It is easy to imagine the difficulties that could occur in terms of demotivation and a sense of lack of trust among his emotions.

2 **Feedback.** Feedback will also improve the quality of reflection, for without it there would be few ways of measuring performance and benchmarking what had or had not been achieved. For Ted, feedback was received from his manager, marketing and sales staff, and retailers. It is not sufficient to know where you are going; you need also to know how well you are doing on the journey.

3 **Interactions with other people.** In Hall's book *The Career is Dead, Long Live the Career* (1995) he maintained that 'other people' were essential to supporting reflection-in-action. Seibert identified three types of interaction between the manager and others:

   – Access to others: a manager's work situation needs to provide interaction with others who have important information.
   – Connections to others: this category is not the same as 'access to others' since it concerns a 'meaningful supportive relationship' (Seibert, 1999: 60) in which bosses, peers, mentors and even spouses give emotional support.
   – Stimulation by others: the need for others to provide information, new ideas and perspectives, which encourage the development of ideas.

4 **Pressure.** Promotive pressure is the situation in which managers have a high workload with little time in which to complete it. 'Not surprisingly,

this reflection was highly concentrated and of brief duration, often lasting for only a few moments' (Seibert, 1999: 61). Directive pressure is related to the pressure people experience as a result of undertaking a highly visible assignment that focuses attention on their project.

5 **Momentary pressure.** This refers to those few occasions managers have when they can reflect on their work. These occasions are often when the person is involved with other activities such as walking to a meeting, waiting for an answer on the telephone, or even in the lavatory!

The categories described by Seibert above illustrate some of the circumstances when people reflect in the workplace. However, he does not discuss the quality of the reflective process and, in particular, how effective the insights are. The finding that managers have significant time pressures is nothing new and their limited time to reflect, sometimes only in the toilet, indicates that personal management of time and the creation of thinking time is an essential ingredient if reflection-in-action is to deliver satisfactory results.

Single- and double-loop learning

Allied to the process of reflective practice is Kolb's learning cycle and also Argyris and Schön's (1974) single-loop learning and double-loop (or deutero) learning. They drew on the work of Bateson's (1972) *Steps to an Ecology of Mind*, which discussed single-loop learning and deutero learning. Single-loop learning involved planning the action, undertaking it, evaluating it and, finally, learning from the previous stages (see Figure 9.3). Essentially, it is not too different from the learning cycle and quality improvement cycle, which we saw in Chapter 2. What the learner asks is, 'Am I doing the thing right?'

Figure 9.3 Single-loop learning

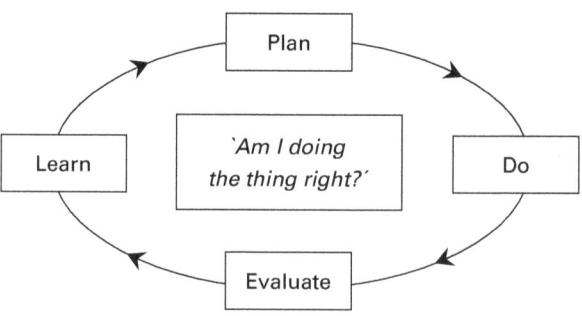

Figure 9.4 Deutero or double-loop learning

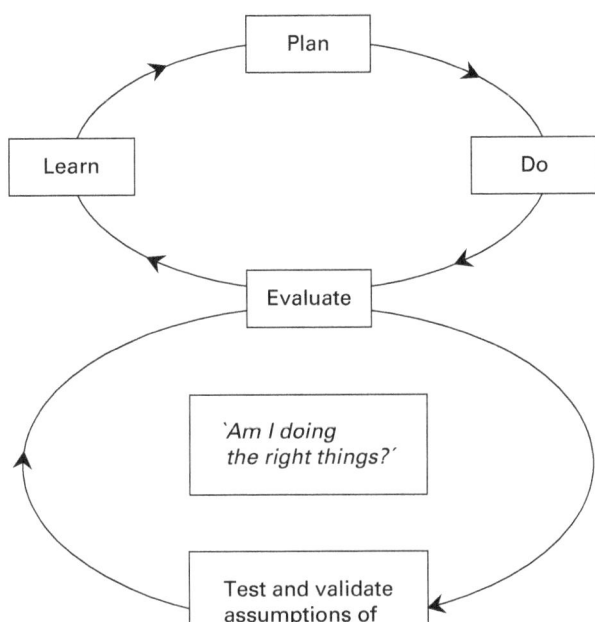

Double-loop learning, or deutero learning, is similar to single-loop learning. However, in this case the learner steps out of the single loop in order to assess whether the activity he or she is involved with is appropriate and asks, 'Am I doing the right things?' (see Figure 9.4). For example, a traditional watchmaker might be operating within the single-loop learning process and progressively improving what he does. However, it may be that he should have been asking himself whether he should consider digital technology. It was this single-loop learning that caused the Swiss watchmaking industry so much trouble until they asked themselves, 'Are we doing the right things?' This may be a historical example, but when looking through the financial pages of newspapers it is not difficult to find illustrations of industries and organizations that have failed to reflect more widely on what they are doing.

Using problems and challenges

Freire's (1982) concept of banking education described how the teacher 'narrated' and pupils were passive receptacles into which information could be poured. Freire was very critical of this approach, saying that not only did it dominate the pupils with a way of thinking but it inhibited them from thinking and learning properly.

To counteract the banking concept Freire (1982: 54) proposed 'problem-posing education'. Rather than banking education with its anaesthetizing effect, 'problem-posing education involves a constant unveiling of reality' and it 'strives for the emergence of consciousness and critical intervention in reality'.

Freire (1982: 54) stated that the teacher 'does not regard cognizable objects as his private property, but as the object of reflection by himself and the students. In this way, the problem-posing educator constantly reforms his reflections in the reflection of the students. The students – no longer docile listeners – are now critical co-investigators in dialogue with the teacher.' This approach involved the teacher and the pupils working alongside one another rather than being divided by desks and, more importantly, being divided by didactic and organizational barriers (at this point it may be useful to return to the case study on XP School in Doncaster, Chapter 3). By reflecting together he believed learning was best achieved through providing pupils with problems rather than solutions. Freire (1982: 54) stated:

> Students, as they are increasingly faced with problems relating to themselves in the world and with the world, will feel increasingly challenged and obliged to respond to that challenge. Because they apprehend the challenge as interrelated to other problems with a total context, not as a theoretical question, the resulting comprehension tends to be increasingly critical and less alienated. Their response to the challenge evokes new challenges, followed by new understandings; and gradually the students come to regard themselves as committed.

This approach to using problems to encourage reflection is a form of Socratic investigation. In effect, the recognition of a problem is the acceptance that there is a gap in performance. Through the process of challenge from either a problem or alternative perspectives from other people, reflection can lead to learning. This is a fundamental part of human nature, and Freire (1982: 56) maintained, 'Problem-posing education bases itself on creativity and stimulates true reflection and action on reality, thereby responding to the vocation of men as beings who are authentic only when engaged in inquiry and creative transformation.'

Problems and problem solving are at the essence of human development, and this theme will be revisited in the consideration of action learning, below and also in Chapter 10. The same principle of problem or challenge is incorporated in Chapter 4 on belonging, where we consider how different environments can be chosen for their impact on the learning objectives.

Problems and painful learning

> Experience is the name everyone gives to their mistakes.
> (Oscar Wilde, *Lady Windermere's Fan*)

Learning from experience has its challenges since not all the circumstances we face in life can be said to be enjoyable. Whilst many learning opportunities can be satisfying, not all learning experiences would be chosen by the individual as a route to learning. Life is often unpredictable and, as a result, presents many opportunities for learning – as long as our minds are open to their potential. Problems are often a great starting point for identifying learning opportunities at a personal level, or at an organizational level, as can be seen in the discussion about action learning below.

It is the case that many painful experiences remain with us for the rest of our lives and become reference points that we take into account before acting again in a similar manner. Indeed, these painful experiences may act as blocks to learning through preventing us from acting in a particular way. This attitude can be a valuable survival mechanism but it can also lead to our own extinction through inhibiting our behaviour.

Snell (1992) investigated experiential learning at work and asked: 'Why can't it be painless?' He concluded that hard knocks and psychological blows are inevitable in the work situation and that these shocks provide the opportunity for moral lessons and character building.

Snell emphasized that for people to learn from hard knocks they had to see them as a learning opportunity. He also drew attention to the fact that if people continued to experience a series of hard knocks then they were likely to be numbed and overloaded by their effects. In cases such as this, a person may withdraw physically and/or emotionally from whatever is causing the challenges and thus limit the potential for learning. It is therefore important to identify optimal learning experiences. Palethorpe and Wilson (2011: 423) stated: 'The management of anxiety is a central concern for learning providers who, if the correct balance is not struck, risk leaving delegates bored and unmotivated or paralysed with fear and anxiety.'

CASE STUDY Working at the 'edge' zone

Whether it is a matter of our ways of knowing, our being or our acting in the world, being challenged often takes us out of our *comfort zone* (Mälkki, 2010, 2011). That is to say, when nothing questions our assumptions and we are able to interpret situations within the light of our previous experiences, we experience ourselves comfortable, in the *comfort zone*. Instead, when our beliefs, attitudes, values, relationships, or sense of understanding the world, for example, become questioned, we experience edge-emotions, ie discomfort and anxiety. These edge-emotions are, therefore, indicators of a threat to our meaning frameworks and current configuration of self (Mälkki, 2010, 2011).

Our emotions support survival by orienting us automatically to concrete action, such as fight, flight or freeze (Damasio, 1999, 2003). We are automatically oriented towards returning to our comfort zone: to feel ourselves comfortable and safe again we tend to avoid dealing with the unpleasant issues that question our ways of knowing or being. We interpret the issues in a way that they no longer appear threatening. We have a natural resistance towards change and a tendency to cling to our current meanings.

If we wish to overcome some of the limitations to learning and change that the edge-emotions present, we need to recognize, in our thinking, this pattern of being automatically oriented towards the comfort zone. Often we wish to remove the unpleasant emotions out of our experience before we even have had time to actually live them through, digest them and hear what they wish to inform us. However, instead of being automatically oriented away from the unpleasantness at the edges of our comfort zones, we may aim to identify, accept and embrace the edge-emotions. With this kind of acknowledgement and tolerance of the edge-emotions that we inevitably encounter in life, we may be better suited to learning and change (Mälkki, 2010, 2011).

Kaisu Mälkki, post-doctoral researcher, Helsinki University, Finland

Action learning

Action learning was originally developed by Reg Revans, a former Olympic long-jumper and Cambridge physicist, who began the process in 1938 while investigating the entry of women into the nursing profession. His main concern was with the divide that occurred between the consultants and administrators (scribes) and the nurses (artisans). Revans, being a scientist, applied an evolutionary model to individual and organizational learning and stated that learning needs to be equal to or greater than the surrounding change:

$$\text{Learning} \geq \text{Change}$$

Revans also stated that learning consisted of two elements: programmed knowledge (traditional teaching and instruction) and questioning insight:

$$\text{Learning} = f(\text{programmed knowledge} + \text{questioning insight}); L = f(P + Q)$$

In his book *Developing Effective Managers*, Revans (1971) described an approach to succeeding in managerial objectives, which he called System Beta and which was based on the scientific method that he used as a researcher at the Cavendish Laboratories:

1 a stage of observation;
2 a stage of hypothesis or theory;
3 a stage of experiment;
4 a stage of inspection;
5 a stage of consolidation.

Revans (1971: 105–06) explained that this System Beta was a cycle that contained the following elements:

1 an attention-fixing event occurring within a framework of experience;
2 a new constructive relationship perceived in or around this event;
3 an attempt to exploit this relationship for some desired purpose;
4 an audit or inspection of the results of this exploitation;
5 the incorporation (or not) of the relationship into the experience of the manager, namely, a process of learning.

This cycle is very similar to Kolb's learning cycle, which was published two years after a visit to Kolb at MIT by Revans and 21 Belgian managers in February 1969. Moreover, Revans's early work on action learning has also been credited by Professor Naoto Sasaki, in his book *Management and Industrial Structure in Japan*, with being the foundation for the quality circle concept in Japan.

In addition to System Beta, Revans developed a contrasting perspective called System Gamma, which considered the 'pre-disposing mental set', ie the subjective consciousness of the manager. Linking the objective System

Beta and the subjective System Gamma is System Alpha, which involved personal values, the external environment and internal resources. It asked (Lessem, 1982: 11):

- By what values am I guided?
- What is blocking their fulfilment?
- What can I do against such blockage?

This consideration of values leads to the core of Revans's work; Pedler (1996: 91) concluded:

> Revans is a radical and it is clear from his writings that he intends action learning to be a deeper, more revolutionary process than just a training method for 'learning by doing'. Action learning, being about individual and organizational development, contains a *moral philosophy* involving:
> - honesty about self;
> - attempting to do good to the world;
> - for the purpose of friendship.

Pedler (1996: 13) explained that defining action learning was very difficult and stated: 'Although the idea may be essentially simple, it is concerned with profound knowledge of oneself and the world, and cannot be communicated as a formula or technique.' Revans (1982: 626–27) provided a long definition, part of which is reproduced here:

> Action learning is a means of development, intellectual, emotional or physical, that requires its subject, through responsible involvement in some real, complex and stressful problem, to achieve intended change sufficient to improve his observable behaviour henceforth in the problem field. 'Learning-by-Doing' may be perhaps a simpler description of this process, although action learning programmes assume a design and organization unnecessary in the everyday actions that supply the learning of young animals and of small children.

A clearer definition is given by McGill and Beaty (1992: 17):

> Action learning is a continuous process of learning and reflection, supported by colleagues, with an intention of getting things done. Through action learning individuals learn with and from each other by working on real problems and reflection on their own experiences. The process helps us to take an active stance towards life and helps to overcome the tendency to think, feel and be passive towards the pressures of life.

The action learning cycle is shown in Figure 9.5.

Figure 9.5 The action learning cycle

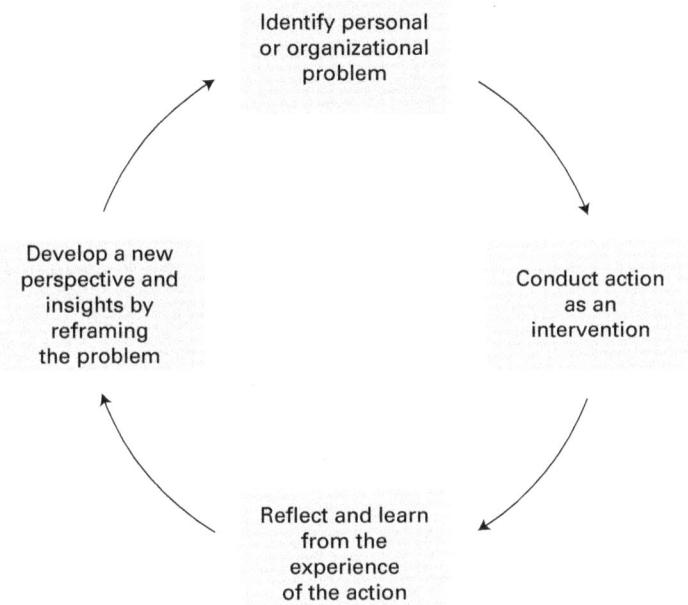

The action learning set

The main starting point for action learning is for each member of the group to bring a problem to the learning set or meeting. Learning sets provide a formalized structure in which people engage with the problem and are challenged, thus encouraging learning. They consist of four main elements:

- the person – who joins the group voluntarily;
- the learning set – the group of people who meet;
- the problem(s) – which each person brings to the meeting;
- the action – which is taken and learnt from.

The process for each individual at each meeting might be:

- action points from the last meeting;
- points completed and deferred;
- objectives to be achieved from this presentation;
- what the presenter learnt from completing and not completing action points.

Many of the activities that occur within an action learning set also occur naturally in the work situation and it is not uncommon for people to say that they learn through discussing things with colleagues. The main difference is that action learning is formalized and thus legitimizes the process and provides a clear focus on a specific problem or group of problems. It also occurs with a specific group of people who meet on a regular basis and not in an ad hoc manner, since the latter can lead to insufficient time and focus being given to the problems and learning opportunities.

The scope of the 'problem' can be small and discrete, or as large and complicated as the individual/group choose it to be. There is also no fixed duration for an action learning set or a project. On many occasions a project is brought to a group and may continue after the group has disbanded. In the reality of working life, problems are rarely completely solved; instead they change shape and/or lead into other related problems. As each issue is explored and addressed, so another surfaces ad infinitum.

The nature of the issues that are brought to the set can be placed on a spectrum from the very personal to those of concern to the organization. In order for the set to function effectively it is necessary for there to be trust and confidence among the members. Through this supportive environment, feelings and emotions can be explored, as well as practical issues, in a confidential environment. This takes time to establish and as confidence builds in the group so more will be shared. Action points may be minuted but the discussion is not normally included in any record of the meeting.

There are two roles in an action learning set: the presenter and the set member (and sometimes a facilitator). While the presenter is providing information about the project, it is the 'contractual duty' of the other set members to explore the project and help the presenter to discover new insights and strategies with the intention of resolving the problem. It is not necessary that the people know each other, nor do they need to be experts on the subject in question. Their role is not to provide advice, albeit this can be of value; rather it is to act as devil's advocates and question and challenge the assumptions that underpin the reflections of others in the learning set.

Although one objective of the meeting is the production of better action and results within the organization, another main purpose is the development of the individual. People actively challenge one another's ideas, encourage people to espouse theories and perceptions that they may not have voiced before, and help people consciously to think about other ideas and concepts that might be applied. The impact of this learning is then likely to have a longer-lasting impact than the transitory influencing of a project.

Revans (1982: 632) argued, 'It is development of the self, not merely development by the self of what is known of the external world.'

It is important, too, that the members carefully analyse the project to identify the 'problems' of the presenter. It is not uncommon for the initial problem to be underlain by a more fundamental problem that is different from the original one. Likewise, the presenter may think he or she has a specific problem and depart from the meeting with a very different one. Feedback techniques such as rephrasing and gently probing can enhance the quality of the interaction between the presenter and the other members of the set.

As with counselling, there is much to be said for each presenter discovering his or her own solutions and new perspectives on the projects. To be provided with an answer dilutes the learning process and may result in the presenter not buying into the solution. The process may take much longer when the answer is not directly provided. Furthermore, an answer may not be the answer that is most appropriate to the situation since the presenter is often the most knowledgeable person about his or her situation.

The learning set needs to be carefully managed to optimize learning in order to avoid the following:

- providing answers too readily;
- allowing certain individuals to coast through the process without really examining their circumstances;
- allowing members to be too vague and not specific with their action plans and presentations;
- members receiving support when they make their presentations but not contributing to the process when others make their presentations.

In addition to the identification of more effective ways of working and also perceiving issues there are other benefits from undertaking the process of action learning, which include:

- enhanced effectiveness in working with the range of relationships at work, including teamworking, developmental roles such as mentoring, and working with and encouraging cultural and transpersonal change;
- capacity to learn, reframe and empower self and others;
- ability to live with uncertainty and ambiguity;
- enhanced capacity to undertake project management;
- developing skills of active facilitation that can be utilized to manage group processes. (McGill and Beaty, 1992: 190)

In summary, the basic elements of an action learning set are:

- Ground rules may be developed by the members.
- Ground rules may be changed following discussion by the members.
- Equal time should be allotted to each member (approx 30 minutes).
- Action plans should be agreed.
- All members should make a commitment to attend.
- Each member's project is dealt with in turn.
- Members need to develop the skill of listening and receiving information.
- The presenter should clearly explain what he or she is looking for from the presentation so that the other members can focus their attention.
- Feedback should be conducted in a constructive and supportive spirit, which may require the development of these skills.
- Issues discussed in the set should be confidential.

The action learning set should also regularly review how effective it is in the process of encouraging development among its members. It should reconsider its ground rules and the culture that is operating in order to identify constraints and limitations that are holding back learning.

Experience and the inner game

The Inner Game of Tennis, a book by Timothy Gallwey (1986), a tennis coach and former junior tennis champion in the United States, has become a classic. Through the medium of tennis, Gallwey has made a number of observations about the nature of learning and experiencing.

His first observation was that the secret of winning a game of tennis was not to try too hard, with the result that the mind became more relaxed and it became easier to make better shots. As a new coach he had also noticed some apparent anomalies when he tried to coach pupils. Namely, some of the errors his pupils made seemed to correct themselves without his intervention or the pupils being aware of the improvement. Gallwey was also conscious of sometimes overteaching his pupils and the fact that on occasions his attempts to improve a particular stroke resulted in a deteriorating performance from the pupil. Telling pupils to lift their shoulder might result in other errors creeping into their game, with the result that they concentrated even more, causing further deterioration.

Gallwey theorized that there would appear to be two elements of the self involved with the game of tennis or other activities, ie the conscious self and the unconscious self. Self 1 is the part of the brain that is the conscious teller, which instructs the body and says such things as, 'keep the racquet head closer to the ground in order to give the ball more topspin'. Self 2, the unconscious automatic doer, carries out the various movements needed to play a game of tennis. It is important to be aware that this part of the brain operates all the bodily functions that are needed to live – it ensures that our heart keeps beating and that our lungs keep breathing without us needing to be consciously aware of it. In many ways our brain is like an iceberg: the conscious brain is like the tip of the iceberg above the water; the unconscious brain, which conducts most of the processing and which we are rarely aware of, is like the greater part of the iceberg, which is under water.

Every time a person hits or doesn't hit a ball, Self 2 is gathering the information and storing this information in the memory. It is aware of how high the ball is bouncing, where the head of the racquet is positioned, where the feet are, how fast the ball is travelling and so on. For a beginner, the most effective way to learn is to experience hitting the ball and avoid detailed instructions that put Self 1 and Self 2 into opposition.

Gallwey suggests that the basic language of Self 2 is not words, since we were learning as infants before we could speak. He maintains that an activity is learnt through feelings and visual images. This consists of stages:

1 **Observation.** In this stage, you see, feel and hear what is happening as you make a stroke.

2 **Programming.** You use visioning to see yourself serving and using supportive elements, such as the sound of the ball as it is hit, how smooth it feels to swing the racket, and the trajectory of the ball as it flies through the air and lands in the service box.

3 **Let it happen.** This stage is just to allow your body to do what is required without concentrating and using Self 1.

4 **Observation.** The cycle is complete and the server continues to be aware of what is happening from the various sources of sight, sound and touch that are available.

When sportspeople make a mistake they evaluate their performance, recognize that it was weak and then sometimes call themselves bad players. You can see this phenomenon on tennis courts, golf courses, football fields, etc, where people are talking and chastizing themselves as they play (this is Schön's reflection-in-action in operation). Not only does this self-criticism undermine their confidence but it also encourages Self 1, the conscious brain, to try to impose itself on Self 2, the unconscious brain, with destructive effect.

Gallwey recommended that we use Self 1 to support Self 2 by being alert and aware of what is happening. With a serve, many muscles are used, and the coordination of all the elements is very complicated; it is extremely difficult for us to concentrate on all these elements at the same time. All Gallwey advised is that when we attempt to serve into the opposite court we are aware and note where the ball landed, ie was it long or short, and was it to the left or the right? Through just letting it happen rather than concentrating hard on what is going on and making it happen the serve will become fluent and accurate. This simple feedback of being aware then allows Self 2 to make the necessary corrections unconsciously, and our game improves. Gallwey (1986: 50) stated, 'It is important not only to understand intellectually the difference between letting it happen and making it happen but to experience the difference.'

Being and peak experience

One of the key skills in playing tennis is the use of concentration. By concentrating we are able to focus more clearly on what is happening within ourselves as well as what is happening around us. This develops our consciousness and allows us to experience even more deeply. Gallwey (1986: 85) explained:

> Whatever we experience on a tennis court is known to us by virtue of awareness – that is, by the consciousness within us. It is consciousness that makes possible awareness of the sights, sounds, feelings and thoughts that compose what we call 'experience'. It is self-evident that one cannot experience anything outside of consciousness. Consciousness is that which makes all things and events knowable. Without consciousness eyes could not see, ears could not hear, and the mind could not think. Consciousness is like a pure light energy whose power is to make events knowable, just as an electric light makes objects visible. Consciousness could be called the light of lights because it is by its light that all other lights become visible.

Gallwey suggests that our focus can be developed in a progressive manner, moving from awareness, to attention, to concentration, to one-point concentration. The more we focus our attention the more we can experience. For instance, your concentration is on the words in this book, but if you disconnect from this stimulus and concentrate on what you can hear you may be able to pick out the sound of a bird or other sounds, and if you listen even more closely you may be able to identify what type of bird and where it is singing.

Similarly, concentrating on an experience and even reflecting on it will often provide us with a deeper and more satisfying sensation through increased understanding and increased awareness of the details that we might have overlooked when it did not fully occupy our consciousness. Thus concentration heightens the experience and enables us to benefit more significantly from events. Gallwey (1986: 125) asserted:

> What makes it possible to learn more from ordinary experience? Two people witness the same sunset; one has a deep experience of beauty, and the other, perhaps because his mind is preoccupied, has a minimal experience. Two people read the same lines in a book; one recognizes a profound truth while the other finds nothing worth remembering. One day we get out of bed and the world looks full of beauty and interest; the next day everything appears drab. In each case the difference lies in our own state of consciousness. In the final analysis it is our state of consciousness that is the determining factor in our appreciation of the beautiful, the true, or the loving.

Appreciation and recognition of beauty may lead to an advanced state of well-being. Most of us will have experienced occasions when we felt totally in tune with ourselves in some activity, perhaps at work, participating in a sport or being with another person. No major effort was required; there was no need to concentrate very hard because everything was very clear and understood. This heightened form of awareness is sometimes called peak experience and equates to Maslow's (1954) self-actualization. A good example of peak experience is given in Orlick's description of night-time skiing below:

Peak experience, being and skiing

One winter night, the sky was clear, the moon was full, the night air crisp. The snow sparkled like dancing crystals under the moonlight. It was a majestic evening as we set out to ski up the mountain trail to a small log chalet nestled in among the trees. We had a fire, had some wine, a bit of stew, joked a little and set out back down the mountain. As I skied down, I became one with the mountain, not knowing where it ended and where I started. I was so close to it, hugging it, it hugging me, as I flowed along that tiny snow-packed trail. I moved in shadows and out of shadows as the moonlight darted through the trees. I was totally absorbed in the experience… it was novel, challenging, sensual, fun, exciting, physically demanding, a meaningful trip with nature… a peak experience, the kind that makes it great to be alive.

SOURCE Orlick (1975: 12)

Orlick's description of being fully absorbed in the experience illustrates how he was fully aware of everything around himself and how he understood it so much that he became part of the mountain. In other words, he was learning to the fullest extent possible. Similarly, the inner game that Gallwey described is really a quest for the person on a journey of self-discovery and actualization. When we experience something very deeply we also know it to the maximum extent and this is a form of peak experience. It becomes very clear that if we wish to maximize learning we should involve people cognitively, affectively and behaviourally in the experiential learning event.

Being, becoming, transforming: the experience economy

The influence of the experience economy was explored in Chapter 2 and we return to this once more here. This chapter – on the dimension of being – has examined: who we are; well-being; mindfulness; reflective practice; and action learning. All of these are designed to lead to personal improvements and 'becoming' someone who has developed further across one or more dimensions. Yet, no one is perfect and can ever be so; therefore, if we are not careful we can turn personal development into an all-encompassing and unachievable obsession. This dilemma between achieving inner peace and tranquillity now, and being dissatisfied with our limitations thus seeking improvement and transformation, is something that needs to be balanced.

The commercial opportunities associated with transformation and change have been identified by numerous individuals and companies. In particular, Pine and Gilmore (1999) noted that economies may evolve through a number of stages that they mapped in their 'progression of economic value' model. The first stage involves commodities that are virtually indistinguishable from one another thus resulting in them being traded in bulk on exchanges with the focus on lowest price. The second stage involves the making of goods using these commodities and thus adding value. This approach offers more options and may be a little less competitive because it is possible to differentiate offerings; however, the volume of manufactured goods is now often greater than demand, putting pressure on selling prices and profit margins. Moreover, 'me too' products offer cheaper versions, increasing the burden on manufacturers. The third stage emphasizes the pre-eminence of services over products in what has been described as the post-industrial society (Bell, 1974).

The fourth stage is experiences that are not the same as services. A service might be a seat (if you are lucky) on a crowded commuter train during rush-hour; an experience would be luxurious first-class travel on the Orient Express to Istanbul with five-star accommodation, cuisine and entertainment. It is these experiences that command the highest prices, with Pine and Gilmore (1999: 11–12) remarking that: 'Commodities are fungible, goods tangible, services intangible, and experiences *memorable*.'

Four realms of experience were identified using a quadrant with dimensions of passive participation–active participation, and, absorption–immersion:

- Passive participation and absorption = entertainment
  (eg theatre, cinema, lecture theatre)
- Active participation and absorption = educational
  (eg co-production with learners)
- Passive participation and immersion = aesthetic
  (eg art gallery, museum)
- Active participation and immersion = escapist
  (eg theme parks, virtual reality)

The most relevant quadrant for this discussion is the active participation and absorption quadrant of the 'educational', which involves the learners interacting with the providers of the experience, eg schools, colleges, universities, training centres etc, to jointly co-produce a learning experience. This is where many educational institutions have placed a great deal of attention in enhancing the student experience and even establishing 'student experience offices'.

But, as Pine and Gilmore (1999: 244) explain, an experience can become commodified resulting in a 'been there done that' refrain from jaded consumers. In order to accommodate this concern, they added a fifth stage to their progression of economic value model, which is 'transformation'. In essence the customer becomes the product, ie they become transformed by the experience they have undergone. This is especially relevant to educational experiences that transform a person from the relatively naive young person who arrives to the mature individual who graduates. It is the quality of the experience that leads to this transformation.

Conclusion

We began this chapter by considering what it means to be human and this led to an exploration of the philosophical meanings of being and experience. The prisoners described in Plato's cave allegory interpret shadows as reality, but their experiences may only be a milder form of myopia in comparison to our own. It would appear that we never fully experience things with which we come into contact; hence Plato asking whether we can fully experience a bed and Dewey how we experience a chair.

Another dimension of our being is to create a healthy and rewarding life, which we call well-being. We can enhance this through practising mindfulness and reflecting on our sensory experiences and transient thoughts rather than living in the past or the future. This steered us to reflective practice and Schön's reflecting-on-action and reflecting-in-action. Allied to this is Revans's action learning, which focuses on real-life problems and uses these as vehicles for learning.

We then considered the experience economy and the importance of experiences for adding value, particularly when they result in the transformation of a person, through learning. It is this change and transformation to higher levels of being that drives us on – and we should not fear change. As Handy (1990: 44) advised:

> Change, however, does not have to be forced on us by crisis and calamity. We can do it for ourselves. If changing is – as I have argued – only another word for learning, then the theories of learning will also be the theories of changing. Those who are always learning are those who can ride the waves of change and who see a changing world as full of opportunities – not dangers.

PART THREE
Experiential learning and the future

Imagining, experiencing and learning from the future

10

As a society, we don't recognize or embrace the critical role of imagination. It is very difficult for people to understand things they have not experienced, and without being able to use and apply imagination to its fullest, we have become paralyzed. REICH (2017: 21)

Introduction

In his book *The Fifth Discipline*, Senge (1993: 23) described what he called the 'delusion of learning from experience'. He acknowledged the importance of learning from direct experience but then went on to argue that this was limited because of the extended timescales that may elapse before the impact of behaviour can be observed:

> But what happens when we can no longer observe the consequences of our actions? What happens if the primary consequences of our actions are in the distant future or in a distant part of the larger system within which we operate? We each have a 'learning horizon', a breadth of vision in time and space within which we assess our effectiveness. When our actions have consequences beyond our learning horizon, it becomes impossible to learn from direct experience.

Herein lies the core *learning dilemma* that confronts organizations: *we learn best from experience but we never directly experience the consequences of many of our most important decisions.* The most critical decisions made in organizations have system-wide consequences that stretch over years and decades.

Senge was right, to a point, that we cannot learn from direct experience about things far into the future but we can learn by extrapolating from the present and imagining the future. Indeed, many of the actions we undertake and the thoughts we process have at least one eye on the future; as *The Economist* (1999) observed: 'In every way that people, firms or governments act and plan, they are making implicit forecasts about the future.'

In this chapter we move away from exploring past and present experiences and consider the future through the following areas:

- imagination;
- a chronology of experiential learning;
- temporal limitations of Schön's reflective practice;
- reflecting on the past, present and future;
- virtual and augmented reality.

We are imagining all the time

In the analogue world of video recording, still images are sequentially recorded onto film in a linear manner and, when shown at 12–14 frames per second, give the impression of movement. In the brain, the recording of memories is not so simple and straightforward. Instead, memories are stored and distributed around the brain rather than in one place and when we recover these memories we reconstruct the individual fragments into a composite recollection (Lashley, 1951).

Engrams or memory traces, unlike books on a shelf, are not stored and read one word after another as they have been printed. Rather, they are reconsolidated, combining visual, auditory, tactile, olfactory, taste and emotional impressions from the event. In this way we can re-experience and relive events in our lives that have significance for us. In some ways this is a little like digital recordings on a hard disk, which are distributed across the disk rather than sequentially. Likewise, scratches to the disk can damage and disrupt access to the data just as brain injuries can with the brain. Yet there are differences – memories are often duplicated across the brain and so damage to one part of the brain does not necessarily mean that the whole memory is irretrievable. Also, harm to one part of the memory does not necessarily prevent the brain using the other components to re-create the event and fill in the gaps. Indeed, it is believed that this is what happens each time we remember something.

It is not just vision that is reconstructed. Consider how we engage in a conversation in a very noisy environment in which some of the words said by our conversational partner are interrupted or distorted by louder sounds. The fragmented sounds that we receive are then reassembled in our brains and the gaps are filled in from our experience to form the illusion of a continuous string of words.

Quite simply, our brains are constructing or reconstructing our experience of the world all the time by interpreting the signals of sight, sound, taste, touch and smell. In other words, it is 'imagining', ie turning a jumble of signals into a coherent whole, which enables us to perceive and interact with the world.

Imagination

Imagination is one of the most powerful mental tools we have at our disposal. Without this ability to speculate about what might be we would be imprisoned in a world of fatalism, waiting for whatever might befall us. We would be buffeted by whatever forces with which we came into contact and would just react rather than attempting to shape our destinies at least to some degree.

Without the ability to project our thoughts into the future we would be like a ship without a rudder; there could be no direction other than drifting at the mercy of the tides. If we lacked the ability to imagine the future there could be no plans, no hopes, no aspirations, no wants, no dreams and no desires (Wilson, 2012). There would only be ennui and a nihilistic approach to living life now with no regard to the consequences for the future. This would be a very negative existence, and indeed it is hard to think how the human species could have survived without the power to investigate the myriad futures that might be possible.

Fortunately, the world is not as bleak as that which has been described in the preceding paragraphs. We are able to use our imagination to 'mental time travel' (Tulving, 1972); we can speculate about possible alternatives; and we are able to select a course of action that can lead towards the achievement of our goals and objectives. Circumstances may intervene to hinder or prevent the achievement of our goals, not least our own limitations, but at least we have the ability to weigh up the possibilities of success by taking into account our own strengths and weaknesses. Sailing around the world like Ellen MacArthur may be a dream for those who are more adventurous, but the majority would recognize their limitations and fears, and opt for something more achievable such as sailing a dinghy on a relatively calm lake, or taking a sightseeing boat along the River Seine in Paris.

It is only through imagination that individuals and society have advanced and prospered. It enables us to learn from the future. Dewey (1934: 267), recognizing this importance, stated:

> [Imagination] designates a quality that animates and pervades all processes of making an observation. It is a way of seeing and feeling things as they compose an integral whole. It is the large and generous blending of interests at the point where the mind comes into contact with the world. When the old and familiar things are made new in experience, there is imagination. When the new is created, the far and strange become the most natural inevitable things in the world. There is always some measure of adventure in the meeting of mind and universe, and this adventure is, in its measure, imagination.

Our imagination is extraordinarily powerful and it provides us with the capability to explore possible options and potentially outline different future pathways – this is a form of focused imagination. There is also absent-minded imagination or daydreaming, which Killingsworth and Gilbert (2010) said was '"stimulus-independent thought" or "mind-wandering" and [which] appears to be the brain's default mode of operation'. Given that the brain naturally spends a significant proportion of the day either consciously imagining or in absent-minded explorations, more attention should be given to building upon these natural processes. Organizations and the education system should encourage people to develop their skills of imagination, vision, creativity and foresight rather than criticizing people for daydreaming.

There is a relatively clear process through which we investigate and act on our intentions. Dewey (1938) maintained that when we become aware of an impulse it becomes translated into a desire – something that we wish to achieve. However, neither an impulse nor a desire is the same thing as a purpose, which represents an achievement or outcome. Acting on an impulse or desire requires an examination of the potential consequences to determine whether they will have a positive or negative result. This examination requires the frontal cortex of the brain to assess whether desires and emotions that feed through the amygdala (which activates the emotional parts of the brain) are appropriate (Goleman, 1996). Dewey (1938) explained that a purpose is a complex operation and involves three main stages:

- Observation of the circumstances and environmental factors in operation at the time.
- Knowledge of what has occurred in similar circumstances in the past is applied to the observation of current factors. This knowledge is based upon personal experience and that of others, together with advice and what we have read and learnt about second-hand.
- Application of judgement. This takes into account the observations and recollections to assess their importance and determine which is the most appropriate course of action. Judging what is realistic and achievable, and the potential consequences of a course of action, is a critical part of the process.

In 1938, Dewey was aware of the importance of thinking about a desire or impulse before acting upon it. This use of judgement was an important one from an educational perspective, and he (1938: 81) stressed, 'The crucial educational problem is that of procuring the postponement of immediate action upon desire until observation and judgement have intervened.'

The process of thinking about the consequences of a desire before acting upon it is hugely important. Mischel's (2014) classic experiment that invites young children to postpone eating one marshmallow now in exchange for two marshmallows sometime later sums up the dilemmas we all face. Also, we often talk about the difficulty of choosing between 'heart' and 'mind', ie the distinction between what our emotions are encouraging us to do and the more analytical reasoning of the brain. Drawing on neurological research, we now know that the emotions originate in the limbic system, while the neocortex allows us to think more rationally about the facts before responding. Evolutionary physiology suggests that it was the emotional parts of the brain that developed first, thus allowing us to respond with alacrity to threats from the likes of sabre-toothed tigers. However, as the threats diminished it became more important to think through a course of action about a possible threat before responding. For example, our boss attempting to bully us may cause an instinctive desire to punch him or her, but in most cases, hopefully, reason will take over and we will address the issue through more appropriate means, eg a grievance procedure. More significantly, the 9/11 Commission Report stated:

> There were failures of imagination, policy, capabilities and management. The most important failure was one of imagination.

Imagination versus action

When people are accused of daydreaming it is usually in a pejorative sense, ie they are wasting time doing nothing or idly speculating about things that could never have any concrete reality. Of course, there is a danger that we can become lost in daydreams that are unattainable, as happened to Walter Mitty (Thurber, 1939) and Billy Liar (Waterhouse, 1959). In some respects this may be a waste of mental energy since the brain might be used for more constructive purposes. Indeed, perpetually wishing for things that are highly unlikely to materialize may be demotivating and harmful in its effects. Dewey (1938: 81) succinctly summed up this potential for wasting mental energy with the statement, 'If wishes were horses, beggars would ride.'

Alternatively, the process of daydreaming may be viewed more positively because it allows the brain to relax and enables it to structure, and store in the memory, information that might be used at a future date. Furthermore, daydreaming may be a means of energizing and exercising the brain when external stimuli are limited (Christoff *et al*, 2009).

The notions of daydreaming and imagination are not too disparate and may sometimes be interchangeable. However, on investigating them more closely it can be argued that daydreaming in its more negative sense implies futile speculation about unachievable objectives. Imagination, on the other hand, is perceived as being much more positive; hence the accusation that someone lacks imagination is seen as rather critical.

We saw earlier how the stages of an impulse may be translated ultimately into an action through a consideration of the requirements and demands needed to achieve an objective. Unfortunately, not all learning experiences are positive ones and these can mentally scar the individuals concerned. Peter Honey and Michael Pearn at the CIPD's Human Resource Development Conference in London looked at the nature of mistakes and stated that there were three types of behaviour by people who have made a mistake: some people recognized the mistake, learnt new behaviour and so avoided the mistake in the future; some did not learn and continued to make the same mistake time after time; and some were so traumatized by an experience that they avoided any potential of involving themselves in a similar experience again.

Staying within a safe and familiar comfort zone does have its benefits in the short term, but in the longer term it can also cause claustrophobia and stagnation. The lack of challenges minimizes the chances we have to learn new things and develop new conceptual frameworks. Failing to move from the comfort zone into the challenge zone removes most of the opportunities for learning. Postle (1993: 35) stated that:

> We often cling, with the intensity of addiction, to the comfort that comes from staying with our preferred mode and keeping away from the other modes. I remain convinced that this is usually because at some point in our history, one or another – or all – of the four modes of learning may have become debilitated or ruined. If this debilitation or damage was severe, whether locally or generally, then staying with the preferred mode may also successfully defend us against the feelings associated with that early hurt. If so, then our interest in action, *or dreaming up futures* [our emphasis], or caring, or arguing, whichever most keeps quiet our painful history, can indeed come to have the intensity of addiction.

It would appear, therefore, that we should add an element of caution to the use of imagination. While it fires our motivation it can also constrain our activity by locking us into idle speculation that may achieve very little. However, on the whole, the limitations of imagination are relatively small in comparison to the numerous benefits that can accrue from attempting to chart our future.

Mental fitness for the future

Have you ever broken an arm, leg or some other part of your anatomy and had it bound up in a plaster cast for a period of time? When the plaster was removed you would probably have noticed that the muscles surrounding the break were much weaker than before. Neurological researchers have discovered that not only are the muscles weaker but so too is the brain tissue associated with the movement of those muscles. The longer the body part is encased in plaster, the greater the shrinkage of the brain.

As the development of scanning and imaging technology has grown, so too has our knowledge of how the brain operates. In one experiment, research was conducted into the effect of physical and mental practice of tensing a finger in the left hand. During a four-week period involving five sessions per week, half the participants carried out physical exercises. The other people undertook a similar number of exercises but this was all done mentally. At the end of the period the ones who had done the physical exercises had increased their strength by 33 per cent. A control group who had done nothing showed no change. The virtual exercisers improved their finger strength by 22 per cent (Yue and Cole, 1992)! The increase in strength had resulted from changes in the brain.

In another exercise, participants mentally rehearsed a five-finger piano exercise for two hours a day over five days (Pascual-Leone *et al*, 1995). Brain scans revealed that the area of the brain associated with the fingers had expanded over the period of the exercises. Thus, it becomes clear that if we project ideas into the future we are likely to increase the number of connections within the brain and thereby increase the chances of us being more effective. When we consider imagination in this light it is possible to view it as a form of mental exercise designed to increase the chances of success in a future activity.

Imagining the future

> Imagination is more important than knowledge. To raise new questions, new possibilities, to regard old problems from a new angle, requires creative imagination and marks a real advance in science. (Albert Einstein)

Morgan (1997b: 2), in his book *Imaginization*, explains that: 'Imaginization is about improving our abilities to see and understand a situation in new ways.' The book provides a number of strategies to develop the mind and encourages the development of new perspectives and ways of thinking:

> In the most basic sense, imaginization invites a way of thinking. It encourages us to become our own theorists and to feel comfortable about acting on the basis of our insights. It invites us to develop a skill that I believe we all have, even though we may not realize that this is the case. By recognizing this, and thinking creatively and intelligently about ourselves and our situations, we can 'push the envelope' on our realities and reshape them positively. (Morgan, 1997b: 16)

To push the envelope on our realities and positively reshape them requires us to reflect and see past experiences in a new light – in other words this is a form of retrospective learning. It also requires us to place ourselves in new situations that present new challenges and opportunities for learning, ie prospective learning.

The difficulty is that we frequently fail to push the envelope and become entrapped in repetitious behaviour or habit, which Dewey described as 'the great flywheel of society' (Miettinen, 2000: 68). Revans expressed the danger of getting trapped in a particular routine or habit of which we were not aware and thus being unable to see or comprehend other ways of acting.

Imagination and the child

The power of imagination is strong, especially in children, who are sometimes unable to distinguish between fact and fantasy. The value of play enables children to rehearse skills and thoughts in a safe environment before venturing out into the real world where lessons are learnt in harder ways. Using their imagination allows children to project ideas into the future to test their viability and also allows the development of creativity. Developing the ability to imagine can unleash a powerful tool, as Alison Uttley (1943: 199), the children's writer, illustrated:

> Have you any toys? Toys! We play with anything, with sticks, stones and flowers, and we run about and look at things and find things and sing and shout. We don't have toys.
>
> The fields were our toyshops and sweetshops, our market and our storehouses. We made toys from things we found in the pastures. We ate sweet and sour food of the wild. We hunted from hedge to hedge as in a market, to find the best provisions, and we had our wild shops in corners of fields, or among the trees.

The benefits of prospective learning or imagination can be very powerful for the child and far exceed the testing of ideas and the development of creativity. Cohen (1987: 136) summarized the cognitive benefits:

> The well-imagining child would learn to integrate experience, work out what was inner and outer, learn to organize information better, become more reflective, elaborate perceptions and cognitions, recognize mistakes quicker and develop better concentration... The 'social benefits of imagery' included becoming more sensitive to others, increased empathy, poise, acculturation, self-entertainment, reducing fear and anxiety, improved emotional well-being and self-control.

Parents frequently encourage their children to become more mature. However, children have a great ability to live for the moment and experience the joy of just being, whereas adults often say that they will be happy when they own a new car or house, have completed a piece of work, etc. We need to remember as adults that this also means that we need to travel in the opposite direction and meet the child in us to appreciate fully the nature of being.

Tower and Singer's (1980: 36) perspective is very similar:

> When a child engages in imaginative play with a parent, a very special phenomenon is taking place: the child is generating and executing ideas based on its own experience in a context of mutual respect, interest and absence of criticism. Parent and child are free to experience each other in terms of possibilities. Constraints inherent in the usual roles they play in relation to each other may be temporarily put aside. The give and take of laughter and of shared 'dangers' and 'rescues' may enhance a positive sense of communion. Parents often have lost touch with their own childhood joys in fantasy play and can regain some of that excitement through play.

A child's development begins at a very early stage; the case study below demonstrates this clearly and shows how this may have significant implications for the future.

CASE STUDY Antenatal and postnatal development

During my pregnancy with twins we had an interesting experience. In one of my antenatal visits to the hospital I had an ultrasound scan, which showed that one of the babies was a girl. (We later found that the other was a boy.) Calum, the boy, was very active throughout the pregnancy while Eilidh, the girl, was quiet and slept a lot.

During the scan Calum was moving around and kicking vigorously while Eilidh was quite passive. As we were watching, Calum kicked out and came into contact with Eilidh, who responded by spinning 180 degrees to turn her back on him, all the while continuing to suck her thumb.

Now that they are born I can observe them more closely and take note of their personalities. One year on, Eilidh still loves her sleep whilst Calum is a very early riser. Calum enjoys the rough-and-tumble of play while Eilidh likes more gentle play.

We tried to ensure that both babies were given equal care and stimulation, even alternating which parent put each baby to bed at night. They also shared the same toys. Despite this, both Calum and Eilidh are developing in quite different ways. Eilidh courts attention from others, especially adults. She treated me to her first real smile when she was less than four weeks old and learnt at a very young age that a smile would get the reaction and attention that she loves. Eilidh was first to recognize and sing along with her favourite songs. Calum, on the other hand, prefers things to people. He treats strangers with indifference, preferring to play with his toys. He quickly became very adept at recognizing and sorting shapes and exploring the mechanisms of his toys.

Although the twins were very close and became upset when they were separated, they behaved as if the other was an extension of themselves. They sucked each other's thumbs and toes but they did not interact with each other in the same way as with ourselves and other adults until one incident when they were around five months old. They were lying side by side on the floor and Eilidh had her hand in Calum's mouth. Calum sneezed and Eilidh pulled away, giggling. She put her hand back and he sneezed again, eliciting another giggle. For the next 20 minutes, both babies watched, smiled, touched and giggled with each other. It appeared to me that each baby suddenly recognized the other as a separate person. From that day, they became a team, interacted, played and communicated with each other, often sharing a private joke that no one but themselves could understand.

One day I was teaching them to give me a kiss by kissing each of them in turn. A few minutes after the game was over, they started giggling and kissing each other. Since then, without any prompting from ourselves, they spontaneously give each other a kiss and cuddle every morning, as we do with them.

Although the only evidence I have is observing just two babies, from their behaviour I can only conclude that their learning is not driven solely by nature, nurture or environmental factors but a combination of all three.

Rosie MacIntyre

A chronology of experiential learning

While undertaking research for the first edition of this book, an epiphany occurred to the author. While reading a book, a diagram was noticed that described the internal processes or skills that people use to learn from experience, ie willing, sensing, intuiting, feeling, reasoning and, in particular, it depicted a temporal consideration of remembering and imagining (Mulligan, 2000). Around the same time, Robertson's book (2000: 14) *Mind Sculpture* described how all the interactions we have leave a trace in our brains so that: 'Your brain is changed physically by the conversations you have, the events you witness and the love you receive.' The two insights from Mulligan and Robertson resonated strongly and were imaginatively and creatively combined together to develop the theory that we learn from the future. Essentially, the process of thinking about what might happen in the future develops new neural pathways in the brain, which is the essence of learning. Robertson added:

> For who 'you' are arises from the restless murmuring and urging of the world at the gates of your senses. Through your senses, and in the trembling weave of your brain, this energy is transmuted into the electricity of you. And you, in turn, give this energy back to the universe by what you choose to do and say. Thus you are locked into an intimate embrace with the universe, the universe transforming you and you changing it.

A chronological consideration of experiential learning (see Figure 10.1) enables us to analyse it retrospectively, concurrently or prospectively, ie with reference to the past, the present or the future. When we undergo an event it is possible to learn from that experience at different times, ie:

- learning from a past event when reflecting on it later;
- learning more about a past event when thinking about it further;
- reinterpreting the past event differently in the light of further experience(s);
- learning from an event at the time it occurs;
- learning from a consideration of future scenarios.

We will now consider retrospective learning, concurrent learning and prospective learning, ie from the past, present and future.

Figure 10.1 A chronological perspective of experiential learning

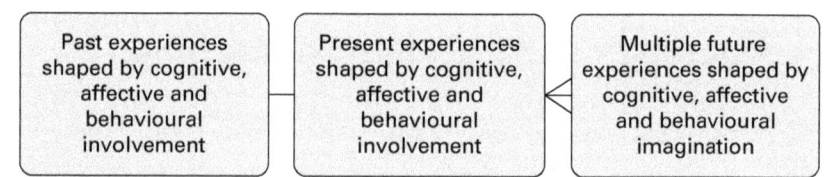

Retrospective learning

Much experiential learning involves looking back at an event and analysing it (what Schön, 1983, termed reflection-on-action). Often when we are undergoing an experience there is insufficient time and/or we are too close – physically, chronologically or emotionally – to have the ability to make sense of what is happening. These processes of thinking about a past event may be illustrated when we say, 'If only I had...' What we are doing is reflecting about the experience and making sense of it in our own mind – in effect we are attempting to fit the experience into our mental schema, adjusting the schema or replacing them altogether.

Another form of retrospective learning is to look back at an event and recollect even more closely what happened and thus learn in even greater depth. For instance, we may rewind the mental tape of a conversation we had to try to get more detailed insights into why another person behaved in a particular way.

Yet a further way of learning retrospectively is when an event can be reinterpreted in the light of subsequent experiences and there is the potential for its meaning to be considerably different to that at the time. One example is a parent rapidly lifting a child to safety before the child burns him- or herself on a stove. The child may be shocked and cry as a result of the sudden action or the frustration at not being allowed to do what he or she wants, but when the child is older the interpretation is much different, particularly so if the child has subsequently burnt him- or herself.

Not only can we learn from a new experience as we relate that experience to our existing ones, but we can also find new meanings hidden in old experiences. These old experiences may be drawn from any time in our history, and although we may have incorporated them within a particular mindset we may change them as a result of our new experience.

It is possible to use learners' previous experiences to add depth, colour and a concrete reality to the more abstract environment of learning of the classroom or training room. This may involve revisiting a past experience in light of the theoretical and structured learning that has just been delivered.

Concurrent learning

When we perceive a stimulus, either external to us or even within ourselves, this can be regarded as a form of learning from experience. For example, when we are driving in a car and slowing down for some traffic lights ahead we will continuously adjust the pressure on the brake pedal to ensure that we come to a halt just behind the car in front rather than crashing into it. This learning is almost instantaneous and the frequent responding to accommodate the external environment is described as concurrent learning.

Many of our physical actions, as well as our mental ones, are in a continual process of assessment and change. In the classroom, training room and workplace we often learn immediately from the experience and this may involve adjusting our tone of voice or demeanour so that people respond in the desired manner. The next time you reach for that cup of tea or coffee just think about how you are temporarily learning in the moment as your movements are finely coordinated to allow you to grasp the mug and drink from it without spilling the contents.

Similarly, if we notice that there is frost on the ground we may drive more carefully to avoid skidding and having an accident. Alternatively, we may adjust the pressure that we exert with our fingers on a new computer keyboard. Both these adaptations to the external environment are a form of learning, albeit short term; as soon as the temperature rises above freezing or we return to our old keyboard we are likely to return to our previous behaviour.

The quality of the immediate learning in formal situations may be enhanced by coaching the learner to stand back from the experience he or she is undergoing and consider what is happening. This form of activity and reflection is common in team and management development activities where the participants are encouraged not only to succeed in the task but also to consider their own and others' behaviours and interactions. This behaviour was termed by Schön (1983) as reflection-in-action.

Temporal limitations of Schön's reflective practice

Remarkably, Schön did not discuss the application of prospective reflection or reflection-on-the-future, which is an essential ingredient of almost all actions – if we do not have an intention, a plan that we have conceived, then actions will have little or no directive purpose. By imagining what might be possible we are then able to develop operational strategies that hopefully will deliver the concrete reality.

The process of investigating possible futures and learning from them involves a similar process to that of learning from past and present experience. This process of imagining, dreaming, mental rehearsal or visualizing happens when we make plans, perhaps for a holiday or a business project (Wilson, 2012). Visualizing is increasingly being used by athletes and other people trying to achieve high levels of performance, where they positively visualize a successful outcome so that they are fully prepared when the event happens (Morris, Spittle and Watt, 2005).

Reflection-on-the-future, or reflection-before-action, would appear to be little discussed in spite of it appearing to be a natural human condition. There are a few acknowledgements in the literature, eg Van Manen (1991) who discussed the notion of 'anticipatory reflection', which involved consideration or planning of an event. Also, Greenwood (1998: 1049) wrote that: 'This Schönian model of reflective practice is essentially flawed in that it fails to recognize the importance of reflection-before-action.' The important practical application of this future reflection has applications across all areas of life, particularly health care:

> To begin with, Schön's emphasis on reflection-in-and-on-action implicitly undervalues reflection-before-action. It is at least arguable, however, that much of the suffering in the world, including that caused by nurses' errors, could have been avoided had practitioners stopped to think about what they intended to do and how they intended to do it before they actually did it. (Greenwood, 1993: 1186)

Wilson (2008) identified five main reasons why reflection-on-the-future has been little discussed in the literature, with the result that it has not been codified within reflective practice. First, reflecting on past and present actions has an inherent and tacit recognition that the purpose of this action is to improve future performance. That this is so obvious that it need not be considered might be considered as the 'reflective elephant in the room syndrome'. What is the purpose of reflection if not to improve subsequent performance or understand events? Thus, Moon (2000: 49) suggested that:

> Anticipation may imply a combination of reflection and imagination. In this combination, reflection-on-action – the revisiting of prior experiences of the same or similar events – is stretched into the future with the use of imagination. Imagination may work with the outcomes of reflection-on-action, but would not be considered to be part of reflection.

A similar perspective is illustrated by MacDonald *et al* (2005: 2) who stated:

> Two objectives drive student portfolios. One objective looks back and the other looks forward. Looking back involves reflecting on achievement and learning. Looking forward involves identifying gaps and future development opportunities based upon reflection… As with student portfolios, both past and future reflection is an element of teacher portfolios.

Moreover, Doncaster and Thorne (2000: 397) discussed reflection and planning as part of professional doctorates and stated: 'This task focuses heavily on the processes of planning. It is forward looking, but builds on both the research capability that candidates by this time must have demonstrated.'

Second, the semantic understanding of reflection suggests a consideration of what has happened rather than what might happen. It is not possible to reflect on something that has yet to happen without the use of imagination, as Moon (2000: 97) argued:

> Reflection could be said to be involved in anticipation and planning, but it needs to be combined with imagination to extend its application into the future. The word 'reflection' has the connotation of a link to the past – going back over ideas and experiences or gathering current ideas so that thinking or learning may be progressed.

Third, reflection is generally considered to deal with concrete reality. We cannot address or change behaviour if something has yet to happen. Both reflection-on-action and reflection-in-action are rooted in the notion of experiential learning. That is, they both link theory and practice in a cycle. Theory informs and is tested by putting it into practice. The practice exposes the theory to intense scrutiny, identifying which parts of the theory work and which don't work. Thus, the theory is refined and improved through practical application (Dewey, 1938). Dewey (1938: 9) also defined reflective thought as:

> Active, persistent and careful consideration of any belief or supposed form of knowledge in the light of the grounds that support it and further conclusions to which it leads… it includes a conscious and voluntary effort to establish belief upon a firm basis of evidence and rationality.

Another writer who emphasized the importance of developing knowledge through real interaction with the world was Freire (1982: 56) who maintained that: 'Problem-posing education bases itself on creativity and stimulates true reflection and action on reality.'

A fourth reason for there being little emphasis on the future is that the very terms 'practice' or 'practitioner' both imply practice, ie the act of doing something. Thinking or reflecting about something ethereal is not doing.

Fifth, there may be a self-fulfilling prophecy in operation. Because there has been little exploration of the future temporal dimension it has not entered the mainstream of reflective practice. It is argued here that this reduced level of thought about the future constrains a holistic consideration of reflection and thereby inhibits the full development of professional practice.

A sixth point can be added. How can we use existing forms of reflection, ie reflection-on-action and reflection-in-action, to help with new and original problems and randomness (Taleb, 2007)? We cannot depend solely upon reflection on past or even current events that are largely of benefit for incremental improvements. Creating new and innovative solutions to future challenges requires us to speculate on the future, not rely upon the past.

Finally, if we accept the argument that reflective practice involves a consideration of the future then it should be made explicit. Reflection on the past and present is strongly emphasized in the literature but the future tends to be less considered. Given that the future is where we are all heading it demands more systematic consideration and this will now be considered in the next section.

Prospective learning: reflecting on the future

> Faith in the power of intelligence to imagine a future in which the projection of the desirable in the present, and to invent the instrumentalities of its realization, is our salvation. And it is a faith that must be nurtured and made articulate.
> (Dewey, 1917: 69)

The third and final stage in this chronological consideration of reflection is to look at how we might reflect on the future. This is achieved by considering or imagining various possibilities and the strategies that are required to achieve them. By imagining or reflecting on what might be possible we are then able to develop operational strategies that hopefully will deliver the concrete reality.

When we reflect or speculate about ideas and the way things might be in the future, we are often exploring the potential to achieve them and their possible consequences (Markman, Klein and Suhr, 2009; Bar, 2011). This speculation is often driven by desires and impulses to improve upon current circumstances and they have a clear purpose, eg to find a more effective way of achieving work targets; to plan a holiday that takes into account all the family's wishes; to examine what might be the best response when our boss asks why a certain task has not been achieved, etc.

Figure 10.2 illustrates how we are frequently assessing and benchmarking our performance. Often there is a desire or pressure to improve and we use our imagination to identify what might be achieved and how we might get there.

Figure 10.2 Using imagination to bridge the learning gap or performance gap

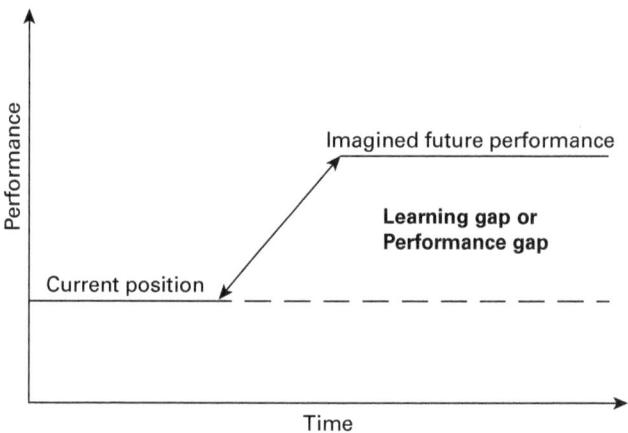

All these examples are testimony to a natural human condition, which is to speculate or reflect on what the future might bring and, importantly, be influenced. Although it is not possible to reflect on concrete experiences that have yet to happen, it is possible to give deep consideration to trends and future scenarios. One relatively successful application of scenario planning was that conducted in South Africa towards the end of apartheid. There was concern that the country might face serious civil disturbance and therefore the Mont Fleur scenarios were constructed and then discussed among all the main actors (Kahane, 2004). Four main pictures were painted of what the future might hold, including the continuation of apartheid, weak government, economic collapse, and inclusive democracy and economic growth. Through discussion and examination of future possibilities a consensus was developed that enabled a smoother transition to an open democracy.

Unlike the past, which cannot be changed, only reinterpreted, it is possible to have a variety of futures. There is not, as many people subconsciously believe, only one future but there are many possible alternatives unless one is a fatalist who believes that one has no real control over destiny and that all is preordained. Many people, on the other hand, believe that they possess the power to influence their own future and that of their organization. In order to create a future we need first to be able to identify where we wish to go. Through reflection on current and former experiences we may project a variety of scenarios and examine what might happen. It is a form of future reflection and it allows us to examine pathways without the necessity of expending energy and other resources on inefficient or futile courses of action.

We are able to use our reflection to speculate about possible alternatives and we are able to select a course of action that can lead towards the achievement of our goals and objectives. Circumstances may intervene to hinder or prevent the achievement of our goals, not least our own limitations. But, at least we have the ability to weigh up the possibilities of success by taking into account our own strengths and weaknesses.

Greenwood (1993) maintained that human action was intentional, ie it was purposive and directional. In order to achieve an objective we first have to plan what needs to be done to achieve the objectives. She used the example of someone wanting to go to London. In order to get there one first had to catch a train; to catch the train one first had to get to the station, etc. In other words, our actions are determined from our intentions. Argyris, Putnam and Smith (1985: 82) stated that people 'do not just happen to act in a particular way. Rather, their action is designed; and as agents, they are responsible for the design.' This case was also presented by Greenwood (1993: 1186) who stated, 'Reflection-in-and-on-action, by contrast, requires the agent to reason from her actions to her intentions.' She also added that it was necessary for human beings to respond to action feedback in an iterative manner.

The case for reflecting on the future is well made by Greenwood (1993). Moon (2000: 49), too, appeared to warm to the concept, particularly later in her book. In spite of earlier scepticism suggesting that 'Imagination... would not be considered to be part of reflection', she (2000: 180) suggested a series of guided phases to encourage reflective practice, the last one being particularly pertinent:

Phase 1: develop awareness of the nature of current practice.

Phase 2: clarify the new learning and how it relates to current understanding.

Phase 3: integrate new learning and current practice.

Phase 4: anticipate or imagine the nature of improved practice.

Furthermore, later in the book Moon (2000: 207) once again returns to a consideration of the future by briefly discussing guided fantasy. She wrote, 'Leaders might be led to imagine themselves performing effectively in a situation that they fear, such as examinations or a difficult professional situation.'

By now it should be evident that reflecting-on-the-future should be a key component of reflection; therefore, to provide more precision a definition would be helpful:

Future reflection is the act or process of reflecting on desirable and possible futures with the purpose of evaluating them as well as considering strategies intended to achieve the objective(s).

Grooving your skills

The more we physically or mentally practise an action or skill the more we strengthen the links between neurons, which results in more fluent and improved performance. Much mental rehearsal, whether for an examination or an important meeting, is intended to make us better. The more we practise the easier it becomes to repeat the task because the neural connections have been increased and developed. Gallwey (1986: 67) described this in slightly different terms:

> One hears a lot about grooving one's strokes in tennis. The theory is a simple one: every time you swing your racquet in a certain way, you increase the probabilities that you will swing that way again. In this way patterns, called grooves, build up which have a predisposition to repeat themselves. Golfers use the same term. It is as if the nervous system were like a record disk. Every time an action is performed, a slight impression is made in the microscopic cells of the brain, just as a leaf blowing over a fine-grained beach will leave a faint trace. When the action is repeated, the groove is made slightly deeper. After many similar actions there is a more recognizable groove into which the needle of behaviour seems to fall automatically.

Functional equivalence and virtual reality

When we think about doing something it activates the same areas of the brain as if we are actually physically doing it (Holmes and Collins, 2001). The more we mentally rehearse a physical action the stronger the neural connections become, enabling us to perform more proficiently. This is why sports psychologists encourage sportsmen and women to visualize being in the arena and to see, hear, touch, taste and smell the imagined experience. In this way, when the event really happens, they are more relaxed and are less likely to have anxiety and fear of failure, which negatively affect performance.

In many respects we possess our own virtual reality system, which enables us to imagine and reflect thereby assisting us to learn more effectively. Virtual and augmented reality is becoming increasingly life-like and it is now used extensively in the world of work. New breakthroughs in immersive technologies, including other three-dimensional formats and gestural interface-based technologies, are transforming the experience of learning. Walmart, the world's leading retailer, has adopted VR approaches to improve the leadership skills of front-line supervisors and department managers, using simulations of complex customer-facing situations that are difficult or unsafe to create in real life, such as natural disasters, black Friday, crowd behaviours. McDonald's also use a VR-enabled gaming approach to help shift managers to learn on the job, and the car manufacturer Nissan is creating a digital version of its Sunderland factory so that processes and systems can be learnt more easily. Within education, medical students can now utilize bodily gestures (gesture-based technologies) to see through, pull out, inspect and analyse bodily organs, veins and nerves, muscles and tendons, and explore their functions and disfunctions. There are also developments in the revisioning of processing power that can be generally distributed within the environment, such as wearable computing, smart buildings, smart street lighting, and smart clothing. These changes will bring changes to our daily life and our experience of the world. Greenfield, the author of *Everyware*, a book about the dawning age of ubiquitous computing, notes how we might:

> point to an unfamiliar word in a text, and a definition appears. You sit down to lunch with three friends, and the restaurant plays only the music that you have all rated highly. (2006: 26)

He continues:

> In all of these scenarios, there are powerful informatics underlying the apparent simplicity of the experience, but they never breach the surface of awareness: things Just Work. Interactions with everyware feel natural, spontaneous, human.

These changes will, in turn, affect what and how we humans learn, experience and imagine the world.

Conclusion

Throughout this book we have emphasized the importance of using the concept of experiential learning as a means of drawing together theory and practice. It is probably the single unifying feature that integrates the neurological processes of the brain with the various theories and strategies for encouraging learning. It involves action learning and reflective practice; it involves the emotional aspects of learning, and incorporates the various environmental considerations that add to the learning experience. Also, we possess a natural desire to improve and become better – a becoming and transforming on our journey to a higher level of being.

The nature versus nurture debate has long been entrenched with protagonists making strong points from each perspective and, perhaps, the majority of people believing that both factors have an impact. Nurture, or experience, has a major impact – as this book has emphasized – and it would now appear to have an even bigger one. Remarkable evidence is beginning to accumulate that experience can influence gene activity without changing a person's genetic code. For example, research by Bygren, Kaati and Edvinsson (2001) in Sweden has revealed that the diet of ancestors after rich and poor harvests can impact on the longevity of succeeding generations. We do not have to wait for the human genome to evolve slowly over longer periods of time.

Reflecting on past, present and future events enables us to enhance the world for ourselves and for others. Moreover, education is probably the most valuable tool we can give people, thus enabling them to respond to the demands of the future. We will leave the final words to Freire (1982: 57):

> Problem-solving education is revolutionary futurity. Hence it is prophetic (and, as such, hopeful), and so corresponds to the historical nature of man. Thus, it affirms men [humans] as beings who transcend themselves, who move forward and look ahead, for whom immobility represents a fatal threat, for whom looking at the past must only be a means of understanding more clearly what and who they are so that they can more wisely build the future.

REFERENCES

Abbot, C (1987) The good, the bad and the ugly: the role of outdoor programmes in working with young drug abusers, *Autumn School of Studies in Alcohol and Drugs*, proceedings of Seminar and Scientific Sessions, St Vincent's Hospital, Melbourne, Australia

Abram, D (1997) *The Spell of the Sensuous*, Vintage Books, New York

Adler, P S (1975) The transitional experience, *Journal of Humanistic Psychology*, **15** (4), pp 13–23

Agor, W H (1991) The logic of intuition: how top executives make important decisions, in *Creative Management*, ed J Henry, pp 163–76, Sage, London

Allison, P (2000a) Authenticity and outdoor education, *Values and Outdoor Learning*, Association for Outdoor Learning, Penrith, Cumbria

Allison, P (2000b) Research from the ground up, *Brathay Occasional Papers*, **1**, Brathay Hall Trust, Cumbria

Amabile, T (1983) *The Social Psychology of Creativity*, Springer-Verlag, New York

Applebaum, S, Bregman, M and Moroz, P (1998) Fear as a strategy: effects and impacts within the organisation, *Journal of European Industrial Training*, **22** (3), pp 113–27, MCB University Press, Bradford

Argyris, C (1994) Good communication that blocks learning, *Harvard Business Review*, July–August, pp 77–85

Argyris, C, Putnam, R and Smith, D M (1985) *Action Science*, Jossey-Bass, San Francisco, CA

Argyris, C and Schön, D (1974) *Theory in Practice: Increasing professional effectiveness*, Jossey-Bass, San Francisco, CA

Arran, A (1998) Personal communication on the design of Spider Club awards

Assagioli, R (1980) *Psychosynthesis*, Wildwood House, London

Attard, P (2001) The use of drama-based training as a learning medium, unpublished master's thesis, Department of Continuing Education, Sheffield University, Sheffield

Attarian, A (1999) Artificial climbing environments, in *Adventure Programming*, ed J C Miles and S Priest, pp 341–45, Venture Publishing, Andover, MA

Bacon, S (1987) *The Evolution of the Outward Bound Process*, Greenwich Outward Bound, United States

Baddeley, A, Eysenck, M W and Anderson, M C (2009) *Memory*, Psychology Press, Hove

Badger, B, Sadler-Smith, E and Michie, E (1997) Outdoor management development: use and evaluation, *Journal of European and Industrial Training*, **21** (9), pp 318–25, MCB University Press, Bradford

References

Bagshaw, M (2000) 17 tried and tested activities for understanding the practice and applications of emotional intelligence, *Using Emotional Intelligence at Work*, Fenman Ltd, Cambridgeshire

Bandler, R and Grinder, J (1990) *Frogs into Princes: Neuro linguistic programming*, Real People Press, Utah

Bank, J (1994) *Outdoor Development for Managers*, 2nd edn, Gower, Aldershot

Bar, M (2011) *Predictions in the Brain*, Oxford University Press, Oxford

Barbalet, J (1998) *Emotions, Social Theory and Social Structure*, Cambridge University Press, Cambridge

Barnes, P (2000) *Values and Outdoor Learning: A collection of papers reflecting some contemporary thinking*, Association for Outdoor Learning, Penrith, Cumbria

Barnett, R (2000) University knowledge in an age of supercomplexity, *Higher Education*, 40 (4), pp 409–22

Barrett, J and Greenaway, R (1995) *Why Adventure? The role and value of outdoor adventure in young people's personal and social development*, Foundation for Outdoor Adventure, Coventry

Bateson, G (1972) *Steps to an Ecology of Mind: Collected essays in anthropology, psychiatry, evolution, and epistemology*, University of Chicago Press, Chicago

Baumeister, R F and Leary, M R (1995) The need to belong: desire for interpersonal attachments as a fundamental human motivation, *Psychological Bulletin*, 117 (3), pp 497–525

Beard, C (1998) The outdoor leisure industry and the environment, *Horizons*, 2, Cumbria

Beard, C (2003) The circle and the square – nature and artificial adventure environments, in *Whose Journeys? Where and Why? The 'Outdoors and Adventure' as a Social and Cultural Phenomena: Critical explorations of relations between individuals, 'others' and the environment*, ed B Humberstone, H Brown and K Richards, pp 187–98, Fingerprints, Barrow in Furness

Beard, C (2005) The design of effective group-based training methods, in *Human Resource Development*, ed J Wilson, pp 342–64, Kogan Page, London

Beard, C (2008) [accessed 9 April 2018] Experiential Learning: The Development of a Pedagogic Framework for Effective Practice, unpublished doctoral thesis, *Sheffield Hallam University* [Online] http://shura.shu.ac.uk/13095/

Beard, C (2010) *The Experiential Learning Toolkit: Blending practice with concepts*, Kogan Page, London

Beard, C (2012) Spatial ecology: learning and working environments that change people and organisations, in *Managing Organisational Ecologies*, ed K Alexandra and I Price, Routledge, New York

Beard, C (2013) *Sensory Intelligence*, Morphesus Learning Resources (audio book), Mumbai

Beard, C (2015) Experiential learning: towards a multi-disciplinary approach, in *Routledge International Handbook of Outdoor Studies*, ed B Humberstone, H Prince and K Henderson, pp 425–34

Beard, C (2018) Dewey in the world of experiential education, in *Adult Educators on Dewey's Experience and Education*, New Directions for Adult and Continuing Education #158, ed A Mandell and X Coulter, pp 27–38, Jossey-Bass, San Francisco, CA

Beard, C M (1996) Environmental awareness training: three ideas for greening the company culture, *Eco-Management and Auditing*, **3**, pp 139–46

Beard, C M (1997) The future for eco-design: new business products, conference proceedings of Business Strategy and the Environment, 18–19 September, Leeds

Beard, C M (2000) A brave new environmental vision for the millennium, Euro Environment 2000 conference: Visions, Strategies and Actions Towards Sustainable Industries, 18–20 October, Aalborg Congress and Culture Centre, Denmark

Beard, C and Goode, M (2013) Contributing to a more sustainable world? Business product innovation and the development of an industrial ecology, in *Enhancing Education for Sustainable Development in Business and Management, Hospitality, Leisure, Marketing, Tourism*, ed R Atfield and P Kemp, The Higher Education Academy, York

Beard, C and McPherson, M (1999) Design and use of group-based training methods, in *Human Resource Development: Learning and training for individuals and organizations*, ed J P Wilson, pp 342–64, Kogan Page, London

Beard, C and Price, I (2012) Learning spaces that change people and organisations, in *International Human Resource Development*, ed J P Wilson, pp 465–80, Kogan Page, London

Beard C and Price, I (2013) Room for improvement, *Journal of the Royal Society of Arts*, Spring, pp 38–41

Beard, C and Russ, W (2017) Event evaluation and design: human experience mapping, *Event Management: An international journal*, **21** (3), 365–74

Beard, C and Wilson, J (2002) *The Power of Experiential Learning*, Kogan Page, London

Beard, C, Wilson, J P and McCarter, R (2006) Towards a theory of eLearning: experiential eLearning, *Journal of Hospitality, Leisure, Sport and Tourism Education*, **6** (2), pp 3–15

Becher, T (1989) *Academic Tribes and Territories: Intellectual enquiry and the cultures of disciplines*, Society for Research into Higher Education, Open University Press, Milton Keynes

Bee, F and Bee, R (1998) *Facilitation Skills*, Institute of Personnel and Development, London

Behuniak, S (2005) Finding solitude: the importance of silence and space for thinking, paper presented to Design For Learning, the Twelfth International Conference on Learning, 11–14 July, Granada, Spain

Belbin, M (1981) *Management Teams: Why they succeed or fail*, Butterworth-Heinemann, Oxford

Bell, D (1974) *The Coming of Post Industrial Society*, Routledge and Kegan Paul, London

References

Benson, J (1987) *Working More Creatively with Groups*, Routledge, London

Berger, R (2007) Nature Therapy: developing a framework for practice, unpublished PhD thesis, Abertay University, Scotland

Berger, R, Rugen, L and Woodfin, L (2014) *Leaders of Their Own Learning*, Wiley, United States

Berne, E (1973) *Games People Play*, Penguin, Harmondsworth

Best, B and Thomas, W (2007) *The Creative Teaching and Learning Toolkit*, Continuum Publishing, London

Binstead, D and Stuart, R (1979) Designed reality into management learning events, *Personnel Review*, **8** (3), pp 12–19

Bishop, S R, Lau, M, Shapiro, S, Carlson, L, Anderson, N D, Carmody, J and Devins, G (2004) Mindfulness: a proposed operational definition, *Clinical Psychology: Science and practice*, **11** (3), 230–41

Bitner, M J (1992) Servicescapes: the impact of physical surroundings on customers and employees, *The Journal of Marketing*, **56** (2), pp 57–71

Black, M (1979) More about metaphor, in *Metaphor and Thought*, ed A Ortony, Cornell University Press, Ithaca, NY

Black Mountain Ltd (1996) Developing your human dimension, commercial publicity brochure

Blackie, M A L, Case, J M and Jawitz, J (2010) Student-centredness: the link between transforming students and transforming ourselves, *Teaching in Higher Education*, **15** (6), pp 637–46

Bloom, B S et al (1956) *Taxonomy of Educational Objectives: The classification of educational objectives, handbook 1: cognitive domain*, Longmans, Green & Co, London

Boler, M (1999) *Feeling Power: Emotions and education*, Routledge, London

Bolton, G (1985) Changes in thinking about drama in education, *Theory into Practice*, **24** (3), Summer, pp 151–57

Boniface, M (2000) Towards an understanding of flow and other positive experience phenomena within outdoor and adventurous activities, *Journal of Adventure Education and Outdoor Learning*, **1** (1), pp 55–68

Booth, B F and Moss, I (1994) *A Social History of Sport*, HPA Inc, Ottawa

Boud, D, Cohen, R and Walker, D (1993) *Using Experience for Learning*, Open University Press, Buckingham

Boud, D and Miller, N (eds) (1996) *Working with Experience: Animating learning*, Routledge, London

Boud, D and Walker, D (1990) Making the most of experience, *Studies in Continuing Education*, **12** (2), pp 61–80

Boud, D and Walker, D (1993) Barriers to reflection on experience, in *Using Experience for Learning*, ed D Boud, R Cohen and D Walker, pp 73–86

Boydell, T (1976) *Experiential Learning*, Manchester Monograph 5, University of Manchester, Department of Adult Education, Manchester

Brew, J M (1946) *Informal Education: Adventures and reflections*, Faber and Faber, London

Britzman, D P (1998) *Lost Subjects, Contested Objects: Towards a psychoanalytic inquiry of learning*, State University of New York Press, New York

Brooks, J G and Brooks, M G (1993) *The Case for Constructivist Classrooms*, Association for Supervision of Curriculum Development, Alexandra, VA

Bryman, A (1999) The Disneyization of society. *The Sociological Review*, 47, pp 25–47

Bryson, B (2000) *An Introduction, the English Landscape*, Profile Books, London

Bull, N (1951) *The Attitude Theory of Emotion*, Nervous and mental disease monographs, New York, Coolidge Foundation

Burns, G (1998) *Nature Guided Therapy: Brief integrative strategies for health and well-being*, Brunner/Mazel, Philadelphia

Burr, V (2003) *Social Constructionism*, 2nd edn, Routledge, London

Butcher, G B (1991) Creating the right environment for training managers, *Training and Development*, 9 (6), pp 26–30

Buzan, T (2000) *The Speed Reading Book*, BBC Worldwide Ltd, London

Bygren, L O, Kaati, G and Edvinsson, S (2001) Longevity determined by parental ancestors nutrition during their slow growth period, *Acta Biotheoretica*, 49 (1), pp 53–59

Carlson, R (1998) *Don't Sweat the Small Stuff with Your Family*, Hyperion, New York

Cell, E (1984) *Learning to Learn from Experience*, State University of New York Press, Albany

Charlton, C (1992) Developing leaders using the outdoors, in *Frontiers of Leadership: An essential reader*, ed M Syrett and C Hogg, pp 454–61, Blackwell, Oxford

Child, G (1993) *Mixed Emotions*, The Mountaineers, Seattle

Chopra, D (1996) *The Seven Spiritual Laws of Success: A practical guide to the fulfilment of your dreams*, Bantam Books, London

Christoff, K, Gordon, A M, Smallwood, J, Smith, R and Schooler, J W (2009) Experience sampling during fMRI reveals default network and executive system contributions to mind wandering, *Proceedings of the National Academy of Sciences May 26, 2009*, 106 (21), pp 8719–24

Coffield, F, Moseley, D, Hall, E and Ecclestone, K (2004) *Learning Styles and Pedagogy in Post-16 Learning: A systematic and critical review*, Learning and Skills Research Centre, London

Cohen, D (1987) *The Development of Play*, New York University Press, New York

Collins, S (2016) *Neuroscience for Learning and Development: How to apply neuroscience and psychology for improved learning and training*, Kogan Page, London

Collison, C and Mackenzie, A (1999) The power of story in organisations, *Journal of Workplace Learning*, 11 (1), pp 38–40

Consalvo, C (1995) *Outdoor Games for Trainers*, Gower, Aldershot

ContactBabel (2005) *The UK Contact Centre Operational Review*, ContactBabel, Sedgefield, Co Durham

References

Cooper, G (1998) *Outdoors with Young People: A leader's guide to outdoor activities, the environment and sustainability*, Russell House Publishing, Dorset

Cornell, J (1989) *Sharing the Joy of Nature*, Dawn Publications, California

Coursera [accessed 8 March 2018] [Online] https://www.coursera.org/about

Covey, S R (1990) *The Seven Habits of Highly Effective People*, Simon & Schuster, New York

Cronon, W (1995) The trouble with wilderness, or getting back to the wrong nature, in *Uncommon Ground: Rethinking the human place in nature*, ed W Cronon, pp 60–90, Norton & Co, New York

Cronon, W (1996) *Uncommom Ground: Rethinking the human place in nature*, Norton Publications, New York

Crosby, A (1995) A critical look: the philosophical foundations of experiential education, in *The Theory of Experiential Education*, ed K Warren, M Sakofs and J Hunt, Association for Experiential Education, Kendall/Hunt Publishing, Dubuque, IA

Cuffaro, H K (1995) *Experimenting with the World: John Dewey and the early childhood classroom*, Teachers College Press, New York

Curriculum Corporation (1994) *Statements and Profiles for Australian Schools*, Melbourne, Australia

Dainty, P and Lucas, D (1992) Clarifying the confusion: a practical framework for evaluating outdoor development programmes for managers, *Management Education and Development*, 23 (2), pp 106–22

Dale, E (1969) *Audiovisual Methods in Teaching*, Dryden Press, New York

Damasio, A R (1996) *Descartes' Error: Emotion, reason and the human brain*, Papermac, London

Damasio, A R (1999) *The Feeling of What Happens: The body and emotion in the making of consciousness*, Harcourt Brace, New York

Damasio, A R (2003) *Looking for Spinoza: Joy, sorrow, and the feeling brain*, Harcourt, Inc, Orlando

Darwin, C (1872) *The Expression of the Emotions in Man and Animals*, University of Chicago Press, Chicago

Daudelin, M (1996) Learning from experience through reflection, *Organizational Dynamics*, 24 (3), pp 36–46

Davies, W (1997) *One River: Science, adventure and hallucinogenics in the Amazon Basin*, Simon & Schuster Ltd, New York

Davis, B and Sumara D J (1997) Cognition, complexity, and teacher education, *Harvard Educational Review*, 67 (1), pp 105–25

Davis-Berman, J and Berman, D (1999) The use of adventure-based programs with at-risk youth, in *Adventure Programming*, ed J C Miles and S Priest, pp 365–72, Venture Publishing, PA, USA

de Bono, E (1991) Lateral and vertical thinking, in *Creative Management*, ed J Henry, pp 16–23, Sage, London

DEEP (1999) [accessed 8 March 2018] Definitions, Ethics and Exemplary Practices (DEEP) of Experiential Training and Development (ETD) [Online] http://www.etdalliance.com/Resources/Documents/DEEP.pdf

De Freitas, S and Maharg, P (2011) *Digital Games and Learning*, Continuum, London

De Lubicz, I S and Lamy, L (1954) *Her-Bak: The living face of ancient Egypt*, Hodder and Stoughton, London

Design Council (2005) Kit for purpose: design to deliver creative learning, report of the Design Council, London

Dewey, J (1916) *Democracy and Education*, Macmillan, New York

Dewey, J (1917) A recovery of philosophy, in *Creative Intelligence*, ed J Dewey *et al*, pp 3–69, Henry Holt, New York

Dewey, J (1925) *Experience and Nature*, The Paul Carus Foundation Lectures 1, Open Court Publishing Company, Chicago

Dewey, J (1934) *Art as Experience*, Allen & Unwin, London

Dewey, J (1938) *Experience and Education*, The Kappa Delta Pi Lecture Series, Macmillan, New York

Dillon, P (2007) A pedagogy of connection and boundary crossings: methodological and epistemological transactions in working across and between disciplines, a paper presented at Creativity or conformity? Building Cultures of Creativity in Higher Education, University of Wales and the Higher Education Academy, Cardiff, January 8–10

Doncaster, K and Thorne, L (2000) Reflection and planning: essential elements of professional doctorates, *Reflective Practice*, **1** (3), pp 391–99

Duhigg, C (2012) *The Power of Habit: Why we do what we do, and how to change*, RH Books, London

Dunn, D and Chaput de Saintonge, M (1997) Experiential Learning, *Medical Education*, **31**(supplement 1), pp 25–28

Edwards, R (1994) Are you experienced?: postmodernity and experiential learning, *International Journal of Lifelong Learning*, **13** (6), November–December, pp 423–39

Egan, G (2002) *The Skilled Helper*, 7th edn, Brooks/Cole, Pacific Grove, CA

Elgood, C (1984) *The Handbook of Management Games*, Gower, Aldershot

Everly, G S and Lating, J M (2002) The anatomy and physiology of the human stress response, in *A Clinical Guide to the Treatment of the Human Stress Response*, ed G S Everly and J M Lating, pp 15–48, Springer Science and Business Media, Berlin

Experience Creative Development (2000) Promotional leaflet, Leatherhead, Surrey

Eyal, N (2014) *Hooked: How to build habit forming products*, Penguin, London

Falconar, T (2000) *Creative Intelligence and Self Liberation*, Crown House Publishing, Carmarthen

Feilden, R (2004) *The Impact of School Environments: A literature review*, The Design Council and the Centre for Learning & Teaching, University of Newcastle, Newcastle

Feldman Barrett, L and Salovey, P (eds) (2002) *The Wisdom in Feeling: Psychological processes in emotional intelligence*, The Guilford Press, New York

Fenwick, T J (2000) Expanding conceptions of experiential learning: a review of the five contemplations of cognition, *Adult Education Quarterly*, 50, pp 243–72

Fenwick, T J (2003) *Learning Through Experience: Troubling orthodoxies and intersecting questions*, Krieger Publishing Company, Malabar, Florida

Ferrucci, P (1982) *The Visions and Techniques of Psychosynthesis*, Turnstone Press, Wellingborough

Fineman, S (1997) Emotion and management learning, *Management Learning*, 28 (1), pp 13–25

Fox, R (1999) Enhancing spiritual experience in adventure programs, in *Adventure Programming*, ed J C Miles and S Priest, pp 455–61, Venture Publishing, Andover, MA

Frank, L S (2011) Maxine Greene: the power of the possible, in *Sourcebook of Experiential Education*, ed T E Smith and C E Knapp, Routledge, Oxford

Fraser, B (2001) Twenty thousand hours: editor's introduction, *Learning Environments Research*, 4, pp 1–5

Freire, P (1982) *The Pedagogy of the Oppressed*, Penguin, Harmondsworth

Frijda, N and Mesquita, B (1994) The social roles and functions of emotions, in *Emotion and Culture*, ed S Kitayama and H R Markus, American Psychological Association, Washington, DC

Fritchie, R (1988) in *Working with Assertiveness*, BBC training video booklet, BBC Enterprises Ltd, London

Furedi, F (2004) *Therapy Culture: Cultivating vulnerability in an uncertain age*, Routledge, London

Gabriel, Y (1998) The use of stories, in *Qualitative Methods and Analysis in Organisational Research*, ed G Symon and C Cassel, Sage, London

Gagne, R M (1974) *Essentials of Learning Instruction*, Dryden Press, Hinsdale, IL

Gallagher, S (2005) *How the Body Shapes the Mind*, Oxford University Press, Oxford

Gallo, C (2016) *The Story Teller's Secret*, Macmillan, London

Gallwey, T (1986) *The Inner Game of Tennis*, Pan Books, London

Gardner, H (1983) *Frames of Mind: The theory of multiple intelligences*, Basic Books Inc, New York

Gardner, H (1993) *Frames of Mind: The theory of multiple intelligences*, 2nd edn, Basic Books, New York

Gardner, H, Csikszentmihalyi, M and Damon, W (2001) *Good Work: When excellence and ethics meet*, Basic Books, New York

Gass, M (1992) WebCare international: using the Spider's Web with business populations, in *Book of Metaphors*, ed M Gass and C Dobkin, AEE, Boulder, CO

Gass, M (1995) *Book of Metaphors Volume II*, Kendall/Hunt Publishing, Dubuque, IA

Gass, M and Priest, S (1998) Using metaphors and isomorphs to transfer learning in adventure education, in *Outdoor Management Development*, ed C Loynes, Adventure Education, Cumbria

Gattis, M (ed) (2001) *Spatial Schemas and Abstract Thought*, MIT Press, Cambridge MA

Gillis, H L and Thomsen, D (1996) quoted in Ringer, M (2000) Adventure therapy: a description, in *Therapy Within Adventure*, ed K Richards and B Smith, pp 19–20, Proceedings of the Second International Adventure Therapy Conference, University of Augsburg, Augsburg

Gilsdorf, R (2003) Experience-adventure therapy: an inquiry into professional identity, in *Therapy Within Adventure*, ed K Richards and B Smith, pp 51–75, Proceedings of the Second International Adventure Therapy Conference, University of Augsburg, Augsburg

Gladwell, M (2005) *Blink: The power of thinking without thinking*, Little, Brown, New York

Goffman, E (1971) *The Presentation of Self in Everyday Life*, Penguin, Harmondsworth

Gold, G (1996) Telling stories to find the future, *Career Development International*, 1st quarter, pp 33–37, MCB University Press, Manchester

Golding, B (2005) *Listening to Men Learning: An exploration of men's learning preferences in community contexts*, paper presented to Design For Learning, the Twelfth International Conference on Learning, 11–14 July, Granada, Spain

Goleman, D (1996) *Emotional Intelligence*, Bantam Books, London

Goodall, J (1971) *In the Shadow of Man*, Houghton Mifflin, Boston and London

Gray, J (1993) *Men are from Mars – Women are from Venus*, Thorsons, London

Gray, J (1999) *Children are Heaven*, HarperCollins, New York

Greenaway, R (1993) *Playback: A guide to reviewing activities*, The Award Scheme Ltd, Duke of Edinburgh's Award and Endeavour, Scotland

Greenaway, R (1996) *Reviewing Adventures, Why and How*, NAOE, Sheffield

Greenaway, R (1999) [accessed 14 July 1999] [Online] http://www.users.globalnet.co.uk/-rogg/activities/outdoor_indoor.htm

Greenaway, R and Hilditch, D (1993) *Playback: A guide to reviewing activities*, The Duke of Edinburgh's Award in association with Endeavour Scotland

Greenfield, A (2006) *Everyware: The dawning age of ubiquitous computing*, New Riders: Berkeley, USA

Greenwood, J (1993) Reflective practice: a critique of the work of Argyris and Schön, *Journal of Advanced Nursing*, **19**, pp 1183–87

Greenwood, J (1998) The role of reflection in single and double loop learning, *Journal of Advanced Nursing*, **27**, pp 1048–53

Griffiths, J (2006) *Wild: An elemental journey*, London, Penguin Books

Gross, R (2001) *Psychology: The science of mind and behaviour*, 4th edn, Hodder & Stoughton, London

Gwilt, I (2013) Data-objects: sharing the attributes and properties of digital and material culture to creatively interpret complex information, in *Digital Media Technologies for Virtual Artistic Spaces*, ed D Harrison, IGI Global, Hershey, Pennsylvania, USA

Gwilt, I, Yoxall, A and Sano, K (2012) Enhancing the understanding of statistical data through the creation of physical objects, 2nd International Conference on Design Creativity (ICDC2012), Glasgow, UK, 2012, proceedings published by the design society UK

Hager, P (1999) Robin Usher on Experience, *Educational Philosophy and Theory*, **31** (1), pp 63–75

Hall, D and Associates (1995) *The Career is Dead, Long Live the Career*, Jossey-Bass, San Francisco

Hall, E and Moseley, D (2005) Is there a role for learning styles in personalised education and training?, *International Journal of Lifelong Education*, **24** (3), pp 243–55

Hall, J (2004) Phoenix House therapeutic conservation programme: underpinning theory, English Nature Research Reports, no 611, English Nature, Peterborough

Handy, C (1989) *The Age of Unreason*, Business Books, London

Handy, C (1990) *The Age of Unreason*, Century Business, London

Handy, C (1994) *The Empty Raincoat*, Hutchinson, London

Hardingham, A (1998) *Psychology for Trainers*, Institute of Personnel and Development, London

Hartmann, R and Beard, C M (2000) Environmental training: a strategic tool in an organisation's environmental management, proceedings of the Euro Environment 2000 conference: Visions, strategies and actions towards sustainable industries, 18–20 October, Aalborg Congress and Culture Centre, Denmark

Harwood, A (2005) Reaching the parts: the use of narrative and storytelling in organisational development, in *Organisational Development in Healthcare*, ed E Peck, pp 219–43, Radcliffe Publishing, Oxford

Heap, N (1993) Bridging the learning gap, *Training and Development*, January, pp 16–17

Henry, J (1991) *Creative Management*, Sage, London

Heron, J (1990) *Helping the Client: A creative, practical guide*, Sage, London

Heron, J (1999) *The Complete Facilitator's Handbook*, Kogan Page, London

Heron, J (2001) *Helping the Client: A creative practical guide*, Sage, London

Higgins, P (1996) Connection and consequence in outdoor education, *Journal of Adventure Education and Outdoor Leadership*, **13** (2), pp 34–39

Higgins, P (1997) Outdoor education for sustainability: making connections, *Journal of Adventure Education and Outdoor Leadership*, **13** (4), pp 4–11

Holman, D, Pavlica, K and Thorpe, R (1997) Rethinking Kolb's theory of experiential learning in management education, *Management Learning*, **28** (2), pp 135–48

Holmes, P S and Collins, D J (2001) The PETTLEP approach to motor imagery: a functional equivalence model for sport psychologists, *Journal of Applied Sport Psychology*, **13** (1), pp 60–83

Honey, P and Mumford, A (1992) *Manual of Learning Styles*, 3rd edn, Honey Publications, Maidenhead

Hopfl, H and Linstead, S (1997) Learning to feel and feeling to learn: emotion and learning in organisations, *Management Learning*, **28** (1), pp 5–12

Hovelynck, J (2000) Recognising and exploring action-theories: a reflection-in-action approach to facilitating experiential learning, *Journal of Adventure Education and Outdoor Learning*, **1** (1), pp 7–20

Hughes, C and Lury, C (2013) Re-turning feminist methodologies: from a social to an ecological epistemology, *Gender and Education*, **25** (6), pp 786–99

Hunt, C (1999) Reflective practice, in *Human Resource Development: Learning and training for individuals and organizations*, ed J P Wilson, pp 221–40, Kogan Page, London

Illeris, K (2002) *The Three Dimensions of Learning*, Krieger Publishing, Malabar, FL

Illeris, K (2009) Lifelong learning as a psychological process, in *The Routledge International Handbook of Lifelong Learning*, ed P Jarvis, pp 401–10, Oxford: Routledge

Ingleton, C (1999) Emotion in learning: a neglected dynamic, paper presented at the HERDSA Annual International Conference, Melbourne, July

Irvine, D and Wilson, J P (1994) Outdoor management development – reality or illusion?, *Journal of Management Development*, **13** (5), pp 25–37

Itin, C M (1999) Reasserting the philosophy of experiential education as a vehicle for change in the 21st century, *Journal of Experiential Education*, **22** (2), 91–98

James, T (2000) Can the mountains speak for themselves?, *Scisco Conscientia*, **2** (2), pp 1–4

Jarvis, P (1999) *International Dictionary of Adult and Continuing Education*, Kogan Page, London

Jarvis, P (2006) *Towards a Comprehensive Theory of Human Learning*, Routledge, Oxford

Jarvis, P (ed) (2009) *The Routledge International Handbook of Lifelong Learning*, Routledge, Oxford

Jeffs, T (2018) The origins of outdoor and adventure education, in *Rethinking Outdoor, Experiential and Informal Education: Beyond the confines*, ed T Jeffs and J Ord, Routledge, Oxford

Jeffs, T and Ord, J (2018) (eds) *Rethinking Outdoor, Experiential and Informal Education: Beyond the confines*, Routledge, Oxford

Johnson, B (1996) Feeling the fear, in *Working with Experience: Animating learning*, ed D Boud and N Miller, pp 184–93, Routledge, London

Johnstone, K (1981) *Impro*, Methuen, London

References

Kabat-Zinn, J (1990) *Full Catastrophe Living: Using the wisdom of your body and mind to face stress, pain, and illness*, Delacourt, New York

Kabat-Zinn, J (1994) *Wherever You Go, There You Are: Mindfulness meditation in everyday life*, Hyperion, New York

Kahane, A (2004) *Solving Tough Problems: An open way of talking, listening and creating new realities*, Berrett-Koehler, San Francisco, CA

Kahneman, D (2011) *Thinking Fast and Slow*, Penguin Books, London

Kellert, S R (1993) The biological basis for human values of nature, in *The Biophilia Hypothesis*, ed S R Kellert and E O Wilson, Island Press, Washington, DC

Kidner, D (2001) *Nature and Psyche: Radical environmentalism and the politics of subjectivity*, State University of New York Press, New York

Killingsworth, M A and Gilbert, D T (2010) A wandering mind is an unhappy mind, *Science*, **330**, 12 November, p 932

Kirk P (1986) Outdoor management development: cellulose or celluloid?, *Management Education and Development*, **17**, pp 85–93

Kirton, M J (1976) Adaptors and innovators: a description and measure, *Journal of Applied Psychology*, **61**, pp 622–29

Kitayama, S and Markus, H R (eds) (1994) *Emotion and Culture*, American Psychological Association, Washington, DC

Knight, S (2002) *NLP at Work*, Nicholas Brealey Publishing, London

Koestler, A (1967) *The Ghost in the Machine*, Arkana, London

Kolb, A and Kolb, D A (2008a) *Experiential Learning Theory Bibliography: Volume 1 1971–2005*, Experience Based Learning Systems, Cleveland, OH

Kolb, A and Kolb, D A (2008b) *Experiential Learning Theory Bibliography: Volume 2 2006–2008*, Experience Based Learning Systems, Cleveland, OH

Kolb, A Y and Kolb, D A (2009) The learning way: meta-cognitive aspects of experiential learning, *Simulation and Gaming*, **40** (3), pp 297–327

Kolb, D A (1971) Individual learning styles and the learning process, working paper #535-71, MIT Sloan School of Management, Cambridge, MA

Kolb, D A (1976) *The Learning Style Inventory: Technical manual*, McBer, Boston, MA

Kolb, D A (1984) *Experiential Learning: Experience as the source of learning and development*, Prentice Hall, Englewood Cliffs, NJ

Kolb, D A, Boyatzis, R and Mainemelis, C (2001) Experiential learning theory: previous research and new directions, in *Perspectives on Thinking, Learning, and Cognitive Styles*, ed R Sternberg and L Zhang, pp 227–47, Lawrence Erlbaum, Mahwah, NJ

Kraft, U (2005) Unleashing creativity, *Scientific American Mind*, **16** (1), pp 16–23

Krouwel, B and Goodwill, S (1994) Achieving your aims in the outdoors, *Training Officer*, September, pp 220–21

Kull, R (2008) *Solitude: Seeking wisdom in extremes*, New World Library, California

Lackney, J and Fielding, A (1998) [accessed 8 March 2018] School Design Studio [Online] http://Schoolstudio.typepad.com/school_design_studio/2007/01/12_design_princ.html

Lakoff, G and Johnson, M (1999) *Philosophy in the Flesh*, Basic Books, New York

Lamplugh, D (1991) *Without Fear: The key to staying safe*, Weidenfeld & Nicolson, London

Lashley, K S (1951) The problem of serial order in behavior, in *Cerebral Mechanisms in Behavior*, ed L A Jeffress, pp 112–36, New York: Wiley

Lave, J and Wenger, E (1991) *Situated Learning: Legitimate peripheral participation*, Cambridge University Press, Cambridge

Learning from Experience (2012) [accessed 8 March 2018] [Online] http://learningfromexperience.com/

Leberman, S I and Martin, A J (2005) Applying dramaturgy to management course design, *Journal of Management Education*, **29** (2), pp 319–32

Lessem, R (1982) A biography of action learning, in *The Origins and Growth of Action Learning*, ed R W Revans, pp 4–17, Chartwell-Bratt, Bickley, Kent

Lewin, K (ed) (1951) *Field Theory in Social Science*, Harper & Row, New York

Lewis, C S (1980) *The Chronicles of Narnia: The lion, the witch and the wardrobe*, Collins, London

Lewis, D (2013) *Impulse: Why we do what we do without knowing it*, Random House, London

Lin, T (2005) Information design for learning: a visual communication perspective, *International Journal of Technology, Knowledge, and Society*, **1**, Common Ground

Lindsay, A and Ewert, A (1999) Learning at the edge: can experiential education contribute to educational reform? *Journal of Experiential Education*, **22** (1), June, pp 12–19

Lindstrom, M (2005) *Brand Sense*, Kogan Page, London

Linehan, M M (1993) *Skills Training Manual for Treating Borderline Personality Disorder*, Guilford Press, New York

Lippit, R (1949) *Training in Community Relations: A research exploration toward new group skills*, Harper & Brothers, New York

Loeffller, B and Church, B T (2015) *The Experience: The 5 principles of Disney service and relationship excellence*, Wiley, New Jersey

Lombard, A (2007) *Sensory Intelligence: Why it matters more than IQ and EQ*, Metz Press, South Africa

Loynes, C (2000) The values of life and living: after all, life is right in any case, in *Values and Outdoor Learning*, ed P Barnes, Association for Outdoor Learning, Penrith, Cumbria

Loynes, C (2002) The generative paradigm, *Journal of Adventure Education and Outdoor Learning*, **2** (2), pp 113–25

Luft, J (1961) The Johari Window, *Human Training News*, **5** (1), pp 6–7

Lumsdaine, E and Lumsdaine, M (1995) *Creative Problem Solving: Thinking skills for a changing world*, McGraw-Hill, New York

Macala, J C (1986) Sponsored experiential programs: learning by doing in the workplace, in *Experiential and Simulation Techniques for Teaching Adults*, ed Linda H Lewis, pp 57–70, Jossey-Bass, San Francisco

MacDonald, L, Liu, P, Lowell, K, Tsai, H and Lohr, L (2005) [accessed 8 March 2018] Graduate Student Perspectives on the Development of Electronic Portfolios [Online] https://uascentral.uas.alaska.edu/onlinelib/Spring-2005/ED698-JD1/13705737.pdf

MacLennan, N (1995) *Coaching and Mentoring*, Gower, Aldershot

Maguire, E A *et al* (2000) Navigation-related structural change in the hippocampi of taxi drivers, *Proceedings of the National Academy of Science USA*, **97**, pp 4398–403

Malinen, A (2000) *Towards the Essence of Adult Experiential Learning*, Jyväskylä University Printing House, Jyväskylä, Finland

Mälkki, K (2010) Building on Mezirow's theory of transformative learning: theorizing the challenges to reflection, *Journal of Transformative Education*, **8** (1), pp 42–62

Mälkki, K (2011) Theorizing the nature of reflection, doctoral dissertation, University of Helsinki, Institute of Behavioural Sciences, Studies in Educational Sciences

Mallia, G (1997) The use of comic strips in adult education practice, in *Beyond Schooling*, ed G Baldacchino and P Mayo, Mireva Publications, Msida, Malta

Mallinger, A and De Wyze, J (1993) *Too Perfect*, HarperCollins, London

Mannell, R C (1984) The playful side of laughter, *Journal of Leisureability*, **11**, pp 4–7

Mannell, R C and Kleiber, D A (1997) *A Social Psychology of Leisure*, Venture Publications, Pittsburgh, PA

Markman, K, Klein, W M P and Suhr, J A (2009) *Handbook of Imagination and Mental Simulation*, Psychology Press, Hove, Sussex

Marlatt, G A and Kristeller, J L (1999) Mindfulness and meditation, in *Integrating Spirituality into Treatment*, ed W R Miller, pp 67–84, Washington, DC, American Psychological Association

Martin, A, Franc, D and Zounkova, D (2004) *Outdoor and Experiential Learning: An holistic approach to programme design*, Gower, Aldershot

Martin, A J (2001) Dramaturgy: an holistic approach to outdoor education, *Australian Journal of Outdoor Education*, **5** (2), pp 34–41

Martin, A J (2011) The dramaturgy approach to education in nature, *Journal of Adventure Education and Outdoor Leadership*, **11** (1), pp 67–82

Martin, A J, Leberman, S I and Neill, J T (2002) Dramaturgy as a method for experiential programme design, *Journal of Experiential Education*, **25** (1), 196–206

Maslow, A (1954) *Motivation and Personality*, Harper & Row, New York

Maslow, A (1971) *The Farther Reaches of Human Nature*, Viking, New York

McGill, I and Beaty, L (1992) *Action Learning*, Kogan Page, London

McIntyre, N and Roggenbuck, J W (1998) Nature/person transactions during an outdoor adventure experience: a multi-phasic analysis, *Journal of Leisure Research*, **30** (4), pp 401–22

McLeod, J (1997) *Narrative and Psychotherapy*, Sage, London

Megginson, D (1994) Planned and emergent learning: a framework and a method, *Executive Development*, **7** (6), pp 29–32, MCB University Press, Manchester

Michelson, E (1999) Carnival, paranoia, and experiential learning, *Studies in the Education of Adults*, **31** (2), pp 140–54

Miettinen, R (2000) The concept of experiential learning and John Dewey's theory of reflective thought and action, *International Journal of Lifelong Education*, **19** (1), January–February, pp 54–72

Miles, J (1995) Wilderness as a healing place, in *The Theory of Experiential Education*, ed K Warren, M Sakofs and J Hunt, Association for Experiential Education, Kendall/Hunt Publishing, Dubuque, IA

Miles, J and Priest, S (1990) *Adventure Education*, Venture Publishing, State College, PA

Miller, N and Boud, D (1996) Animating learning from experience, in *Working with Experience: Animating learning*, ed D Boud and N Miller, pp 3–13, Routledge, London

Mischel, W (2014) *The Marshmallow Test: Understanding self-control and how to master it*, Random House, New York

Mohawk, J (1996) A nature view of nature, *Resurgence*, **178**, pp 10–11

Moon, J (2000) *Reflection in Learning and Professional Development*, Kogan Page, London

Moon, J (2004) *A Handbook of Reflective and Experiential Learning*, RoutledgeFalmer, London

Morgan, G (1997a) *Images of Organisations*, Sage, London

Morgan, G (1997b) *Imaginization: New mindsets for seeing, organising, and managing*, Sage, London

Morris, D (1967) *The Naked Ape: A zoologist's study of the human animal*, Jonathan Cape, London

Morris, D (1969) *The Human Zoo*, Corgi Books, London

Morris, T, Spittle, M and Watt, A P (2005) *Imagery in Sport*, Human Kinetics, Champaign, IL

Mortiboys, A (2002) *The Emotionally Intelligent Lecturer*, SEDA Publications, Birmingham

Mortlock, C (1984) *The Adventure Alternative*, Cicerone Press, Milnthorpe, Cumbria

Mossberg, L (2007) A marketing approach to the tourist experience, *Scandinavian Journal of Hospitality and Tourism*, **7** (1), pp 59–74

Mulligan, J (2000) Activating internal processes in experiential learning, in *Using Experience for Learning*, ed D Boud, R Cohen and D Walker, pp 46–58, SRHE/Open University Press, Milton Keynes

Mulligan, J and Griffin, C (1992) *Empowerment Through Experiential Learning: Explorations of good practice*, Kogan Page, London

Mumford, A (1991) Individual and organisational learning: the pursuit of change, *Journal of Industrial and Commercial Training*, **23** (6), pp 24–31

Neulinger, J (1974) *The Psychology of Leisure*, Charles C Thomas Publishers, Springfield, IL

Neuman, J (2004) *Education and Learning through Outdoor Activities*, Duha Publishing, Prague

Nolan, R (2004) *Compatibility or Conflict: The sustainability of ecotourism consumerism*, unpublished thesis, MSc Environmental Management and Conservation, Sheffield Hallam University

Norris, J (2011) Crossing the threshold mindfully: exploring rites of passage models in adventure therapy, *Journal of Adventure Education and Outdoor Learning*, **11** (2), pp 109–26

OECD (2011) *Education at a Glance 2011: OECD indicators*, OECD, Paris

Ogilvie, K (1993) *Leading and Managing Groups in the Outdoors*, NAOE Publications, Sheffield

Ord, J (2018) Mountains, climbing, and informal education, in *Rethinking Outdoor, Experiential and Informal education: Beyond the confines*, ed J Jeffs and J Ord, Routledge, Oxford

Orlick, T (1975) *In Pursuit of Excellence*, Human Kinetics Publishers/Coaching Association of Canada, Champaign, IL

Osborne, A F (1963) *Applied Imagination*, Scribners, New York

O'Sullivan, E L and Spangler, K J (1998) *Experience Marketing*, Venture Publishing, State College, PA

Palethorpe, R and Wilson, J P (2011) Learning in the panic zone: strategies for managing learner anxiety, *Journal of European Industrial Training*, **35** (5), pp 420–38

Palmer, J (ed) (2001) *Fifty Modern Thinkers on Education*, Routledge, London

Parkin, M (1998) *Tales for Trainers*, Kogan Page, London

Parr, J (2000) *Identity and Education: The links for mature women students*, Ashgate Publishing, Aldershot

Pascual-Leone, A, Nguyet, D, Cohen, LG, Brasil-Neto, JP, Cammarota, A and Hallett, M (1995) Modulation of muscle responses evoked by transcranial magnetic stimulation during the acquisition of new fine motor skills, *Journal of Neurophysiology*, **74**, pp 1037–45

Pavlov, I (1927) *Conditioned Reflexes: An investigation of the physiological activity of the cerebral cortex*, trans G V Anrep, Oxford University Press, London

Peard, G (1999) Spirit of the earth: Chief Seathl's speech, *Horizons*, **4** (4), pp 9–13

Pedler, M (1996) *Action Learning for Managers*, Lemos and Crane in association with The Learning Company Project, London

Peterson, R and Getz, D (2009) Event experiences in time and space: a study of visitors to the 2007 World Alpine Ski Championships in Are, Sweden, *Scandinavian Journal of Hospitality and Tourism*, **9** (2–3), pp 308–26

Piaget, J P (1927) *Conditioned Reflexes*, Oxford University Press, Oxford

Pinchot, G (1991) Conference Tapes, Institute of Personnel and Development Annual Conference, 23–25 October, Harrogate

Pine, J and Gilmore, B H (1999) *The Experience Economy, Work is Theatre and Every Business is a Stage*, Harvard Business School, Boston, MA

Pine II, B J and Gilmore, J H (2011) *The Experience Economy*, Harvard Business School Publishing, Boston, MA

Pinker, S (1989) *Learnability and Cognition: The acquisition of argument structure*, MIT Press, Cambridge, MA

Pinkney, L (1999) [accessed 20 May 2005] Sensory Therapy [Online] www.sophp.soton.ac.uk/neuro/SENSORY.htm

Plato (1953) Laws, in *Plato's Modern Enemies and the Theory of Natural Law*, ed J D Wild, p 24, University of Chicago Press, Chicago, IL

Plutchik, R (1980) *Emotion: A psychobioevolutionary synthesis*, Harper & Row, New York

Pollock, L (2000) That's infotainment, *People Management*, 28 December, pp 19–23

Porter, T (1999) Beyond metaphor: applying a new paradigm of change to experiential debriefing, *Journal of Experiential Education*, **22** (2), pp 85–90

Postle, Dennis (1993) Putting the heart back into learning, in *Using Experience for Learning*, ed D Boud, R Cohen and D Walker, pp 33–45, Open University Press, Buckingham

Priest, S and Ballie, R (1995) Justifying the risk to others: the real razor's edge, in *The Theory of Experiential Education*, ed K Warren, M Sakofs and J Hunt, pp 307–16, Association for Experiential Education, Kendall/ Hunt Publishing, Dubuque, IA

Priest, S, Gass, M and Fitzpatrick, K (1999) Training corporate managers to facilitate: the next generation of facilitating experiential methodologies, *The Journal of Experiential Education*, **22** (1), p 50

Priest, S and Rohnke, K (2000) *101 of the Best Corporate Team-Building Activities We Know!*, Kendall/Hunt Publishing, Dubuque, IW

Proudman, S (1999) Urban adventure in 1989 and reflections ten years after, in *Adventure Programming*, ed J C Miles and S Priest, Venture Publishing PA, USA

Rackham, N and Morgan, T (1977) *Behaviour Analysis in Training*, McGraw-Hill, London

Rae, L (1995) *Techniques of Training*, 3rd edn, Gower, Aldershot

Randall, R and Southgate, J (1980) *Co-Operative and Community Group Dynamics*, Barefoot Books, London

Ray, M and Myers, R (1986) *Creativity in Business*, Doubleday, New York

Reed, C (1999) A weekend in the country: the outdoors, the earth and drama therapy, *Horizons*, **3**, pp 20–21

Reich, B (2017) *The Imagination Gap*, Emerald Publishing, Bingley

Reid, M and Barrington, H (1999) *Training Interventions*, IPD, London

Revans, R W (1971) *Developing Effective Managers: A new approach to business education*, Longman, London

Revans, R W (1982) *The Origin and Growth of Action Learning*, Chartwell Bratt, London

Reynolds, M (1997) Learning styles: a critique, *Management Learning*, **28** (2), pp 115–33, Sage, London

Ritchhart, R, Church, M and Morrison, K (2011) *Making Thinking Visible: How to promote engagement, understanding, and independence for all learners*, Jossey-Bass, San Francisco

Ritzer, G (2001) *Explorations in Social Theory: From metatheorising to rationalisation*, Sage Publications, Thousand Oaks, CA

Roberts, J (2012) *Beyond Learning by Doing: Theoretical currents in experiential education*, Routledge, Oxford

Robertson, I (1999) *Mind Sculpture*, Bantam Books, London

Robertson, I (2000) *Mind Sculpture: Unleashing your brain's potential*, Bantam Books, London

Rodwell, J (1994) *Participative Training Skills*, Gower, London

Rogers, A (1996) *Teaching Adults*, Open University Press, Buckingham

Rogers, C R (1969) *Freedom to Learn: A view of what education might become*, Charles E Merrill, Columbus, OH

Rosenberg, M (2003) *Nonviolent Communication: A language of life*, PuddleDancer Press, California

Rowland, S (2000) *The Enquiring University Teacher*, SRHE/Open University Press, Milton Keynes

Salaman, G and Butler, J (1990) Why managers won't learn, *Management Education and Development*, **21** (3), pp 183–91

Salovey, P and Mayer, J D (1990) Emotional intelligence, *Imagination, Cognition and Personality*, **9**, pp 185–211

Samra-Fredericks, D (1998) Conversation analysis, in *Qualitative Methods and Analysis in Organisational Research*, ed G Symon and C Cassel, Sage, London

Sasaki, N (1981) *Management and Industrial Structure in Japan*, Pergamon Press, London

Saunders, D (1988) Simulation gaming: three aspects, *Training Officer*, May, pp 134–36

Schank, R C (1992) Story-based memory, in *Minds, Brains and Computers*, ed R Morelli *et al*, Ablex Publishing Corporation, Norwood, NJ

Scheff, T (1997) *Emotions, the Social Bond, and Human Reality*, Cambridge University Press, Cambridge

Schein, E H (1992) *Organizational Culture and Leadership*, 2nd edn, Jossey-Bass, San Francisco

Schetter, M (1992) Comic strips in Belgium, in *Belgium, Economic and Commercial Information*, ed Borgerhoff Mulder *et al*, Belgium Foreign Trade Office, Brussels, quoted in G Mallia (1997) The use of comic strips in adult education practice, in *Beyond Schooling*, ed G Baldacchino and P Mayo, p 89, Mireva Publications, Msida, Malta

Schmitt, B H (1999) *Experiential Marketing: How to get customers to sense, feel, think, act, relate to your company and brands*, The Free Press, New York

Schoel, J, Prouty, D and Radcliffe, P (1988) *Island of Healing: A guide to adventure-based counselling*, Project Adventure Inc, Hamilton, MA

Schön, D (1983) *The Reflective Practitioner*, Basic Books, New York

Schön, D (1987) *Educating the Reflective Practitioner*, Jossey-Bass, San Francisco

Schueller, G (2000) Thrill or chill, *New Scientist*, **2236**, 20 April, pp 20–24

Schull, N (2012) *Addiction by Design: Machine gambling in Las Vegas*, Princetown University Press, NJ

Schultz, G (1992) *Die Erlebnisgesellschaft: Kultursoziologie der Gegenwart*, Campus Verlag, Frankfurt am Main

Seibert, K W (1999) Reflection in action: tools for cultivating on-the-job learning conditions, *Organizational Dynamics*, Winter, pp 54–65

Senge, P M (1993) *The Fifth Discipline: The art and practice of the learning organization*, Century Business, London

Senge, P, Scharmer, C, Jawaorski, J and Flowers, B (2005) *Presence: Exploring profound change in people, organizations and society*, Nicholas Brealey Publishing, London

Sheets-Johnstone, M (2009) *The Corporeal Turn, An Interdisciplinary Reader*, Imprint Academic, Exeter

Siegler, R, Deloache, J and Eisenberg, N (2006) *How Children Develop*, Worth Publishers, New York

Sinetar, M (1992) Entrepreneurs, chaos and creativity: can creative people survive large company structure?, in *Frontiers of Leadership: An essential reader*, ed M Syrett and C Hogg, pp 109–16, Blackwell, Oxford

Skinner, B (1974) *Adult Behaviourism*, Jonathan Cape, London

Smith, P K *et al* (1986) Play in young children: problems of definition, categorisation and measurement, in *Children's Play: Research developments and practical applications*, ed P K Smith, pp 37–54, Gordon & Breach, New York

Smith, R and Betts, M (2000) Learning as partners: realising the potential of work-based learning, *Journal of Vocational Education and Training*, **52** (4), pp 589–604

Smith, T E and Knapp, C E (eds) (2011) *Sourcebook of Experiential Education: Key thinkers and their contributions*, Routledge, Oxford

Snell, R (1992) Experiential learning at work: why can't it be painless?, *Personnel Review*, **21** (4), pp 12–26

Sterling, S (2001) *Sustainable Education: Re-visioning Learning and Change*, Green Books, Totnes

Sterling, S (2003) Whole systems thinking as a basis for paradigm change in education: explorations in the context of sustainability, unpublished PhD thesis, University of Bath

Stevenson, J (2000) *Eastern Philosophy*, Alpha Publishing, New York

Stiglitz, J, Sen, A and Fitoussi, J P (2009) The measurement of economic performance and social progress revisited: reflections and overview, Commission on the Measurement of Economic Performance and Social Progress, Paris

Stonehouse, P, Alison, P and Carr, D (2011) Aristotle, Plato, and Socrates: ancient Greek perspectives on experiential learning, in *Sourcebook of Experiential Education: Key thinkers and their contributions*, ed T E Smith and C E Knapp, Routledge, Oxford

Stouffer, R (1999) Personal insight: reframing the unconscious through metaphor-based adventure therapy, *Journal of Experiential Education*, **22** (1), June, pp 28–34

Strangaard, F (1981) *NLP Made Visual*, Connector, Copenhagen

Stringer, L and McAvoy, L (1995) The need for something different: spirituality and wilderness adventure, in *The Theory of Experiential Education*, ed K Warren *et al*, pp 57–72, Kendall/Hunt Publishing, Dubuque, IA

Surtees, M (1998) New frontiers in outdoor development: evaluating the personal development outcomes of expeditions, unpublished master's thesis in HRD, Sheffield Business School, Sheffield

Swaab, D (2014) *We are Our Brains: From the womb to Alzheimer's*, Penguin, London

Swarbrooke, J, Beard, C, Leckie, S and Pomfret, G (2003) *Adventure Tourism: The new frontier*, Butterworth-Heinemann, Oxford

Taleb, N N (2007) *The Black Swan: The impact of the highly improbable*, Penguin, London

Taylor, H (1991) The systematic training model: corn circles in search of a spaceship?, *Journal of the Association for Management Education and Development*, **22** (4), pp 258–78

Tenant, M (1997) *Psychology and Adult Learning*, 2nd edn, Routledge, London

Terrell, C (2000) Cartoon review cards, *Horizons*, **12**, Winter, AfOL, Penrith, Cumbria

Thayer, R (1996) *The Origin of Everyday Moods: Managing energy, tension and stress*, Oxford University Press, Oxford

The Economist (1999) [accessed 8 March 2018] We Woz Wrong, 16 December [Online] http://www.economist.com/node/268752

Thom, J M and Clayton, N S (2013) Re-caching by Western scrub-jays (Aphelocoma californica) cannot be attributed to stress, *PloS One*, **8** (1), e52936

Thorne, F C (1963) The clinical use of peak and Nadir experience reports, *Journal of Clinical Psychology*, **19** (2), pp 248–50

Thurber, J (1939) The secret life of Walter Mitty, *The New Yorker*, 18 March

Tolle, E (1997) *The Power of Now: A guide to spiritual enlightenment*, Vancouver: Namaste Publishing

Tolle, E (2006) *A New Earth: Awakening your life's purpose*, Plume, London

Tomlinson, M (2017) Introduction: graduate employability in context: charting a complex, contested and multi-faceted policy and research field, in *Graduate Employability in Context: Theory, research and debate*, ed M Tomlinson and L Holmes, pp 1–40, Palgrave Macmillan, London

Tower, R B and Singer, J L (1980) Imagination, interest and joy in early childhood, in *Children's Humour*, ed P E McGhee and A J Chapman, Wiley, Chichester

Trules, A (2005) Personal storytelling bridges the great divide: changing the world one story at a time, paper presented to the Twelfth International Conference on Learning, University of Granada, Spain

Tulving, E (1972) Episodic and semantic memory, in *Organization of Memory*, ed E Tulving and E Donaldson, pp 381–403, Academic Press, London

Turner, T (2005) Video games as education and literacies: what we have to understand about video and computer games and technological environments to accomplish learning and literacies, workshop presentation Abstract, Design For Learning, The Twelfth International Conference on Learning, 11–14 July, Granada, Spain

Tversky, B (2001) Spatial schemas in depictions, in *Spatial Schemas and Abstract Thought*, ed M Gattis, pp 79–112, MIT Press, London

Ulrich, D (1974) Aesthetic and effective responses to natural environments, in *Behaviour and the Natural Environment*, ed I Altman and J Wohlwill, Plenum Press, New York

UNDP (2010) Human development report 2010: 20th anniversary edition: the real wealth of nations: pathways to human development, UNDP, New York

Usher, R and Edwards, R (1994) *Postmodernism and Education*, Routledge, Oxford

Uttley, A (1943) from *Country Hoard*, in J S Bruner, A Jolly and K Sylva (1976) *Play*, Penguin, Harmondsworth

Van Manen, M (1991) *The Tact of Teaching*, The State of New York Press, New York

Van Matre, S (1978) *Acclimatisation*, American Camping Association, Martinsville, IN

Van Matre, S (1979) *Sunship Earth*, American Camping Association, Martinsville, IN

van Ments, M (1994) *The Effective Use of Role Play*, Kogan Page, London

Vanreusel, B (1995) From Bambi to Rambo: towards a socio-ecological approach to the pursuit of outdoor sports, in *Sport in Space and Time*, ed O Weiss and W Schulz, Vienna University Press, Vienna

Vygotsky, L (1978) *Mind in Society: The development of higher psychological processes*, Harvard University Press, Cambridge, MA

Walter, G and Marks, S (1981) *Experiential Learning and Change*, John Wiley & Sons, New York

Walker, R (1999) Fire in the sky: from big bang to big money, *Horizons*, **4**, pp 5–7

Warren, K, Sakofs, M and Hunt, J S (1995) *The Theory of Experiential Education*, Kendal Hunt, Colorado

Waterhouse, K (1959) *Billy Liar*, Michael Joseph, London

Whitehead, J and McNiff, J (2006) *Action Research: Living theory*, Sage, London

Whitton, N (2014) *Digital Games and Learning: Research and theory*, Routledge, London

Wickes, S (2000) The facilitators' stories, *Organisation Development*, Brathay Topical Papers, 2, pp 25–46, Brathay, Cumbria

Wilkes, F (1999) *Intelligent Emotion*, Arrow Books, London

Willett, J (1977) *Brecht on Theatre,* Eyre Methuen, London

Williams, A (2012) Taking a step back: learning without the facilitator on solo activities, *Journal of Adventure Education and Outdoor Learning*, **12** (2), pp 137–55

Williams, M (2017) [accessed 8 March 2018] Mindfulness [Online] https://www.nhs.uk/Conditions/stress-anxiety-depression/Pages/mindfulness.aspx

Williams, R (2012) The impact of residential adventure education on primary school pupils, unpublished PhD thesis, University of Exeter

Willis, A (2011) Re-storying wilderness and adventure therapies: healing places and selves in an era of environmental crisis, *Journals of Adventure Education and Outdoor Learning*, **11** (2) pp 91–108

Wilson, J P (2008) Reflecting on the future: a chronological consideration of reflective practice, *Journal of Reflective Practice*, **9** (2), pp 177–84

Wilson, J P (2012) *Dream: Your life, your future*, Burton in Kendal, Cumbria

Wilson, P (1997) *Calm at Work*, Penguin, London

Winston, R (2003) *The Human Mind*, Bantam Press, London

Wood-Daudelin, M (1996) Learning from experience through reflection, *Organizational Dynamics*, **24** (3), pp 36–46

Woodruffe, C (2001) Promotional intelligence, *People Management*, 11 January, Chartered Institute of Personnel and Development

Woollett, K and Maguire, E A (2011) Acquiring 'the knowledge' of London's layout drives structural brain changes, *Current Biology*, **21**, pp 2109–14

Yaffey (1993) The value base of activity experience in the outdoors, *Journal of Adventure Education*, **10** (3), pp 9–11

Yardley-Matwiejczuk, K (1999) *Role Play: Theory and practice*, Sage, London

Yerkes, R M and Dodson, J D (1980) The relation of strength of stimulus to rapidity of habit formation, *Journal of Comparative Neurological Psychology*, **18**, pp 459–82

Young, M (2008) *Bringing Knowledge Back In: From social constructivism to social realism in the sociology of education*, Routledge, London

Yue, G and Cole, K J (1992) Strength increases from the motor program: comparison of training with maximal voluntary and imagined muscle contracts, *Journal of Neurophysiology*, **67**, pp 1114–23

INDEX

Note: bold page numbers indicate figures; italic numbers indicate tables.

2 × 2 experiential learning quadrant 3–4, **4**
three Cs concept 280–84

Abbot, C 116
Abram, D 178, 182, 257, 263
action learning 292–98, **295**
activities for experience learning
   adventure learning 126–27
   adventurous journeys 132–36
   art and images, use of 164–67, **167**, **168**
   brain, engaging the 138–39
   community/environment connections 161–62
   construction/deconstruction 141–42
   drama and role play 156–61
   dramaturgy 127–29, **129**
   eco-adventure travel 133–34
   escape simulations 125–26
   expeditions 133, 134–36
   fantasy 150–53
   journeys, learning 130–31, **131**
   objects, handling 142–43
   obstacles in 140–41
   outcomes, determining required 130
   planned/unplanned experiences 123–25, **124**
   play and reality 153–56
   post-expedition readjustment 135–36
   reality and 143–62
   reflective practice 168–69
   reviewing 169–71
   rules for 140–41
   sequencing 136–37, **137**
   storytelling 162–64, 165
   typology for programmes 131–32
addictive experiences 47
Adler, P S 210
adventure therapy 115
adventurous journeys 132–36
Allison, P 55, 58, 135–36
alphabets 181–82
amplification of sensory experiences 174
amygdala 201
anchoring 196–97
Anderson, Ray 89
anger 227–28

antenatal and postnatal development 316–17
Argyris, C 223–24, 325
art and images, use of 164–67, **167**, **168**
artificial spaces 104–08
Assagioli, R 142
Attarian, A 105
aural flooding 187–88
awareness, sensory 173, 177–78

Badger, B 126–27
Bagshaw, M 207
Barrett, J 58
Beard, C M 3, 25, 65, 76, 244–46
Beaty, L 294
Becher, T 94
Beck, Harry 64
behaviourism 33, **34**
Behuniak, S 187–88
being dimension
   action learning 292–98, **295**
   cave, Plato's allegory of 275–76
   debriefing after activities 274–75
   edge emotions 292
   human, being 273–74, 275–76
   inner game 298–302
   life, examination of 273
   mindfulness 277–79
   peak experience 301–02
   problem-posing education 289–91
   problems, painful learning and 291
   single/double-loop learning **288**, 288–89, **289**
   three Cs concept 280–84, **281**, **282**
   well-being 276–77
belonging dimension
   artificial spaces 104–08
   boundaries, indoor/outdoor 98–100, **101**
   city spaces 101–02
   ecological approach 94
   environmental issues in outdoor learning 112–13, 117–18, **119**
   gender issues 94
   health, natural environment and 113–17

belonging dimension (*continued*)
   indoor learning environments 91–96
   nature, attitudes towards 85–87
   new designs for learning environments 94–96
   outdoor learning 96–98
   private spaces 95–96
   simulated environments 110–12
   space, importance of 87–91
   spatial ecologies, evolution of 87–91
   sustainable learning environments 117–18, **119**
   territoriality 94
   'The Four Steps' 112, **112**
   video gaming 95
   workplace design 90–91
Benson, J 227, 234
Best, B 71
Betts, M 50
bibliography of experiential learning 37
Binstead, D 148
biographical work 168–69
biological functions 30
Bishop, S R 278
Black, M 233
Black Mountain 127
Bloom, B S 33
bodily learning 63, 65, 66, 197
   bodily knowing 242–43
   body-brain connections 181
Bokova, Irina 53
Boler, M 256
Bolton, G 157
Boud, D 4, 8, 29–30, 32, 55, 125, 199
boundaries, indoor/outdoor 98–100, **101**
Boydell, T 4–5
brain, the
   amygdala 201
   body-brain connections 181
   brainwaves 220
   construction/reconstruction of memories 308–09
   damaged 239
   engaging 138–39
   functioning/feeling/thinking brains 201, 242–43
   hippocampus 239
   learning and 239–40
   neurotransmitters 239–40
   physical/mental practice 313–14
Brew, J M 57
Brooks, J G 32
Brooks, M G 32
Bryson, B 104
Bull, N 181, 200

Burns, G 114–15, 117, 173, 193
Burr, V 30
Butcher, G B 143, 145
Butler, J 208

calm, emotional **210**, **211**, 212–14, **214**
cartoons 164–67, **167**
case studies
   antenatal and postnatal development 316–17
   art and images, use of 164
   Coffee and Papers experience 87–89
   creativity and self-expression 268–70
   drama and role play 158–61
   dramaturgy 128–29, **129**
   edge emotions 292
   experience mapping 78–80
   industrial ecology (IE) 244–46
   Kadoorie Farm and Botanic Garden, Hong Kong 9–10
   KidZania 48–49
   law clinics 146–47
   leadership competencies in Malaysia 159–61
   masks 194–96
   reality 149–50
   reviewing 170–71
   rowing camps 109–10
   self, exploration of 194–96
   Sparks Consulting 109–10
   tall ship experience 103–04
   'The Four Steps' 65
   three Cs concept 280–84, **281**, **282**
   workplace design 90–91
   XP School, Doncaster 71–72
categorization
   of learning 1, 24
   by the mind 243–46
cave, Plato's allegory of 275–76
Cell, Edward 2
Chaput de Saintonge, M 50
Charlton, C 113
Child, G 260
children and imagination 315–17
Chinese aphorism 26, 121
Chopra, D 260–61
chronology of experiential learning 317–26, **318**, **324**
Church, B T 47
city spaces
   artificial spaces 104–08
   as learning opportunity 101–02
   outdoor programmes 102
   wildlife spaces 102
classification of learning 1, 24

climbing walls 104–08
coaching *see* delivery of experiential learning
codes 69
Coffee and Papers experience 87–89
Coffield, F 39, 41
cognitivist theories 33, **34**
Cohen, D 155, 315
Cohen, R 4, 8, 29–30, 125, 199
Collison, C 162
colour 193
comfort zone 292, 312–13
comics 165–67, **167**
communication
 blockages 223
 compassionate 203–06
 with feeling 202–06
 non-violent communication (NVC) 203
 triangle **223**, 223–24
community connections with activities 161–62
compassionate communication 203–06
competencies in leadership, Malaysia 159–61
concentration 300–02
concurrent learning 319–20
conditioning 33, 280–81, **281**, **282**
conduct **281**, 281–84, **282**
Consalvo, C 97, 165
conscious/unconscious mind 299–300
consciousness **281**, **282**, 282–84
 of experience 11
construction/deconstruction
 activities 141–42
 experience 31
 memories 308–09
consumer experience, dimensions of **45**, 45–46
continuity of experience 29, 43
continuous improvement 40–41, **41**
control
 fear of losing 225–27
 and power in interventions 60–62, *61–62*
Cooper, G 262–63
Coral Cay 133
Covey, S R 44
creative intelligence (CQ) 264–70
creative thinking 244–46
Crosby, A 206
Csikszentmihalyi, M 215, 216, 251
Cuffaro, H K 5

Dale's Cone of Experience 26, 121, **122**
Damon, W 251
Darwin, C 256
Daudelin, M 212

Davies, W 260
Davis, B 36
daydreaming 312
de Freitas, S 191
de Wyze, J 153–54
deeper learning
 action learning 292–98, **295**
 cave, Plato's allegory of 275–76
 debriefing after activities 274–75
 edge emotions 292
 human, being 273–74, 275–76
 inner game 298–302
 life, examination of 273
 mindfulness 277–79
 peak experience 301–02
 problem-posing education 289–91
 problems, painful learning and 291
 single/double-loop learning **288**, 288–89, **289**
 three Cs concept 280–84, **281**, **282**
 well-being 276–77
delivery of experiential learning
 categories and names 54–55
 complexity of 54
 deprofessionalization of educators 53–54
 design of learning experiences 55, 62–72
 interventions 56–62, *61–62*
 see also activities for experience learning; Learning Combination Lock
Deming, W E 40–41, **41**
design of learning experiences
 addictive experiences 47
 bodily learning 63, 65, 66
 codes 69
 complexity of 55–56
 expeditionary learning 71–72
 gestures 63
 habits, learning 70–71
 ingredients, juggling 62–63
 language, impact on experience 67–68
 maps 63–64, 66–67
 movement 63, 65, 66
 navigational tools 63–64, 66–67
 objects and props 68–69
 outcomes, determining required 130
 performative approach 65
 seven aspects of **56**
 sophistication, increase in 47
 sound and film bites 69–70
 stories 69–70
 thinking out loud 68
 typology for programmes 131–32
 XP School, Doncaster 71–72
 see also activities for experience learning; Learning Combination Lock

Index

Dewey, J 4, 5–6, 28, 29, 37, **37**, 44, 50, 53, 199, 251, 285, 310–11, 312, 322, 323
dimensions of human experience 51, **76**, **77**
  see also being dimension; belonging dimension; doing dimension; feeling dimension; knowing dimension; sensing dimension
disillusionment after experiences 58
Disneyfication of experiences 47–48
distressed learning 145
doing dimension
  adventure learning 126–27
  adventurous journeys 132–36
  art and images, use of 164–67, **167**, **168**
  brain, engaging the 138–39
  community/environment connections 161–62
  construction/deconstruction 141–42
  drama and role play 156–61
  eco-adventure travel 133–34
  escape simulations 125–26
  expeditions 133, 134–36
  fantasy 150–53
  journeys, learning 130–31, **131**
  link to purpose and will 123
  meaning of doing 121–22
  objects, handling 142–43
  obstacles for activities 140–41
  outcomes, determining required 130
  planned/unplanned experiences 123–25, **124**
  play and reality 153–56
  post-expedition readjustment 135–36
  reality and 143–62
  reflective practice 168–69
  reviewing activities 169–71
  rules for activities 140–41
  sequencing of activities 136–37, **137**
  storytelling 162–64, 165
Doncaster, K 321
dopamine 240
double/single-loop learning **288**, 288–89, **289**
drama and role play 156–61
dramaturgy 127–29, **129**, 144
Duhigg, C 70–71
Dunn, D 50

E C Harris 90
e-learning 95
Earth Centre, Doncaster 259–60
Eastern philosophies 26–27
ECHQ 90
eco-adventure travel 133–34
ecological theories **34**, 35–36

ecologies, spatial
  evolution of 87–91
  see also environments for learning
ecology of experience 31–32
economy, experience 46–50, 302–03
ecotherapy 115
edge emotions 292
edventure 133–34
Edwards, R 49
ego 225
Einstein, Albert 23, 27, 238, 314
Elgood, C 151
embodied cognition 242–43
embodied learning 190–91
  bodily learning 63, 65, 66
  body-brain connections 181
emotions
  ability to learn 43
  accessing, tools for 219–36, **223**, **226**
  anger 227–28
  aptitude in 200
  calm, emotional **210**, **211**, 212–14, **214**
  communicating with feeling 202–06
  edge 292
  evolution and 311
  experiential learning and 206–09
  fast/slow thinking 201–02
  fear 208, 216–17, 221–27
  flow learning 214–16
  higher education 202
  humour, use of 229–31
  identifying and classifying 256–57
  identity and education 218–19
  intelligence, emotional (EQ) 200, 205–06, 207, 254–57
  in life and learning 199–200
  mapping 224–27
  metaphors 231–36
  moods 208–09
  optimum experience 209–10, **210**
  positive/negative 217–18
  pride 257
  primary 208
  rational-emotional debate 202
  relaxed alertness 219–21
  sensing dimension 193
  shame 257
  spiritual intelligence (SQ) 257–61
  therapy and 256
  trilogies in emotional work 227–29
  waves **211**, 211–12, 213
employability learning 50
endorphins 240
energy waves 213–14, **214**

environment connections with
    activities 161–62
environmental issues in outdoor
    learning 112–13
environments for learning
    artificial spaces 104–08
    boundaries, indoor/outdoor 98–100, **101**
    current, issues with 94
    defined 93
    design principles 91–92
    ecological approach 94
    environmental issues in outdoor
        learning 112–13, 117–18, **119**
    gender issues 94
    importance of 87
    indoor 91–96
    new designs 94–96
    outdoor learning 96–98
    physical issues 93
    private spaces 95–96
    simulated 110–12
    space, importance of 87–91
    sustainable 117–18
    territoriality 94
    'The Four Steps' 112, **112**
    video gaming 95
    workplace design 90–91
Erickson, M 115
escape simulations 125–26
ethics of interventions 58
expeditions 71–72, 133, 134–36
experience economy 46–50, 302–03
experience learning
    reviewing activities for 169–71
    see also activities for experience learning
experience society 46–50
experience(s)
    addictive 47
    as bridge 5–6, **6**
    as central 2–3
    commodification of 303
    consciousness of 11
    construction of 31
    consumer, dimensions of **45**, 45–46
    continuity of 29, 43
    defining 27–28
    Disneyfication of 47–48
    ecology of 31–32
    inner-outer worlds interactions 28, 30
    inner private world 3
    language, problem of 11–12
    mapping 78–80
    memories of as dynamic 29
    outer public world 3
    philosophy of 29
    quality of and for learning 3
    as resistant to description 30–31
    theory of 28
    uniqueness of 29–30
experiential education 24–27
experiential learning
    2 × 2 quadrant 3–4, **4**
    bibliography 37
    chronology of 317–26, **318**, **324**
    criticisms of 41–44
    defined 2, 3–5, 6–8, 24, 25, 42, 51–52
    as experience plus learning 27–32
    experiential education and 24–27
    fluidity of 7
    foundations of 26–27
    incoherence of 7
    interactional dynamics 4
    as liberating 7–8
    metaphors used to describe 7
    models explaining 32–41, **34**, **37**, **38**,
        40, **41**
    as natural form of learning 13
    parameters of 6–7, 12–13
    purpose of 53
    see also activities for experience learning;
        delivery of experiential learning;
        design of learning experiences; future,
        the; Learning Combination Lock
Experiential Learning Toolkit, The (Beard) 3

facilitation *see* delivery of experiential
    learning
Falconar, T 266, 267
fantasy 150–53
fast/slow thinking 201–02, 243
fear 208, 216–17, 221–27
feedback 37, **38**
feeling dimension
    accessing emotions, tools for 219–36,
        223, **226**
    anger 227–28
    calm, emotional **210**, **211**, 212–14, **214**
    communicating with feeling 202–06
    emotional aptitude 200
    emotional waves **211**, 211–12, 213
    experiential learning and 206–09
    fast/slow thinking 201–02
    fear 208, 216–17, 221–27
    flow learning 214–16
    higher education 202
    humour, use of 229–31
    identity and education 218–19
    intelligence, emotional (EQ) 200,
        205–06, 207
    life and learning 199–200

feeling dimension (*continued*)
  metaphors 231–36
  moods 208–09
  optimum experience 209–10, **210**
  positive/negative emotions 217–18
  primary emotions 208
  rational-emotional debate 202
  relaxed alertness 219–21
  trilogies in emotional work 227–29
Feilden, R 85
Fenwick, T J 24, 44
film bites 69–70
Findhorn Foundation 259–60
Fineman, S 207–08
First Nation peoples and nature 85–86
Fitoussi, J P 276–77
flow learning 214–16
Fox, R 258
Franc, D 127, 128, 129, 144, 216, 265
Frank, L S 121
Freire, P 289–90, 322
Freud, S 193
Frontier 133–34
Furedi, F 256
future, the
  children and imagination 315–17
  chronology of experiential learning 317–26, **318**, **324**
  concurrent learning 319–20
  consequences of experiential learning 307–08
  imagination 309–13
  mental fitness for 313–14
  reflection on 320–26
  retrospective learning 318–19
  virtual reality 326–27

Gallo, C 69–70
Gallwey, T 298–302, 326
games
  fantasy 151–53
  Great Escape Game 126
  for play 154
  sensory experience 191
  simulation gaming 98–99
  video, as environment for learning 95
Gardner, H 196, 249–51, 255
Gass, M 234–35
GCHQ 90–91
gender, environments for learning and 94
gestalt cycle **214**
gesture-based technologies (GBT) 178
gestures 63, 182
Getz, D 45
Gilbert, P 205

Gilmore, J H 46, 302, 303
Gilsdorf, R 116
Gladwell, M 197
Golding, B 94
Goleman, D 207, 208, 254–55
Goodwill, S 144
graphical displays 63–64
Great Escape Game 126
Greenaway, R 58, 99–100, 169
Greene, M 123
Greenfield, A 327
Greenforce 133
Greenwood, J 321, 325
Griffiths, J 184, 202
Gross, R 246, 247
guided fantasy work 136

habits, learning 70–71, 239
habituation of sensory experiences 174
Hahn, K 184, 251
Handy, C 19, 54
Hardingham, A 266–67
Harwood, A 143
health, natural environment and 113–17
Henry, J 264–65
Heron, J 36, 59, 214, 231–32
hierarchical models of learning 33
hierarchy of needs 258
higher education
  emotions 202
  senses 187–91
hippocampus 239
Hobson, J A 212
Holman, D 42–43, 145, 225
Honey, P 39, 312
Hughes, C 32
Human Experience Mapping 78–80
humanist theories 33–34, **34**
humans, being a human 273–74, 275–76
humour, use of 229–31
Hunt, J S 28

identity and education 218–19
Illeris, K 8, 31, 36
images, use of 164–67, **167**, **168**
imagination
  and action 312–13
  children and 315–17
  construction/reconstruction of memories 308–09
  future, imagining the 314–15
  intentions, investigating and acting on 310–11
  mental fitness for the future 313–14
  mental rehearsal 326

physical/mental practice 313–14
  use of 309–10
indigenous cultures
  learning 57–58
  and nature 85–86
indoor learning environments 91–96
industrial ecology (IE) 244–46
informal education 56
Ingleton, C 257
inherited behaviours 30
inner game 298–302
inner private world 3
  interaction with outer world 28, 30
  interface with outer world 73–74
  sensory work 196–97
  talk 225–27
intelligence
  assessment technique 251–52
  convergent/divergent thinking 264
  creative (CQ) 264–70
  defining, difficulties in 246
  in education 247, **248**
  emotional (EQ) 200, 205–06, 207, 254–57
  forms of 249–71
  higher levels of 270–71
  IQ tests 247
  multiple intelligences 196, 249–51
  naturalistic (NQ) 261–64
  neglected forms of 253–70
  qualitative view 249
  sensory (SI) 173, 177–79, 253–54
  spiritual (SQ) 257–61, 264
  tests 247
  wisdom 270–71
interventions 56–62, *61–62*
intuition 247
IQ tests 247
Irvine, D 141
Itin, C M 25, 55

Jarvis, P 8, 25, 176
Jeffs, T 56
Johari Window 226, **226**
Johnson, B 221, 243
Johnson, M 1, 66
journeys, learning 130–31, **131**

Kadoorie Farm and Botanic Garden, Hong Kong 9–10
Kahneman, Daniel 201–02, 243
Kant, I 255
Kellert, S R 114
KidZania 47–49
Kirk, P 148

knowing dimension
  bodily knowing 242–43
  brains 239–40
  categorization by the mind 243–46
  convergent/divergent thinking 264
  creative intelligence (CQ) 264–70
  creative thinking 244–46
  defining intelligence, difficulties in 246
  emotional intelligence (EQ) 254–57
  forms of intelligence 249–71
  IQ tests 247
  multiple intelligences 249–51
  naturalistic intelligence (NQ) 261–64
  neglected forms of intelligence 253–70
  spatial metaphors 244
  spiritual intelligence (SQ) 257–61, 264
  tests of intelligence 247
  theories of learning 240–41, **241**
  wisdom 270–71
Kolb, A Y 43
Kolb, D 5, 36–37, 39, 43, 44, 225, 285
Kraft, U 265
Krishnamurti, Jiddu 280
Kristeller, J L 278
Krouwel, B 144
Kull, Robert 12, 30, 176, 182, 183

Lakoff, G 1, 66, 243
language
  alphabets 181–82
  complexities, expression of 244
  impact on experience 67–68
  (mis)interpretation of words 183–84
  more-than-human world, separation from 181–82
  post-kinetic period 180–81
  pre-linguistic period 180–81
  problem of 11–12
  sensing dimension 179–84
law clinics 146–47
leadership competencies in Malaysia 159–61
learning
  as argumentation process 43
  brains 239–40
  concurrent 319–20
  experience, quality of and for 3
  retrospective 318–19
  single/double-loop **288**, 288–89, **289**
  stages of 39
  theories of 33–36, **34**, 240, 241, **241**
  see also experiential learning
Learning Combination Lock
  dimensions of human experience **76**, 77
  inner-outer worlds, interface between 73–74

Learning Combination Lock (*continued*)
  model 75
  presentation of 73
  six tumblers metaphor 74, 75
  sustainable learning environments 118, **119**
  see also being dimension; belonging dimension; doing dimension; feeling dimension; knowing dimension; sensing dimension
learning cycle 37, **38**, 42–43
learning objects 189
learning spiral 43
learning styles 39–41, **40**, **41**
leisure
  learning and 219
  work as 265
Lewin, K 37, **38**, 123, 284–85
life, reflection on 168–69
Loeffler, B 47
Lombard, A 191–92
London Underground map 64
Loynes, C 46, 57–58
Lury, C 32

Macala, J C 57
MacDonald, L 321
Mackenzie, A 162
Maharg, P 191
Malinen, A 42
Mallia, G 165
Mallinger, A 153–54
maps
  experience mapping 78–80
  fear maps 224–27
  as navigational tools 63–64, 66–67
market processes 45–50
Marlatt, G A 278
Martin, A 127, 128, 129, **129**, 144, 216, 265
masks 194–96
Maslow, A 258
McAvoy, L 258
McGill, I 294
McLeod, J 59, 163, 168
meditation 213, 277–79
Megginson, D 124–25, 209–10
memletic state 197
memories
  construction/reconstruction of 308–09
  senses as triggering 253–54
meta-cognition 68
metaphors 162
  describing experiential learning 7
  emotions, accessing through 231–36
  spatial 244
  use of generally 11
Michelson, E 7
Michie, E 126–27
Miettinen, P 44
Miles, J 113, 215
Miller, N 55, 199
mind
  body-brain connections 181, 197
  conscious/unconscious 299–300
  engaging the 138–39
  meaning of 274
  see also brain, the; knowing dimension
mindfulness 277–79
Mischel, W 311
Mohawk, J 86
moods 208–09, 219–21
Moon, J 30, 321, 322, 325
'more-than-human world' (MTHW)
  interactions with 8–10
  language, and separation from 181–82
  and learning 96–98
  reciprocity with 263–64
Morgan, G 233, 314
Morris, D 209
Mortiboys, A 255
Mortlock, C 112
movement 63, 65, 66
Mulligan, J 317–18
multidisciplinary approach 8–11
multiple intelligences 196, 249–51
Mumford, A 39, 171
music 220

Nansen, F 123
national health service (NHS) 88–89
Native Americans and nature 85–86
naturalistic intelligence (NQ) 261–64
nature 57–58
  health and 112–17
  indigenous cultures and 85–86
  and learning 96–98
  nature-guided therapy 193–94
  sensing dimension 184–87
  Western culture and 86–87
navigational tools 63–64, 66–67
Neulinger, J 265
neurolinguistic programming (NLP) 188–89
neurotransmitters 239–40
Nolan, R 133
non-violent communication (NVC) 203
Norris, J 184

object-based learning (OBL) 142–43
objects and props 68–69

obstacles in activities 140–41
Ogilvie, K 112
OLS Unique Solutions 158–59
Operation Raleigh 134, 135
optimum experience 209–10, **210**
Ord, J 56, 96
organization by the mind 243–46
Osborne, A F 265
outcomes, determining required 130
outdoor learning 96–98
    adventure learning 126–27
    city spaces 102
    dramaturgy 127–29, **129**
    environmental issues 112–13, **113**
    health, natural environment and 113–17
    metaphors 234–35
    reality 144, 145
    sensing dimension 184–87
    sophistication, increased 127
outer public world 3
    interaction with inner world 28, 30
    interface with inner world 73–74
Outward Bound intervention formats 56

Palethorpe, R 291
Parkin, M 162, 165, 232, 233
Parr, J 218–19
Pavlica, K 42–43, 145, 225
peak experience 301–02
Pearn, M 312
Pedler, M 294
performative approach 65, 268–70
Peterson, R 45
philosophy of experience 29
photographic images 167–68, **168**
Piaget, J P 154, 249
Pine, B J 46, 302, 303
Pinkney, L 192
planned/unplanned experiences 123–25, **124**
planning 324–26
Plato 153, 202, 255, 275–76
play
    creativity and 265
    reality and 153–56
Plutchik, R 256–57
Pollock, L 156
Porter, T 213
post-expedition readjustment 135–36
post-kinetic period 180–81
Postle, D 207, 217–18, 313
postnatal and antenatal development 316–17
power and control in interventions 60–62, 61–62

pre-linguistic period 180–81
presence 196
pride 257
Priest, S 215
private spaces for learning 95–96
problems
    education by posing 289–91
    painful learning and 291
props 68–69
prospective learning 323–26, **324**
psychosynthesis 142
Putnam, R 325

Rae, L 62
rational-emotional debate 202
reading in reflective practice 169
reality
    community/environment connections 161–62
    complexity of 145
    degree of in activities 143
    dimensions of 148
    drama and role play 156–61
    dramaturgy 144
    high/low levels of 148–50
    law clinics 146–47
    outdoor learning 144, 145
    perception of 145
    play and 153–56
    reading to reflect on 169
    real projects 161–62
    video gaming 144–45
    virtual reality 326–27
    work environment 145
    writing to reflect on 168–69
Reed, C 186
reflection 168–69, 212, 284–86, 286, 320–26
reframing 266–67
Reich, B 307
relaxed alertness 88, 172, 219–21
retrospective learning 318–19
Revans, R 292–94, 297, 314–15
reviewing activities for experience learning 169–71
Reynolds, M 42
risk 133
Roberts, J 25, 27, 47
Robertson, I 221, 317–18
Rockface 105–06
Rodwell, J 126
Rogers, A 30
Rogers, C 33–34, 61
role play 156–61
Rosenberg, M 202–03, 204–05

rowing camps 109–10
rules for activities 140–41

Sadler-Smith, E 126–27
Sakofs, M 28
Salaman, G 208
Saunders, D 98
scenario planning 324–26
Schmitt, B H 45
Schön, D 285, 320–21
Seibert, K W 286, 287–88
self, exploration of 194–96
self-directed experiences 57
  planned/emergent learning **124**, 124–25
self-disclosure 163
self-expression 268–70
Sen, A 276–77
Senge, P 196, 263, 307
senses *see* sensing dimension
sensing dimension
  amplification of senses 174
  aural flooding 187–88
  awareness, sensory 173, 177–78
  body-brain connections 181
  colour 193
  digital games 191
  embodied learning 190–91
  emotions and mood 193
  experiential learning, importance
    for 175–76
  flooding 187–88, 189
  gesture-based technologies (GBT) 178
  habituation of senses 174
  higher-education teaching 187–91
  importance of senses 173, 174
  inner sensory work 196–97
  intelligence, sensory (SI) 173, 177–79, 253–54
  language 179–84
  learning experiences 188
  learning objects 189
  memories, senses as triggering 253–54
  music 220
  nature and wilderness 184–87
  nature-guided therapy 193–94
  neurolinguistic programming
    (NLP) 188–89
  number of senses 174–75
  perception and experience of the
    world 174
  processed v raw sense appreciation 176, 182–83
  self, exploration of 194–96
  smells 220
  therapy 191–93
  VAK analysis 188
  walking and talking the learning 190–91
sequencing of activities 136–37, **137**
serotonin 240
Shabab Oman 103–04
shame 257
sharing of experiences 58
Sheets-Johnstone, M 30, 176, 179–80, 183
simulation gaming 98–99
Singer, J L 316
single/double-loop learning **288**, 288–89, **289**
skills
  intervention 58–60
  see also activities for experience learning;
    delivery of experiential learning;
    design of experiential learning
slow/fast thinking 201–02, 243
smells 220
Smith, D M 325
Smith, P K 155
Smith, R 50
Snell, R 291
social constructivist theories 31, **34**, 35
society, experience 46–50
sociological perspective 8
solo experiential programmes 57
solo performance 268–70
sound bites 69–70
SpaceKraft 192–93
spaces
  importance of for learning 87–91
  learning 91–93
  see also environments for learning
Sparks Consulting 109–10
spatial ecologies
  evolution of 87–91
  see also environments for learning
spatial metaphors 244
Sperry, R 265
spiral, learning 43
spiritual intelligence (SQ) 257–61, 264
stages of learning 39
Sterling, S 53
Stiglitz, J A 276–77
stories 69–70
storytelling 162–64, **165**, 268–70
Stringer, L 258
Stuart, R 148
styles of learning 39–41, **40**, **41**
subconscious, engagement of 196–97
Sumara, D J 36
Surtees, M 135
sustainable learning environments 117–18, **119**

tall ship experience 103–04
Taylor, H 43
teaching *see* delivery of experiential learning
technology
    aural flooding 187–88
    digital games 191
    gesture-based technologies (GBT) 178
    photographic images 167–68, **168**
    virtual reality 326–27
'Tell-Show-Do' pyramid 26
Tenant, M 58
territoriality 94
Thayer, R 209
'The Four Steps' 65, 112, **112**
The Market Place 244–46
therapy
    compassion-focused 203–06
    emotions and 256
    metaphors 233–34
    natural environment and 113–17
    sensory spaces 191–93
thinking
    bodily 242–43
    convergent/divergent 264
    fast/slow 201–02, 243
    out loud 68
    see also brain, the; knowing dimension; mind
Thomas, W 71
Thorpe, L 42–43, 321
Thorpe, R 145, 225
three Cs concept 280–84, **281**, **282**
Tolle, Eckhart 200, 273, 278
Tower, R B 316
transfer of learning 58
trilogies in emotional work 227–29
typology for programmes 131–32

Ulrich, D 114
unconscious/conscious mind 299–300
unconscious learning 196–97
United Nations Human Development Index 277
unplanned/planned experiences 123–25, **124**
urban environment
    artificial spaces 104–08
    as learning opportunity 101–02
    outdoor programmes 102
    wildlife spaces 102

urban-wilderness duality 183–84
Usher, R 49
Uttley, A 315

VAK analysis 188
Van Matre, Steve 145
van Ments, M 158
video gaming 95
virtual reality 326–27
voice, student 49–50
Vygotsky, L 67

Walker, D 4, 8, 29–30, 32, 125, 199
Walker, R 186
wallking 66
Warren, K 28
waves, emotional **211**, 211–12, 213
well-being 276–77
Western culture and nature 86–87
Western philosophies 26
Whitton, N 33, 144, 191
Wickes, S 59
wilderness
    sensing dimension 184–87
    urban-wilderness duality 183–84
    see also outdoor learning
Wilkes, F 213, 215, 216, 225
Williams, M 279
Willis, A 184
Wilson, J P 141, 291, 321
Wilson, T 205
Winston, R 238
wisdom 270–71
Woodruffe, C 207
words
    impact on experience 67–68
    (mis)interpretation of words 183–84
    problem of 11–12
    see also language
workplace design 90–91
writing in reflective practice 168–69

Yaffey, D 210
Yardley-Matwiejczuk, K 157

Zabak-Zinn, J 278
Zounkova, D 127, 128, 129, 144, 216, 265

CPSIA information can be obtained
at www.ICGtesting.com
Printed in the USA
JSHW021915070222
22647JS00008B/439